Martin Joseph
Sociology for Everyone

Second Edition

Preface by
ANTHONY GIDDENS

Polity Press

Copyright © Martin Joseph 1986, 1990

This edition first published 1990 by Polity Press
in association with Basil Blackwell

Editorial office:
Polity Press, 65 Bridge Street,
Cambridge CB2 1UR, UK

Marketing and production:
Basil Blackwell Ltd
108 Cowley Road, Oxford OX4 1JF, UK

Basil Blackwell Inc.
3 Cambridge Center
Cambridge, MA 02142, USA

ISBN 0 7456 0708 X (pbk)

British Library Cataloguing in Publication Data
A CIP catalogue record for this book is available from the British Library.

Library of Congress Cataloging in Publication Data
Joseph, Martin
    Sociology for everyone/Martin Joseph; preface by Anthony
Giddens – 2nd ed,
        p.   cm.
    Includes bibliographical references (p.347).
    Summary: A comprehensive introduction to sociology, examining such
aspects as family life, politics, inequality, and social control.
Includes self-examination questions, discussion topics, and
suggested projects.
                                    ISBN 0–7456–0708–X (pbk.)
    1. Sociology. [1. Sociology.] I. Title.
HM66.J64   1990   90–354
301–dc20   CIP
                                                       AC

Typeset in 11 on 13 pt Times and Helvetica
by Joshua Associates Ltd., Oxford
Printed in Great Britain by
Page Bros (Norwich) Ltd.

For Maureen and Simon, Jonathan and Sarah

Contents

Detailed Chapter Contents

PART III POLITICS AND MATERIAL INEQUALITY

PART VI   RESEARCH

Acknowledgements

I am grateful for all the unstinting help I have received from friends and colleagues in producing this second edition of *Sociology for Everyone*. Firstly I must mention the staff at Polity Press, including David Held for his help generally, and Tracy Traynor and Helen Jeffrey for their editorial help. I would also like to thank Tony Giddens for writing the preface.

I am most grateful to my college, Oxford Polytechnic, for the use of their facilities and for its moral support. In addition I must thank my colleagues who have read the draft chapters for this edition and have made useful comments. Here I must mention Maggie Wilson, Alastair Neilson, Philip Davies, Peter George and especially Keith Lambe and Frank Webster.

Permissions Acknowledgements

Every effort has been made to trace all copyright holders, but if any has been inadvertently overlooked, the publishers will be pleased to make the necessary arrangements at the first opportunity.

The illustrations on the following pages are reproduced by kind permission of the artists: 16, 61, 64, 142, 191, 237, 300.

The author and publishers would like to thank the following organizations for their permission to reproduce material for which they hold either US, UK or world rights:

New Society and Statesman for the pictures on pp. 28 and 32, and the extracts on pp. 51, 266–7, 267–8, and 338–9
Penguin Books Limited for tables 2.2, 3.3, 3.4, 3.5, 3.6, 3.7, 8.6, 10.6, 13.2, 13.3, 13.4, 14.1, 14.2, 14.3
Routledge and Kegan Paul for the picture on p. 19 and table 2.3
The Trades Union Congress for the picture on p. 115
Grafton Books for table 11.3
Express Newspapers for the cartoon on p. 239
Ballière Tindall Ltd for table 12.5

University of Chicago Press for the diagram on p. 255

George Brazillier Inc. and the Corbusier Foundation, Paris for the pictures on pp. 260 and 261

Hodder and Stoughton Ltd for tables 6.2 and 6.3

Oxford University Press for table 11.3

Collins for the extract from Sir Michael Edwardes, *Back from the Brink* on pp. 130–1

Policy Studies Institute for material used in chapter 9 *passim*

Faber and Faber for the extract from A. Fox, *Beyond Contract* on p. 122.

The Commission for Racial Equality for table 9.5 and the picture on p. 165

Allen and Unwin for table 10.5 and for the extract from Sara Delamont, *The Sociology of Women* on pp. 150–1

McGraw-Hill, New York for diagrams 1 and 2 on p. 299

Gower Publishing Group for the extract from *The Islington Crime Survey* on pp. 291–2

BBC Books for the extract from *Out of the Doll's House*, by Angela Holdsworth, on pp. 136–8

Her Majesty's Stationery Office for tables 9.3, 9.4, 11.4, 13.5, 14.4; reproduced with the permission of the Controller of Her Majesty's Stationery Office.

Central Statistical Office for tables 4.1, 5.2, 5.3, 5.4, 6.7, 9.1, 9.2, 9.3, 12.3, 14.4, 14.5, 14.6, 14.7, 14.8, 15.1; reproduced by permission of the Controller of Her Majesty's Stationery Office.

Office of Population Censuses and Surveys for tables 2.1, 8.5, 9.1, 9.3, 12.2, and in Item B on p. 35

Employment Gazette for tables 5.2, 5.3, 7.1, 7.3, 8.1; reproduced by permission of the Controller of Her Majesty's Stationery Office.

Department of Employment for tables 9.1, 9.3, 9.5

Questions from GCE 'O' and 'A' level papers and sample GCSE papers are reproduced by permission of the following examination boards:

The Associated Examining Board
Joint Matriculation Board
The London East Anglian Group
Midland Examining Group
Northern Examining Association
Southern Examining Group
University of Cambridge Local Examinations Syndicate
University of Oxford Delegacy of Local Examinations

The exam boards accept no responsibility whatsoever for the accuracy of method of working in the answers given.

Preface

The study of sociology is of essential importance for anyone who would regard themselves as an informed citizen in today's world. In identifying both the continuity and the diversity of human experience, sociology teaches us sympathy for the cultures of others at the same time as it helps us better understand the institutions of our own society. No field is more demanding than sociology, yet none at the same time is so able to change and deepen our view of ourselves. Studying sociology should not be merely a neutral process of learning, but one which unsettles pre-existing assumptions, challenging our prejudices and preconceptions.

Precisely because it deals with activities and events which are central to human life, and because it demands an effort of breaking free from preconceived habits of thought, sociology is a difficult subject to introduce to a beginning audience. An introductory sociology text is of little use if it does not capture the imagination, and if it does not harness that quest for self-understanding which is probably in some form or another basic to all human experience. *Sociology for Everyone* is outstanding because the author has built the whole work around the perception that sociology can only be satisfactorily taught if it stimulates a commitment to rational debate about issues which may for centuries have been settled by tradition, by unthinking habit or by coercion. The common sense beliefs which individuals hold both about their own societies and those of others, can frequently be shown either to be bluntly mistaken, or to be at least contentious. By identifying some of the most frequently held assumptions about social life, Joseph is able to demonstrate in a direct and forthright manner the significance of learning a sociological perspective. Although the book contains a great deal of interesting empirical material and illuminating conceptual analysis, the emphasis throughout is placed upon learning to think in a sociological way. Joseph's presentation and discussion of common sense assumptions immediately engages the interest of the reader. The perceptive way in which common beliefs are then subjected to reinterpretation provides an immediately accessible and highly compelling rationale for the sociological enterprise. The result is a distinctive text, distinguished both by its easy readability and by the wealth of information which it provides.

In this new edition, Joseph has updated his material thoroughly in the light of current developments and social changes. The pace of change today has accelerated and we seem to live in a period of major institutional transition. Sociology is the prime intellectual discipline which seeks to group the nature of such changes. It is a complex and difficult subject; *Sociology for Everyone* provides an introduction to the discipline which is accessible but does justice to that complexity.

Anthony Giddens

Part I

The Introduction

1   Introduction

Plan of the book

This is an introductory book intended both for the interested lay person and for students preparing for exams, including GCSE, A level and other exams requiring some knowledge of sociology. It is written in non-technical language and should be easily understood at first reading.

There are three main themes in the book. Firstly, there is a question that is asked throughout – *what is really going on here?* What is really going on within this family, or at this school or office? This in turn leads to further interesting questions, for example: how do teachers and pupils view their school? How do workers and managers view their factory or office? By contrasting differing viewpoints of the same situations the sociologist demonstrates that there is not just one reality, one truth, but different and conflicting definitions of reality (see Glossary for 'social reality').

This leads to the second theme of this book – *ideologies*. We need to ask what people *believe* they are doing compared with what they are *actually* doing. Beliefs may be ideological not because they are inherently untrue – often there is a strong element of truth in them – but because they are exaggerations of the truth; or they do not actually accord with the facts; or they are based principally on belief rather than careful observation and real evidence; or they are used to justify the position of the powerful. Usually all these elements are present. One of the main tasks of sociology is to criticize ideologies by demonstrating how they distort reality and how they really serve the interests of the powerful. Specific examples of ideologies will be considered as the book proceeds (see also Glossary for a fuller definition of 'ideology').

The third theme of this book can be summed up in the phrase '*doing sociology*'. Readers need to use their imagination, their 'sociological imagination', rather than passively absorb a mass of knowledge. The insights gained from reading and thinking about the book should be applied to listening to the news, making decisions, analysing conversations, under-standing crime statistics, understanding politics, analysing the distribution of power and wealth and so on. The goal is not just to acquire technical skills but to be able to make sense of the social world we all share. In other words, it is to improve the quality of thinking through a widening of social

---

Three examples of ideologies

Sexism – discrimination against women. Among other things it includes the belief that women cannot do certain kinds of work. The last war proved how untrue this was when women did virtually any job previously done by men. The ideology of sexism serves the interests of men, who occupy most of the positions of power in society.

Ageism – discrimination against the elderly, which has the effect of excluding them from society – for example compulsory retirement, which is almost universal now in Britain. Compulsory retirement serves the interests of the majority in work by reducing the work force and hence the possibility of unemployment.

Racism – discrimination against people because of their race. Most usually this serves the interests of whites over other racial groups.

Three basic themes of this book
1 the question: what is really going on here?
2 ideologies: how they distort our view of what is really happening and how they serve the interests of the powerful.
3 'doing sociology': the book invites active participation rather than passive assimilation, thinking and criticizing, rather than just remembering and accepting

---

awareness. The insights gained *are* the knowledge; they belong to the readers of the book.

One of the approaches used in this book is the constant questioning of common assumptions – assumptions which most (or many) people make, and which appear to be common sense. For example, many people assume that social class differences are less important nowadays than they used to be, or that there is a greater equality of opportunity in education, or that the young reject the standards of their seniors, or that trade unions and shop stewards are too powerful and so on. Frequently these assumptions are false, or are exaggerations, so that decisions based on these false assumptions may in turn be incorrect. One way of gaining insights into social behaviour, such as strikes, crime, divorce and the exercise of power, is to turn assumptions into questions. Instead of assuming that trade unions are too powerful, the reader could ask: how much power in fact do they have, and what type of power is it? What are the limits to their power? Instead of assuming that television influences the viewer, the reader could ask: what evidence exists that attitudes are changed by the viewing of particular types of programme? Do viewers influence broadcasters rather than the other way around? Again, instead of asking why street riots occur, the sociologist might ask: why are they so rare? Or: why are we so law abiding? Part of the skill of the sociologist is to ask the right questions.

Each chapter of the book aims to give the reader an overall view of the topic covered, examining closely such common assumptions. In some chapters common questions are examined instead of common assumptions. As an exercise, and in accordance with one of the main themes – 'doing sociology' – it would be a good idea for readers to pause at each common assumption (or common question) and see how far they agree with it, perhaps making notes on the cases for and against the assumption. As a further exercise readers could ask themselves: what are the implications for the policy maker (governments, managers etc.) if the assumption is true or if it is untrue?

There are further exercises in which the reader may like to take part. At the end of most of the chapters there are self-examination questions, the answers to which are in the text. There are also discussion topics which readers may like to consider on their own or with others. These exercises will help students to answer examination questions. Readers are also invited to try their hand at past exam questions and project work (again with the emphasis on 'doing' sociology).

Project work

Projects are set at the end of many chapters. Rather than tackling these on your own, why not form groups, with each member specializing in one aspect of the problem; this will spread the burden of the work. It may be interesting, for example, to split a class into small sub-groups of, say, three or four. Each of these sub-groups then reports back to the whole group.

In any case, do all you can to make the course come alive for yourself and others.

The book is designed to be easily understood at first reading. Each chapter is designed to be read on its own and be self-sufficient. However, a list of further reading is also given for each chapter. Some of the books are difficult for a beginner. The more straightforward reading is marked with an asterisk.

It will be seen that there is little direct mention of theory until the end of the book. This is because social theory is dealt with in a practical way throughout the text. The insights that social theories yield are applied to the practical problems examined here. Thus theories about the work ethic are discussed when the problems of premature retirement are examined; social theories about race are discussed when the practical problems of racial discrimination are examined and so on.

This section has outlined the plan of the book. The remaining three sections seek to answer the questions:

What is sociology?
What do sociologists do?

What are some of the difficulties involved in making progress in studying
  sociology?

What is sociology?

One way to answer this question as clearly as possible is to list some of the
ways in which the sociologist views people and society.

1   The individual is seen as a social person. He or she has been socialized
    (brought up) by society and is guided by society's norms and values (see
    Glossary for definition of 'norms and values'); these are absorbed by us
    – they are 'within' us. (Generally we are less individual than we think, we
    are moulded to a large extent by society, and we have less free will than
    we think.)

2   We are basically learning animals. Almost everything we are we have
    learned.

3   Because we are what we have learned, it follows that there can be a wide
    range of variation in human types between societies and within them.
    Societies differ according to the cultures of the groups within them. It is
    these cultures that are learnt and taken over by the individual group
    members. Within Western societies one of the important cultural
    groupings is social class. Infants are brought up differently (socialized)
    according to the social class of their parents. (Other cultural groups
    include race, religion, gender and age.)

4   Following from point 3, we may compare different human types to
    show, for example, how far variations in belief and conduct are learned
    rather than genetically inherited. Studies of different societies show, for
    example, that the position and expected behaviour of women, as
    contrasted to that of men, varies widely from society to society. So the
    role of being a woman is very probably a socially learned role rather
    than a biologically determined one. (This is not to deny the biological
    basis of human action based on instinct, but merely to show that the

---

Socialization
Men and women are socialized, or prepared for their position or role in
society, by learning from parents, teachers and others the 'correct' values
and attitudes that go with that position. But not everyone accepts their role
in society. Women may seek greater equality in a male dominated world;
working class people may try to improve their conditions of life, racial
minorities may refuse to accept inferior status and so on. ('Role distance'
is a concept used by Erving Goffman to refer to the detachment of a
performer from the role he or she is performing; see also 'role' and
'socialization' in Glossary.)

sociologist stresses that behaviour is mainly learnt rather than mainly inherited.)

5 It follows from point 4 that in order to find out more about ourselves and our society we must try to 'stand outside ourselves' and our society. One way to do this is to examine our taken for granted world: to examine and criticize what passes for 'common sense'. This is one of the main themes of the book.

What do sociologists do?

The last section suggested sociologists should stand outside our society and examine what passes for 'common sense'. The assumption that it is not as important for women as men to go to university and have careers should, for example, be examined; as should the fact that allowance is rarely made in our society for women's careers which are disrupted by childcare. Another task of the researcher is to ask: in whose interest are these assumptions made? In other words, who has the power and who is relatively powerless?

To answer these questions we must first of all observe and analyse what is going on in a particular social situation – the family, classroom, factory or hospital. The sociologist is often asking simply: what is going on here? This may make sociologists unpopular because people do not want others to know what is really going on; professions, firms, trade unions and governments do not like being investigated. Sociologists also make themselves unpopular by questioning official versions of the 'truth'. They may study a school from the viewpoint of the pupils rather than the head teacher, a hospital through the eyes of the patient, a factory from the perspective of the shop floor rather than from management's viewpoint and so on.

Taking the school as an example, the researcher may view the head teacher's version of what is going on as questionable – as itself something to be investigated. Thus the head teacher and his colleagues in a 'slum school' may see the maintenance of discipline as a key problem. But the pupils may see things quite differently.

The sociologist as questioner

Peter Woods in his book *The Divided School* has a chapter entitled 'Having a laugh'. He comments: 'in their lives (pupils') laughter has a central place either as a natural product or as a life-saving response to the demands of the institution – its boredom, ritual, routine, regulation, oppressive authority.' By discovering the viewpoint of both pupils and teachers the sociologist can demonstrate that order in the classroom is *negotiated*. If the pupils are expected to cooperate, so too must the teacher by presenting a meaningful curriculum.

What is going on here?

Although sociology often appears to be a questioning of those in author-ity, it should be emphasized that the subject is open to all and that many of the most important sociologists could be described as conservatives in the political sense.

The reader's task at this stage is to develop what C. Wright Mills called the 'sociological imagination', to see the connection between the ideas and activities of individuals and the beliefs and values of the community to which they belong. One way of acquiring a sociological imagination is through constant curiosity. We must be prepared to question beliefs, to listen to ourselves and others more carefully and perhaps to eavesdrop on conversations – to look (metaphorically!) behind the lace curtains!

Finally, sociologists must not shirk criticism of each other. Sociologists often question the assumptions of other sociologists. Several important examples of this appear in the subsequent chapters.

What are the difficulties involved in studying sociology?

Students in some cases are their own worst enemies. They cannot progress because they are afraid of seeing the world from a different viewpoint from that to which they are accustomed. New knowledge may conflict with what people already 'know' (or think they know) and this is disturbing. After all, how many people regularly buy a newspaper which promotes political views to which they are opposed?

Since studying sociology means questioning many common sense assumptions, held over a lifetime, it demands a considerable revision to previously held views. The student may be tempted to adopt various procedures to deal with disturbing ideas presented during a sociology course. The following list indicates some of the ways:

1 Selective perception – the person hears only what he or she wants to hear, new and discordant items being lost or distorted. Hence phrases like 'there's none so blind as those who will not see', or 'he doesn't want to understand.'

2 The person may not be able to remember new (discordant) knowledge and may only remember what he or she wants to remember. This is known as selective recall.

3 So-called 'common sense' is often used as a means of dismissing new ideas. It is common sense that the best will rise to the top; that we are all middle class now; that everyone gets the same medical treatment in the National Health Service; that the moral fibre of society is crumbling – look at the crime rate, look at the divorce rate and so on. Yet all these statements are questionable. They are what the sociologist enquires into. They are starting points, not final statements. One of the main enemies to progress in sociology is what could be called 'saloon bar sociology' – endlessly repeating the statements made above. If, for example, in any exam essay you find you are writing down 'what everyone knows', then you are probably on the wrong track. The lay person's common sense knowledge is actually part of the main subject matter of sociology.

4 Many people overestimate change. 'It is all different now,' they will say, referring for example to public schools, state schools, the army, training for nursing, factory life, patterns of infant care, society's treatment of women, premarital sex and so on. On every one of these items there are many studies showing that it has not 'all changed'. What appears to be a change is often little more than a change in fashion. Beatings may be phased out in public schools, yet the institution itself is basically the same.

5 Following from point 4, students frequently comment: 'Isn't this research (or study or book) out of date?', 'Surely this isn't the case now'

and so on. Again this might be a 'ploy' to avoid new insights. Many aspects of society change little because it is in the interests of the powerful that the status quo should be preserved.

6 Students frequently ask of sociology: what is the practical use of this? Quite often sociology's independent stance is particularly useful. Thus a manager may seek answers to the problem of control of the work force. The sociologist may show that the work force in turn is using shop floor (that is, workplace) strategies to counteract management's control (such as restricting output, or absenteeism). In short, you cannot get the 'right' answer by asking the wrong sort of questions and not seeing that there are other questions.

7 Students frequently overstress the individual's power over his or her own destiny. They underestimate the importance of social influences, in particular the influence of parents, teachers, the peer group such as friends, classmates, and colleagues, and society generally. We are basically role players and the roles are provided by society. The role connects the individual to society. Roles include close personal ones like father, husband, son, as well as less personal ones like manager, teacher, nurse etc. The prescribed role tells us how to behave. It tells us our duty (as father etc.). This is sometimes hard to accept. Surely we have personal likes and private selves? Really what we think of as a private self is in large part a social self. We are to a large extent determined by society and our free will is limited.

8 There is a tendency to overstress instincts; the will to achieve, the sex drive and so on. We tend to attribute too much to human nature. A good example of this is to be found in William Golding's book, *Lord of the Flies*, in which a group of school boys is shipwrecked on a desert island so that the veneer of civilization is stripped away. The boys behave barbarously towards each other, and the author implies that this is reverting to human nature. But is it? Probably it is not 'human nature' so much as a reflection of the morals of a certain section of society (in this case public schoolboys).

To a large extent this book is an explanation of the taken for granted social world. It should be an interesting and enjoyable experience. I hope it is!

A note on exam questions

The questions you will find at the end of each chapter of this book are drawn from a variety of examinations; from GCSE to A level papers. The non A level student should not worry about trying to tackle an 'A level type' question. It will shed new light on the particular topic of a chapter and help generate a better understanding of the material. Conversely, the A level student should well be able to cope with all those questions which are from

GCSE papers. Responding to them will help to clarify some basic and fundamental matters.

Self-examination questions

1 How would you define ideology? Give examples.
2 What is meant by: 'role', 'socialization', 'common sense'?
3 What is meant by 'the sociological imagination'?

Discussion topics

1 Give a common sense account of what goes on at school and then try to explain what really goes on at school from
   a) the teacher's viewpoint;
   b) the pupil's.
   Try to do the same for the hospital, factory and prison.
2 It was suggested in this chapter that human actions are shaped more by what people learn than by their biology and the book by Golding was discussed in this context. Drawing on books, television, films, magazines and other sources give examples of
   a) an assumption that human actions are biologically determined;
   b) an assumption that they are learnt.

Further reading

(The more straightforward reading is marked with an asterisk. This applies throughout the book.)

*P. Berger, *Invitation to Sociology*
*C. Wright Mills, *The Sociological Imagination*
'Setting the Agenda', *New Society*, 19 May 1983 (asks what the important social issues are today)
*'The Middle Class', *New Society*, 20 January 1983 (Society Today series)
*'The Working Class', *New Society*, 12 October 1982 (Society Today series)
Macmillan Student Encyclopedia of Sociology or *Penguin Dictionary of Sociology* (for reference purposes throughout the book)

Two social journals can be recommended:

Social Studies Review, University of Leicester, University Road, Leicester, LE1 7RH
New Statesman and Society, Foundation House, Perseverance Works, 38 Kingsland Road, London, E2 8DQ

Part II

Family Life

2 Family

All happy families resemble one another, but each unhappy family is unhappy in its own way.

Leo Tolstoy, *Anna Karenina*

Most people have families. We all know about families and so make certain common sense assumptions about the family. We assume that family relationships are and should be intimate, but that our extended family, of grandparents, uncles, aunts and cousins, is less important now than it was in the past. We also assume that a mother's role is a deeply personal one. By talking of maternal *instincts*, we suggest that maternal care is part of 'human nature' and not an acquired pattern of behaviour. Moreover, because we are accustomed ('socialized') to family life, we take much of it for granted as being 'natural' and this in turn makes it difficult for us to investigate it. Many of us also assume that it is human nature that couples should marry for life; that the individual chooses a spouse with similar qualities; that the couple want children; that the woman usually wants to stay at home to care for the children; that the couple stand on their own feet; and so on.

All these common sense assumptions seem to be part of a taken-for-granted world. They are therefore usually accepted and taken as the last word. But for the sociologist these assertions and assumptions are the subject matter of investigation. They are the starting points of research into what is really going on in the family.

After reading these opening comments, some readers may still be wondering what the significance of all this is. Why should this kind of research be funded with taxpayer's money? How will clearing up the myths surrounding the family affect us? One practical answer is that our common sense understanding of the family does affect everyday decision making. Take, for example, the Department of Social Security official dealing with a one parent family. Where the mother is the single parent the Department tends to encourage her to stay at home and care for the children. Where the father is the single parent he is encouraged to work. But these decisions may be based on a false idea of family life. Table 2.1 suggests that we must be very careful in our ideas about the family: the conventional image of mother, father and two children with the father as sole breadwinner is only

Table 2.1   People in households: by type of household and family in which they live (percentages)

Type of household	1961	1987
Living alone	3.9	9.9
Married couple, no children	17.8	21.5
Married couple with dependent children	52.2	44.1
Married couple with non-dependent children only	11.6	11.8
Lone parent with dependent children	2.5	4.7
Other households	12.0	8.0
All households	100.0	100.0

Source: Office of Population Censuses and Surveys

true of a minority of households. Thus Table 2.1 shows a steep increase in people living alone and a steep increase in lone parent households. These trends are likely to continue into the next century.

Caution: great care must be taken in interpreting statistics, even (or especially) official, government statistics. In the case of Table 2.1, the apparently steep increase of 100 per cent in lone parent households comes from a small base; doubling a small number may not be very significant. On the other hand, the third item in the table does show that less than half the people in the UK live in households that conform to the 'conventional image of the family', i.e. married couple with dependent children. (See also project 4 in Chapter 16, p. 337, for a critique of official statistics.)

Again, a belief in the supposed values of Victorian family life in which the mother cared for the young and the handicapped may be false. Many Victorian families were desperately poor and mothers often died before the youngest child had grown up. Nevertheless, the belief in Victorian values persists. What does it really mean then when some politicians advocate a return to Victorian values? It means:

1   the mother should stay at home and look after the children, and any other dependants;

2   less money need be paid by the state to care for these dependent people.

Apart from its practical usefulness, sociological research on the family helps to show what is happening within the family. It may demonstrate, for example, that rediscovery of the extended family (which is discussed later in the book) is a result of the comparatively recent increase in life expectancy which has meant that most people live long enough to have grandchildren.

As suggested earlier, it is because we are all experts on the family that the family is difficult to study. Yet the contrast between a family in India, Japan or Africa and an English or American family clearly shows different patterns of behaviour. However, because a family is so intimate a unit, it is difficult to research into it. Three methods of research suggest themselves:

1 to stay in another family and carefully observe the interaction (a popular BBC series some years ago did this);
2 to contrast family life in different countries and cultures (for example W. J. Goode – *World Revolution and Family Patterns*);
3 to study the history of the family (for example *The Symmetrical Family* by M. Young and P. Willmott).

By following this type of research and constantly questioning common sense assumptions the true nature of these assumptions may become clearer; we may see that the assumptions are culturally confined in space and time and that they reflect our view of the world.

Some of the common assumptions that people in our (Western) society make regarding the family may be summarized as follows.

1 Through motherhood a woman expresses her natural maternal instincts.
2 Only a stable family life can ensure the successful upbringing of children.
3 The family unit consists primarily of parents and children – the nuclear family – rather than the wider (extended) family of grandparents, uncles, aunts, cousins, etc., which apparently characterized earlier times.
4 The family is, or should be, warm, intimate and satisfying.
5 Marriage is more companionable now. Husband and wife share duties.
6 The Victorian family had stricter morals; was less likely to break up through divorce; and cared more for its young and old.

Common assumption one: *through motherhood a woman expresses her natural maternal instincts*

Elisabeth Badinter in her book *The Myth of Motherhood* surveys child rearing practices in Europe over the past 300 years. She questions the existence of a 'maternal instinct'. For example, she shows that in Paris in 1780 only 1000 of the 21,000 babies born each year were breast fed by their mothers – the rest were fed by wet nurses. In spite of evidence like this people continue to think of mother love as an instinct; the mother who does not love her child is regarded as abnormal. Badinter's study shows that maternal love has varied over history; it is not necessarily deeply rooted in women's nature. Badinter shows that throughout the period mothers failed to live up to the standards that idealists expected.

Coupled with the common assumption that motherhood is a natural instinct is an over-romanticized view of motherhood. Though the image of the loving, caring mother is true of many women, it does seem to set a daunting standard for many prospective mothers. In her book *From Here to Maternity* Ann Oakley shows that motherhood came as a shock to most mothers. Although most enjoyed the experience, they were unprepared for it because of myths surrounding it, as Table 2.2 suggests.

Table 2.2   Becoming a mother

Was difficult	36%
Was different from expected	84%
Is too romanticized	84%

Source: Oakley, *From Here to Maternity*

In *Inventing Motherhood* Ann Dally shows that while mothers have always existed, 'motherhood' is a comparatively recent invention. Only in the Victorian era did the word emerge as an ideal to be admired rather than a mere statement of fact. The idealization of motherhood has led to a crisis because the reality now falls short of the ideal. (Examples of this idealization are television advertisements portraying the perfectly competent, loving mother.) In addition there are increasingly alternatives to the career of motherhood. There is no advantage in having babies too young. It may be much better to gain experience of life and of supporting yourself and discover what is satisfying and fulfilling. Rather than accepting an idealized concept of motherhood with all the isolation that this involves (the exclusiveness of the mother–child relationship etc.), Dally suggests that each member of the family is responsible (or potentially responsible) for himself or herself. Each individual receives what he or she needs from the family and contributes to it according to capabilities. Dally concludes:

> A successful family today is an institution for mutual support and enjoyment, not one in which a slave–mother cherishes her privileged husband and children and sacrifices or avoids her own life by taking over theirs.

While animals may have a maternal instinct, there seems to be plenty of evidence that in human beings motherhood is a learned set of activities, into which women are socialized.

Ann Oakley speaks of the institution of motherhood rather than the maternal instinct. Childbirth, masculinity and femininity all follow different patterns according to the culture of different societies. In Western societies women are supposed to have attained equality, yet they do not usually take the lead. Often women are portrayed as waiting for someone or something: in shopping queues, in antenatal clinics, for men to come home, at the school gates etc. The problem is that motherhood is not a passive role – the children are dependent on the mother; she has to make the decisions. Contentment with motherhood is more likely among active independent women than 'feminine' women. Trying to live up to the ideal of the wife and mother is therefore difficult, as the culture provides conflicting ideals. Ann

Oakley found in her research that one woman in three is suffering from depression and that the likelihood of becoming depressed is crucially related to motherhood. The act of childbirth itself is much safer but it is now medicalized and therefore out of the control of women. She pleads for a return to woman-controlled childbirth. Women should have the choice on whether they should have children, how many, where they should have them, and whether they would prefer to pursue a career or stay at home. All these things are changeable, because motherhood is a social institution, not an instinct, and therefore is capable of being changed.

Common assumption two: *only a stable family can ensure the successful upbringing of children*

Since the increasing divorce rate has produced a higher number of broken homes, the effect on the children is quite rightly a topic of interest. Studies show, however, that many children from intact homes suffer from family insecurity and emotional deprivation. Conversely many children from broken homes lead happy and normal lives. On this issue it is interesting to look at the *kibbutz* in Israel, where the care of children is a communal rather than a parental responsibility.

The *kibbutz* is a self-contained agricultural community. Within it the family is not a separate unit. Each child belongs to a group of its own age. Children visit their parents for about two hours a day. Community care of the children is intended to give men and women equal status and freedom to play their full part in the work and life of the *kibbutz*. The children are seen as children of the *kibbutz*. *The Children of the Dream* by Bruno Bettelheim suggests that children are not harmed by this experience, and indeed the practice is seen as protecting children from 'bad mothering'.

On the other hand there are some disadvantages arising from a *kibbutz* upbringing. The children may find true intimacy with non-*kibbutzniks* difficult as they grow older. According to research collected by Elizabeth Irvine (in *The Family in the Kibbutz*), mothers would sometimes prefer to bring up their own children, especially after the first child, though she found no evidence of a 'maternal instinct' in operation.

The example of the *kibbutz* indicates that the upbringing of children is not solely an instinctual matter: it varies greatly from society to society with the result that there is a wide variation in human personalities. This is demonstrated further in the

There are more one parent families now

Source: *New Society*, 14 June 1984

next chapter, which studies different patterns of infant care within Britain.

The previous section suggested that motherhood is not necessarily a 'natural' or instinctive phenomenon, but rather learned behaviour – behaviour that fits the particular society of the day. The same may be true too of childhood. It seems natural to see children as quite different from adults – almost as creatures apart. Yet Philippe Ariès (in *Centuries of Childhood*) shows that children in seventeenth century Europe lived like adults; they dressed like them and played adult games like cards with them. Ariès suggests that 'adolescence' is not a natural period but was invented by Western society to cope with the longer expectation of life (and the longer period of full time education).

In other words these 'stages' in life such as childhood, adolescence, adulthood, retirement and old age are not inevitable stages; they vary from society to society. The chapter here on old people shows how over this century we have invented the idea of retirement, so that now we expect men to retire at the arbitrary age of 65 and the men concerned know that this is expected of them. People are socialized to be their age ('act your age', we say). As we grow older, we learn to play the part of an older person with fewer ambitions and quieter holidays, and generally withdraw from society.

Common assumption three: *the predominant family type in Western society is the nuclear family – the extended family is no longer important*

The nuclear family is the 'two generational' family comprising mother, father, and children. The extended family is 'three generational', including grandparents and possibly also uncles, cousins, etc.

Parsons and Bales in *Family Socialization and Interaction Process* argued that the isolated nuclear family is *functional* to modern industrial society. This means (among other things) that the nuclear family serves the needs of modern industrial society. The reasons for this are set out in the accompanying box.

However social research indicates that the extended family in contemporary Western society is more widespread than is commonly supposed. One of the most famous studies on this question, *Family and Kinship in East London*, by Young and Willmott, showed that the extended family was still very strong in working class Bethnal Green in London in the 1950s. It centred on the link between mother and married daughter, and showed that about half the daughters saw their mothers every day. The neighbourhood was characterized by low population turnover, high density housing, low occupational advancement, little outside interaction and generally intense family contact. It may be thought that with large scale redevelopment of the inner city this picture is no longer true; but a follow up

---

Why the nuclear family is functional to modern industrial society

1 The nuclear family is small and mobile.

2 It performs the essential functions of the family – the procreation and care of children – and provides for the bond between the husband and wife.

3 The other functions that the extended family of the past was said to have had, such as education, health care etc., have been removed from the home and are provided universally by public bodies such as schools and hospitals.

4 As well as being geographically mobile the modern nuclear family is more socially mobile too. In the past the child's status was tied to that of the family. Today the child can sometimes rise above that.

5 In the past the emphasis was on *ascribed status* – you were born to a certain status and stayed there, for example peasant or lord. A monarch would be an example of an ascribed status, so too would be an untouchable in the Hindu caste system. In contrast, *achieved status* implies individual effort to rise in a modern, open, industrial society; it implies that with hard work and effort the higher positions of society are open to all.

6 In the nuclear family there are no definite rules laying down what the relationship ought to be between members. In the extended family a man may get a job, say, because the manager is his uncle.

---

study by Willmott and Young (*Family and Class in a London Suburb*) showed that this cultural system can adapt. It showed that the mother–daughter link, though weaker, is unbroken and the old are not neglected. Further, the researchers showed that for the second generation the old patterns of strong family interaction reemerge.

Young and Willmott's first study was done in the 1950s and readers may question its relevance today. In fact the findings of many older studies are still true now. Consider the comments of one of the authors, Peter Willmott.

Despite a decline in the proportions of people living with or very near relatives, kinship remains an important force in the lives of most people. Just as the old stereotype of the traditional extended family (pre-Laslett) was wrong in overstating the role of relatives, the new one (post-Bethnal Green) is wrong in understating it. Parents and married children can keep in regular contact partly because they can often arrange their housing so that they live near enough to each other to be able to do so. A small scale but important study in the Greater London area compared the kinship patterns of people originating from mainly Victorian areas who had stayed in the same district since before they got married with people from similar areas who had moved out. Many of the second group turned out to have remained in close touch with their parents and siblings; they saw as much of them each week as those who had stayed put. This had come about because clusters of relatives –

How important is the extended family today?
Source: M. Young and P. Willmott, *Family and Kinship in East London*

particularly parents and their married children – had moved out to suburban districts where they were within reasonable visiting distance of each other. (P. Willmott, 'Urban Kinship Past and Present', *Social Studies Review*, November 1988.)

It might be objected that this picture applies to working class families but not middle class, where the nuclear family is thought more likely to be typical. However, nearly all the studies of middle class families indicate the prevalence of the extended family. Rosser and Harris studied families in Swansea. Their findings clearly demonstrated the existence of a strong mother–daughter link in both middle class and working class families, as shown in Table 2.3, from *Family and Social Change*. The study concluded that the extended family is a social entity which gives some sense of identification.

Another study, by Firth (*Families and their Relatives*) in the Highgate area of London, was based on a sample of 176 middle class families. It showed a high degree of contact between kin outside the nuclear family even though they lived far apart. People turn to kin in emergency of course, and Firth concluded that industrial society itself gives rise to the need for the extended family from which to select contacts to relieve difficulties.

Similarly Bell, in a sample of 120 middle class families in Swansea, showed that despite geographic dispersal the extended family still provided a strong link, this time between married son and father or father-in-law.

Table 2.3 Frequency of contact between married child and parent (percentages)

	Contact with mother				Contact with father			
	Middle class		Working class		Middle class		Working class	
	Sons	Daughters	Sons	Daughters	Sons	Daughters	Sons	Daughters
Contact in last 24 hours	39	44	27	56	37	39	26	48
Contact in past week	35	32	43	27	26	28	45	31
All contact within last week	74	76	70	83	63	67	71	79

Source: C. Rosser and C. C. Harris, *Family and Social Change*

Through this link the older generation channels material aid. To give aid apparently confers status on the father, and of course aid is important in the family building stage of life. (C. Bell, *Middle Class Families: Social and Geographic Mobility*.)

Clearly then this is one of the many instances where not all sociologists agree. Some, such as Parsons and Bales, agree with the popular image of the pattern of family life – that in the past the extended family was the norm, but that now the norm is the nuclear or conjugal family. Generally, though, this 'functionalist' view of the family is not supported by the evidence on extended family ties. In addition there is also evidence that in the past the extended family was weaker than is commonly thought. It seems that it did not provide for the welfare of all its members and act as a joint production unit as it is supposed to have done (in agriculture and cottage industries). Often in the past the extended family did not function because of the death of key members (life expectancy at birth in 1690 was 32 years) and because economic hardship led to the break-up of the extended family. Thus Goode (*World Revolution and Family Patterns*) shows that the extended family applied mainly to the wealthy. Only the rich farmer could offer sufficient prospects for his sons and grandsons to stay with him. Again, Laslett in *The World We Have Lost* argues that to perform all welfare functions required, the extended family of olden times would have had to be large. But often the families were *not* large: these families could not for instance support elderly parents living at home (in contrast 21 per cent of the families in the Bethnal Green study were housing elderly parents).

Perhaps we could conclude that despite the fact that the nuclear family appears to be the natural family unit in modern Western society (although with increasing divorce there is a rising number of one parent families), the extended family is more important than is commonly supposed. Similarly, in the past the extended family was perhaps less important and less capable of performing wider functions than is generally assumed.

QUESTION: Do you belong to an extended family? How often do you see your grandparents? Do your friends belong to extended families?

Common assumption four: *the family is or should be warm, intimate and satisfying*

Ideally the family should be warm, intimate and satisfying; it should be a haven from the tensions of the world. But how far is this true; is the family sometimes a prison rather than a haven?

It might be a good idea to emphasize the negative side of the family first, since the positive side seems to be part of our taken for granted world – as shown for example by the idealized picture of the family and our constant surprise at news items showing violence and misery in some families.

The defects of the family can be considered under three headings: firstly, violence in the family; secondly, male dominance in the family; and thirdly, the family as a trap or a kind of prison.

Violence in the family

One of the most vivid portrayals of violence in the family comes in Erin Pizzey's well known book *Scream Quietly or the Neighbours will Hear*, containing personal stories from the wives who suffered such violence.

Since that book was published in 1974 there have been several more on the same theme. J. P. Martin remarks that the home can be a violent place (in the book he edited: *Violence and the Family*). In the same book Dennis Marsden asks: is violence between family members such an individual matter as to be outside the scope of sociological study? Marsden thinks there is a job here for the sociologist – to analyse what goes on inside the family. He suggests that while there may be less violence now in public life, this is not yet true of the family. People may believe violence has declined; this makes them less likely to believe it exists and more reluctant to intervene. In the short term we should be more vigilant and provide refuges for victims of violence. In the long term we need to strengthen social policies that will release children, and women, and grannies, from their society-created status as the 'victims' of violence and domination.

One example of violence in the family in recent years has been the Cleveland Affair. In May and June 1987 the number of referrals of suspected victims of child sexual abuse rose dramatically in Cleveland from about 30 a month to 81 in May and June (reported in *Social Work Today*, 7 July 1988, and in *New Statesman and Society*, 15 July 1988).

Here are some facts to emerge from the Butler-Sloss Report on child abuse in the Cleveland area.

1 According to Michael Bishop, Cleveland's social services director:
   a) 118 place of safety orders were taken out;
   b) 83 of these resulted in further court orders or the family voluntarily accepting supervision by a social worker;
   c) in only 26 cases did the High Court clear the families concerned.

2 According to Sue Amphlett, director of the pressure group Parents Against Injustice (PAIN):
   a) there are 27 families involving 66 children who deny sexual abuse by a father and have effectively been cleared;
   b) of the 66 children, 63 have been returned home.

3 According to the Enquiry Panel:
   a) 121 cases were originally observed;
   b) of these, 98 had returned home.

4 General findings of the Enquiry briefly:
   a) all the caring professions should cooperate more fully;
   b) they should have a clearer idea of what is suspicious.

QUESTION: how would you account for the big difference in the versions of what happened?

Suggestions

1 Read the accounts given in the press and journals at the time (including the facts quoted here) and *Keesing's Record of World Events*.
2 It seems each group (social workers, police, etc.) has its own distinct version of events. You could use the literature on the sociology of the professions to account for this, or show how members of an opposing group stick together in conflicts – as reported in the press – and that this leads to poor communication between the groups. (See, for example, M. Joseph, *Sociology for Business*, Chapter 4, for reasons for poor communication and for an overview of the sociology of the professions.)

QUESTION: who do you think is to blame for these cases?

Suggestions

In analysing these cases the sociologist should be less concerned with apportioning blame to individuals and more concerned with the question – in what sort of society can this type of cruelty take place? (See, for example, Chapter 14, 'Deviance'. Thus Table 14.3 shows that the homicide rate varies from society to society, in a similar way as cruelty to children may vary from society to society.)

What further insights can sociology offer in the study of violence in the family? J. P. Martin believes that women are more likely to be subordinate in societies where the degree of individual security is low, where women cannot get out to work, where in effect women and children are trapped and where the law can be disobeyed because it does not accord with public opinion (hence the need to take wife beating seriously rather than as a topic for callous male jokes). Martin also believes that violence in the family is a reflection of violence in society as a whole. An improvement in standards will come about from criticism of the prevailing ethic (and here the chapters on old people and race relations in this book are relevant), and from advances in the economy as a whole. Improvements in the economy and more employment for women would give women more independence; this would encourage a move away from the idea that the wife and children are the husband's property. (The notion of inherent male superiority has been questioned by the fact that some women have risen to the top in almost every profession, and yet 'patriarchy' prevails, as the next section shows.)

This leads to the question of male domination of the family.

QUESTION: do you think violence in the family is widespread? Consult the recommended reading at the end of the chapter and newspaper reports, etc.

Male dominance in the family – patriarchy

Feminists campaigning for equality for women often criticize the idealized picture of the family. They point to the domination of women by men in the

Violence in the family in the past

A sociological explanation of violence in the family may concentrate on the dominance of the family by the male – patriarchy – and the lower status of the wife and children. Consider now the following extract – it comes from the *North British Review*, 1856.

> Echoing this mistrust of flogging (the violent husband), a North British Reviewer, in one of the first specific studies of conjugal violence, suggested that preventive measures were as necessary as immediate punishment. Though the roots of domestic violence were manifold, and partly a reflection of women's low social status which encouraged abuse, practical remedies could be applied. The immediate cause lay in the ignorance and negligence of the working class wife. Rather than providing the husband with a comforting refuge from the frustrations of work she neglected their home, driving him to the pub, and inflamed him further by a stream of household complaints. The solution to the inevitable quarrel, when nagging wives were often silenced by blows, lay, as Miss Brewster's experiments in Scotland showed, in domestic training for the wife, and, in the longer term, an improvement in working class housing. (*North British Review*, 1856, quoted in J. P. Martin (ed.), *Violence and the Family*.)

Firstly, the date is very significant for anyone who believes that society was substantially less violent in some golden past. Secondly, the extract illustrates the lower status of and the lower regard for women. As Margaret May says, commenting on this extract in the same book, 'the tendency to blame the woman for her failure to conform to the cherished ideal of wifely self-denial and forbearance remained a common theme in discussions of conjugal violence.' Thirdly, it does at least show an awareness that meeting violence with violence is probably ineffective.

family. Men control the money and make most of the decisions affecting the family. It has also been suggested that it is men who control sexual activity and again, this concerns the power of men over women. This has been called 'sexual politics'. An example of the power of men over women is the fact that it is still impossible to convict a man of raping his wife, unless she has taken out a legal injunction against him. One writer in this area is Beatrix Campbell. In her chapter in *What is to be Done about the Family?* (ed. L. Segal), she argues that while improved methods of birth control have freed women from unwanted pregnancies, they have not freed women from unwanted sex. It would seem that the common assumption that the family is, or should be, warm, intimate and satisfying needs to be questioned on the grounds that there is considerable sexual inequality both in the family and throughout society.

Of course, sometimes we get examples where it does appear that the marriage partners are equal. Take for instance the book by Rhona and Robert Rapoport entitled *Dual-Career Families*. In this they show both husband and wife having fulfilling professional careers; wives were just as involved in their careers as husbands were in theirs. Further they forecast that this was the shape of things to come.

Lately these findings have been questioned by Harold Benenson in the *British Journal of Sociology*. Benenson argues that the Rapoport sample was not representative, it was 'up market'; for example, the couple might be two doctors or two lawyers. You cannot generalize from these elite families to the whole population, most of which could not, for instance, afford home helps. Benenson's study showed that even within 'upper crust' dual career families the female half got less money and had less responsibility at work. For example, women doctors got only 56 per cent of the earnings of their male colleagues. Furthermore, these women still had to 'service' the husband for work (cook and clean for him, etc.) and take responsibility for the children. (Generally the evidence shows there is a strong tendency for top career women to be single or divorced, says Benenson.)

How does male dominance or patriarchy arise and why does it continue? According to C. C. Harris in his book *The Family and Industrial Society*, it is the family that is the origin of sexual division in society; any understanding of women's oppression in society requires a knowledge of what happens within the family.

It may be interesting to try to see what is happening through the eyes of one of the members of a family, say a daughter aged twelve. She sees her mother performing certain tasks such as cleaning, preparing meals and tending the baby. The daughter is expected to help in some of these tasks. She also sees her father going out to work each day and realizes he has an important career and a life outside the family with his friends as well as a life within the family as, apparently, leader and decision maker.

What is happening is that the girl is observing and learning the roles of her mother and father and copying the mother's role; the mother is providing a role model to copy. The role is 'structural' because it applies to the general society outside this particular family. The role is also historical because it is learnt and repeated generation after generation. The role of woman and mother is thus socially inherited. What appears in the family to be private and particular is in reality public and general. One task of the sociologist is continually to make this connection between the private and the public, between what C. W. Mills called 'private troubles' and 'public issues'.

In summary, *patriarchy* is a concept that describes the dominance of men over women, especially in the household. To most sociologists it is not a natural or biological phenomenon. Rather it is a social relationship. Referring to the definition of ideology given in Chapter 1, patriarchy is an *ideology* for two main reasons. Firstly, the belief in male superiority (which represents women as inherently different from men) is only a belief; and secondly, this belief serves the interests of the powerful, in this case the male. The power of the male consists of a number of components. It is economic in the sense that the male is serviced, his clothes are cleaned and his meals prepared; it is sexual in the form of compulsory heterosexuality, including marriage and motherhood; it is cultural in the sense that it is a devaluation of women's work, achievement and worth generally. Many examples of patriarchy have already been given in this section.

QUESTION: in your view, is 'patriarchy' widespread?

The family as a trap or prison

So far it has been shown that in some families there is a problem of violence and that in most families there is male dominance. Continuing in this pessimistic vein, two psychiatrists, R. D. Laing and David Cooper, have argued that most families seem to stifle their members psychologically, and they see the family as a kind of prison rather than a haven. Laing (in *The Politics of the Family*) sees the family as a system which comprises the relationships between the members. The system's social patterns of behaviour are inherited from generation to generation and its characteristics are internalized in the minds of the individual members of the family. Essentially, being in a family means being trapped in a relationship. What holds the family together is not a common goal but the continued presence of its members. The world outside the family may seem strange and threatening but it is the family itself that so defines it and sets itself up as the only refuge; and so the grip of the family is tightened.

There is plenty of evidence that for some the family is more a prison than a haven. The study of the family is a study of power: the power of men over women, of parents over children, of stronger over weaker, of elder over younger. This has its counterpart outside: employer over employed, white over black and the powerful over the powerless in general. (See the comments on 'patriarchy' on pp. 23–6.) There has been some criticism of Laing and Cooper on the grounds that they concentrate too much on the interior of the family and say little on the relationship between the family and economic and social life (see D. H. J. Morgan, *The Family, Politics and Social Theory*, pp. 224–6).

Common assumption five: *marriage is more companionable now; husband and wife share family duties*

This would follow from the previous common assumption (if it were true), and husband and wife would share the family duties. In their book, *The Symmetrical Family*, Young and Willmott sought to show that inside the family the role of the sexes had become less segregated. Husbands and wives shared the work, with the husband increasingly doing work hitherto regarded as women's work. Elizabeth Bott in *Family and Social Network* uses the idea of 'joint conjugal role' where husband and wife plan family matters together. They do each other's work and spend much leisure time together.

Bott uses the term 'segregated conjugal role' where husband and wife have different tasks and interests and there is a clearly defined division of labour – the wife works in the kitchen and the husband does the practical jobs around the house. Bott then shows that the joint conjugal role is associated with a dispersed network of friends and aquaintances where these people, although known to the family, may not know each other. In contrast, where there is a segregated conjugal role there may be a 'highly connected network' in which people known to the family also know each other, and this is said to typify the working class families. Joint and segregated conjugal roles are summarized in Table 2.4.

Table 2.4   Conjugal roles

Joint conjugal role	Segregated conjugal role
Husband and wife share tasks and interests.	Husband and wife have different tasks and interests.
Dispersed network where people known to the family may not be known to each other.	Highly connected network where people known to the family also know each other.
Husband and wife have similar interests.	Husband and wife have separate interests.
Typical of middle class families.	Typical of working class families.

There seems to be a general assumption that we are moving towards a society in which marriages will be companionable, especially in view of the break-up of many working class communities. (See C. C. Harris, *The Family*, pp. 169–75, for a critique of Bott.) Nevertheless we should not underestimate the continuance of segregated conjugal roles, as a study by Dennis, Henriques and Slaughter clearly showed – *Coal is our Life*. In the Derbyshire mining village studied the male mystique (associated with hard work and heavy drinking) predominated. Women were considered lucky as they did not have to go down the pit. There was strict segregation of roles and a strong sense of community, typical of the highly connected network.

Perhaps the best known study describing the isolation of women is Hannah Gavron's book, *The Captive Wife: Conflicts of Housebound Mothers*, in which she portrays the wife as trapped in the home. Gavron pleads for a reintegration of the mother and young child back into society, for example by providing more nursery places and by allowing mothers to take their young children with them to work.

Common assumption six: *the Victorian family had stricter morals, was less likely to break up through divorce, and cared more for its young and old*

With so many hazards to family life today it is not surprising that people look back to a golden past. But was family life so much better in Victorian times? In his *New Society* article entitled 'How much has the family changed?', Michael Anderson disputes these common assumptions. In the 1851 census 18 per cent of family households were single parent households compared with 9 per cent in 1981. One in three couples had their marriage broken by death within 20 years.

Victorian sexual morality was not all that strict under the surface of society, and prostitution, used to supplement low incomes, was rife. More than half of all first births were conceived out of wedlock. 6 per cent of births in England in the 1850s were officially illegitimate compared with 8.4 per cent in 1980.

Wife beating, family neglect and brutality towards children were probably more widespread then, and hard drinking was also more widespread, peaking in the 1870s. This does not imply that patriarchy has declined. Probably patriarchy takes a more subtle form now. For example, more married women go out to work compared with Victorian times, and this causes greater questioning of the authority of the male. He may seek new ways to assert his authority.

Again, the Victorian family did not necessarily look after their old folk better than we do. In 1851 about 20 per cent of the over-65s lived apart from all relatives, about the same as in Britain in 1962. In 1907 about 6 per cent lived in institutions compared with 5 per cent in 1981.

There was much less privacy in the Victorian family; in 1861, 34 per cent of all Scottish families were living in a single room.

At the root of the myth? A Victorian family poses
Source: *New Society*, 27 October 1983

The emphasis today is on happiness and personal satisfaction in marriage rather than on marriage as being basically for survival, hence the higher divorce rates now. Again, it may be a myth that children then were better controlled; in any case we stress personal development in children rather than strict obedience. Anderson concludes: 'few people who are alive today would wish to live in the Victorian family. To suggest otherwise is to foster a dangerous illusion.'

The future of the family

Four views of the family in society

1 *The family is in decline and this is detrimental to society.* According to this view the decline of the family and the lack of parental influence will bring about indiscipline and riots, drug abuse and more crime generally. The emphasis here would be on a return to old-fashioned values – Victorian values: love and discipline for the young, care for the old and handicapped, and independence for the family generally, more or less free from state support.

2 *The family is in decline and this is all to the good.* The decline of the family is seen as a natural stage in social evolution. The alleged decline of the extended family could be seen as a stage in this process. The evolving of new forms of communal life can also be seen in this way: the commune, living together before marriage and so on. However, marriage is still popular and there is little long term evidence of a decline in the family.

3 *The family is not in decline and this is all to the good.* This is the view taken by functionalist sociologists who see the nuclear family as functional to industrial society. Thus Parsons argues that the family relieves the tensions of life in a complex industrial society. In such a society most relationships are necessarily shallow and calculative. Family relationships are the exception. Many sociologists feel that more is expected of the family now. Thus the rising divorce figures are not necessarily seen as a decline in the popularity of marriage as an institution, but rather as a sign that couples are less inclined to put up with an unsatisfactory marriage. Ferdinand Mount in his book *The Subversive Family* suggests that the family is part of human nature and will endure when he says:

> Marriage and the family make other experiences, both pleasant and unpleasant, seem a little tame and bloodless. And it is difficult to resist the conclusion that a way of living which is both so intense and so enduring must somehow come naturally to us, that it is part of being human.

4 *The family is not in decline and this is unfortunate.* Taking this view would be radical psychiatrists like R. D. Laing (in *Politics, Madness and the Family*) and D. Cooper (*Death of the Family*). These writers view the family as a sort of prison for members and an important source of guilt and neurosis generally. Many feminists see the family as part of the apparatus for the exploitation of women (e.g. H. Gavron in *The Captive Wife*, and M. Barrett and M. McIntosh in *The Anti-Social Family*). A third group taking a similar view are Marxist commentators on the family. They emphasize firstly, the exploitation of women by men in the family (F. Engels, *The Origin of the Family, Private Property, and the State*) and secondly, the exploitation of the family by society. The family socializes the future worker for his or her job and the employer does not have to pay the cost of the worker's socialization and preparation for work. The worker in turn, when supporting a family, must behave well at work to retain the job – in which he or she is trapped; and so the cycle of exploitation continues. In all, the family is a cheap producer of labour, the basic commodity of the capitalist system. (It is interesting to contrast this theory of the family with that advocated by functionalist sociologists such as Parsons and Bales mentioned earlier in this chapter.)

Concluding studies

In conclusion, the following summary of a *New Society* series called 'The Family in Crisis' (6 March to 10 April 1987) may prove useful in demonstrating how sociologists look at the family and its problems.

'The Woman's Place' by Ann Oakley

Oakley, a well known sociologist and feminist, discusses the relationship between feminism and the woman's role as a mother. (Feminists advocate equal rights for men and women – see Glossary, 'feminism', 'patriarchy', 'sexism'.) Oakley asks if women are expected to withdraw from the world and confine their lives to the family. She then suggests three approaches on feminism and the family:

a) If you have feminism you cannot have the family.
b) If you have the family you might as well forget about feminism.
c) A family form which can adjust to women's changing role is one of the achievements of our time.

According to Oakley, all three approaches assume that feminism has had a disruptive effect on family life – but has it? Dissatisfaction with marriage existed long before feminism. Between 1487 and 1653, 200 marriage manuals dealing with the problems of marriage and family life were published in England, well before feminism was on the scene.

However, marriage and family life are still popular, says Oakley. Nine out of ten men and women marry and nine out of ten women have at least one child. (*New Society*, 6 March 1987.)

QUESTION: what is a woman's place?

Suggestions

You could argue that a woman's place is both at home and in society generally, and that this should be the same for men too. Then show the difficulties in achieving this (see 'feminism' in Glossary, and Chapter 8).

'Wedlocked Britain' by David Clark

Clark is another writer who stresses the popularity of marriage despite all difficulties. For example, so-called rebellious youth assiduously seeks marriage. By the early seventies one in three spinsters marrying was a teenager. Conversely, a quarter of women marrying for the first time between 1979 and 1982 had cohabited with their husbands beforehand. However, Clark felt that these couples were committed to sexual fidelity rather than any more open form of relationship. Cohabitation should therefore be seen as a form of trial marriage – a final phase of courtship rather than an alternative to marriage.

Clark sees marriage as the doorway to adult status and independence. However, men tend to see marriage as something which supports them in the world of work but which also leads to tension between the demands of paid work outside and the demands of unpaid labour at home (see previous section and also 'role conflict' in Glossary). (*New Society*, 13 March 1987.)

'Family Ties' by Janet Finch

Finch (like M. Anderson above) argues that the idea of a golden age in the past when people were much more willing to support kin is likely to be inaccurate, simply because in harsh conditions carers have not got the capacity to support them.

Today it is mainly women who are the carers for the infirm. This position, though, is increasingly threatened by feminists who ask – what is the man doing? Why should he not be a carer too? Also, changing demography means there will be fewer unmarried daughters to act as carers. (*New Society*, 20 March 1987.)

QUESTION: why do we seem to hanker after a golden past where a harmonious family cared for the old and infirm?

Suggestions

See 'Further reading' at the end of the chapter, including Finch, Anderson and Laslett.

It could be argued that there is an ideology of a golden past in the family. Emphasizing this would suit the interests of governments and taxpayers since the burdens of caring then become the responsibility of the family and not the state.

'Parents and Kids: The New Thinking' by Martin Richards

In this study Richards is seeking to answer the question: what is the effect of divorce on the children? He found that visits by the non-custodial father were seen by social workers etc. as disruptive. He shows that there is a presumption that custody should go to the mother, but this just reflects the fact that the mother provides the bulk of the child's care. It seems that children resent their parents' separation and may hold fantasies about a reunion. Mothers may become more authoritarian after a divorce while the children, especially boys, may become more aggressive (*New Society*, 27 March 1987.)

QUESTION: the writer of this article is a psychologist and stresses the effect of divorce on the children. How might a sociologist approach the issue?

Suggestions

See Chapter 4 on divorce. A sociologist might stress the effect of society on the individual. A greedy society influences the individual's behaviour; and this in turn affects the marriage.

'The No Longer Working Class' by Lydia Morris

The long held tradition of the man as breadwinner and his wife as house-keeper is being challenged by the prevalence of male unemployment and the rise of part-time employment for women, says Morris.

Thus, in some areas, male unemployment stands at 30 per cent of the male working population.

Table 2.5 Percentage of women as employees

1948	1980	1984
34%	42%	43%

Source: adapted from L. Morris, 'The No Longer Working Class'

Table 2.6 Percentage of married women in the female work force

1951	1971	1984
38%	63%	69%

Source: adapted from L. Morris, 'The No Longer Working Class'

'I can't afford it but I let him have a night out. He has to get out you know. You need at least one night out a week when you're in the house so much.'

Source: *New Society*, 3 April 1987.

Morris shows that despite these major changes in the female work force, traditional male attitudes still prevail in the home. Men feel they are the breadwinners and should go out to work and may disparage their wives' work. For example, one man remarked of his wife's part-time job, 'It's not that we need the money, it's just that it helps her a bit with the house-keeping.' Overall, this study shows that changes in the economic structure do not necessarily lead to changes in the attitudes of men and women. (*New Society*, 3 April 1987.)

QUESTION: why are gender based attitudes so hard to change?

Suggestions

This is a theme of Chapter 8. See also 'gender' in the Glossary.

'Married Happiness' by Jacqueline Burgoyne

Burgoyne poses the question – are the joys of married life largely reserved for the better off? With increasing home ownership and the increasing consumer demand for goods and houses it would be easy to believe that Britain is becoming a home-centred classless society. There is a strong notion of the 'normal' family with a nice house, children, domestic goods and affection, and a deep feeling that riches do not necessarily lead to happiness.

These assumptions about the nature of the normal family may be largely a product of post-war affluence. But poorer families and recent recruits to home ownership may see family life differently. They may have been forced to buy an inferior house, and they may have difficulties with the mortgage repayments; for example, in 1979 there were 2500 repossessions by banks and building societies; by 1985 this had risen to 17,000. Thus a survey by Mack and Lansley (*Poor Britain*) showed that the items listed as important by poorer families included self-contained accommodation; three meals a day; toys; carpets; items the average British family can take for granted. Increasing investment in a certain kind of 'normal' family means that in the process a growing minority gets left behind. (*New Society*, 10 April 1987.)

Conclusions

1 The structure of the family has changed. Less than half the households in Britain comprise a married couple with dependent children.

2 Motherhood may not be a matter of instinct, or human nature. Rather it may vary from society to society.

3 The nuclear (two generation) family appears to be the 'norm' in advanced societies yet many sociological studies show that the three and four generation extended family is still important.

4 In some families there is violence and sex abuse. It is difficult to estimate the extent of this; even disregarding actual physical violence the family seems to act as a kind of prison sometimes (further sociological research is needed here).

5 The government should help families more; for example, maintain family allowances, improve housing, crack down on violent fathers.

Self-examination question

What is meant by: 'nuclear family', 'extended family', 'maternal instinct', 'socialization', 'achieved status', 'ascribed status', 'patriarchy', 'joint conjugal role', 'Victorian values'?

Project

Read the following passage and then answer these questions:

1 How far does the family live up to the conventional image of mother, father and children?

2 What changes in the family do you foresee by the year 2000?

The family: old and alone
The idea of 'the family' has long been a powerful one. It conjures up an image of domestic warmth and happiness, the evocative power of which is constantly used by advertisers to sell everything from cornflakes to washing powder. The message is unequivocal. A family consists of a father, a mother and children.

In the last few years 'the family' has also returned to the political agenda. The family has become one of the ideological weapons in the government's campaign to reassert Victorian values. But the latest 1981 census volume (*Household and Family Composition*, HMSO, £10) will provide ammunition both for Mrs Thatcher and the opposition parties.

One thing is clear. The 'traditional' family – the married couple with dependent children – is proportionately, if not absolutely, in decline. From 37% of all households in 1961, this type of family fell to 34% in 1971, and 30% in 1981.

The most dramatic increase has been in the proportion of one person households – from 12% in 1961 to 22% in 1981. In absolute terms, single people living alone increased from 1.8 to 3.8 million, or by well over 100%. What has caused this increase? It is not principally that more young people are setting up home on their own, nor that more married couples are divorcing. The number of one person households under pensionable age nearly doubled from 684,000 in 1961 to 1.34 million in 1981. And the number of pensioners living on their own increased from around one million to more than 2.5 million. As a proportion of the total, they increased from 7% in 1961 to 14% in 1971.

But what about single parent families? Over the 20 years, they increased by roughly 50% – from just under one million to nearly 1.5 million. As a proportion of all households they increased from 6–9%. There is one scrap of comfort in the census for the defenders of Victorian values. Despite the increase in the divorce rate, no less than 87% of husbands and wives are still on their first marriage. (Chris Hamnet, *New Society*, 14 June 1984).

Past examination questions

1   **'Of all human institutions the family is definitely the most adaptive; therefore its future is secure.' Discuss.**

University of London, A Level, Paper 2, Summer 1984.

Suggestions

Show change and show stability of old norms.
With the aid of Chapter 4 on divorce, show that in spite of the rising divorce rate marriage as an institution is still as popular as ever. (See F. Mount, *The Subversive Family*.)

2

Item A

There is evidence that an increasing number of fathers are taking an active share in the rearing of their children and enjoying it. This is very different from the role of the Victorian father who was in most cases a distant figure to his children and whose attitude was much more formal. This may be part of the changes in Western society, where differences in role between male and female generally are declining. No longer is the male the provider and the female the home-maker and child-rearer. Inside and outside the home, work is being shared and performed by both.

Item B

Families with dependent children, 1971–84, Great
Britain (percentages)

Family type	1971–73	1982–84
Married couple	92	87
Lone mother	7	12
Lone father	1	1
All lone parents	8	13

Source: Office of Population Censuses and Surveys Monitor
GHS85/1, July 1985

1   In Item B which family type has increased the most?   (1 mark)
2   In Item B which family type has decreased?   (1 mark)
3   Look at the extract given as Item A and state two changes in the role of father which are referred to.   (2 marks)
4   Item B draws our attention to a variety of family types. Identify and describe two types of families which sociologists have observed.   (4 marks)
5   Identify and explain two aspects of family life which have changed since the onset of the Industrial Revolution.   (4 marks)
6   Briefly explain two reasons for the popularity of remarriage given that divorce is now quite common.   (4 marks)
7   Give two reasons why the family may be undergoing change at the present time.   (4 marks)

Southern Examining Group, GCSE, Paper 1, Summer 1988.

Suggestions

You will find *The Symmetrical Family* and *Family and Kinship in East London* by Young and Willmott useful in helping to deal with questions 4 and 5. You could compare the nuclear with the extended family. On question 6, see Chapter 4 on divorce. On question 7 you could suggest that the requirement of an industrializing (modernizing) society leads to greater equality between the spouses. On the other hand you could argue marriage is essentially unequal because women are in a weaker position in society as a whole.

3

Item A

Parsons argues that urban industrial societies are typified by relatively stable, but isolated nuclear family units. This is because the occupational system demands that the individual is both geographically and socially mobile. Linton agrees that the isolated nuclear family is becoming dominant but stresses that these changes follow from the fact that industrialization allows both men and women greater freedom. In consequence, Linton argues, family relationships become potentially more fragile in modern industrial societies. (Adapted from M. Anderson, *Sociology of the Family*.)

Item B

Extended kin appear to play an important part in contemporary family life. Such relationships may be disrupted by aspects of contemporary industrialism – e.g. by geographical relocation – but they appear to be capable of surviving this sort of temporary disruption; indeed, contrary to some views, such kinship ties may facilitate geographical and social mobility by providing assistance for individuals and nuclear families who need it. (Adapted from Bilton et al., *Introductory Sociology*.)

Item C

Popular images of the Asian family, like so many commonsense constructs, are often highly selective, prejudiced and riddled with contradictions. For anyone who wishes to look, popular images do not match the reality. It is clear that Asian families show similarities and differences across as wide a range as others in Britain, and that racism, class relations and the importance of gender and generation all have a bearing upon how families are formed.

The supermarket image of the British family beams from cornflake packets and the banks. It is an image of a white, middle class family, a wife and husband and two children, a boy and a girl. This, it suggests, is a normal family.

The situation for Asian families is one of change, in which patterns of family life are being modified. The dynamic nature of Asian families is not dissimilar to the changing nature of British families generally, and this underlies our understanding of Asian families as part of the overall pattern of diversity in Britain today. (Adapted from Westwood and Bhachu, *Images and Realities*.)

1   Identify two reasons given in Item A to support the argument that isolated nuclear family structures are typical of advanced industrial societies.   (2 marks)
2   Items A and B offer contrasting accounts of family structure in industrial societies. Assess the extent to which each of the views is supported by sociological evidence and arguments.   (7 marks)
3   Item C suggests that popular images of the Asian family do not match reality. How would you explain this?   (6 marks)
4   Assess the view, put forward in Item C, that there is an 'overall pattern of diversity' in family structure in Britain.   (10 marks)

Associated Examining Board Specimen A Level Question for 1991 Syllabus

Suggestions

1   The nuclear family assists geographical and social mobility essential in industrial society.
2   While Item A stresses the importance of the nuclear family, item B shows why extended kin are still important as shown in the text (Young and Willmott etc.).
3   We tend to apply our own images of reality.
4   See for example Table 2.1. Also, in a multi-racial society there will be several different types of family structure.

4 **'Domination has been replaced by partnership.' Assess this view in relation to families today.**

University of Cambridge Local Examinations Syndicate, A Level, Paper 1, June 1987

Suggestions

In the past the father was portrayed as an authority figure. Nowadays the hidden assumption of patriarchy may be more important, with the father making most of the decisions affecting the family. See also Table 8.6.

Use the various case studies quoted in this chapter.

5 **The family is the source of all our discontents. Discuss this assessment of 'the modern family'.**

University of Cambridge, A Level, Paper 2, June 1987

Suggestions

Use books critical of the family, especially by David Cooper, R. D. Laing, P. Laslett, etc. See box headed 'Four views of the family in society'. (See also question 6.)

6 **Explain the ways in which families fulfil their functions in any *one* society.**

London and East Anglian Group, A Level, Paper 1, May 1988

Suggestions

You could refer, for example, to Laslett, *The World We Have Lost*, or to Young and Willmott, *Family and Kinship in East London*, etc. Show that often the family does not perform the functions it is supposed to.

7 **Referring to the quotation from Tolstoy at the opening of this chapter, what might a sociologist say are the obstacles to family happiness?**

Suggestion

Discuss patriarchy in the family, sexism, socialization to sex roles, bad parenting (see next chapter).

Further reading

(easier reading marked*)

*G. Allen, *Family Life*

*M. Anderson, 'How Much Has the Family Changed?'

M. Anderson (ed.), *Sociology of the Family*

E. Bott, *Family and Social Network*

J. Burgoyne, 'Married Happiness'

D. Clark, 'Wedlocked Britain'

S. Cochrane, 'Torn Apart at Home', *New Statesman and Society*, 1 July 1988

A. Dally, *Inventing Motherhood*
*M. Farmer, *The Family*
J. Finch, 'Family Ties'
R. Fletcher, *The Shaking of the Foundations*
*D. Gittins, *The Family in Question*
C. C. Harris, *The Family and Industrial Society*
*A. Holme, 'Family and Homes in East London' (for an update of the classic
    studies of Young and Willmott)
P. Laslett, *The World We Have Lost*
J. Laurance, 'Statistics of a Taboo', *New Statesman and Society*, 1 July 1988
M. Macleod and E. Saragu, 'Against Orthodoxy', *New Statesman and Society*,
    1 July 1988
D. H. J. Morgan, *The Family, Politics and Social Theory*
L. Morris, 'The No Longer Working Class'
F. Mount, *The Subversive Family*
A. Oakley, 'The Woman's Place'
R. N. Rapoport et al., *Families in Britain*
M. Richards, 'Parents and Kids'
L. Rimmer, *Families in Focus*
Y. Roberts, 'It Can Happen Here', *New Statesman and Society*, 1 July 1988
*L. Segal (ed.), *What is to be Done about the Family?*
E. Shorter et al., 'The Unholy Family'
J. Wayne, 'Blaming the Messenger', *New Statesman and Society*, 1 July 1988
P. Wilson and R. Pahl, 'The Changing Sociological Construct of the Family'
*M. Young and P. Willmott, *Family and Kinship in East London*
M. Young and P. Willmott, *The Symmetrical Family*
Families in the Future
Happy Families?
Values and the Changing Family

3   Infant Care

The structure of this chapter is similar to Chapter 2. It sets out some common assumptions concerning infant care and then attempts to show what really happens in the care of children. We all, of course, have personal experience of infant care from our own childhood and also possibly as parents. We are all experts on this subject – or are we? Are the experts – teachers, doctors, health visitors – really the true experts? Is the development of the child mainly to do with hereditary factors or are environmental factors crucial?

The theme of this chapter is that 'we are what we have learnt'. We are what we have *socially* inherited rather than just what we have *genetically* inherited. Further, we learn to be ourselves very early in life.

Drawing on the evidence of studies of infant care over the last 30 years, the chapter shows that common assumptions on this subject are questionable and based on ideologies. The main common assumptions seem to be:

1   that children take after their parents and inherit their parents' characteristics;

2   that there are fewer class differences in the upbringing of children;

3   that working class children are 'culturally deprived';

4   that there is more maternal deprivation now (that is, that mothers care less for their children);

5   that there are fewer differences now between the ways boys and girls are brought up.

These common assumptions will now be examined in turn. But first of all, do you agree that these are common assumptions?

Common assumption one: *that children take after their parents and inherit their parents' characteristics*

What is more important: what a child inherits from its parents, or how it is brought up? (This is known as the nature–nurture argument.) Really there can be no final answer to the question, so let us assume, for the moment, that common assumption one is true.

At first sight this appears to be a reasonable assumption. Many of us

Which characteristics do we inherit, and which do we learn?

believe children will take after their parents; we look at a baby and say it has got its mother's eyes or its father's stubbornness. It is but a short step from here to believing that it will inherit its parents' intelligence. Indeed, the belief that intelligence is inherited underlies the rationale of intelligence tests and other forms of psychological testing, which are so prevalent in Western society in allocating children to different kinds of education, and adults to jobs. These tests select, allocate and exclude; by assuming that intelligence is inherited, they virtually exclude the possibility of people learning to be more 'intelligent'. (The ideological nature of IQ tests is discussed in Chapter 11.)

There can probably be no final answer to the question of genetic inheritance versus learnt characteristics. Table 3.1 is intended to highlight some of the main differences between the two views. (Which viewpoint do you favour?)

Common assumption two: *that there are fewer class differences now in the upbringing of children*

The two main classes in advanced society are the middle class and the working class. The middle class ranges from professional and managerial people down to routine office workers, while the working class ranges from skilled manual workers down through semi-skilled to unskilled manual workers. As a general rule, people from different social classes have different patterns of behaviour and different lifestyles.

Table 3.2 points to some of these differences. How would you complete it? Think about the first six items. (This book may help to provide some of the answers, for example, Chapter 12 on medicine looks at the different health and life expectancies of middle class and working class people.)

Table 3.1 Differing views on inheritance

Views held by some psychologists	A sociological view
1 Infant care by parents is instinctual.	We are what we have learnt. Infant care is a learnt pattern of behaviour for the most part.
2 Children take after their parents mainly because of genetic inheritance.	Children resemble their parents because of their upbringing.
3 You cannot do much to improve ability. (Therefore there is no need for state intervention – therefore I need not pay more taxes for better state services for others, such as better schools.)	New habits can be learned. (There is room for the state to develop full potential, for example through better schools.)
4 Intelligence tests are a fair measure of innate intelligence.	Intelligence tests do not measure innate intelligence. They measure what a particular culture values most, for example reading ability and mathematical ability (rather than mechanical skills, such as repairing a car).
5 Stress on: nature genetic instinct intelligence innate behaviour born	Stress on: nurture cultural learning interest acquired and learned behaviour made

However, it is the seventh item in the table that this chapter will examine: the contrast between the way working class and middle class parents bring up their children.

It is clear that different social classes have different views on what is desirable in children. The conception of what is desirable is the bridge between the family and the larger social structure. In other words, the parents prepare the child for the world as experienced by the parents. The differences between the different social classes in the way children are brought up are generally greater than most people think.

In the study of patterns of child care the concept of *socialization* is particularly important. Socialization can be seen as the learning of a *culture*. Culture can be defined briefly as the *norms* and *values* of a society as learnt (or internalized) by the individual. (Norms and values can in turn be defined as 'means' and 'ends' in society; for example, achieving financial

Table 3.2   A basis for comparing middle class and working class life styles

	Professional or managerial person	Unskilled manual person
1 How much money do they have?		
2 Where do they live?		
3 What kind of work do they do?		
4 Where do they spend their holidays?		
5 What kind of food do they eat?		
6 What are their different health and life expectancies?		
7 How do they bring up their children?		

success is a value, working hard for this is a norm. See Glossary for a fuller definition of terms.) This process of learning a culture begins in infancy and continues throughout life. To a large degree parents act as agents for society, passing on to the child those values and attitudes which are required for the position in society which that child is 'destined' to fill. In this way society could be said to reproduce itself.

Perhaps the best known work on childhood socialization is the series of studies by John and Elizabeth Newson. The first main study was called *Patterns of Infant Care in an Urban Community* and it was a survey of 700 mothers with one-year-old children in Nottingham. The researchers considered that middle class mothers had a 'better attitude' to pregnancy, and this was measured by the percentage of mothers attending antenatal relaxation classes, the willingness to seek professional advice as distinct from using traditional remedies and so on. A general finding was that middle class mothers would punish according to principle whereas working class mothers tended to punish according to the consequences of an act. Middle class fathers seemed to take their role more seriously whereas the working class father might reject his role; often he was not available. These and many other differences show that socialization (as defined here earlier) is quite different between middle class and working class families.

The first of the accompanying tables is based on *Patterns of Infant Care* and the remaining tables are based on later surveys. Try to see what these findings mean in terms of the material circumstances of the children, the values and attitudes passed on to the children, and in particular the differences between middle class and working class children.

These tables are based on the Newson studies of child care and have been confirmed by later studies. For example, a study by the National Foundation for Education Research entitled *The Young Child at Home* showed

Table 3.3 Class differences in the care of children from birth to 12 months

	Social class I and II[1] %	Social class V[2] %
Still breast feeding at 1 month	60	34
Dummy given at some time	39	74
Normal bedtime before 6.30 pm	47	31
Child sleeps in own room	54	3
Diet judged inadequate in protein or vitamin C	5	32
Mother checks genital play	25	93
Generally smacks the child for offences	39	58
High participation in child care by father	57	36
Couple seldom go out together	25	59
Mother's age 21 or less at first birth	24	53

[1] Social Class I and II = professional and managerial
[2] Social class V   = unskilled manual

Source: J. and E. Newson, *Patterns of Infant Care in an Urban Community*

Table 3.4 Class differences in the care of children at 4 years old

	Social class I and II %	Social class V %
One child only (at time of interview)	17	1
Mother's age 27 or less	9	27
Strong desire for quiet, neatness and cleanliness	3	10
Mother participates in children's play	71	45
Mother/father regularly reads bedtime stories	56	14
Mother gives false information 'where do babies come from?'	8	66
Punitive response to bedwetting	10	88

Source: J. and E. Newson, *Four Years Old in an Urban Community*

that 57 per cent of a sample of middle class mothers sent their children to a play school twice a week compared with only 29 per cent of working class mothers.

In general it seems working class parents marry younger, have more children and have far fewer material advantages (the child is unlikely to have its own room). More importantly so far as the child's attitudes are concerned, the methods of child care are quite different.

It must be emphasized that the differences in child care should be seen as

Table 3.5   Class differences in the care of children at 7 years old

	Social class I and II %	Social class V %
Child described as 'outdoor'	44	71
Mother threatens external authority	6	39
Mother threatens withdrawal of love for misdemeanour	6	30
Child (boy) considered destructive	4	35
Mother believes toys should be communally owned	7	22

Source: J. and E. Newson, *Seven Years Old in the Home Environment*

Table 3.6   Class differences in the care of children at 7 years old

	Social class I and II %	Social class V %
Child has been to theatre with parents	77	27
Child has been to museum with parents	89	52
Child has been to zoo with parents	89	64
Child has been to exhibition with parents	31	7
Child has been to sporting event with parents	37	14
Child has been to religious service with parents	57	19

Source: J. Newson, E. Newson and P. Barnes, *Perspectives on School at Seven Years Old*

part of a total way of life – that middle class parents espouse some values and working class parents others; and this is due to the different conditions of life they experience. A logical place to begin is with occupational difference.

Middle class people tend to have *careers*, which have promotion prospects. Think of the young chartered accountant who hopes one day to become a partner in a large firm of chartered accountants; or the bank clerk who hopes to become a bank manager. It seems many middle class people have a 'ladder' view of life, always striving to *become* something better.

Working class people tend to have *jobs*, where the main motivation to work is money. Often they do not expect to get much promotion. Getting ahead in a middle class occupation is dependent on one's own actions; while in working class occupations getting ahead is often dependent on collective action, e.g. membership of a trade union. Again, there is a link between parental values, patterns of child care and occupational requirements in the various social classes. Thus the home prepares the child for the school, which in turn prepares the child for the occupational structure. The links between home, school and occupation are demonstrated more fully later in the book (for example in Chapter 11 on education).

Common assumption three: *that working class children are 'culturally deprived'*

The previous section may have given the impression that working class children were somehow culturally deprived: that middle class children are given more encouragement to learn and have a more fluent command of the language. All this leads in turn to further assumptions, that the middle class home prepares the child for school better than the working class home and so on.

But are working class children really deprived? Do they really suffer from cultural deprivation? Nell Keddie asks these questions in the book she edited, *Tinker, Tailor . . . The Myth of Cultural Deprivation*. In her introduction she asks what culture these families are deprived of, since no group can be deprived of its own culture. Perhaps the idea of cultural deprivation is based on the assumption that children who do not come from homes where the mainstream middle class culture prevails are culturally deprived and therefore less educable. This implies that it is the school's function to impart the values of this mainstream culture and that failure to acquire these values has led to these children's ineducability through lack of preparation – cultural deprivation. Thus the children's failure is located in the home, rather than the school and its curriculum.

Are children culturally deprived because they do not learn what Bernstein called an elaborated code of speech? W. Labov in a paper in Keddie's book ('The Logic of Non-Standard English') argues that non-

---

Labov on 'verbal deprivation'

The notion of 'verbal deprivation' is a part of the modern mythology of educational psychology, typical of the unfounded notions which tend to expand rapidly in our educational system. In past decades linguists have been as guilty as others in promoting such intellectual fashions at the expense of both teachers and children. But the myth of verbal deprivation is particularly dangerous, because it diverts attention from real defects of our educational system to imaginary defects of the child; it leads its sponsors inevitably to the hypothesis of the genetic inferiority of black children that it was originally designed to avoid. The most useful service which linguists can perform today is to clear away the illusion of 'verbal deprivation' and to provide a more adequate notion of the relations between standard and non-standard dialects. (W. Labov, 'The Logic of Non-Standard English'.)

standard English has its own logic. The non-standard English which some working class and black children may speak is discouraged by the school since it is not part of the mainstream culture and the formal communication of the school. Yet these children are not really culturally deprived and their language is capable of sophisticated argument and logic and is as rich as 'mainstream speech'.

The question of home background and the school curriculum is explored further in Chapter 11, on the sociology of education.

Common assumption four: *that there is more maternal deprivation now*

The previous section considered the allegation that working class and non-white children may be culturally deprived due to their upbringing. This section looks at the assumption that there may be greater maternal deprivation (lack of love and care by the mother) now; this could be due, for example, to the fact that an increasing number of mothers in all social classes go out to work. There is a further assumption here, that children are deprived as a result of inadequate or bad mothering. How true is this?

A good starting point might be John Bowlby's book *Child Care and the Growth of Love*. Bowlby thought that a child was 'deprived' if its mother could not give the loving care an infant needs. This maternal deprivation would seriously affect the child, for example in later life it would not be able to form a relationship with another person. (The deprivation might be due to bad mothering or the absence of the mother.)

Michael Rutter, in *Maternal Deprivation Reassessed*, agrees that many of Bowlby's findings have been confirmed. However, deprivation can cover a wide range of adversities. For example, admission of a young child to hospital may cause distress due to the temporary loss of parents, but also due to the effects of a strange and frightening environment, a disturbance effect after the return home, intellectual retardation because of a lack of mental stimulation, and so on – maternal deprivation is not the only factor. Rutter also suggests that it is bond formation that is important, rather than solely mother–child bond formation. It is in the child's interest to encourage attachment to several people, not just the mother.

Probably the main focus of interest is whether it is harmful for the child if the mother goes out to work. Summarizing the evidence, Rutter shows that working class mothers were less anxious about having substitutes while they were away and less anxious about separation generally. Secondly, fathers in these cases took a more active interest in family life (and the children took on more household responsibilities). Thirdly, Rutter found that the experience of having a paid job outside the home may have a beneficial effect on the mother's wellbeing.

Apart from the effects on the children, it will be obvious that the question of maternal deprivation is an important one for the rights of women, the right to work, and sexual equality generally. The evidence produced by Rutter and others suggests that there are substitutes and complements for maternal care. Many, perhaps most, women obtain intense satisfaction from being full time mothers. Nothing said here is intended to suggest otherwise. What is important is not to see maternal care as a purely instinctive matter – it is probably learnt behaviour; and secondly to realize that perhaps some of the arguments against women working may be advanced for ideological reasons, to keep women in their place! In the home.

Common assumption five: *that there are fewer differences now between the ways boys and girls are brought up*

This question will also be discussed in Chapter 8, on gender, which shows how the upbringing of children is based on ideas and values which exaggerate sexual differences and put women in an inferior and subservient role, a role that is learnt in childhood and practised throughout life.

John and Elizabeth Newson (in *Seven Years Old in the Home Environment*) comment that girls' play tends to mirror fairly closely the roles of those adult women who the children can observe in everyday life. These are either mothers' roles or roles like them, such as nurse or teacher (two of the games popular with young girls). Boys frequently adopt heroic roles such as cowboy or astronaut, roles unconnected with everyday life. In any case there is a big difference between the play of boys and of girls. This point, and the differing attitudes of parents to boys and girls, is clearly show in Table 3.7.

Table 3.7 Differences in the upbringing of boys and girls

		Boys %	Girls %
1	Child described as 'outdoor'	67	52
2	Child fetched from school	15	30
3	Rough and tumble type of play preferred	55	33
4	Imaginative role playing preferred	38	65
5	Child smacked once a week or more	41	25
6	Mother carries out threats against child	48	56
7	Child considered aggressive	37	24
8	Children considered aggressive		
	with mother	33	49
	with father	68	40
9	Child helps regularly with household chores	27	32
10	Child earns pocket money from parents	59	50

Source: mainly J. and E. Newson *Seven Years Old in the Home Environment*

Table 3.7 shows there are big differences in the upbringing of boys and girls. How could you summarize these differences? What do you think the likely consequences of all this would be? It seems, for example, that mothers are harder on girls (item 6); girls are not encouraged to play boisterous games (items 1, 3 and 4); and it is the girls mainly who are taught to do the housework by copying mother (items 8 and 9). From all this the girl is likely to learn that woman's place is in the home, that the woman plays second fiddle and so on. In whose interests is all this? It appears to be in the interests of the male, hence the ideological nature of such ideas as 'a woman's place is in the home' and the idea that it is less important for a woman to go to university or to have a career. Do you agree?

Conclusions

1   The theme of this chapter is the concept of socialization; how children are socialized for their role in society; how class attitudes and gender differences persist through socialization (see 'socialization' in Glossary).

2   More emphasis should be placed on what the child learns in infancy than on what it inherits.

3   More attention should be given to class differences in the upbringing of children (rather than assuming that these class differences are somehow disappearing).

4   More attention ought to be given to possible wrong assumptions made by schools, rather than assuming that working class (and black) pupils fare badly at school because they are 'culturally deprived'.

5   Finally there needs to be greater awareness of the differences in the upbringing of boys and girls, as this will help to show that many of the gender differences are culturally learnt rather than genetically inherited.

Self-examination questions

(Answers can be ascertained from the text.)

1   What is meant by: 'socialization', 'social class', 'culturally deprived', 'role model', 'maternal deprivation', 'nurture', 'instinct', 'intelligence'?

2   What are the arguments for and against Bowlby's view of maternal deprivation? Why should sociologists be interested in this debate?

Discussion topics

1 Is there or can there be a correct method of child care?
2 In what respects do parents act as agents of social control?

Projects

1 **The following table has been extracted from the book *Seven Years Old in the Home Environment*, by J. and E. Newson.**

What do you consider the findings indicate about the differences in patterns of child care as between (a) different social classes (b) boys and girls?

What do you consider the implications are (a) for performance at school (b) for occupational choice?

What do you think women's rights campaigners would find interesting in these figures.

Collect further evidence which supports or refutes the trends suggested by this table (you will find useful: *New Statesman and Society*, books by campaigners for women's rights such as Ann Oakley and Juliet Mitchell, *Social Class Difference in Britain* by Ivan Reid).

Table 3.8

	I and II	III White Collar	III Manual	IV	V
	%	%	%	%	%
1 Child owned ten or more books					
boys	98	70	48	43	28
girls	95	69	50	44	10
2 Rough and tumble play preferred					
boys	41	43	58	63	60
girls	2	21	34	39	39
3 Child smacked less than once a month					
boys	35	22	23	26	19
girls	52	43	34	38	28
4 Father's participation in family is high					
fathers of boys	58	62	46	47	46
fathers of girls	37	24	34	25	23
5 Child fetched from school					
boys	22	21	13	7	16
girls	45	20	29	28	26

Suggestions

As in other questions here, you could start with a definition of socialization: that it is the internalizing of the norms and values comprising the culture of a society. Then show that the socialization patterns for boys and girls are consistently different. The same is true of class differences. Then show why the class differences favour the middle class child at school. Finally show why women's rights campaigners might advocate the same socialization for boys and girls (see for example *Just Like a Girl* by Sue Sharpe or *Subject Women* by Ann Oakley, or many other books on this subject).

2   **After reading the passage, attempt the following questions.**

Unhappy childhood

But it would be facile to blame politics alone for modern society's comparative indifference towards children. Such attitudes become possible only when in tune with popular prejudice. While the British probably love their own offspring as much as do parents in any other nation, there is a certain remoteness in this relationship, combining an odd mixture of sentimentality and fear of over-indulgence.

Thus, sending small children away to boarding school so they can 'learn to stand on their own feet as soon as possible' continues to surprise other nationalities. As does the famous telegram Arthur Ransome's child characters received from their otherwise loving absent father, on requesting his permission to go sailing: 'Better drowned than duffers. If not duffers, won't drown.' Sink or swim indeed. Elsewhere our long attachment to corporal punishment at school testifies to a lingering, curiously puritanical fear that failure to confront the young with harsh realities will somehow fatally spoil them.

Such traditional attitudes apply now only in a minority of homes, yet their shadow still falls across many of the ways in which the rest of us relate to children. Some otherwise caring parents will be reluctant to pick up a crying baby even in the first week of its life for fear of encouraging more sobbing and thereby, 'making a rod for your own back'. The same fear of spoiling children is also reflected in society's tendency to go on ignoring their needs.

Mothers still search in vain for facilities beyond the home for feeding or changing a baby, or for toilets in their local children's library where the other infants can pee. In crowded streets, traffic islands are usually too small to get a pram on to, and in the shop the same pram may either be forbidden or else involves a struggle with swing doors, stairs or lifts whose doors cannot be held open until everyone is safely inside. Trying to get the pram on to a bus or tube on the journey home is fraught with problems. Once at home, places outside suitable for a child to play will be at a premium, as cars have been allowed to steal roads and pavements, making any tolerably safe children's game impossible.

It doesn't have to be like this. Some other European nations set a far better example in all these areas. There are even special parks that include miniature tracks and movable baby cars to help children learn better road safety at an early age. (N. Tucker, *New Statesman and Society*, 8 July 1988.)

1 Would you say child rearing practices in Britain are harsh? Illustrate your answer with examples.

2 In what ways could child care in its widest sense be improved?

3 Should child care be taught in school? If so, what are the obstacles to its introduction?

Suggestions

Show that there are different methods of child rearing and that these seem to vary according to class.

How are we to judge what is good child care?

Many childhoods are unhappy due to poverty and lack of facilities, poor housing, etc. Refer to 'Further reading'.

3 **Read the passage and answer the questions that follow.**

Feelings of inadequacy and self-blame are extremely common among mothers. Mothers who do no paid work often feel inadequate as adult members of society and thus unworthy as mothers, while women who have paid employment feel guilty. Whichever choice they take, mothers tend to feel that their children's entire development is affected by their choice. In fact mothers often seem to feel that the good bits about their children are inborn aspects of their personalities, while the bad bits are their mothers' doing! Most mothers accept the myth of a possible perfect mother, whose children would effortlessly behave 'well' just because of her perfection. When a mother sees her children screaming in the supermarket for the sweets which the management has deliberately placed at eye level, or wetting their pants on auntie's best rug, she does not see them as separate people, but as little bits of herself, reflections of her mothering being judged and found wanting. Motherhood as an institution is at once inside us and outside, and feels enormously powerful and all-encompassing. Mothers will find it easier to see through the myth of the perfect mother when non-mothers join with them to insist on better conditions for rearing children. (C. New and M. David, *For the Children's Sake*, pp. 194–5.)

1 Why do some mothers feel unworthy while others feel guilty, according to the writer?

2 What is the myth of the perfect mother? Whose interest does this benefit? Whose ideologies (if any) does it support?

Suggestions

Mothers are made to feel guilty whether they work or not. Why is this? Is it to keep them out of the labour market (where they would compete with men)?

Discuss the views of Bowlby (*Child Care and the Growth of Love*) and Rutter (*Maternal Deprivation Reassessed*). Consult Bibliography and 'Further reading'.

Discuss relevant ideologies, such as 'patriarchy'.

4   **Read the passage and answer the questions that follow.**

Children at play

Iona and Peter Opie, the foremost anthropologists in the field of British children's culture, always maintained that child's play was a social world which resisted adult incursion. In 1959 they wrote of a 'self-contained community in which children's basic lore and language seem scarcely to alter from generation to generation' and their conviction had not changed twenty years later. Other writers, though, have dwelt on adult intervention in the child's world of play and the ideological implications of this; consider toys, for example.

Toys first appeared in Britain in large numbers during the latter half of the last century: the first clockwork trains, for instance, were made in 1865 and construction sets, teddy bears, and toy soldiers all go back to the turn of the century. There is a minimal sociological literature on toys but what writing there is is generally leftish and disapproving. Peter Wollen's work is typical of this disapproval, arguing that toys, although for children, are seldom designed, made or bought by them; that toys are for private use and do not feature in the (more desirable) 'collective product' of public play; and that toys colonize the imagination, discouraging creativity. (S. Wagg, 'Perishing Kids? The Sociology of Childhood', *Social Studies Review*, March 1988.)

1   Why would sociologists be interested in the toys children play with?
2   In what ways do boys' toys differ from girls' toys?

Suggestions

Show that toys can be seen as part of the socialization process – that, for example, parents use toys to socialize their children and pass on the parents' views on society. In effect toys can be seen as helping to prepare children for their role in society. J. and E. Newson in *Seven Years Old in the Home Environment* show how working class mothers stress that toys should be shared. Expensive toys could be seen as announcing the parents' status – (or sometimes a substitute for love).

Past examination questions

1   **The bundle of drives which is a human baby develops as a person only through relationships with others. What are the principal aspects of this process?**

University of Cambridge Local Examinations, A Level, Summer 1983.

Suggestions

Stress the importance of socialization and then use Table 3.1 in this chapter to highlight the sociological approach to this question. Mention that we are what we have learnt to be and this comes from our interaction with others, at first our parents, later our peer group.

2

Item A

Item B

> Boys and Girls can do woodwork or needlework . . . In needlework you can make a doll, skirt or night-dress case . . . In woodwork you can make a model of a plane, car or boat . . .

Of course it is not just school subjects which keep up traditional gender divisions. The family, neighbourhood and peer group place equally strong, if not greater, pressures on young people to be 'typical' girls and boys.

It seems to me that very little has changed during the growth of comprehensive education [see Chapters 8 and 11]. Girls still rarely take the subjects which have been done traditionally by boys. Even at a school which prides itself on offering equal chances and choices to both sexes traditional gender differences remain. What hope is there then for young people in schools which have more narrow-minded practices?

Item C

Subject choices, by sex: 4th and 5th year, 1985/86 (percentages)

Year	Subject	Boys doing subject	Girls doing subject
4th	Craft Design Technology	80	8
4th	Home economics Needlework	–	70
5th	Metalwork Woodwork	70	–
5th	Home economics Needlework	10	50

(Items B and C adapted from 'Sugar and Spice . . .', Frances Pinney, *The Social Science Teacher*, Summer 1986.)

1   Study the cartoon, Item A, and then describe how children are socialized into becoming 'typical' girls and boys.   (2 marks)

2   Study Item B. Identify and explain briefly any one form of pressure which is placed upon young people to keep to their traditional gender roles.   (2 marks)

3   a) Explain the expression 'traditional gender divisions'.   (2 marks)
    b) How does the information presented in Item C show 'traditional gender divisions'?   (2 marks)

4   Items B and C show that girls and boys often choose different subjects in schools. Identify and explain three reasons for their subject choices.   (6 marks)

5   How have both legal and social changes helped to improve the status of women in our society during this century?   (6 marks)

Southern Examining Group, GCSE, Paper 2, Summer 1988

Suggestions

Stress that we are socialized to our roles as man or woman; certain subjects at school are considered girls' subjects, others are for boys.

See also Chapter 8 on gender – especially 'Why do sexual inequalities persist?' – and Chapter 11 for the hidden curriculum.

Sexual inequalities persist. They seem to start in the home (Chapter 8).

Further reading

As usual, the easier reading is marked*
 P. Ariès, *Centuries of Childhood*
 J. Bowlby and M. Fry, *Child Care and the Growth of Love*
 C. E. Davies et al., *The Young Child at Home*
 M. Hoyles (ed.), *Changing Childhood*
 C. Jenks (ed.), *The Sociology of Childhood*
 N. Keddie (ed.), *Tinker, Tailor . . . The Myth of Cultural Deprivation* (especially the Introduction and the chapter by Labov)
 J. Klein, *Samples from English Cultures* (especially summary at the end of Volume II)
 M. Mead, *A Coming of Age in Samoa*
 M. Mead, *Growing Up in New Guinea*
*J. Newson and E. Newson, *Four Years Old in an Urban Community*
*J. Newson and E. Newson, *Patterns of Infant Care in an Urban Community*
 J. Newson and E. Newson, *Seven Years Old in the Home Environment*
 J. Newson and E. Newson, *The Extent of Parental Physical Punishment in the UK*
*J. Newson, E. Newson and P. Barnes, *Perspectives on School at Seven Years Old*
 I. Opie and P. Opie, *The Lore and Language of Schoolchildren*

*M. Rutter, *Maternal Deprivation Reassessed*
S . Scarr and J. Dunn, *Mother Care Other Care*
N. Tucker, 'Unhappy Childhood'
S. Wagg, 'Perishing Kids? The Sociology of Childhood'
P. Wollen, 'Do Children Really Need Toys?'

4   Divorce

Introduction

The divorce rates are going up in most industrialized countries. There was a fall from a wartime peak (when many marriages were quickly contracted), but since the fifties the trend is clearly upwards. Since the war the age of marriage has fallen in most developed countries, but in about 1976 the trend reversed. People are now marrying later and the proportion of unmarried people in their twenties is increasing. The rise in the number of single people is also partly due to the higher divorce rates. Table 4.1 illustrates divorce trends in Europe.

This chapter looks at some of the possible causes of the higher divorce rates and then considers a few of the common assumptions concerning

Table 4.1   Divorce rates, European Community comparisons

Country	Divorce per thousand existing marriages	
	1981	**1986**
UK	11.9	12.9
Belgium	6.1	7.3
Denmark	12.1	12.8
France	6.8	8.5
Germany (FR)	7.2	8.3
Greece	2.5	3.0
Irish Republic	0.0	0.0
Italy	0.9	1.1
Luxembourg	5.9	7.5
Netherlands	8.3	8.7
Portugal	2.8	–
Spain	1.1	–

Source: Statistical Office of the European Community, reprinted in *Social Trends 1989*

these apparently disturbing statistics. Firstly though, what conclusions would you draw from Table 4.1?

Table 4.2 Petitions by husbands and wives

	1961	1976	1987
Petitions (in thousands) in England and Wales			
Filed by husbands	14	43	50
Filed by wives	18	101	133
	32	144	183

Source: adapted from *Social Trends 1989*. *Social Trends* is an important source of government statistics.

Table 4.2 seems to show:

1   A large overall increase in the number of divorces.
2   A pronounced increase in the number of wives petitioning for divorce. In earlier years most petitions were brought by husbands. What does this mean? Could it be that in this respect women are gaining more independence? This seems unlikely especially as in most areas of social life – the family, work etc. – there is still much discrimination against women.
3   Although there has been some increase in divorces between 1976 and 1987 the rate seems to have slackened. The reason for this is examined later.
(NB: about four-fifths of petitions end in divorce.)

Table 4.3 Age, class and divorce (1979)

Social class of husband	Divorce rate per thousand husbands, age 20–29	Divorce rate per thousand husbands, age 50–59
Professional	10	too few cases to estimate a rate
Skilled non-manual	19	10
Unskilled manual	55	9

Source: adapted from *Social Trends 1985*

Table 4.3 seems to indicate two main points:

1   The rate of divorce declines with age.
2   The rate of divorce is higher among the working class (although in the past it was only the wealthy who could afford a divorce).

Some 'causes' of the rising divorce rate

It is not hard to guess at some of the prevailing common assumptions on divorce: that the figures indicate some serious social pathology – in plain words, society is becoming rotten; that the figures reflect a casual attitude to sex; that marriage is under threat; that individuals are selfish; that the children are neglected; and so on. These assumptions are quite understandable, especially considering that the high divorce rates are also accompanied by high illegitimacy rates, high cohabitation rates and so on.

Before dealing directly with these common assumptions it might be useful to look sociologically at some of the possible causes of the increasing divorce rates. Perhaps 'causes' is the wrong word; rather, one should look at all the concomitants of industrialization in society (that is, all the social changes in society that accompany industrialization) that might be linked to the increase in divorce. These may be listed as follows:

1 the decline of strict religions (the secularization of society);
2 legal toleration of divorce;
3 some increase in the independence of women;
4 urbanization;
5 birth control;
6 increased geographic mobility;
7 increased social mobility;
8 increased heterogeneity of the population;
9 higher expectations of the marriage partners;
10 The increasing effect of social class on divorce in industrial society.

These 'causes' of the higher divorce rates (or concomitants of industrialization) will now be considered in turn.

The secularization of society

The importance of religious explanation is reduced and people seek 'rational' or 'scientific' answers rather than a religious explanation (for example, a religious view of marriage is that it is a sacrament and therefore cannot be broken).

Increased legal toleration of divorce

Between 1921 and 1979 the number of divorces rose more than forty fold. It would be easy to demonstrate this just by showing the divorce figures year by year. However, it might be more interesting to try to get the figures to tell a story, as in Table 4.4. Each of these Acts made it easier to get a divorce, for example the Divorce Law Reform Act 1969 laid down the irretrievable breakdown of marriage as grounds for divorce. The petitioner no longer had to prove a matrimonial offence (such as adultery or cruelty). Thus every time the law made it easier to get a divorce, the divorce rate

Table 4.4 Divorce petitions in the UK and changes in the law

		Annual average number of petitions
1923 Matrimonial Causes Act	1921–5	2,848
	1926–30	4,052
1937 'Herbert' Act	1931–5	4,784
	1936–40	7,535
1950 Matrimonial Causes Act	1946–50	38,901
	1951–4	33,131
1969 Divorce Law Reform Act	1964–8	40,381
	1972–6	122,859
	1983	169,000
	1987	183,000

Source: O. R. McGregor, *Divorce in England*, and *Social Trends 1989*

increased. (The exception is the 1946–50 figure, which was high because of the dissolution of many hurriedly contracted wartime marriages.) What perhaps these figures indicate is that in the past many couples were living in unsatisfactory marriages, unable to obtain a divorce for legal reasons.

Increasing independence of women

Since 1931 the number of married women at work has trebled and this has tended to free women from dependence on men. In addition there has been an increasing commercialization of services – cleaning, meals, etc. This has reduced the dependence of men and women on the home, since it has reduced the number of cooperative activities in the home. Because of this and the independence that work gives married women generally, the authority of the male has deteriorated (and therefore is resented).

Urbanization

In towns there are fewer social controls, since the individual is in the company of comparative strangers. Probably this explanation is less applicable now than it was earlier in the century when there was a greater difference between town and country, but it might be important when considering developing nations.

Birth control

As the size of the family declines, so the likelihood of divorce increases. There seems to be a connection between divorce and deliberate childlessness.

The Divorce Act 1969 did not require petitioners to prove a matrimonial offence (such as adultery).
Source: *New Society*, 19 January 1984.

Increased geographic and social mobility

Increased geographic mobility may mean, for example, that people are more likely to move away from the district in which they were born and brought up. Increased social mobility may mean, for example, that the son of a working class father may be more likely to enter a middle class occupation and perhaps meet more middle class people, from whom he might select a mate. There are two possible results of this increased geographic and social mobility. Firstly, the single person is more likely to meet and marry someone who comes from a different area or who comes from a different social class and this may lead to incompatibility. Secondly, increased geographic and social mobility reduces the influence of local and informal controls. If you are living among 'strangers' you are less worried about what they may think, for example whether they disapprove of divorce.

Increased heterogeneity of the population

This follows from the last point. Because industrial societies are more mixed, there is an increasing chance of marriage between people from different cultural backgrounds and hence a greater risk of divorce.

Higher expectations of the marriage partners

Industrial society is impersonal and life in this type of society may be more stressful. For these reasons people expect more from marriage, which has to make up for these deficiencies.

The increasing effect of social class on divorce

Table 4.3 shows the connection between social class and divorce. At the beginning of the century most petitions were brought by middle class husbands. Now most petitioners are working class (more usually wives).

Having briefly outlined some possible causes for, or social changes linked to, the increase in the divorce rate, some everyday assumptions can now be considered.

Common assumption one: *the increasing divorce figures indicate something is seriously wrong with society*

This assumption may derive from the view that marriage is a divine institution and an inviolable contract. Divorce was associated with sin. The legal position was based on this view: that a divorce would be granted only if some 'matrimonial offence', such as adultery, could be proved. As mentioned earlier, it was only in 1969 that the doctrine of the irretrievable breakdown of marriage was instituted as grounds for divorce. Certainly it would be difficult to prove that society is more decadent now than in the past. Consider the conspiracy of silence that surrounded marriage and sex in the past and the widespread prostitution in Victorian society.

Common assumption two: *the high divorce rate indicates a casual attitude to sex and this is further confirmed by the increasing incidence of pre-marital and extra-marital sexual relations and by the increasing illegitimacy and abortion rates*

In fact the evidence shows that there is no rush to divorce. 60 per cent of divorces take place after ten years of marriage. Secondly, the increase in pre-marital and extra-marital sexual relationships does not necessarily mean a more casual attitude to sexual morals. In the case of pre-marital sex evidence suggests that many couples intend to marry. Extra-marital relations may be less hidden now because we are less secretive. (On the other hand, the advent of AIDS may have reduced extra-marital sexual relations.) Here, as with other social phenomena, it is not the actual act itself which interests the sociologists, but the meaning of the act to the actors. Thus the true researcher should try to discover how genuine the actors' feelings and intentions are, rather than just the rate of pre-marital sexual relations.

Common assumption three: *the high divorce rate indicates that marriage as an institution is threatened, especially as more unmarried couples are living together*

This assumption must also be challenged. 90 per cent of divorced people remarry. It could be argued not that marriage breakdown is increasing, but that we are getting close to the normal or expected divorce rate. In the past, on the other hand, because of the obstacles to divorce (particularly cost and the need to prove a matrimonial offence) the divorce rate was abnormally low. Nor can it be assumed that marriage as an institution is threatened by the increase in unmarried couples living together, as many of these couples intend marriage or come round to it eventually. The sociologist should not pass judgement on what is happening, but seek greater understanding.

Common assumption four: *the high divorce rate indicates that people are becoming more selfish and generally seeking their own pleasure or happiness*

This common assumption has been dealt with already to some extent in discussing the intentions of couples. The increase in the divorce rate is partly explained by the removal of religious, legal and financial obstacles and is not necessarily due to increased selfishness.

Common assumption five: *as a result of adult selfishness children suffer – parents are neglecting their responsibilities*

Though divorce can be tragic for the children, there is little evidence that parents are neglecting their responsibilities wholesale. One third of all divorces are of childless couples – in another third of divorces there is only one child under the age of 16. As mentioned earlier, there is a strong connection between deliberate childlessness and divorce.

Common assumption six: *perhaps marriage is too difficult for many people*

Finally some people, especially perhaps divorcees, may feel that really men and women were not made to live together. It is a persuasive proposition. Many novelists, notably Thomas Hardy, dwell on this. On the other hand, the sociologist should reject the 'human nature' implication underlying this assumption. It is not human nature that husbands and wives should constantly quarrel and be unable to see each other's viewpoint – though it may be a common occurrence in the type of society we live in, where

There is no real evidence that couples are becoming more irresponsible.
Source: *New Society*, 21 June 1984.

exploitation, cruelty, selfishness and general lack of consideration of others is taken for granted. However, as Chapter 3 explained, the basic sociological position is that we are learning animals; almost everything we are is what we have learnt and is not instinctual or genetic or human nature. In a different kind of society we might learn to be better. In a different kind of society there might be less exploitation of women. In such a society men might be less thoughtless and women less 'attracted' to the role of martyr. This is not utopian. A comparison of different kinds of societies shows how differently the roles of husband/wife, father/mother, man/woman can be played.

Conclusions

1   There has been a substantial increase in the divorce rate in Britain and in industrialized society generally.

2   It seems that the social changes associated with industrialization are also associated with this increasing divorce rate, for example the decline of strict religions, legal toleration and other items listed at the beginning of this chapter.

> **Boredom and growing apart**
> Infidelity, violence and sexual difficulties, even relentless nagging or studied rejection and indifference: all these are forms of marital behaviour that are generally regarded as potential threats to a partnership. There is probably much less agreement, however, about the degree to which such behaviour should be tolerated before steps are taken to end the marriage. For some, the events concerned are much less dramatic and cannot easily be equated with any of the legal 'facts' necessary to demonstrate that their marriage has broken down irretrievably. Such couples often describe a gradual realization that they have grown apart, that once the goals and preoccupations of early married life – making a home, having children – were over, they had little in common. In retrospect their reasons for getting married in the first place now seem insubstantial: their friends were all getting married, they wanted to leave home and their chosen partner was simply the person they were dating at the time. (J. Burgoyne et al., *Divorce Matters*, p. 94.)

3   Two important changes in the pattern of divorce have occurred. Firstly, women are much more likely to petition for divorce now. Secondly, working class couples are much more likely to separate now.

One theme of this chapter has been to examine the view that the high divorce rate indicates a deep social malaise. It has suggested that the higher divorce rate may be partly due to the fact that divorce is easier now and that in the past there were many couples who stayed together in an alienated marriage solely because divorce was not practical. The increasing divorce rate is not an indication that the family is disintegrating, although it may be a sign of the strain on the family. Overall it cannot be accepted that the high divorce figures herald the breakdown of marriage as an institution, still less that society is becoming 'rotten'.

Self-examination questions

1   What is meant by: 'divorce rate', 'industrialized society', 'illegitimacy rate', 'cohabitation', 'geographic mobility', 'social mobility', 'heterogeneity'?
2   It was suggested that rather than talk of the causes of rising divorce, we should see it as an aspect of industrialization. What does this mean?

Past examination questions

1   Examine the major causes and social consequences of the increasing frequency of divorce.

Oxford Local Examinations, A Level, Summer 1981

Suggestions

Most of the answer is in the text. On consequences, emphasize that it does not appear that couples are shirking their parental responsibility, even though one parent families are more common now. It seems couples are expecting more of marriage now. (See also comments on common assumptions.)

2   Using the information in Table 4.5:

1   Identify and describe the main trends and changes.   (10 marks)

2   What changes would you predict more recent data will demonstrate?   (6 marks)

3   Outline sociological reasons for the trends you have identified.   (14 marks)

In all cases present the data in a form appropriate to your answers.   (Total 30 marks)

Suggestions

1   The biggest increase in the divorce rate came between 1969 and 1971 as a result of the Divorce Reform Act 1969, which allowed the irretrievable breakdown of a marriage as grounds for divorce. If the parties consented, two years separation was grounds for divorce, and the table demonstrates the increase in divorce on these new grounds. On the other hand, adultery, which was the grounds cited in half the petitions in 1969, formed only a quarter of the petitions in 1979 since now a matrimonial 'offence' no longer needed to be proved.

2   Further changes may include an increasing proportion of wives petitioning for divorce and more petitions citing separation as the grounds for divorce.

3   The sociological reasons for these trends have been dealt with in this chapter.

3   What can the divorce statistics tell us about the nature of change in society?

Health Visitors' Examination, Oxford Polytechnic, June 1985

Suggestions

The 'answer' to this question has been the main theme of this chapter (see, for example, section headed 'Some "causes" of the rising divorce rate').

Table 4.5 Divorce proceedings in England and Wales, 1969–1979

	1969	1970	1971	1972	1973	1974	1975	1976	1977	1978	1979
Dissolution of marriage[1]											
Petitions field	60,134	70,575	110,017	109,822	115,048	129,993	138,048	143,698	167,074	162,450	162,867
On grounds of:											
Adultery	29,891	36,474	27,284	30,920	32,261	35,736	37,650	38,231	43,095	43,257	44,092
Desertion	11,490	12,266	11,277	8,650	7,626	6,712	5,847	5,263	6,113	5,495	4,449
Behaviour[2]	14,538	17,534	20,604	25,424	30,468	37,012	42,869	46,238	62,579	56,333	60,846
Separation (2 years and consent)			16,057	20,187	24,203	30,201	33,085	34,173	36,399	40,167	38,714
Separation (5 years)			29,911	19,270	16,593	16,445	13,987	14,572	14,586	14,959	12,957
Adultery and desertion	1,397	1,376	989	756	594	414	44	36	343	238	84
Adultery and cruelty[2]	1,397	1,563	1,722	1,977	2,113	2,367	2,923	2,912	2,925	1,450	1,219
Desertion and cruelty[2]	1,064	988	1,382	1,615	830	740	87	76	317	113	92
Adultery, desertion and cruelty[2]	92	95	148	565	104	93	13	5	119	42	36
Separation (consent and 5 years)			549	433	242	259	1,536	35	96	47	50
Other	265	279	94	25	14	14	7	1,157	502	349	328
By husbands	22,270	25,543	43,792	38,745	38,792	41,002	41,651	42,866	44,411	46,844	45,589
By wives	37,864	45,032	66,225	71,077	76,256	88,991	96,397	100,832	122,663	115,606	117,278

[1] Excluding petitions in which divorce is asked for in alternative to nullity.
[2] Grounds of behaviour were introduced from 1 January 1971 to replace grounds of cruelty.
Sources: Lord Chancellor's Department.

University of London, A Level, Summer 1984.

4 **Why is divorce becoming more common in modern society? Does this phenomenon provide support for those who have argued that the nuclear family is 'dysfunctional'?**

University of Cambridge Local Examinations Syndicate, GCSE, Paper 2, June 1988

Suggestions

See Chapter 2 for description of nuclear family and that it appears to be functional to modern industrial society (dysfunctional would be the opposite).

Although the divorce rate is high, marriage seems to be as popular as ever. It may be that people still want marriage but they expect more from it – discuss.

Further reading

*Ambrose et al., 'Men After Divorce'
 J. Bernard, *The Future of Marriage*
 J. Brannen and J. Collard, *Marriages in Trouble*
*J. Burgoyne and D. Clark, 'Why Get Married Again?'
*J. Burgoyne, R. Ormrod and M. Richards, *Divorce Matters*
*N. Hart, *When Marriage Ends*
*B. Thornes and J. Collard, *Who Divorces?*

Part III

Politics and Material Inequality

5   Stratification

Oh let us have our occupations
Bless the squire and his relations
Live upon our daily rations
And always know our proper stations
                                    Dickens

Introduction

For the moment stratification can be taken to mean social *class*. Mention of 'class' raises hackles in many people. Class seems to pigeonhole us. 'I do not belong to any class in particular – I am an individual.' Surely class is much less important than it was? We do not now have the division of 'upstairs downstairs' which is illustrated in the television series of that name. We seem to be all middle class now. We do not feel inferior to people who are supposed to be in a higher class than us. Sociologists seem to be obsessed with class. Don't we now live in a classless society?

Sociological studies show that class divisions are very strong in Western society and that many of the common assumptions about the declining importance of class are just untrue.

The evidence set out in this book shows that in the higher social classes, for example professionals and managers, as compared to lower class groups, there are:

1   a longer life expectancy;
2   lower mortality rates in all major diseases;
3   a lower infant mortality rate;
4   a lower suicide rate;
5   better working conditions;
6   better housing;
7   better education facilities;
8   better health provision;
9   less likelihood of divorce;
10   less smoking;
11   more natural teeth; and so on.

The facts show that class differences on the above items are as wide as ever.

Class is usually based on your occupation (or your father's occupation). Thus in government statistics the definition of social class is as follows:

I   professional occupations;
II   intermediate occupations (including most managerial and senior administrative occupations);
III N   skilled occupations (non-manual);
III M   skilled occupations (manual);
IV   partly skilled occupations;
V   unskilled occupations.

This classification is used by the Office of Population, Censuses and Statistics but there are many other classifications in use.

It is true that class is usually defined in terms of a person's occupation, but this is only part of the story. Sociologists show that class consciousness, class awareness and class identification are important; that people of the same social class think and act similarly; that class is really a central feature of our lives whether we are aware of it or not; that we live according to the fashions and values of our class; that it affects almost everything we do; and that we are reminded of it from the cradle to the grave.

The continuing importance of class

Now as an exercise, study the following tables and judge their significance. What do they say about social class? Then ask yourself: is class still important? Does it help to explain differences in health, for example? What causes these class differences? What are the consequences of these class differences?

Table 5.1 Sickness and class

	Non-manual workers	Manual workers
Get paid when sick (males)	98%	69%
Covered by private pension scheme	63%	38%

Source: *Social Trends 1985*

Significance of Table 5.1: this table shows that non-manual workers are more likely to be paid when absent from work through sickness and to be covered by a pension scheme when they retire. However, it shows more than this; it is really an indication that the working conditions of the non-manual worker are much better generally than those of the manual worker.

Table 5.2   Average weekly male
earnings

Occupation	1982	1988
Manual	£131	£196
Non-manual	£178	£292

Source: *Employment Gazette*, March 1989

Significance of Table 5.2: the table clearly shows that the manual working
class receive lower wages. It also shows that this class gap is widening.

Table 5.3   Unemployment rate by
occupation, Great Britain, spring
1987 (persons over 16)

Occupation	Men	Women
Manual	9.7%	8.3%
Non-manual	3.7%	5.0%

Source: *Employment Gazette*, October 1988,
Table 8

Significance of Table 5.3: this shows a higher rate of unemployment for
those in manual occupations. Note the lower rates of unemployment for
women, but many women work in part-time jobs with little career
prospects.

Table 5.4   Distribution of disposable income

	1976	1986
Bottom fifth of population	7%	7%
Top fifth of population	38%	42%

Source: *Social Trends 1989*

Significance of Table 5.4: the table shows, for example, that in 1986 the
bottom fifth of the population received only 7 per cent of the nation's
income. The table also shows that the gap between rich and poor widened
between 1976 and 1986. Social class relates to income, so that the bottom
fifth of the population comprises to a large extent the unskilled manual
working class.

Note: Table 6.7 in the following chapter shows the distribution of *wealth*.

Theories of class

When they view the society around them most people seem to accept what is going on at a fairly superficial level. Often they do not see the inequalities and the injustices referred to in the previous section. Why is this? The answer may be that people only see what they want to see, closing their eyes to inequality – until it becomes too noticeable, in the form of crime, street riots, football disturbances and disorder in classrooms (all of these occurrences can be seen as aspects of inequality).

But what is it that hides this inequality from our eyes? Perhaps the answer is that it is ideology that hides all this. The ideology of class, that distorts and hides what is really going on.

Thus according to Marxists, the state, the law, beliefs, values and even religion serve the interests of the ruling class, justifying its position while hiding what is really going on. This is the key to understanding Marx's theory of class, which will be dealt with now. This will be followed by considering Weber's theory of class.

Marx's theory of class

Marx's theory of class is basically quite simple. According to Marx there are two main classes in capitalist society: of people who own the means of production (called the capitalists or bourgeoisie) and those who do not (called the proletariat or workers).

In capitalist society there is competition among the bourgeoisie. Thus, for example, each producer tries to gain a bigger share of the market, by selling its goods cheaper than its competitors. As smaller producers drop out in this competition the bourgeoisie becomes smaller with power concentrated in the hands of the fewer producers.

The competition among the bourgeoisie forces down wages and also leads to a worsening of working and living conditions. This increasing 'immiseration' of the proletariat leads to a greater class consciousness – a greater awareness of the workers' true position in society and of their identification with other workers. In due course this would allegedly lead to revolution and eventually to a new type of classless society. In this new society all property would be owned collectively and distribution would be based on Marx's maxim: 'from each according to his ability; to each accord-ing to his needs.' It is to this kind of society that Marx's term 'communism' truly applies. Marx argued that this process is inevitable, and is hastened by the periodic crises, slumps and wars, that beset capitalism. The process is depicted in Diagram A. Diagram B shows that as capitalism matures, so the old classes become absorbed into one of the two main class groupings. Society becomes 'polarized' into these two groups (as the right-hand part of

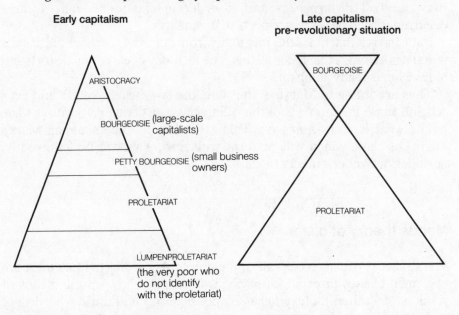

Diagram A   class, conflict and change

Increasing   Increasing   Increasing   TRUE
COMPETITION → IMMISERATION → CLASS CONSCIOUSNESS → COMMUNISM
among the   of the proletariat   among the
bourgeoisie   proletariat

Diagram B   the polarizing of capitalist society into two main classes

the diagram shows). This polarization of society makes revolution more likely, according to Marx.

One question that could be asked here is: are clerks (who do routine non-manual work) members of the working class (since they do not own the means of production) or could they be considered members of the middle class? What do you think?

David Lockwood in his study entitled *The Blackcoated Worker* examines the alleged false consciousness of the clerk. 'Black coated worker' means the same as white collar worker or clerk. 'False consciousness' is a Marxian term, deriving from the fact that clerks neither own nor control the means of production, yet identify with management. Lockwood explores three aspects of the clerk's world, the market situation, the work situation and social status.

In terms of his or her market situation (that is, economic circumstances) the clerk is still better off than the manual worker, who may be on shift work or piece work and has less job security and less occupational mobility.

In the work situation – the physical setting in which an individual works – the office worker is part of a hierarchy of management. On the factory shop floor workers are quite separate from the management groups and feel distinct from them. Factory work gives rise to a 'them and us' image of society, which accords with a Marxist theory of class conflict.

Clerical workers, like white collar workers generally, often feel themselves to be superior in the eyes of society – to have a higher status than manual workers.

Lockwood concludes that clerks tend to identify with their employers and feel they are on the same side as management. (It will be interesting to see if the new information technology with computerized ledger keeping alters this picture.) Clerks are less supervised and generally have better conditions and more rights than manual workers.

On balance it seems clerks are middle class, though with increasing unionization of white collar workers the picture could change. What, do you think, are the implications of this view for Marx's theory of class?

Criticisms of Marx

There have, of course, been many criticisms of Marx and Marx's view of class. Table 5.5 gives some of them.

Table 5.5 Criticisms of Marx

Criticisms of Marx's view of class	Possible counter-arguments
1 Increasing immiseration of the proletariat (described earlier) has not taken place over the long run. Society has become more middle class. Diagram B above should be diamond shaped to depict the growth of the middle class, thus: UPPER CLASS MIDDLE CLASS WORKING CLASS	This immiseration has been shifted from the industrialized countries to the ex-colonial peoples of the third world, many of whom eke out a precarious living. In any case there is still great class inequality in Western societies, as this book has indicated. Even in advanced Western societies there is still considerable exploitation of labour, where the employer is not paying the full, fair wage.
2 Worldwide revolution has not taken place as predicted by Marx.	This is true. In fact the first main Marxist revolution took place in Russia, a mainly backward country,

Table 5.5 (*Cont.*)

Criticisms of Marx's view of class	Possible counter-arguments
	not a mature capitalist society (as Marx had predicted). Several Marxist writers have revised Marx's own theory of revolution. Thus, for example, Lenin thought that the proletariat alone could not bring about revolution; that the emergence of revolutionary class consciousness required leadership and this had to be drawn from all classes, in particular from the revolutionary elite or Vanguard Party. Lenin believed that workers by themselves could only reach the stage of 'economism'; of trade union consciousness, involving for example striking for more pay.
3 The bourgeoisie do not own the means of production. In the West there is a separation of ownership and control. Thus the owner of a factory may employ a manager to run it on the grounds that the manager has the professional expertise. James Burnham called this the 'managerial revolution'.	Studies show that management and ownership are often combined, that higher managers often have a substantial share holding in the companies they manage and come from what would be called a dominant class. (Baran and Sweezy describe this in their book *Monopoly Capital*.)
4 Being 'propertyless' (and thus part of the proletariat) fails to distinguish between workers and managers, or workers and professionals.	Managers and professionals could be seen as helping the owners of the means of production to run their affairs. Thus the 'house accountant' could be seen as part of the bourgeoisie (see also the Lockwood on clerks described earlier).
5 Many American sociologists (e.g. Davis and Moore) say that reward at work is according to skill and effort. If you work hard you get on, and receive higher wages.	Sociological studies of occupational choice show that it is difficult to get into many higher occupations (see Chapter 6 on politics). Also many young people are not aware of occupations outside their own or their parents' or peers' immediate experience. The theme of Paul Willis's book *Learning to Labour* is how the 'slum' schools prepare

Criticisms of Marx's view of class	Possible counter-arguments
	(socialize) working class children for a lifetime of manual labour (assuming now there are the jobs anyway). Marxists argue that the employer pays minimum wages and that the surplus goes to the employer as surplus value, hence exploiting the employee.
6 The ownership of the means of production is not important now, argues Daniel Bell in *The Coming of Post-Industrial Society*. The key question now is who owns and controls the knowledge: knowledge stored in a computer, professional knowledge and so on.	Really this does not invalidate Marx's argument, since knowledge could be regarded as part of the means of production. Typically it is only the large corporations, which have the capital, that can afford to turn 'knowledge' into profitable products.
7 Marxism says little about gender inequality – domestic inequality and the exploitation of women, resulting in the fact that in the home and outside women's work has lower status. Male Marxists fail to show how gender differences are socially constructed and socially maintained.	Friedrich Engels, a nineteenth-century Marxist, wrote of the subjugation of women in the family in *The Origin of the Family, Private Property and the State*, Engels demonstrated the existence of patriarchy – the domination of the male in the home (see Chapter 8). He felt that legal reforms would help to show up patriarchy, although they would not eliminate it. (Many leading feminists today are Marxists themselves.)
8 There are other means of stratification in society besides class, for example, inequalities arising out of race, power and status. Marx seems to concentrate on material inequality.	Most differences in society are based firstly on material differences. Other inequalities flow from basic imbalances of wealth and property. Thus the power of the bourgeoisie arises from the fact that they own the means of production, according to Marx. Many sociologists, however, are attracted to the theories of Max Weber who showed the importance of status and power as well as class. Weber deserves a section of his own.

Weber's theory of class

Max Weber defines a 'class' as a group of people who share a similar position in a market economy; they receive similar economic rewards (pay) and they therefore have similar life chances in common. Individuals with scarce skills or more education or possessing capital would have a higher class position. In Weber's view there are four main classes:

I the propertied class;
II white collar workers;
III the petty bourgeoisie (shopkeepers and small proprietors);
IV the working class.

Class conflict can occur between these various classes. It is more likely to occur between adjacent classes, for example between II and III rather than I and III.

It will be seen that Weber has a more complex view of class than Marx. It is not based solely on the ownership or non-ownership of the means of production. Even among those without property there are important differences; different skills have different market values.

Skill in the market economy
An interesting example of a loss of skill leading to a loss of status is the case of newspaper typographers. Their high status was due to their skill on the typesetting machines. This skill was kept scarce through tight recruitment, virtually keeping the craft to those in the family. The skill became obsolete with the introduction of computers and thus the typographers' status fell too.

Weber, however, was not content to classify society solely by class. He also classified social life by *status*. A status group referred to all those occupying a common status. Those in the status group had the same honour accorded them, for example army officers. Status reflects manners, education, family origin (often immigrants have low status), race and how you made your money (from 'trade' or inheritance).

The third criterion by which Weber classified social activity was power (discussed more fully in Chapter 6). Power is the probability that one actor can carry out his or her will against another. Power involves a relationship, for example between husband and wife, or parents and children, or employer or employee, or teacher and student. To have power you have to be able to control what the other person needs. For Weber the chief source of power was not to be found in the ownership of the means of production. Rather, the increased complexity of modern industrial society leads to the development of vast bureaucracies and increasing centralization, for example the all-powerful state.

Table 5.6 Weber's view of social stratification

	Social order	Economic order	Legal/political order
Definition	Honour	Market situation	Power
Stratification system	Status	Class	Party
Key concept	Life style	Life chance	Organization for achieving power

Thus in Weber's view there were three stratification systems in society, as shown in Table 5.6 (note: strata or stratification refers to layers, in this case the layers of society as in Weber's four classes on the previous page).

QUESTION: using Weber's theory outlined above, how would you classify the following people in terms of status, class and party (power): a black doctor, a cabinet minister from the working class, a headmistress, a headmaster, a duke's son who has no money – make up a few examples of your own. (The black doctor may be low in status (or lower than a white doctor); high in the market situation, that is, able to earn a good income, and therefore of higher class with better life chances; but may perhaps have little power, unless he or she holds an important position in, say, a Regional Health Authority.)

Thus while Marx tried to analyse stratification in society by one system (the ownership of the means of production), Weber showed that there are at least three possible ways of stratifying society and that there is interplay between status, class and party (that you can be high on one measure and low on another).

Who is right on class, Marx or Weber? Marx's theory of class has been very influential. Weber's analysis of class, status and party is richer, more complicated and difficult to assess. The test is really which is most useful in explaining a situation, for example a situation of conflict.

Thus it is shown in Chapter 11 that a Weberian view of class is useful when analysing what is really happening in schools. Those learning 'higher' skills (such as abstract, non-practical knowledge) generally come from higher class homes (in the Weberian sense) and usually go on to higher education, where they continue to acquire higher skills which thereby confirm them in their higher class positions.

Another Weberian approach to class is revealed in Chapter 6 on politics, in which it is demonstrated that there is a strong connection between class, status and power. The dominant class holds high positions, in the class sense, in industry, banking, the Civil Service etc. These dominant class people also have high status and power. Clearly Chapter 6 illustrates a Weberian approach in which status and power are important as well as class.

Finally, the approach adopted in Chapter 7, 'Industrial Relations', illustrates a Marxian-type analysis. It describes the constant struggle between management and work force, showing how management (the owners of the means of production) try to control the work situation and how workers attempt to resist this control. Two other concepts closely associated with the Marxian view of class are highlighted in Chapter 7. Firstly, *ideology* – in this case managerial ideology, which says that management must manage and that all members of the organization share the same interests (whereas management and workers might have quite different goals). Secondly, *alienation* – workers are separated from their true creative selves and their labour becomes a mere commodity sold by the hour (see Glossary for definitions of 'ideology' and 'alienation').

It will be noticed that in the Marxian analysis of class the middle class seldom appears. There are basically only two classes in most Marxist analyses; they derive from the bourgeoisie and the proletariat.

It must be stressed again that sociology is open to all, whatever your political views. Thus you might find it useful to adopt a Marxian approach to class in order to analyse what is really going on in, say, a factory or office, but this does not mean that you are a Marxist in the political sense; merely that you find a Marxian approach *useful* in a particular study.

On the whole the author has found the Weberian approach to class the most flexible and the most able to encompass a wide range of issues. On the other hand he also realizes that a Marxian approach to class can be useful in some circumstances for shedding light on what is really going on.

The next section looks at other ways in which societies are stratified.

Other forms of stratification in society

It will be seen, then, that societies can be analysed in terms of power and status as well as class. Nevertheless, class is usually considered the most important division in Western societies. It may be useful to describe here a few of the terms commonly used in addition to, or as an alternative to, class.

Stratification, it should be recognized, is a general term for ranking groups of people in a hierarchical order (with the highest group at the top); the ranking may be in terms of class, status and power, or perhaps income, wealth, race (ethnicity), age, etc. (The analogy is with the way rocks are often found in strata with a layer of soft rock over a layer – or stratum – of hard rock.)

Caste is a form of stratification. In Indian Hindu society, there is a hierarchy of castes based on ritual purity. Haryans, members of the lowest castes, are known as the untouchables because they are excluded from the performance of rituals which confer religious purity. In caste society all other forms of ranking (stratification) are based on this ranking for ritual purity.

Usually you stay in the caste into which you are born. There is also occupational specialization. Only a limited range of lowly occupations are open to the untouchables. Castes may have originated from the subjugation of one group or race by another. The highest caste in Hindu society is the Brahmin or priestly caste, followed by the warrior and landlord caste (Vaishay).

Estates, like class and caste, are another form of social stratification. An example of this occurred in feudal times. The main estates in descending order of power and prestige were the monarch, the nobility (lords etc.), the clergy, the burghers (or citizens of the towns) and the serfs. Like caste society, this was a closed society. The main means of escape was to the towns or by entering the clergy. The rights and duties of each estate were laid down by law and custom, for example the serf held his land from his lord and in return performed specified duties such as tilling part of the lord's land.

Ascribed status (or *ascription*) means the individuals' positions in society are given and fixed. They are born into this position. They have no control over this. They cannot, for example, work harder to achieve a higher estate.

QUESTION: to what societies would you apply the term 'ascription'?

Achieved status – this is the opposite of ascribed status. Individuals can achieve a higher position through hard work. Many immigrants to the USA seem to have had this view of American society.

QUESTION: is British society characterized by 'Achieved status'? (Note the limitations in occupational choice, the unfair treatment of blacks who cannot get a job, the discrimination against women.)

Social mobility

How easy is it for the son or daughter of a working class father to enter a middle class occupation? How likely is it that the son or daughter of a father in the professional and managerial class will end up as an unskilled labourer? This is what studies of social mobility are about.

Intergenerational mobility compares the present position of individuals with their parents'. Intragenerational mobility compares the positions attained by individuals in the course of their own lifetime.

The question of social mobility interests sociologists because it indicates how open our society is. Can people from lower positions make it to the top? There have been two major studies in Britain since the war. The first, by David Glass, published on research carried out in 1949, showed that there was a considerable amount of short range mobility coupled with a higher degree of rigidity and self-recruitment at the extremes, particularly at the upper levels of society. In other words, although the son of a labourer might become a supervisor, he was very unlikely to become a doctor or lawyer. Labourers tended to be the sons of labourers, professionals the sons or daughters of professionals. As shown in the tables in Chapter 6, it is very difficult for those who have not been to public school and Oxford or Cambridge University to get into the ruling elite.

The second well known study was by J. H. Goldthorpe et al. (*Social Mobility and Class Structure in Modern Britain*), sometimes known as the Nuffield Study. This study showed that there have been more openings at the top, due to the fact that more positions have been created higher up the scale, for example, there are many more professionals now.

However, despite these changes, there has not really been a significant reduction in class inequalities. Relative mobility rates have remained fairly stable. The chances of someone from a privileged class ending up in the working class are not very great. Advantaged groups can use their resources to preserve their privileged positions.

Mobility through education

Sponsored mobility. This term was used by the American sociologist, Ralph Turner, to describe the British education system, in which more able children who passed the 11+ exams (or IQ tests and A levels) were chosen to progress further in the education system. They were sponsored – helped and encouraged to go on.

Contest mobility. This is the opposite and was thought by Turner to characterize the American education system, which Turner considered to be more open because it left selection as late as possible. (What actually happens in the American education system is that disadvantaged students drop out earlier, so really a form of selection (self-selection) does operate in the USA too.)

Trends

Is class here to stay or is its importance declining? One sociologist has shown that in recent years there has been a decline in the working class so that for the first time this century it is less than 50 per cent of the population (see Table 6.8 for changing voting habits of the working class). There has also been a decline in manual occupations and communities, for example, a decline in mining and steel making with a corresponding expansion of white collar occupations. (See G. Marshall, 'What is Happening to the Working Class?', *Social Studies Review*, January 1987.)

Daniel Bell, the well-known American sociologist, sees this as part of the process of embourgeoisement (see Glossary), with work becoming less routine.

In contrast, Harry Braverman (in *Labour and Monopoly Capital*) offers a Marxist interpretation: society is becoming proletarianized, as there is de-skilling of the work and increasing alienation (see Glossary) and close management control.

Stephen Lukes argues that we should look at class in terms of consumption rather than production, distinguishing, for example, between:

1   those having sufficient housing and those who have not;

2   those who are self-sufficient on wages and those who are not;

3   those who are in bourgeois regions and those in declining regions (see Glossary, 'embourgeoisement').

Thus class conflict could be seen as restructured and is characterized by:

1   *Sectionalism*: people seek and support their own group.

2   *Instrumentalism*: people work just for the money with little interest in the job (or class solidarity).

3   *Privatism*: people spend their time and money on the home, again with little feeling of class solidarity.

Finally, Marshall still believes that Britain remains a class society rather than a post-industrial or post-class society. Class is important in giving people a sense of identity.

Conclusions

It may be interesting to conclude this chapter by comparing common assumptions made about class with the likely reality. As mentioned in Chapter 1, the task of the sociologist is to examine the common assumptions made by most or many people. *Suggestion*: do not look at the 'Likely reality' column until you have considered your own views first.

Common assumption	Likely reality
1 Class is less important now than it was 50 or 100 years ago.	Class is still important. Take a simple example – mortality rates. It is true that life expectancy has increased for all, yet mortality rates for working class people are still much higher than for middle class people on all major diseases. Why is this? (See Chapter 12 on medicine.)
2 Really we are all middle class now. We buy our clothes from similar chain stores, most people own a car. Nearly 70 per cent of householders are owner-occupiers.	A famous study by Goldthorpe et al., *The Affluent Worker*, showed that even when manual workers earned very high wages they did not take up middle class attitudes. They saw their work as a means of getting

Common assumption	**Likely reality**
	money rather than as a career. They did not mix with middle class people.
3 We can achieve a higher class position if we strive hard enough.	Really society is much less open than we think. Most upward mobility is short range and it is very difficult to enter elite occupations.
4 Marx was completely wrong in his forecasts. Increasing immiseration of the workers has not occurred (at least, not in the West). There has been no communist revolution in an advanced capitalist country (although there have been revolutions in East European countries).	Marx may still be a useful guide in showing what is really happening: for example that ownership of the means of production is in relatively few hands; that many if not most people are alienated in their work, especially manual work; and that powerful groups of people can use ideologies to justify their power and get support from the rest of society. The test of Marx is not whether or not you support his views, or whether his predictions were true, but rather whether his theories are useful in understanding what is going on in society.
5 Sociologists are obsessed with class. Most people feel that they are free individuals: that they are not constrained by class attitudes, that they make their own free choices of what occupation to enter, where to live, where to go for their holidays and so on.	Sociologists are not obsessed with class, they merely describe what is actually happening. Individuals may feel free, yet in reality they are constrained by the customs and attitudes of the groups to which they belong. In Western societies, the most important group is class. Chapter 3 on infant care shows how middle class parents rear their children differently from working class parents and thereby instil in these children different attitudes to work and play, which last a lifetime. We are not free in our occupational choice. Most people choose occupations similar to their parents'. Again, where we live seems to be based on class. Chapter 13 shows it is a question of 'birds of a feather flock together' and neighbourhoods tend to be predominantly middle class or working class rather than mixed.

The nature of Marxism is still changing, as events in Eastern Europe have shown.

Self-examination question

What is meant by: 'class', 'status', 'power', 'caste', 'estate', 'achieved status', 'ascribed status', 'social mobility', 'contest mobility', 'sponsored mobility', 'bourgeoisie', 'proletariat', 'social stratification', 'closed society', 'open society'?

Project

1   **If you are in school or college it might be interesting to take part in the following project.**

Students form pairs, each pair consisting of the son or daughter of a working class father, and the son or daughter of a middle class father. You then ascertain the similarities and differences in your backgrounds, for example, what kind of neighbourhoods do you live in? What kind of education did your respective fathers have? What do your fathers do for a living? Where do you go for holidays? Do your mothers work, if so what at? You could extend the list and then try to account for the differences and similarities you have noted. This chapter and many other parts of the book may help you in your explanation (for example Chapter 12 on medicine tries to show why middle class people enjoy better health).
  Set out your conclusions and try to relate them to the various theories of class described in this chapter.

Past examination questions

1   **Study the information given and then answer the following questions.**

Table 5.7   Percentage of population in each social class

Social class	1931	1971
I	1.8	5.0
II	12.0	18.2
III	47.8	50.5
IV	25.5	18.0
V	12.9	8.4

THE FUTURE OF BABY M

To be born into the working classes is to
be seriously disadvantaged . . . it means the certainty
of poorer nutrition, poorer housing, worse health and a shorter life

[An article caption]

1 a) List two ways in which the working classes may be seriously disadvantaged. (2 marks)
   b) According to the table, which two social classes have declined as a
   proportion between 1931 and 1971? (2 marks)
2 Name two groups of people, other than the working class, who are disadvantaged in our society. (2 marks)
3 Explain three ways in which a person may change his or her social
   class. (6 marks)
4 'Everyone has an equal opportunity to get to the top in Britain today.' To
   what extent do you agree or disagree with this statement? Give reasons for
   your answer. (8 marks)

Midlands Examining Group, GCSE, Paper 2, May 1988.

Suggestions

In looking at working class disadvantages, consider for example the sociology of
education and of medicine. The working class have poor access to higher education and
to health services.

On question 2 above, women and black people are disadvantaged in our society.

On question 3, see discussion of social mobility, sponsored mobility and contest
mobility in this chapter.

On question 4, see 'achieved status' and 'ascribed status' in Glossary. The next
chapter, particularly Tables 6.2 to 6.6, demonstrates that only top people have a chance
to attain top positions in Britain; the picture is similar for other advanced societies,
including the USA.

2 **'The history of all hitherto existing society is the history of class struggle'
(K. Marx and F. Engels). Does this statement provide an adequate basis for
explaining social change?**

University of Cambridge, A Level, Summer 1983.

Suggestions

Is Marx's theory of class and revolution adequate for explaining change? State the
theory, state the criticisms of other Marxists (e.g. Lenin, who believed in the importance
of the Party and said the Revolution could not come from the proletariat alone). Review
other criticisms of Marx (outlined here) and draw your own conclusions. How have
events in Eastern Europe influenced your views?

3   **'Social stratification in industrial societies is based increasingly on individual achievement rather than inherited wealth.' Discuss.**

Associated Examining Board, A Level, Paper 1, June 1988

Suggestions

Show the obstacles against high working class achievement. Use both this chapter and in particular the next which shows that those with high status still get the most prestigious jobs. See also 'achieved status' and 'ascribed status' in Glossary.

4   **'We are all middle class now.' Are we?**

University of Cambridge Local Examinations Syndicate, GCSE, Paper 2, June 1988

Suggestions

See also Chapter 7, pp. 123–4, for a discussion of the embourgeoisement thesis. In particular discuss the work of Goldthorpe et al. on the affluent worker.

5

Item A

The distribution of wealth in Britain, 1980.

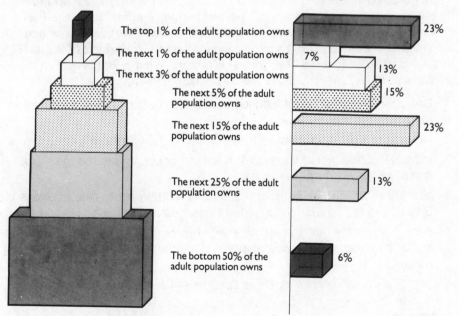

Source: adapted from P. Stanworth, 'Elites and Privilege', in
P. Abrams and R. Brown (eds), *UK Society*.

Item B

But the persistence of dramatic inequalities of wealth is not enough to demonstrate the continuance of an 'upper class', let alone a 'ruling class' . . .

The facts which indicate the continuing existence of a distinctive upper class in British society seem quite indisputable. The public schools – those essentially Victorian organizations which trained 'gentlemen to become businessmen and businessmen to become gentlemen' – continue to play a dominant role in the self-perpetuation of recruitment to elite positions in British society. There is only a tiny minority of non-fee-paying pupils in public schools, and we can be confident that a public school education normally signifies that a person is not of lowly social origins, especially if the school is among the more prestigious. (Adapted from an article by John Scott in *Social Studies Review*.)

Item C

The solidarity of shared lifestyle, culture and common political objectives among the traditional British working class has been undermined since the 1950s by the growth of public-sector employment and of multinational corporations. These twin developments mean that the majority of employees in this country now bargain for wages under conditions other than those imposed by strictly market criteria. This development, together with the increased but uneven participation of women in paid labour, the expansion of non-manual employment, and post-war immigration from the new Commonwealth, has encouraged 'a growing division of workers into sections and groups, each pursuing its own economic interest irrespective of the rest'. (Adapted from an article by Gordon Marshall, 'What is Happening to the Working Class?', *Social Studies Review*, January 1987.)

1 Describe the pattern of distribution of wealth in Britain in 1980 as illustrated in Item A.   (4 marks)

2 How might a sociologist obtain the information shown in Item A?   (2 marks)

3 What difficulties would there be in obtaining accurate data on the distribution of wealth?   (4 marks)

4 Item B argues for 'the self-perpetuation of recruitment to elite positions in British society'. To what extent does evidence support this?   (7 marks)

5 Item C suggests that the labour market is increasingly divided. To what extent do either women or ethnic minorities participate in separate labour markets?   (8 marks)

Associated Examining Board Specimen A Level Question for 1991 Syllabus

Suggestions

1 The distribution of wealth is 'skewed' so that the top 10 per cent of the population own 23 per cent of the wealth.

2 Use Inland Revenue statistics, *Social Trends*, etc.

3 Wealthy people hide their wealth. How do you assess 'perks' etc?

4   See text, Tables 6.3 and 6.6, and follow up.

5   See 'reserve army of labour' and 'dual labour markets', pp. 144 and 163–4, and Glossary. Discuss what is meant by women's work.

Further reading

D. Bell, *The Coming of Post-Industrial Society*
H. Braverman, *Labour and Monopoly Capital*
J. H. Goldthorpe et al., *Social Mobility and Class Structure in Modern Britain*
A. Heath, *Social Mobility*
D. Lockwood, *The Blackcoated Worker*
G. M. Marshall, 'What is Happening to the Working Class?'
G. Marshall et al., *Social Class in Modern Britain*
G. Orwell, *Road to Wigan Pier*
*I. Reid, *Social Class Differences in Britain*
R. Tressell, *The Ragged Trousered Philanthropist*
P. Willis, *Learning to Labour*
*'Education and Class', *New Society*, 11 October 1985 (Society Today series)

6　Politics

Political sociology studies power and in particular the social basis of power. What are the social characteristics of those who exercise political power? What are their beliefs and ideologies? What are the effects (sometimes hidden) of what they do? It also studies, among other things, political institutions like Parliament and the political parties, pressure groups and the institutions of the state such as the Civil Service. It is, however, power that is of central concern and the two key questions are: who rules? And how is this rule legitimated, made acceptable?

Power implies the rule of the few over the many. Max Weber believed power had to be legitimated; the few must rule by the consent of the many. Legitimated power is called authority (as distinct from naked power, or force, such as the power of the master over the slave, the warder over the convict).

Power

According to *Weber*, 'power is the probability that one actor within a social relationship will be in a position to carry out his own will despite resistance'. Power always implies power over another person or group. Power is often analysed in terms of the organizations in which it is exercised, for example a factory, office or school. Thus power means a *relationship* between people; think of the mutual dependence of husband and wife, or allied nations during a war. Weber argued that power tends to become institutionalized or *legitimized*, that is, the arrangement comes to be accepted by the parties. It then becomes *authority*. The text shows three ways in which power can be legitimized.

Some political theories

Weber

Weber and other sociologists have looked at the ways in which power is legitimated and becomes authority. Thus Weber distinguished between three types of authority:

charismatic;

traditional;

rational–legal.

Charismatic authority means the personal (or God-given) authority of the leader. Examples in history would include Jesus or Napoleon. More modern examples might include Mikhail Gorbachev and Lech Walesa.

Traditional authority means established authority. The traditions are accepted and handed down from generation to generation. Examples of traditional authority would include the authority of religion, of the tribe, of the caste and so on.

Rational–legal authority means the type of authority which typifies modern industrialized societies, government departments, large commercial firms, trade unions and so on. Actions are based on rational criteria. For example, a firm may have an obvious *goal*, the maximizing of profit, and use logical *means* to achieve this goal, increased efficiency perhaps. Rational–legal authority implies, therefore, a logical means/end relationship.

Weber saw traditional authority as characterizing pre-industrial societies such as parts of the developing world today, and he saw charismatic authority as a temporary stage in society. The charismatic authority of Jesus can be seen as temporary, while the establishment of Christianity can be seen as a form of traditional authority; to quote Weber, 'popes follow prophets'. However, in advanced industrialized societies, traditional authority is not strong enough to hold society together. This is partly because these societies are more heterogeneous (not all members share the same traditions). Hence the need for rational–legal authority where everyone understands the rules.

A democratically elected government is an example of rational–legal authority; some military dictators are examples of charismatic authority; while the priest in appealing to religious loyalties is an example of traditional authority. No doubt the reader can think of many actual examples.

Although rational–legal authority may appear to be the most desirable type of authority in advanced stable democracies, it has some drawbacks. This type of authority is exercised in large scale organizations or bureaucracies such as governments, large commercial firms, and public authorities like Regional Health Authorities. The danger is that bureaucracy can threaten democracy, as was shown by a well known study by Michels.

Michels

Michels noted (in *Political Parties*) that democratic organizations like political parties and trade unions have a tendency to become oligarchies, in which a few powerful people at the top really control the organization. Perhaps China and some of the former regimes of Eastern Europe could be seen in this light.

Pareto

Pareto took a pessimistic view of democracy. In his major sociological work *The Mind and Society* (published in 1916), Pareto put forward his theory of elites in society. He saw the concentration of power in the hands of elites as inevitable. Politics really was the continuous circulation of elites. The circulation of elites occurred because some people were more suited to the maintenance of the status quo while other groups were more innovative and coped better during periods of change.

Talcott Parsons

A functionalist view of society would regard the institutions of society – political, religious, industrial, military, educational and so on – as inter-dependent and working in accordance with shared goals and shared values. These shared views may, for example, stress the need for order and the continuity of the status quo, and for economic advancement. Such a view was advanced by the well-known American sociologist, Talcott Parsons (in *Towards a General Theory of Action*). He suggested that political leaders could be seen as bankers with whom the electors had deposited power. This grant of power could be withdrawn at the next election but meanwhile it would have generated interest for the benefit of the electorate.

Functionalism

Functionalism was one of the major theories in sociology and is based on the following ideas:

1　It sees society as composed of interdependent parts.

2　These parts are the institutions of society: the family, the education system, the military, the political institutions and so on (institution means established form of behaviour – like the family).

3　These institutions share common goals and together work for balance and consensus and order in society, for example the family and the school help to socialize children for their future role in society. (This is similar to the way in which the organs of the body are interdependent and work together for the health of the body.)

Functionalism has been criticized because it over-emphasizes a con-sensus view of society and therefore cannot account for conflict and change.

Dahl

Associated with the functionalist position is the pluralist view of society. This sees power as diffused in a society where many interests (or pressure groups) compete but where society itself is safeguarded by the established institutions of government. In other words, conflict has been tamed through the competition of competing pressure groups. In this view, the power of employers is balanced by that of trade unions; the parties of the right by those of the left and so on. The government itself is a sort of referee or trustee. Accountability is ensured through the ballot box; the party with the vote-winning policies becomes the government. (This view of society is advanced by Robert A. Dahl in his book *Who Governs?* His study (of New Haven, Connecticut) shows that local politics involved a variety of competing local interest groups and that there was no local unified power elite.)

Marx

To the Marxist the basis of power is property; the ownership of the means of production. The owners, the bourgeoisie (or capitalists), will monopolize political power and also dominate the other orders of society: military, economic, religious and so on (but see 'hegemony' in Glossary). In this analysis the government becomes the executive which manages the affairs of the bourgeoisie, as Ralph Miliband explains in *The State in Capitalist Society*. The state is not therefore an impartial referee, but an agent of the bourgeoisie. Such differences as there are in society are about how to run the same economic system. None of the established political parties are really radical, but seek basically to preserve the status quo. In Britain, for example, less than 20 per cent of Labour MPs come from a working class background.

The chapter so far has summarized some of the sociological theories concerning political power. As in other chapters, the intention here has been to use sociological theory to gain insights into our everyday thoughts and behaviour. In particular it has been to examine critically some of the taken for granted, common sense assumptions which regulate this behaviour.

Perhaps the summary in Table 6.1 will help to show how sociological theory can give these insights. It should indicate how sociological theory can show what is really going on, perhaps by exposing some of our common assumptions.

Three such assumptions will then be examined. Firstly, the assumption that in the West we live in an open, pluralistic, democratic society. Secondly, that the coming of the welfare state ensures a fairer and freer society by catering for the needs of the poorest and weakest members of society. Thirdly, that working class people generally support the political parties of the left.

Table 6.1 Political theory and the nature of politics and power

Theory or concept	Insights into politics and power
1 Weber showed that legitimate power becomes *authority*. (As shown below, Weber distinguished between three types of authority: charismatic, traditional, rational–legal.)	Look for examples where power has become authority, such as Parliament. Compare this with an example of naked power or force, for example the taking of hostages. Then compare this with borderline cases such as board room rows. In all cases ask: how is power legitimated to become authority?
2 *Charismatic authority* – the personal or God-given authority of a leader.	Examples might be leaders of new religious cults or possibly a dynamic company director. The charismatic leader may be 'good' or 'bad' – Jesus or Hitler. Do you personally know any people that have this quality of charisma, at least in part? What people in the news possess charismatic authority, would you say?
3 *Traditional authority* – referring to established authority that has lasted for a comparatively long time.	The usual example is the religious leader, such as the Pope. Look at what happens when this traditional authority is challenged, for example by Marxist priests in Latin America (the Pope invokes his traditional authority – while the priests' 'Liberation theology' possibly implies a 'new coming').
4 *Rational–legal authority* – usually applied to the type of authority prevailing in industrialized society. Weber used the concept of the ideal type *bureaucracy* in which for example there was a high degree of specialization, a hierarchy of authority, formal rules, etc. See also Chapter 12 for a description of the hospital as an organization.	Examples of ideal type bureaucracies abound – government departments, large corporations etc. It may be interesting to take a number of organizations with which you are familiar, for example school, college, hospital, and see how far short they fall of Weber's ideal type. You could look for example at what sociologists call 'goal displacement', where the means become more important than the ends, e.g. petty discipline in a school.

Theory or concept	Insights into politics and power
5 Michels's *iron law of oligarchy* – in his book *Political Parties* he argued that in any organization, however democratic, there was a tendency towards oligarchy or rule by the few – 'who says organization says oligarchy'. (But Gouldner counter-argued that democracy tended to reestablish itself.)	Many organizations seem to have this tendency (is it true in schools and colleges?). It might be interesting to look at political parties and trade unions (with which Michels was particularly concerned). The annual conferences of political parties and trade unions are well advertised so there should be plenty of material. You could, for example, ask: how democratic is the Labour Party? Does it carry out conference decisions? Is it ruled in effect by an oligarchy? Then apply the same tests to a trade union and/or other organizations such as commercial companies, Oxfam, the RSPCA, the former governments of Eastern European states, etc.
6 Pareto's theory of *circulating elites* – elites are inevitable. Elites circulate. At one time power may be in the hands of an elite dedicated to maintaining the status quo. This elite may alternate with a group seeking change in society.	It may be interesting to see how far the theory of circulating elites explains the politics of Latin American countries, where governments change from military to civilian rule and back again to military rule. What is the real role of the army in these countries? (Note that armies have sometimes brought about more or less democratic change – in Egypt 1952 and Portugal 1974.) It will be helpful to follow and analyse events in the third world with the aid of a good magazine such as *The New Internationalist*.
7 *Consensus view of society* – for example Talcott Parsons and Dahl. Parsons sees power as the capacity to achieve social ends, while Dahl sees power as influence – the capacity to influence the behaviour of another. Both these writers and others have a consensus view and see society as open. Thus Dahl sees the political system as permitting the whole community to participate in	Is power really diffuse? Is society really open to accommodating newcomers to positions of power? Or is power really concentrated in the hands of a few, of an elite? Before answering this question it might be instructive to peruse the lists of high office holders in Britain (pp. 97–100). Generally it seems that society is less open than most people think.

Table 6.1 (*Cont.*)

Theory or concept	Insights into politics and power
the political process. Both Parsons and Dahl seem to assume a pluralist society, that is, a society where different views, interests and pressure groups may freely compete.	

8 *Conflict view of society* – can be traced back to *Marx*, who saw conflict between the owners of the means of production (the bourgeoisie) and the workers (the proletariat) as inevitable. This conflict would transform society from a capitalist to a communist society.
 	
   L. Coser believed that far from disrupting society, conflict could give it stability because people would form cohesive groups and someone who is an opponent in one dispute may be an ally in another.
 	
   Dahrendorf argued that conflict was natural in society: that it took place between those with authority and those without and that conflict usually took place within organizations (governments, firms, colleges, etc.).
	Analyse the conflicts taking place here and worldwide. Which theory helps best to explain what is really going on, Marx, Coser, Dahrendorf or something else? Analyse the recurrent argument within the Labour Party and many trade unions between 'left' and 'right'. What do the factions really want? Analyse conflicts in the third world. Does Marxian theory or does Pareto best explain what is really going on? Returning to Britain, how would you explain conflicts in industrial relations? (Perhaps workers on strike just want more money and are not really any challenge to 'the system'.)

Common assumption one: *in the West we live in an open, pluralist, democratic society*

Probably most people in the West are reasonably happy with the type of society in which they live, especially after events in Eastern Europe, which showed those regimes as closed societies. Of course, this does not mean that society should not be analysed. By critically examining our society we may be able to arrive at insights which will help to improve that society and generally raise the standard of political decision making.

The pluralistic model of society assumes the government is a neutral referee holding the ring in which competing interest groups confront each other. These competing interests may be incorporated in the established political parties or they may form themselves into pressure groups.

Table 6.2 The social background of cabinet ministers

Cabinet, January 1990	Post	Education
Margaret Thatcher	Prime Minister	Kesteven and Grantham Girls' School; Oxford
Lord Belstead	Lord Privy Seal	Eton; Oxford
Sir Geoffrey Howe	Deputy Prime Minister	Winchester; Cambridge
Lord Mackay	Lord Chancellor	Major School; Cambridge
Douglas Hurd	Foreign Secretary	Eton; Cambridge
Peter Walker	Wales	Latymer
Tom King	Defence	Rugby; Cambridge
Nicholas Ridley	Trade and Industry	Eton; Cambridge
David Waddington	Home Secretary	Sedbergh; Oxford
Michael Howard	Employment	Llanelli Grammar School; Cambridge
Kenneth Baker	Chancellor of the Duchy of Lancaster	St Paul's; Oxford
Kenneth Clarke	Health	Nottingham High School; Cambridge
John MacGregor	Education	Merchiston Castle School; St Andrews
Malcolm Rifkind	Scotland	George Watson's College; Edinburgh
John Wakeham	Energy	Charterhouse; Chartered Accountant
Cecil Parkinson	Transport	Royal Lancaster Grammar School; Cambridge
John Major	Chancellor of the Exchequer	Rutlish
Anthony Newton	Social Security	Friends' School, Saffron Walden; Oxford
Christopher Patten	Environment	Wimbledon College; Cambridge
Peter Brooke	Northern Ireland	Marlborough; Oxford
John Gummer	Agriculture	King's School, Rochester; Cambridge
Norman Lamont	Chief Secretary to Treasury	Loretto; Cambridge

Examples of pressure groups (or interest groups) would include the unions, professions, Confederation of British Industry, the Campaign for Nuclear Disarmament, Friends of the Earth, the Automobile Association and so on.

Pressure groups, it is argued, are part of a pluralist society (that is, a society in which all these interests compete). Pressure groups therefore are said to perform a democratic role by bringing together people with similar interests who thereby gain a voice. Pressure groups promote their interests in a variety of ways. The mass demonstrations of CND may be contrasted with the more subtle methods used by the British Medical Association when it sought to influence the government during the drafting of the National Health Service Act 1946 and by which it still tries to influence government today.

But do we really live in a pluralist society in which, for example, interest groups (or pressure groups) freely compete? How neutral is government anyway? It does appear from the evidence that most societies seem to have a ruling elite. To be admitted to this elite, the applicant has to have certain desirable social characteristics, such as having wealthy parents, attending a high class school, having a university education and so on. If this is so and if societies do have a ruling elite, then this may make them less open than they appear. How open a society is Britain, judging by the accompanying tables? Table 6.2. shows the education and hence the social background of members of the 1990 Conservative Cabinet.

A similar picture emerges when examining the education and social background of the top civil servants, leaders of industry, directors of the largest insurance companies, directors of the large banks and the leading merchant banks and the governors of the Bank of England, governors of the BBC (British Broadcasting Corporation), bishops of the Church of England, etc. Tables 6.3 to 6.6 provide examples illustrating this homogeneity of the elite in Britain in the 1980s.

One could go on giving examples like the ones in these tables. For instance R. Whitley (in an article in *Sociological Review*) has shown how membership of one elite group correlates with membership of others, members of governments and leading MPs have connections with finance and industry and commerce; there are overlapping directorships (directors on more than one board); most leading figures are members of the dozen or so prestigious London Clubs – Carlton, St James, Pratts, the Turf Club etc. No trade union leader has ever led a Royal Commission – these are dominated by high status lawyers, financiers etc. In these circumstances is it really likely that government is neutral? Does it really hold the ring when business and trade unions are in conflict, or would it be more realistic to see such contests in terms of government and business versus the unions?

On the other hand, is the Labour Party that different? It is true that the party started from a working class base early this century. In 1918, 72 per cent of Labour MPs were of working class origin but in the 1980s this figure fell to 20 per cent. The leadership of the Labour Party has become largely self-recruiting (the same group of people get into the leadership) and increasingly distant from the rank and file. There has been a professionalization of politics and a concentration and bureaucratization of power centred on the top civil servants. (How does all this link with Michels' iron law of oligarchy?)

Studies in the USA paint a similar picture. The most famous is by C.

Table 6.3 Leading merchant banks

Founded	Bank	Chairman	Education
1763	Baring Brothers	Sir John Francis Harcourt Baring	Eton; Oxford
1804	Rothschild's	Evelyn de Rothschild	Harrow; Cambridge
1804	Schroder Wagg	Winifred Franz Wilhelm Bischoff	University of Witwatersrand
1810	Brown Shipley	Lord Farnham	Eton; Harvard
1831	Hill Samuel	Richard Ernest Butler Lloyd	Wellington; Oxford
1836	Guinness Mahon	John Richard Sclater	Charterhouse; Cambridge
1838	Morgan Grenfell	Sir Peter Carey	Portsmouth Grammar School; Oxford
1839	Hambros	John Chippendale Lindley Keswick	Eton; University of Aix/Marseilles
1853	Samuel Montagu	Sir Michael Palliser	Wellington; Oxford; Coldstream Guards
1870	Lazard Brothers	Sir John Nott	Bradfield College; Cambridge
1880	Charterhouse Japhet	Maurice Victor Blank	Stockport Grammar School; Oxford
1907	Singer and Friedlander	Anthony Nathan Solomons	Chartered Accountant
1919	Rea Brothers	The Earl of Dartmouth (Managing Director)	Eton; Coldstream Guards
1946	S. G. Warburg	Lord Roll of Ipsden and Sir David Gerald Scholey (joint Chairmen)	University of Birmingham. Wellington College; Oxford

Sources for Tables 6.3 to 6.6: *Directory of Directors*; *Who's Who*; *Company Statements*; A. Sampson, *The Changing Anatomy of Britain*

Table 6.4 Leading insurance companies

Company (in size order)	Chairman	Education
Prudential	Ronald Edward Artus	Magdalen College; Oxford
Legal and General	Professor Sir Robert James Ball	St Marylebone Grammar School; Oxford
Standard Life	Robert Courtney	Sedbergh; Oxford
Commercial Union	Alexander Badenoch Marshall	Glenalmond; Oxford
Norwich Union	Michael Gascoigne Falcon	Stow; Heriot-Watt; Grenadier Guards
Guardian Royal Exchange	John Ernest Harley Collins	King Edward's; Birmingham
Scottish Widows' Funds	Viscount John Campbell Arbuthnott	Fettes; Cambridge
Eagle Star	Sir Jasper Quintus Hollom	King's School, Bruton
Pearl Assurance	Frederick Leonard Garner	Sutton County; Royal Artillery
Sun Life	Gerald James Auldjo Jamieson	Eton; Royal Navy

Table 6.5 High street banks

Bank	Chairman	Education
Barclays	John Grand Quinton	Norwich School; Cambridge
National Westminster	Lord Boardman	Bromsgrove; Northants Yeomanry
Midland	Sir Christopher William McMahon	Magdalen College; Oxford
Lloyds	Sir Jeremy Morse	Winchester; Oxford
Royal Bank of Scotland	Sir Michael Alexander Robert Young Herries	Eton; Cambridge

Table 6.6 Leading British industrial companies

Company	Chairman	Education
Imperial Chemical Industries	Denys Hartley Henderson	Aberdeen Grammar School; Aberdeen
Shell Petroleum	Peter Fenwick Holmes	Cambridge
British Petroleum	Sir Peter (Ingram) Walters	King Edward's; Birmingham
Unilever	Michael Richardson Angus	Marling School, Stroud; Bristol
Vickers	Sir David Arnold Plastow	Culford School; apprenticeship at Vauxhalls
Courtaulds	Sir Christopher Anthony Hogg	Marlborough; Oxford
British Steel	Gordon H. Sambrook	Sheffield University
General Electric Company	James Prior	Charterhouse; Cambridge
British Coal	Sir James Haslam	Bolton School; Birmingham
British Aerospace	Sir Austin William Pearce	Devonport High School for Boys; Birmingham

QUESTION: compare this table with the preceding ones. It looks as if the social status of leading industrialists is lower than that of bankers etc. – they seem to have attended less prestigious schools and universities. Perhaps the reason for Britain's long industrial decline lies here – we accord industry and industrialists lower status.

What do you think?

Wright Mills, *The Power Elite*. Mills shows that the leaders of America's political, economic, military and religious institutions come from similar backgrounds, having for example attended Harvard, Yale and the other top ten American universities.

Why is the political elite so strong? Partly because people are socialized to their position in society whether it be high or low (Chapter 3); partly because, as Miliband argues, elites are self-recruiting (that is, they pick, or attract, their own kind). Scott also presents this view with his idea of an establishment. Poulantzas has rejected this emphasis on social background and has argued that it is the economic power exercised by members of the upper class (as members of the boards of big corporations) and their political participation in the state machine (see Table 6.2) that gives the upper class their power rather than social background alone. The debate

---

Why is the elite self-perpetuating?
'Those who control and determine selection and promotion at the highest level of the state service are themselves most likely to be members of the upper and middle classes, by social origin or by virtue of their own professional success, and are likely to carry in their minds a particular image of how a high ranking civil servant or military officer ought to think, speak, behave and react; and that image will be drawn in terms of the class to which they belong.' (R. Miliband, *The State in Capitalist Society*.)

---

continues – see for example 'hegemony' in the Glossary. (Of course there are other theories of power and for these the reader is referred back to Table 6.1 on the nature of power.)

It could be said that conservatism rules whatever the party in office, and one of the main reasons for this has been given – the homogeneous elite. The parties also seek to present themselves as serving the national interests, especially on law and order, and therefore it becomes necessary to break strikes and end riots without really dealing with their social origins. The Labour Party in particular must show that it is 'fit to rule'; that it is 'moderate' (a highly ideological word). In so far as society is pluralistic, the competition among the various interests and pressure groups is unequal. Governments have to seek the confidence of business (and the International Monetary Fund). The trade unions themselves are divided, serving sectional interests. Strikes are unpopular, and the demands of business can be claimed to be in the national interest.

This discussion has shown that there is great inequality in power in Britain. But there is a corresponding great inequality in wealth and income too (see also Table 5.4 for distribution of income).

Table 6.7 Distribution of marketable wealth in the UK

	1971	1976	1981	1985
Marketable wealth owned by (percentages):				
Most wealthy 1%	31	24	21	20
Most wealthy 5%	52	45	40	40
Most wealthy 10%	65	60	54	54
Most wealthy 25%	86	84	77	76
Most wealthy 50%	97	95	94	93
Total marketable wealth (£ billion)	140	263	546	863

Source: *Social Trends 1989*

QUESTION: what does Table 6.7 really show?

Suggestions

It seems to show there is still great inequality of wealth in Britain. There has been some redistribution of wealth but this has been out of the top 1 per cent and into the top 10 per cent. Greater inequality of wealth might be expected to help the Labour Party, but this is by no means certain. (See 'Common assumption three'.)

The table also indicates that the less wealthy 50 per cent of the population owned only 7 per cent of the wealth in 1985.

Common assumption two: *the coming of the welfare state ensures a fairer and freer society by catering for the needs of the poorest and weakest members of society*

Contrary to popular belief, it is the middle class who are the main beneficiaries of the welfare state. Westergaard and Resler (in *Class in a Capitalist Society*) argue that using public welfare services to try to break down class divisions is unsatisfactory for two reasons. Firstly, they co-exist with competing private welfare provisions (which are financed partly by tax concessions). Secondly, payment for state welfare services bears most heavily on the lowly paid. This is because the burden of national insurance premiums, which are virtually flat rate, hurts the lower paid more. Overall, the welfare services that working class people receive are paid for by them, though they do not control these services and the services are not tailored to fit their interests.

The poor lose out (and the middle class benefit) in many ways from the welfare state. The poor need more help, yet the evidence is that for various reasons they do not take up their entitlements. The forms may be daunting, they are embarrassed to claim means tested benefits, or they may just not know about the benefits (this is a form of rationing welfare). Again, a truly national Health Service should be biased towards the poor because their needs are greater (as Chapter 12 on medicine demonstrates). Instead of this it is biased towards the well-to-do. There are more and better general practitioners and better health facilities generally in higher class areas.

In education, middle class people make better use of the schools, which are geared more to the needs of middle class children (as Chapter 11 on education shows). Middle class children are more likely to attend state further and higher education. (University and polytechnic students are overwhelmingly middle class.)

Many of the services of the welfare state – the police, courts, prisons – are from one point of view a means of controlling the poor rather than primarily benefiting them. However, these are contentious points. Readers might like to test them for themselves through their everyday analysis of news and views.

Common assumption three: *working class people in Britain usually vote Labour*

In their book *The Affluent Worker: Political Attitudes and Behaviour*, Goldthorpe et al. contrast what they call the 'solidaristic collectivism' (or community) of the traditional worker with the 'instrumentalism' (materialism) of the new affluent worker.

Loyalty to the Labour Party is an expression of this social outlook which Goldthorpe and Lockwood term 'solidaristic collectivism'. Support for Labour is 'natural' or 'instinctive'; it is 'the political reflection of a class consciousness which makes a sharp division between the world of "us", the ordinary working-men, and that of "them", the bosses and those in authority generally.'

Examples of traditional workers would be miners, railwaymen, dockers, and steel workers. These people tend to live in 'closely knit cliques of friends, workmates, neighbours and relatives' (though less so now than in the past). This is the hallmark of the traditional working class community. There is a strong sense of solidarity based on mutual aid and shared experiences and the community itself is often isolated (for example the mining village and the railway town).

This image of the traditional worker has perhaps been exaggerated here but is useful as a contrast to the characteristics of the new affluent worker. The three groups of workers sampled in this study can be taken as examples of the affluent worker: they were well paid car workers at Vauxhall's Luton factory, chemical workers at Laporte Chemicals and machining workers at Skefco-Ballbearings. The contrast is between the 'solidaristic collectivism' of the traditional worker and the 'instrumental' orientation of the affluent worker. There is also a move away from 'communal sociability' towards a more privatized form of social existence in which the individual worker and his family become more important than membership of any working class community.

In this study it was shown that these 'affluent' workers tended to vote Labour, especially when they were also members of trade unions. However, their decision to vote Labour was governed by instrumentalism again – a higher payoff could be expected from a Labour government, in the form of higher living standards and better social services for them. Thus although there was a tendency to vote Labour, 'affluent' workers would vote Conservative if it were clearly in their interests to do so.

Although Goldthorpe et al. published their book in 1968, their insights seem just as relevant today. Thus overall there seems to be an increasing tendency for people to vote instrumentally – that is, for the party which will gain the most for them – and this seems to be confirmed by Table 6.8 (see also suggestions for answering question 4 towards the end of this chapter).

Table 6.8 The divided working class: the parties' shares of the vote among different groups of manual workers (percentages)

	New working class				Traditional working class			
	Lives in South	Owner-occupier	Non-union member	Works in private sector	Lives in Scotland or North	Council tenant	Union member	Works in public sector
Conservative	46	44	40	38	29	25	30	32
Labour	28	32	38	39	57	57	48	49
Liberal/SDP Alliance	26	24	22	23	15	18	22	19
Conservative or Labour majority in 1987	Con +18	Con +12	Con +2	Lab +1	Lab +2	Lab +32	Lab +18	Lab +17
Conservative or Labour majority in 1983	Con +16	Con +22	Con +6	Lab +1	Lab +10	Lab +38	Lab +21	Lab +17
Category as percentage of all manual workers	40	57	66	68	37	31	34	32
Change since 1983	+4	+3	+7	+2	−1	−4	−7	−2

Note: figures have been rounded to the nearest whole number, so totals do not always add up to 100 per cent.
Source: I. Crewe, 'Why Mrs Thatcher was Returned with a Landslide'

Conclusion

One of the main themes of this chapter has been inequality and power.

Why does inequality persist?

Why are political elites self-perpetuating?

Is there more inequality now than in the past?

Why do we believe the trade unions are too powerful?

Why do we believe that the welfare state has made us a more equal society?

To answer these questions it may be useful to repeat Marx's view that the dominant ideas in society are those of the ruling class. These ideas then justify the existing arrangements in society, including the rule by the few of the many, the justification for inequality (or the denial that inequality exists). These dominant ideas are a distortion of reality and serve the interests of the powerful. Most people seem to accept or fail to notice the inequalities mentioned here because it is part of our common sense world to assume that, for example, society is fairly open, getting more equal and so on. This view of the world is reinforced by the media, by governments, by influential and powerful people and indeed by our everyday conversations.

Whether or not one accepts Marx's views on ideology and inequality is of course for the individual to decide. Perhaps the question is not whether Marx was right or wrong but rather, whether his theory is *useful* in understanding the social world.

The chapter can be summarized by briefly restating and then examining some of the common assumptions considered already, together with a few others.

Common assumption	Likely reality
1 That most societies in the West are open and democratic (especially when compared with some Eastern European states).	True to a point, but this leaves out the caste-like nature of the political elite, whose members have similar social backgrounds. New entrants become assimilated into (or socialized into) the elite.
2 Those who cannot get to the top in politics can enter other fields, for example industry, commerce, the arts, the academic world.	Again only true to a point. Leading members in most of these fields come from the elite strata of society. Most leading businessmen and industrialists have been to public school and Oxford or Cambridge Universities, or similar. This is true of members of the Arts Council, University Vice Chancellors, Presidents of the leading professional institutions and so on.

Common assumption	Likely reality
3 Extra-parliamentary activity can bring about changes in government policy, for example pressure groups, trade unions, professional bodies and even street riots.	The influence of a pressure group depends on how near its views are to those of people with power, for example, the BMA is likely to be more influential than CND. In the more prestigious groups it is likely that leading members will come from backgrounds similar to those of the political elite. To a large extent violence is the weapon of the weak. It has little effect unless the ruling circle feels threatened. Trade unions are weaker than is commonly supposed. They represent their own members, for whose interests they strive.
4 There are fewer inequalities in society now. The welfare state helps to care for the poor.	Although wealth and income are less unequal now, the tables here show there is still great inequality. Poverty is still widespread and is constantly being rediscovered (for example Townsend's book *Poverty in the UK*). The wealthier middle class seem to benefit more from the welfare state than the poor, for example most university and polytechnic students are middle class. This chapter shows there is still great inequality in access to political power.
5 Most working class people vote Labour.	With the decline of the traditional working class who usually voted Labour, voting intention is now guided more by instrumental consideration – which party will do best for me?
6 Most middle class people will vote Conservative.	Even this is now questionable. Labour will have to recruit increasingly from the middle class in order to compensate for the decline of the older traditional working class, its principal support in the past. Maybe it should seek votes from the growing number of old people in the electorate.

Self-examination questions

Refer to the text for the answers.

1 What is meant by 'power', authority', 'charismatic authority', 'traditional authority', 'rational–legal authority', 'bureaucracy', 'oligarchy', 'solidaristic collectivism', 'instrumentalism', 'pluralist', 'pressure group'?

2 Using Weber's three ideal types of authority (charismatic, traditional, rational–legal), how would you classify the authority of the following:

the Pope	the President of the USA	the Board of Marks
Queen Elizabeth II	the American Congress	and Spencer
the present Prime Minister	Adolf Hitler	a hospital

Projects

(The following past exam question can be used as a project.)

1 **Read the passage and answer the questions that follow.**

From research carried out mainly in Britain and the United States we can make the following generalizations: that policy issues have little effect on how the elector uses his vote and that voters inherit party loyalties from their families, usually based on such factors as social class. It is doubtful whether the electors have a clear conception of which parties are 'left' or 'right'. Surveys in Britain show that the level of acceptance and even knowledge of party policies by the voters for that party is remarkably low. In fact it has been argued that a considerable minority is more in agreement with the opposing party's policies than their own.

Voting behaviour is more easily explained by emphasizing party loyalty, this loyalty being determined by various factors including social class and religion. Class is an obvious factor in electoral behaviour; the National Opinion Poll findings on the October 1974 British General Election showed that 'class is strongly correlated with party'. (Source: A. Ball, *Modern Politics and Government*.)

1 In the above passage, what two examples are given of factors that determine party loyalty? (1 mark)

2 According to the above information:
   a) what part do policy issues play in voting behaviour? (1 mark)
   b) what is the level of acceptance and knowledge of party policies by voters for a particular party? (1 mark)

3 Identify three factors, other than those given in part 1, which influence voting behaviour. (3 marks)

4 Identify and explain three reasons why the conclusions reached by pre-election opinion polls may not always coincide with the election results. (6 marks)

5   Social class is an important influence on voting behaviour, but many people
    do not vote along traditional class lines. These people are often referred to
    as 'deviant voters'. Examine the reasons for deviant voting.   (8 marks)

                                          Associated Examining Board, Summer 1984

2   Read the passage and answer the questions that follow.

Voting with your slippers

Whereas MPs vote with their feet in the division lobbies of parliament, an
increasing number of British electors are voting with their slippers in the
privacy of their living rooms. Rather than putting on a pair of shoes to walk to
the nearest polling station, they stay at home instead. The British turnout at
the first direct election of the European parliament in 1979 was low, even by
the standards of a deep-sea diver – 32.6 per cent, less than half the average
for the rest of the EEC's members. Forecasts of how Europeans will vote on
Sunday in this year's European election suggest that continental turnout will
again be nearly double the turnout of Britons voting today.

   In local government elections, the majority of registered electors are stay-
at-home citizens, who would rather reach for a cup of tea or a TV knob than a
ballot paper. Local turnout is normally less than 40 per cent. Most people will
still vote for (or against) a Westminster MP. But the 1983 general election
turnout of 72.7 per cent was the second lowest since the end of the war.

   Why do Britons increasingly prefer the antics of television comics and hard
men to the antics of political entertainers and hard men – and the Hard
Woman? One explanation, obviously, is political. European elections are not
about anything in particular; national governments, rather than the European parliament, decide what the EEC does. Increasingly, central government tries to decide what local authorities do. At the level of national
parliaments, Britons take free elections for granted, and therefore can leave
them alone. By contrast, Germans and Italians do not take them for granted,
and vote in larger numbers.

   In Britain, turnout has declined with the decline of strong attachments to
political parties. The electoral system also discourages people from voting.
The winner takes all, first past the post system means that half or more of the
popular vote can be wasted. The use of the single transferable vote
proportional representation in Northern Ireland in the 1979 European
election meant that every vote counted (and some voters were counted more
than once). Turnout was 23 per cent higher than in Britain.

   What can be done to make more citizens do their duty and enjoy the
benefits of living in a democracy? There are limits on technical change.
Already it is far easier for Britons today to vote (and far more do) than for
Americans. In the United States, machine politicians have had as much a
vested interest as the Militant Tendency in keeping the number voting down.

   A more efficient electoral register would remove from the list of electors
those who have died, moved away or otherwise become ineligible to vote
since election day. Deleting the 'can't votes' from the register would increase
reported turnout by up to 5 per cent. But few Britons would like to match

continental countries that have an up-to-date register of all electors through compelling citizens to register their address and carry a national identity card.

Holding an election on a Sunday, as in most European countries, would make it easier for people in work to vote. But fixing the polling day on a holiday could be counter-productive if it encouraged people to go to the seaside rather than the ballot box.

Many countries make voting compulsory. This is reckoned to increase turnout by about 10 per cent on average. If this happened in Britain, it would still mean that some six million people would have to be asked to provide a valid reason for not voting (responding to what the Australians call the 'please explain' form). Or else the government would have to try to collect six million fines, if the law was to be enforced.

The surest way to increase turnout is also the least attractive; to increase the stakes of a general election outcome. If a two-party system offered a choice between the Monday Club and the Militant Tendency, then fear would encourage some people to vote. But disappointment in the government is not sufficient to get out the vote. Conservative disillusionment with Mrs Thatcher (like Labour disillusionment with James Callaghan) is more likely just to depress the turnout for the governing party at by-elections.

In short, drastic measures to increase turnout can be objected to. Less than drastic measures have little effect. Civic minded citizens will go out to vote today, regardless. But they shouldn't feel too guilty if they simply relax for once and enjoy staying at home. Many of their very democratic fellow citizens make the same choice, and democracy scarcely seems at risk as a result. (*New Society* Editorial, 14 June 1985)

1　What is the main reason for low turnouts?

2　What are the Monday Club and the Militant Tendency? What are their respective aims?

3　What is meant by 'the winner takes all, first past the post system'?

4　What is the electoral register?

5　In what other ways, apart from voting, can the ordinary citizen affect and influence government?

Past examination questions

1　**Compare and contrast pluralist and Marxist theories of the distribution of power in advanced industrial societies.**

Associated Examining Board, A Level, Summer 1984.

Suggestions

See text of this chapter and Chapter 5 on stratification.

2 **What is the 'iron law of oligarchy'? What evidence could be used to assess the extent to which it applies to control over political decision making in modern industrial societies?**

Joint Matriculation Board, A Level, Summer 1984.

Suggestions

State the law (see text) then show where it may apply (trade unions, companies, governments, etc.). But perhaps say that despite this, democracy still prevails (see Michels).

3 **Examine the evidence for and against the view that there is a ruling class in contemporary Britain.**

Associated Examining Board, A Level, Paper 1, November 1987.

Suggestions

You could quote parts of Tables 6.2 to 6.6 showing the social background of people in high places and the unequal distribution of wealth. Do these inequalities still exist? Have they become institutionalized through socialization etc.

4 **'The concept of "deviant voting" has been replaced by more relevant explanations of voting behaviour.' Explain and discuss.**

Associated Examining Board, A Level, Paper 2, November 1987

Suggestions

The main determinant of voting is still social class; thus an unskilled man or woman is likely to vote Labour. But Table 6.8 shows the rise of a new working class which is likely to vote Conservative. The studies of affluent manual workers by Goldthorpe and his colleagues show that affluent workers are likely to vote 'instrumentally', that is to say for the party that will do them the most good. In this way votes are 'up for grabs' and such workers who normally could have been expected to vote Labour will vote 'deviantly' for a non-Labour candidate. (Consider further Crewe's research, including Table 6.8, and *The Affluent Worker – Political Attitudes and Behaviour* by J. Goldthorpe et al.)

5 **Study Table 6.9 and answer the following questions.**

1 How many by-elections were held in the United Kingdom between May 1979 and June 1983?   (1 mark)
2 How many votes were recorded in these constituencies in the General Election May 1979?   (1 mark)
3 What change took place in the percentage of votes recorded for:
   a) the Labour Party   (1 mark)
   b) the Liberal Party   (1 mark)
   in the constituencies, compared with the General Election May 1979?
4 Name the Nationalist parties mentioned in the chart.   (2 marks)

Table 6.9 Parliamentary by-elections

	May 1979– June 1983	Previous general election, May 1979
Number of by-elections	20	
Votes recorded by party (percentages):		
Conservative	23.8	33.7
Labour	25.7	35.2
Liberal	9.0	8.0
Social Democratic Party	14.2	
Plaid Cymru	0.5	0.4
Scottish National Party	1.7	1.4
Other	25.1	21.2
Total votes recorded (=100%) (thousands)	715	852

Note: Votes recorded in the same seats in the previous General Election.
Source: adapted from *Social Trends 1985*

5 Explain why no votes were recorded for the Social Democratic Party in the General Election May 1979.   (1 mark)

6 Name two different types of pressure group. Give an example of each.   (4 marks)

7 Give four methods used by pressure groups by which they hope to influence government policy and/or public opinion.   (4 marks)

8 Identify and explain two reasons why the results of a poll on voting intentions taken one month before an election may not accurately reflect the actual result of the election.   (4 marks)

Southern Examining Group specimen question (GCSE).

Suggestions

1, 2 and 3 are clear.

4 The nationalist parties in the chart are Plaid Cymru and the Scottish National Party.

5 The Social Democratic Party was not formed until 1981.

6 Protection pressure groups – the AA, trade unions and professions, RSPCA. Promotion pressure groups such as CND, CAMRA.

7 Demonstrations, lobbying MPs, strikes, contacting ministers and higher civil servants.

8 Unrepresentative sample bias, due perhaps to a badly worded question. Respondents may say one thing and actually do another (i.e. vote differently from the way they said they would). (See Chapter 16 on how to conduct surveys.)

6 1 Explain the meaning of the term 'political socialization' and describe the influence of the work place.   (10 marks)

2 Explain why many working class people vote Conservative in British General Elections.   (10 marks)

Southern Examining Group, GCSE Specimen Question.

Suggestions

1 'Socialization' was explained in Chapter 1. It means acquiring 'correct' norms and values – i.e. those norms and values and beliefs which your group (family and friends) approve of. Hence political socialization refers to acquiring 'correct' political norms and values (usually people vote for the same party as their parents voted for). The work place contains the work group and again the voter acquires the values of this group too. Sociologists refer to this as occupational socialization. Newby's study of farmworkers show that they tend to be Conservative, compared with 'traditional' workers such as miners who tend to vote Labour.

2 Newby showed that farmworkers tended to have a 'deferential' attitude to those in authority and this may explain why many of them voted Conservative.

Many car workers voted Conservative and this may be explained by Goldthorpe and Lockwood's concept of 'instrumentalism' (see text). This means they would vote for the party which offered them the most money. The Conservatives' promise of lower taxes and no incomes policy (no control of incomes) seems to have been very appealing to them. They might easily vote Labour again another time.

Finally, many working class people seem to define themselves as middle class, perhaps because they aspire to be middle class, hence they vote for a non-working class party.

Further reading

T. B. Bottomore, *Political Sociology* (relevant parts)
*I. Crewe, 'Why Mrs Thatcher was Returned with a Landslide'
H. M. Drucker et al., *Developments in British Politics*, Chapters 1, 2 and 10
*J. H. Goldthorpe et al., *The Affluent Worker – Political Attitudes and Behaviour*
R. Miliband, *The State in Capitalist Society*
*A. Sampson, *The Changing Anatomy of Britain* (relevant parts)
J. Scott, 'Does Britain Still Have a Ruling Class?'
*'Elections', *New Society*, 13 January 1984 (Society Today series)
*'Power and Authority', *New Society*, 12 February 1985 (Society Today series)

7   Industrial Relations

Introduction

Although industrial relations seem quieter compared with, say, the early eighties, most of the underlying causes of dispute remain. Industrial relations has been defined as a euphemism to describe the constant state of war between labour and management. If there were one word to sum up the theme of this chapter on industrial relations it would probably be – *control*. Management attempt to control the work situation, whether in factory or office, and work people attempt to retain some control over their working conditions and obtain as large a monetary recompense as possible.

What sociology demonstrates is that members of work organizations have their own ideologies, whether these be management ideologies, trade union, professional or craft ideologies. These ideologies are different world views based on different interests. The ideology justifies the interest. It is a device used consciously or unconsciously to maintain control. (See Glossary for definition of 'ideology'.)

A lot of management ideology can be traced back to the theories of scientific management advanced over many years, notably by Frederick Taylor. These hold that management must control all stages of the labour process, not only what is to be done but how it is done; and as this chapter will show, much of the trouble in industrial relations stems from work force reactions to this ideology.

Basically then, management and workers have different viewpoints and interests. What is income to the employee is cost to the employer; what is control and planning to the employer is felt as powerlessness and lack of trust by the employee. Again, managers and professionals have 'careers', while employees have only jobs in which the main interest is often just the money. No wonder disputes abound; it is surprising there are not more.

Industrial relations is a vast subject and to enable it to be seen as a whole, rather than getting bogged down in particular areas, it seems a good idea to examine the sort of 'common sense' assumptions which often cloud the real issues. Here are some of the more prominent of these assumptions.

1   Trade unions are too powerful in industrial relations.
2   Shop stewards are too powerful; shop stewards are trouble makers.
3   Management has the right to manage.

Management and workers have different goals
Source: From *TUC Education*

4 Strikes are one of the main problems in industrial relations.
5 Management and workers should pull together.
6 Unemployment will disrupt society.
7 Affluent workers are more likely than other workers to have middle class attitudes and life styles.
8 'We are all middle class now.'

Each of these common assumptions will now be dealt with in turn.

Common assumption one: *trade unions are too powerful in industrial relations*

An expression frequently used in the media is: 'the trade unions are holding the country to ransom.' Also: unions are 'demanding' more pay, etc., whereas management 'concedes'. The power of the trade unions is usually exaggerated and management and the government is often made to appear helpless in the face of their strength. Unions are 'crippling the country', 'pricing Britain out of world markets', 'pricing their own members out of jobs', 'holding up progress', 'defending restrictive practices', 'being selfish', 'getting unfair advantages for their own members' and so on. Anyone who listens to the radio or television or reads a newspaper is familiar with these pat expressions and could extend the list just given.

What are the social realities of the relationships between union and management?

Firstly, the individual worker is weak against an employer. The employer represents a combination of resources, capital, technology and so on. The firm owns and controls these resources. Workers join trade unions to strengthen their positions, hence you get such phrases as 'unity in strength', and, during a strike, 'one out, all out'. The emphasis is on collectivity and solidarity. (This is why unions strive for 'closed shop' agreements whereby employers agree that only union members will be employed at a firm.) However, it would be wrong to see trade unions solely as a fighting force. Early trade unions were formed for welfare reasons and for mutual support (including compensation for work injury, death grants, education and so on). One of the more important functions of trade unions is in collective bargaining, in which unions and management try to agree wage settlements.

Secondly, although there is talk of 'the two sides of industry' collective bargaining does not mean both sides are equal. In his book, *A Sociology of Work in Industry*, Alan Fox argues that collective bargaining does not deal with fundamentals, for example the basic inequality between employer and worker mentioned above. Collective bargaining deals primarily with pay. It offers no threat to the 'system'. Workers' cooperation is determined by expediency (most workers have family commitments). Trade unions are therefore basically reactive institutions. They have to react to the situation in which they find themselves. In other words, trade unions operate within a 'climate', for example the climate may be one of unemployment and inflation, international competition and falling demand and so on.

Thirdly, it has been argued that far from threatening the 'system', the trade union movement helps to maintain it. Conflict is not necessarily disruptive, it can help to maintain society since conflict helps to create group cohesion. The groups, including trade unions, become institutional-ized, that is to say, they become a permanent feature of society. They also become 'respectable'. Thus trade unions make agreements with employers and even with governments, for example the 'social contract' with the 1974 Labour Government whereby the unions promised wage restraint in return for social reforms. In this way conflict can become 'tamed'. (This view is advanced by L. Coser in *The Functions of Conflict* and by R. Dahrendorf in *Class and Class Conflict in Industrial Society*.) Again, strikes are not a danger to society but are evidence of a diversity of interests. Often these interests cannot be reconciled and strikes may permit the formulation of the issue in a way that permits a solution. In fact, history shows that where trade unions have 'threatened' governments it is because these safety valves have been closed by legislation reducing union power, or where justifiable wage increases have been blocked by a rigidly applied incomes policy (for example the strikes in the public sector in 1979).

Fourthly, it should be remembered that there are dissensions within unions themselves due frequently to a gulf between union leaders and members. Before the First World War, Robert Michels (in *Political Parties*) wrote of the oligarchic tendencies of political parties and trade unions, that is, a tendency for these organizations to be controlled by a few at the top. He wrote of the iron law of oligarchy: 'who says organization says oligarch.' Michels' argument is that it is impossible for trade unions to operate on the basis of direct democracy. The conduct of negotiations and strikes requires organization and bureaucratic leadership. However, when workers become union leaders they come to regard their position as an inalienable right; they cannot return to their former way of life. Inevitably the leaders lose touch with the ordinary members but claim to know what is best for them. In the end the organization itself (and the leader's career) becomes the vital essence rather than the interests of the members.

Finally, the Donovan Commission on trade unions in Britain concluded that far from having too much power, the trade unions have too little. Britain was not particularly strike prone compared with other countries and trade unions helped to regularize discontent by directing it through established channels, whereas unofficial strikes, called by shop stewards, indicated a failure of the formal machinery. This leads to a consideration of the next question.

Common assumption two: *shop stewards are too powerful; shop stewards are trouble makers*

In previous years hardly a week passed without a report about shop stewards in the headlines. But who are shop stewards? Shop stewards are unpaid union officials elected locally by the work people they serve. They are often portrayed in the media as politically motivated dictators, trouble makers, ringleaders and so on. However, Lane (in *The Union Makes us Strong*) describes the shop steward as follows. The shop steward:

1   works alongside the members and knows them;
2   has no power over them because he or she has no sanctions;
3   is watched by the members in his or her dealings with management;
4   must not be ambitious, not a money grabber;
5   should not be too political;
6   must be able to decipher managerial jargon. Managements' messages are often couched in a divide-and-rule language, e.g. the claim is not fair, they are jumping the queue. This is often done in order to set off one group against another.

The shop steward, in working close to the members, carries out the work which the remote paid union official cannot easily do. In this way the canteen and gate meetings are used to do what the formal (poorly attended) union branch meeting cannot do, that is, deal with irritating issues that have arisen that very day in the plant.

Beynon (in *Working for Ford*) comments that the public school idea of the ringleader takes a long time to die. But really the shop steward is not a ringleader or rabble rouser. Shop stewards live and act through the members. Their strength is based on members' support. When shop stewards have this support their authority is useful to both management and workers. Management can get quick decisions while the shop steward can help to give fellow workers what they really want, a voice in decisions that affect their everyday life on the factory floor.

Where does the idea of the ringleader really come from?

Common assumption three: *management has the right to manage*

Phrases frequently used in the media like 'managerial prerogative' and 'management's right to manage' seem natural enough. Surely management ought to manage and be allowed to do so. Strikes, militant shop stewards and government intervention all appear as infringements on management's right to manage. Certainly there is some truth in this belief – management should manage. But, like other ideologies referred to throughout this book, the ideological nature of the belief arises from its exaggeration and the fact that it serves the interests of the powerful: in this case, management. Thus if a politician asserts that management is too weak, that it is not strong enough to stand up to workers' demands, then one must ask by what standards these assertions are made. If it is by this ideological (exaggerated) standard then they may be true – management may not be able to do all that it would like to do.

As mentioned on p. 114 it is considered that there is a managerial ideology that permeates the thinking and decision making of managers in industrial relations. An important component of managerial ideology is the belief in 'scientific' management. A feature of this belief is that management must control every stage of the work process, not just what is done but how it is done. Although Frederick Taylor, one of the leading proponents of scientific management, was writing at the beginning of the century his ideas live today in their emphasis on managerial prerogative, and on control of the task (see his book, *Scientific Management*).

Thus, from a sociological viewpoint, scientific management is not about efficiency of production as Frederick Taylor and his present day supporters claim. Really it seems to be about efficiency of control over the work force. But close management control and the stress placed on managerial prerogative (i.e. 'management's right to manage') means that the work has little interest for the work people. They in turn will react in a number of ways – not necessarily by strikes or seeking more pay. Basically they will seek control of the work situation (which after all is an important part of their lives) by a variety of strategies, which are discussed in the next sections.

Common assumption four: *strikes are one of the main problems in industrial relations*

In fact strikes are not the main problem in industrial relations (although much of the media seems to think they are). Britain is not a particularly strike prone society compared with other countries, as Table 7.1 shows.

As suggested in the preceding section, many of the real problems stem from the overemphasis on managerial prerogative and from the desire of work people to have some control over their working lives. The methods used by work people may be deliberate strategies or unconscious reactions. Here is a list of some of them:

1   establishing group work norms themselves;
2   the strengthening of the shop steward system;
3   absenteeism;
4   high sickness rates;
5   fatigue;

Table 7.1 Working days lost due to industrial disputes, 1977 and 1986 (per thousand
employees)

Country	1977	1986
UK	450	90
Australia	330	240
Canada	380	690
Germany (FR)	200 (1978)	700
Italy	1170	390
Japan	40	10
Sweden	20	170
USA	280	126

Source: *Employment Gazette*, 1988, Table 1

6 high accident rates;
7 high turnover rates;
8 pilfering;
9 sabotage.

These strategies and reactions can now be described briefly.

1 *Establishing group work norms themselves*. It has frequently been
   observed that groups of people working together establish their own
   norms of work output. These work groups will maintain output norms
   in the face of management's attempts to raise output, if the work group
   considers management is behaving unreasonably. The fact that
   management has carried out a careful work study to time the job may be
   irrelevant, it is the work group that decides output norms.

2 *The strengthening of the shop steward system*. Where there is little
   consultation at work, the shop stewards can be seen as part of a search
   for a voice in decisions that affect workers' everyday life on the shop
   floor. Thus, where management seeks to strengthen formal control
   there may be a counterbalancing strengthening of the informal
   authority of the shop stewards. (This matter was discussed earlier in the
   chapter.)

3 to 7 *Absenteeism, high sickness rates, fatigue, high accident rates, high
   turnover rates*. These items can be taken together because they share
   one quality. They are not so much conscious shop floor strategies as
   perhaps unconscious reactions to overzealous managerial control.
   Their incidence is likely to be higher where control is greatest, so that
   the attempt to impose the principles of scientific management is largely
   self-defeating. Thus accidents have been shown to be associated with
   the strain of raising output too high.

8 *Pilfering*. While not in any way condoning pilfering, it can be seen as a reaction to low pay. Thus if labour is valued too low by management, pilfering can be seen partly as an informal attempt to redress the balance. Workers then come to consider pilfering as part of their rights. (Incidentally there are probably more opportunities for pilfering at management level – extra car expenses, entertainment expenses etc.)

9 *Sabotage*. There is little evidence that deliberate sabotage is widespread in industry. (See P. Dubois, *Sabotage in Industry*.) On the other hand the conscious withdrawal of effort (work norms) could be seen as sabotage. Thus working without enthusiasm could be seen as a conscious, or unconscious, reaction to the application of scientific management. In addition, sabotage and the other strategies and reactions described can be expected to increase if formal trade union power is weakened. Hence one writer has noted that sabotage correlates with the lack of a trade union tradition in certain industries. It should be mentioned that employers are also guilty of sabotage sometimes, for example, through lock-outs, withholding patent rights, monopolies, lack of investment in their own firms and so on. (As T. Veblen points out in *On the Nature and Uses of Sabotage*.)

Common assumption five: *management and workers should pull together*

Management theory and actual management practice take a pluralistic view of the business enterprise; that is to say, the various groups in a firm from labourers up to top management are seen as *sharing* certain apparently common sense goals, including the continuing prosperity of the firm, rising output, improving the product and so on. Management plans the enterprise in the interests of all concerned. Again this seems perfectly reasonable – but is it?

In contrast to the accepted orthodoxy of the *pluralist perspective*, Fox in *Man Mismanagement* advances a '*radical perspective*' which concentrates on power and the contrast between those with power in the work organization and those without. Lacking power, employees on the lower rungs of the organization are totally dependent on the organization. They cannot really influence decision making. Their only power is a limited economic power – to strike for more pay. This limited countervailing power is not enough to strike at the roots of management power. Management power is based on:

control of capital (plant, machinery, etc.);
control of the technology (special knowledge);
control of investment;
support from other managements and employers' associations;
a sympathetic public opinion – which is against strikes;

government support – governments will defend the status quo;

the social conditioning of workers themselves, many of whom do not
   support their unions (hence management's preference to appeal to the
   work force direct);

the conservatism of many trade union officials.

The apparent strength of unionized labour and the alleged weakness of
management is perhaps an illusion encouraged partly by biased media.
Nevertheless, it can still be asked: are not the interests of the workers and
management basically similar? 'Common sense' assumes the answer is
'yes'. However, this assumption distorts reality. From the point of view of
workers doing a monotonous job with no career prospects, low status and
no say in decisions that affect their everyday working lives, their only
interest in the job is the money.

When employees accept the basic structure and conventions of work,
they do so not from free choice but from an awareness of the superior
power that supports the organization (as outlined above). This in turn limits
union expectations to what is 'natural' and 'expected'.

At lower levels there is also little trust in the employees and little
discretion accorded to them. Fox concludes:

> When we bind a man with rules which minimize his discretion in a particular
> sphere of behaviour he may, to be sure, accept the constraints willingly as
> legitimate and it is important to work out under what circumstances this is
> likely to be so. But he may perceive the constraints as indicating that we do
> not trust him in which case he is likely to reciprocate with distrust towards us.
> (*Beyond Contract*)

Much of this chapter has been devoted to questioning not so much
managerial authority as managerial ideology and this has been necessary
due to the acceptance of many common assumptions supporting this
ideology. On the other hand it must be stressed that both managers and
workers want more money and management wants greater output and

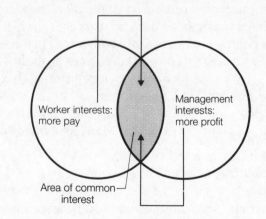

Worker interests:
more pay

Management
interests:
more profit

Area of common
interest

What interests do workers and managers have in common?

productivity (efficiency). This may be depicted as in the diagram, which shows where workers and management have interests in common. Industrial relations based more on this model are perhaps more realistic and likely to be more successful.

Common assumption six: *unemployment will disrupt society*

Behind this assumption is a view that unemployment will somehow rot the social fabric of our society; that there will be more street riots, that youth will lose the will to work, that there will be more suicides and mental illness, that older people made redundant will 'go to pieces' and so on.

Research shows there may be some truth in all these propositions, but there is another way of looking at the problem. Raymond Pahl has argued that we tend to have stereotypes of the unemployed, for example the solid, respectable, not very skilled working class man made redundant through no fault of his own and becoming increasingly depressed and hopeless. Pahl suggests that there is a fallacy in stereotyping like this. The fallacy lies in seeing the unemployed as a separate category from the employed. Rather, there is a flow of workers moving through the status of being unemployed, later becoming employed, then perhaps unemployed again for a time. Even in times of fairly full employment closures and redundancies are part of everyday life in many working class areas. (See Pahl's article, 'Family, Community and Unemployment'.)

Again, 'the idea that workers should be utterly committed to industrial employment that is boring, dirty, noisy and dangerous is not a widely shared idea' – by the work people concerned (Pahl). From this viewpoint, being unemployed is not such a catastrophe since being employed is not all that marvellous either. In addition, the casual nature of the labour market generally is a kind of support for the unemployed.

None of this is meant to make light of unemployment. Rather, as Pahl indicates, the problem of working class unemployment should be seen as part of the problem of poverty, which includes the problem of low pay discussed earlier in this chapter. Thus unemployment, low pay, depressing work and poor education are part of the same problem – poverty.

Common assumptions seven and eight: *affluent workers are more likely than other workers to have middle class attitudes and life styles; and 'We are all middle class now' (sociologists call this the embourgeoisement thesis)*

It might be expected that highly paid manual workers would have similar attitudes to middle class people. On the other hand a theme of this book has been to show the link between class attitudes and work attitudes, that people's work is part of their overall way of life.

An important study of affluent workers in the car, chemical and engineering industries made by Goldthorpe et al. (*The Affluent Worker: Industrial Attitudes and Behaviour*) showed that these affluent workers had what the authors called an '*instrumental*' attitude to their work. Their work was just a means to an end, more money. (82 per cent of the semi-skilled men said their reason for staying at their job was pay.) These workers were motivated to increase their consumption and it was this rather than self-fulfilment at work that motivated them – their job involvement was calculative. This *instrumentalism* affected their attitudes in other situations. Their attitude to the unions was instrumental. Attendance at branch meetings was low and their key interest was: will the unions get us more money? (52 per cent never voted at union branch meetings.) Similarly, they would vote Labour because that was the party that could raise their earnings. Their attitude to education was instrumental: will it help my children to get a well paid job and so on? Another example of this instrumentalism was that many of these workers had moved especially to the area or had left craft or clerical occupations for more money. The money was used to make a more comfortable home – a kind of privatization of non-work life. That is to say, there was no link between home life and work life as there would be, say, in the case of the professional or business person (only 8 per cent participated actively in work based clubs). Furthermore there was also a lack of feeling of solidarity with other workers. Generally these affluent workers did not have middle class attitudes and did not seek promotion or aspire to be middle class, for example the middle class concept of career was weak in this group. They did not see their economic and social advancement coming from work involvement. (74 per cent said they had never seriously thought of becoming a supervisor.)

Generally speaking many of the workers in the sample did not expect much satisfaction from their work. Some of them were engaged in assembly

---

Alienation

Marx argued that the essence of our true nature is that we are creative beings. In so far as we cannot express our true nature through our work we are alienated and our labour is merely bought and sold by the hour. Instead of being creative, labour becomes just a commodity and we are thereby estranged from our true selves.

Blauner has a different view of alienation from Marx. According to Blauner, alienation comprises four elements:

powerlessness – we cannot influence our social surroundings (e.g. alter the pace of work);

meaninglessness – the work has no meaning;

isolation – workers are estranged from society's norms and values;

self-estrangement – workers are separated from their true selves.

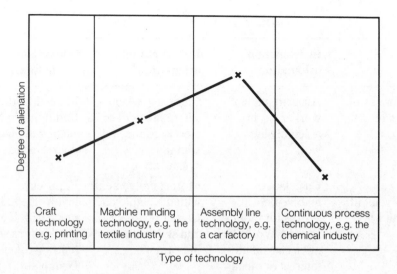

Technology and alienation

line work and this type of work has been seen as an example of '*alienation*'. Blauner in *Alienation and Freedom* advanced the view that alienation was related to the type of technology in use, as the graph depicts. The last stage, continuous process technology, is the most automated and also seen as the least alienating. Blauner's view has been criticized as another example of technological determinism. It is not the technology that causes the alienation; rather, it is the fact that the worker has no control over the work situation, can be transferred from his or her job or fired and so on.

The example of the attitudes of affluent workers is interesting because it shows that even in an extreme case where earnings are high and contacts with traditional workers weak, the group does not adopt middle class attitudes, for example the desire to follow a 'career'. Goldthorpe and his colleagues suggest there are three widespread orientations to work. Firstly, there is the instrumental or calculative orientation of the affluent unskilled worker. Secondly, there is the bureaucratic orientation of the 'faithful clerk'. Thirdly, there is what Goldthorpe calls the 'solidaristic orientation' of the traditional worker in one of the older industries. These three orientations are contrasted in Table 7.2.

The changing scene in industrial relations

Industrial relations are constantly changing and evolving. The eighties have been difficult times for the unions with steadily declining membership, increasing government regulation, unemployment, which of course weakens the unions, coercive measures by some employers and so on. Table 7.3 helps to highlight the decreasing union membership.

Table 7.2   Orientation to work

	Instrumental orientation	Bureaucratic orientation	Solidaristic orientation
Examples of types of worker	Affluent manual worker e.g. in assembly line work.	Clerical worker where the worker is closely connected with the organization	Manual worker in a traditional industry such as mining, docks and railways.
Type of involvement in the work	Calculative involvement. Works for money reward. Work is not a central life interest or means of self-realization.	Moral involvement with the employer. Career prospects and status are important.	Expressive involvement, not so much with the employer as with fellow workers. Group norms and solidarity are important.
Relationship of work and non-work	A split between work and non-work, e.g. workers do not join works clubs or participate in TU activities.	Work gives social status. Work is central life interest. Hence strong link between work and non-work.	The social relationships and shared activities at work are found emotionally rewarding. Strong sense of community both at work and after.

Table 7.3   Trade union membership, 1977–87

	1977	1987
Number of unions at the end of the year	481	330
Total membership at the end of the year (thousands)	12,846	10,475

Source: *Employment Gazette*, May 1989

The membership figures may be the tip of the iceberg, so far as union troubles are concerned. Other trends include:

Firstly, a loss of solidarity; for example, the Nottinghamshire miners who worked during the pit strike of 1984/5 and the members of the Electrical, Electronics and Telecommunications and Plumbing Union (EETPU) who worked during the printers' strike of 1986.

Secondly, the general bargaining power of the unions has been weakened due to this loss of solidarity (mentioned above) and the loss of membership.

Thirdly, it is possible the traditional link between the trade unions and the Labour Party has been weakened; future Labour governments may find it electorally unpopular in the present economic climate to repeal anti-union legislation introduced by the Conservatives.

Fourthly, the power of the shop stewards has been greatly weakened since the seventies.

Finally, there has been a shift to white collar unions as Table 7.4 indicates (though this itself does not necessarily imply a weakening of trade unionism).

Table 7.4 Analysis of trade union membership

Type of occupation	Membership (thousands)	
	1984	1986
Mining etc.	122	91
Metal goods, engineering and vehicles	447	392
Banking, finance, insurance, business services and leasing	344	352

Source: *Employment Gazette*, May 1988

The unions' response to these pressures has varied. Some have emphasized traditional union qualities, such as solidarity, while others have tried to 'sell' themselves to employers; the EETPU, for example, proposed 'no strike' agreements. Some unions are seeking members from newly expanding sectors; for example, the General Municipal and Boiler-makers Union (GMBU) has been making its appeal to what it calls the new servant class (this would include cleaners, catering staff, shop assistants, etc.). There has been a shift to a more flexible work force and the old collectivist unionism has been difficult to sustain.

Other union responses have been the acceptance of more part-time workers, the union training of workers (to make them more valuable on the labour market), the acceptance of core/periphery agreements, whereby core (skilled) workers get more job protection than peripheral workers who come and go. (See D. Thomas, 'New Ways of Working', *New Society*, August 1985, for a definition of core and periphery, etc.)

Conclusions

The aim of this chapter, like the aim of the book, has been to try and show things as they really are. This entails, among other things, looking at industrial relations through the eyes of all the parties concerned. No political view is pressed, no panaceas for industrial relations are offered, no advice to business managers is given: there is only the genuine attempt to try to see the issues clearly.

Table 7.5 summarizes some of the main points.

Table 7.5   Differing views on industrial relations

A common view	A sociological view
1 Management and workers should cooperate more.	Management and workers do not always share the same interests. Often they have differing aims, as shown in this chapter.
2 The unions are too strong.	Management is stronger and workers weaker than is commonly supposed. In the end management has a right to manage.
3 Routine jobs can and should be enriched.	Often this is not possible because management exercises tight control over the work. In many routine jobs the workers' main interest is the money (possibly higher level work could be made more interesting).
4 Workers do not appear to be very loyal to their employers. Often they seek more pay even when the firm is doing badly.	It should not be assumed that career considerations, loyalty to the firm etc. that apply to the managerial and professional levels also apply at the lower levels (where as mentioned the main interest is often just the pay). Anyway, managers are not all that loyal to the employing firm – they may move from firm to firm in order to better their career prospects.
5 Strikes are a serious problem in Britain.	Far from being a serious problem, they could be seen as a healthy aspect of an open society; or a way of taming conflict; on the other hand, strikes could also be seen as a reflection of deep inequalities of wealth and power in society.
6 Many strikes seem senseless (for example demarcation disputes – 'who does what' strikes); or unreasonable (for example where workers object to a vigilant security	It is the task of the sociologist to show that apparently senseless data do in fact make sense. One way of doing this is to reverse the usual 'common sense' question: not to ask

A common view	A sociological view
officer); or due to greed or just 'daft'.	why there are so many strikes but rather why, in view of the alienating work many people do, there are so few strikes. Strikes may reflect genuine conflict in society and for this reason any legislation against them is likely to fail in the long run – because it attacks symptoms and not the real problems. (One aim of this chapter is to deflect the focus of interest away from strikes.)
7 Management must have the right to manage.	True – but when this gets overstressed, workers feel they are being watched and controlled all the time and not really trusted.
8 Many workers could do better. Industrial performance and productivity is poor compared with other countries.	Too much control by management (see above) can result in demoralization, reflected in high absenteeism rates, high labour turnover and poor productivity generally. There are many deeper reasons for Britain's industrial decline, including class divisions manifested in factory and office and the low status accorded to industry and commerce.
9 But surely class distinction is much less important now. Many manual workers earn more than clerical workers, and go on expensive holidays.	The evidence shows that affluent manual workers do not adopt middle class attitudes; do not, for example, see their work as a 'career' and do not aspire to become middle class.

Self-examination questions

(Answers can be checked from the text.)

1 Define briefly: 'trade union', 'shop steward', 'oligarchy', 'industrial relations'.

2 What is meant by: 'alienation', 'instrumentalism', 'Taylorism' (or 'scientific management'), 'institutionalization of conflict', 'work norms', 'pluralist perspective', 'radical perspective', 'embourgeoisement thesis'?

Projects

1 *The following assignment was set for Business and Technician Education Council students as part of their course for the Higher National Award at Oxford Polytechnic, 1985.*

Take as an example a labour dispute currently or recently in the news.

1 Write a very brief history *analysing* the key problems in industrial relations in the example you have taken.

2 *Analyse* the current position from the viewpoint of both management and work force.
NB: Analyse – do not describe.

3 Using sociological insights gained on this course, show how (with the benefit of hindsight) you yourself might have handled industrial relations problems as a manager. Describe how you would tackle current and future problems, carefully justifying every proposal you make (for example by reference to what you have learnt on the course).

4 Highlight the assumptions of the parties involved, paying particular regard to those assumptions concerning the nature of work; the nature of authority; the functions of management and so on.

5 How would you apply the lessons from this assignment to other organizations, for example, local authorities, the Civil Service, health authorities, a professional firm and so on?

Length: maximum number of words 3000.

2 **Read the following passage and answer the questions at the end.**

After the 1981 pay agreement when the TGWU conceded overall control of the negotiating body to the ten other shop floor unions, we moved into a new phase of *employee involvement*. Before this helpful development we had used thousands of man-hours *explaining our strategies on particular issues to employees* direct, through managers at all levels and throughout our factories, and our intention was to continue to do so, in parallel with the union machinery.

An excellent example of direct communication was when Harold Musgrove and his team put the product strategy across to some 18,000 employees – on day and night shifts – talking virtually continuously to groups of 1000 people at a time, prior to Recovery Plan Ballot in 1979. Jaguar have more recently involved their workforce in depth on the new lightweight engine project, and when I went over the engine plant at Radford in mid-1982, the seven stewards who accompanied the plant director, the head of Jaguar, John Egan, and me showed a deep knowledge of the financial, commercial, productivity and manning implications of this new investment.

Rightly so, for it is vital that they should be well versed in facts and statistics that affect jobs. The correlation between disputes and market share shows

how jobs are affected by *mindless industrial action*, and if deeper involvement reduces disputes, then, for this reason alone, it is worth it. At the
employee relations level, this necessitates manager and employee working
directly together – it doesn't benefit from third-party do-gooders or from
government intervention.

With this process goes the need for balance, moderation, and dignity; it
does not justify 'hob-nailed boots', and whenever my senior colleagues have
had evidence that someone has abused his new 'strength', changes have been
made. These unhappy incidents have been the exceptions, but they have on
occasions been publicized, which is fair enough. Abuse must be discouraged
for if men give up some liberty and accept discipline in its place, those
applying the discipline must earn the right to do so. The balance is a fine one;
if management doesn't lead firmly, militant shop stewards will fill the
vacuum, and it will be the moderately minded worker who will be the 'pawn
in the game'. *It is management who have responsibility* for the business; if the
power is to move to the shop stewards, let them find the banks to lend the
money, let them persuade governments of any colour to tide them over bad
times, let them persuade competitors to collaborate; and let the unions
persuade customers to buy the products they design, build and deliver. And
above all, let them create the excellent working conditions – and much
improved bonus earnings – that we are now proud to have in those of our
factories that have come through the management and investment revolution
of the past three years. For you cannot have responsibility and authority
without accountability, and it is at this last fence that the militant falters and
falls. Having learned to exploit, he has not yet learned to create and construct.
(From *Back from the Brink* by Sir Michael Edwardes, former chairman of
BL: the italics are this author's)

1   State briefly the main points of this passage.

2   What does Sir Michael Edwardes mean by 'employee involvement'? What
    are the main difficulties in obtaining employee involvement? What
    comments would you wish to make on the other phrases in italics?

3   To what extent (if any) do you feel this passage reflects the ideology of
    scientific management?

**3   Write a report to the Department of Employment on the latest trends in
industrial relations in Britain. Your report should include some of the
following:**

1   Change in trade union membership.
2   Reasons for the apparent weakness of the trade unions.
3   Non-strike agreement.
4   Core/periphery workers.

Suggestions

Use the text in this chapter and the recommended further reading. *Keesing's Record of
World Events* will help to keep you up to date.

On the reduction in the membership you could mention that many unions have amalgamated to obtain economies of scale (bigger trade unions are cheaper proportionately). Some unions have disappeared because that trade no longer exists.

Look for union *density* – that is, the actual membership as a proportion of total possible membership.

Past examination questions

1 The following is an extract from an interview with a production line worker.

The point about this place is that the work destroys you. It destroys you physically and mentally. The biggest problem is getting people to accept it, to accept being here day in and day out. So you've got low morale from every point of view. You're inflicted with a place of work and you've got to adapt to it because it won't adapt to you. So morale is terribly low. But you can build on this you see. You can't get much lower than hell and so can increase morale through the union. Pull together sort of thing rather than dog eats dog ... We're all in it together like. That's where the union comes in. (H. Beynon, *Working for Ford*.)

1 a) What aspects of work on a production line could be said to 'destroy you physically and mentally'? (6 marks)
  b) 'You've got to adapt to it because it won't adapt to you.' Do you agree? What changes could raise the morale of production line workers? (8 marks)
2 How would you expect an office worker's view of his/her union to differ from this production line worker's view of his union? (6 marks)

University of Cambridge Local Examinations, O Level, Summer 1984.

Suggestions

1 a) The speaker seems to be referring to the relentlessness of the assembly line, especially the fact that he has no control over it. Then relate this to the four component parts of alienation mentioned in this chapter.
  b) The speaker uses words like 'adapt' and 'accept'. Perhaps it is this loss of control that causes the low morale. Two changes could be suggested here. Firstly, 'enrich' the job, giving the worker more responsibility and control. Secondly (or alternatively), pay workers more to compensate them for their alienation. Thus the Goldthorpe studies demonstrated that many workers doing routine jobs had a highly instrumental attitude to their work – their main interest was the money.

  It may be that attempts at job enrichment may not work for this type of job since real control seems to belong to management. Piece work, whereby workers are paid for what they produce, may encourage more autonomy in work groups and lead to better pay. On the other hand piece work is not always favoured by management (possibly because it lessens managment's control over the work situation – see comments on 'Taylorism' in the chapter).

  The speaker seems to expect the union to provide the solidarity that will enhance morale and hopefully lead to improved conditions at work. The Goldthorpe studies however stress an instrumental approach to unions: workers just want the unions to get them more money.

2   Office workers would also want more pay and better working conditions but would probably stress individual advancement more, for example better career prospects, more promotions, better pension schemes, private medical schemes etc.

You could note that many white collar unions are not true unions but 'company unions', really run by the employer.

It could also be mentioned that many white collar workers are as alienated as production line workers, as C. Wright Mills indicates in *White Collar*.

Finally, you could quote from *White-Collar Unionism* by Jenkins and Sherman referring to the year 2000: 'By then the emphasis of the trade unions will have changed from instant reaction to events to one of medium term planning. But the essence, the solidarity and the collectivity will still remain the vital impellers.'

2   Has industrial conflict been institutionalized?

University of Cambridge Local Examinations, A Level, Summer 1983

Suggestions

Say what is meant by institutionalized – that conflict occurs through recognized channels, e.g. a trade union bargains with an employer. Street fighting, violent clashes between pickets and police, damage to property and persons whether during a strike or not would be examples of non-institutionalized conflict. So too would be hidden conflict as explained here, absenteeism, lack of effort, etc. Possibly this is the most serious aspect of industrial conflict – discuss further.

3   Do occupational identities influence behaviour outside the work place?

University of Cambridge Local Examinations, A Level, Summer 1983.

Suggestions

See Table 7.2 in text derived from the Goldthorpe study – instrumental, bureaucratic and solidaristic orientation. For further details see S. R. Parker, *The Sociology of Leisure*.

4   Alienation is a consequence of the way in which work is organized and controlled. Examine this view.

Associated Examining Board, A Level, Paper 2, November 1987.

Suggestion

Compare the views of Marx and Blauner (see this chapter and Glossary).

Further reading

*H. Beynon, *Working for Ford*
 R. Blauner, *Alienation and Freedom*
 H. Braverman, *Labour and Monopoly Capital*

S. Briggs, 'The End of the Nissan Honeymoon', *New Statesman and Society*, 15 July 1988

*D. Farnham and J. Pimlott, *Understanding Industrial Relations*

A. Fox, *Man Mismanagement*

C. Gill, *Work, Unemployment and the New Technology*

J. H. Goldthorpe et al., *The Affluent Worker: Industrial Attitudes and Behaviour*

C. Jenkins and B. Sherman, *White-Collar Unionism*

S. Lonsdale, *Work and Inequality*

C. W. Mills, *White Collar*

S. R. Parker, *The Sociology of Leisure*

S. R. Parker, et al., *The Sociology of Industry*

D. Thomas, 'New Ways of Working'

*T. J. Watson, *Sociology, Work and Industry*

'Database Trade Unions', *New Statesman and Society*, 22 July 1988

*'Education and Work', *New Society*, 18 February 1982 (Society Today series)

*'Organizations', *New Society*, 13 May 1982 (Society Today series); see also Chapter 8

*The Professions', *New Society*, 20 October 1983 (Society Today series); see also Chapter 8

Part IV

Gender, Race and Cultural Inequality

---

8   Gender

Introduction

The three chapters in part IV look at types of cultural inequality. This chapter begins by asking why feminism and the question of women's rights are a matter of sociological concern. It then deals briefly with a number of common assumptions which have a common theme: namely that women's rights have been fought for and won over the last two hundred years and that women basically have the same status and the same rights of citizenship as men. The question, 'why does sexual inequality persist?', is then investigated (see 'feminism' in Glossary).

Firstly then, why are feminism and the question of women's rights of sociological concern? One way of answering this question is to refer to the themes of this book which have been set out several times already:

that we are basically learning animals;

that we are what we have learnt;

that the role of the woman is a *learnt* role – learnt from infancy and reinforced in everyday living;

that the role of woman is therefore socially constructed and supported by *ideologies* about the place of women (shown here in the form of common assumptions about women);

that these ideologies are really an aspect of *power*, the power of men over women summarized in the concept of 'patriarchy' (see below); that it is the task of the sociologist to show 'what is really going on', to show how our social world is constructed and taken for granted.

The examination below of the milestones for women appears to show that great strides have been made in the struggle for equal rights for women. However, the section that follows examines five common assumptions concerning rights for women and shows that women still occupy an inferior position in our male ordered society.

Milestones for women

1848: the Factory Act limited women's and children's working hours in textile mills to ten per day. (Women and children under ten had been excluded from underground work by the 1842 Mines and Collieries Act.)

1857: the Matrimonial Causes Act allowed divorce through the law courts, instead of by the slow and expensive business of a Private Act of Parliament. The husband had only to prove his wife's adultery, but the wife had to prove her husband had committed not just adultery but also incest, bigamy, cruelty or desertion.

1870: the Education Act allowed women not only to vote for the new school boards, but also to be elected to serve on them. Many pioneering feminists seized this first opportunity to do practical public work.

The first Married Woman's Property Act, described by supporters of women's rights as a 'legislative abortion', was nonetheless the first recognition of a new principle: that married women should in certain circumstances own and control their own earnings, savings and legacies.

Girton College, the first women's college at Cambridge, opened but was not recognized by the University authorities.

1903: the Women's Social and Political Union, the second national suffrage movement, was formed by the Pankhursts.

1910: first woman chartered accountant and first woman banker.

1913: the first martyr in the suffrage cause, Emily Wilding Davidson died after throwing herself under the King's horse in the Derby.

1923: the Matrimonial Causes Act made the grounds for divorce the same for men as for women.

1928: the Equal Franchise Act ('Flappers' Vote') gave all women over 21 the vote.

1929: first woman cabinet minister – Margaret Bondfield.

1947: the University of Cambridge finally agreed to award full degrees to women; it was the last university to do so.

1949: the first women King's Counsels (English Bar) – Helena Normanton and Rose Heilbron.

1964: the Married Women's Property Act enabled a divorced wife to keep half of anything she had saved from any allowance given by her husband.

1965: the first woman High Court judge – Dame Elizabeth Lane.

1967: the Abortion Act made abortion far easier as, in addition to medical reasons, social grounds were allowed.

The Matrimonial Homes Act gave both husband and wife the right of occupation of their home. Neither could be evicted during the marriage, except by a court order.

1969: the Divorce Reform Act (implemented in 1971) broadened grounds for divorce. Petitioners had only to prove their marriage had irretrievably broken down.

1970: the Equal Pay Act stipulated that equal pay for men and women doing the same job had to be brought in within five years.

1975: the Sex Discrimination act banned sex discrimination in employment, education and advertising and set up the Equal Opportunities Commission to see that the new act was observed.

The Employment Protection Act made it unlawful to dismiss a woman because she was pregnant and established a woman's right to maternity leave and some maternity pay, as well as the right to return to her job within 29 weeks of giving birth.

1976: the Domestic Violence Act attempted to increase the courts' protection of battered wives and gave police powers of arrest for breach of an injunction in cases of domestic violence.

1979: the first woman Prime Minister in Britain – Margaret Thatcher.

1981: the first woman Leader of the House of Lords – Baroness Young.

1983: the first woman Lord Mayor of London – Mary Donaldson.

1984: the Equal Value Amendment to Equal Pay Act allowed women to claim equal pay to men doing similar but different jobs if they were considered to be of equal value.

1987: 41 women MPs, the highest number ever, but still only 6.7 per cent of the total.

(A. Holdsworth, *Out of the Doll's House*, pp. 12–14.)

These are impressive milestones, great achievements. So why is it that women have not achieved equal status with men? This question is examined in the following section.

Common assumptions one to five: *the rights of women*

It might first be useful to examine some common assumptions which are really a variation on a theme, the theme that women's rights have been fought for and won over the years and that as a consequence women have equal status. The rights of full citizenship (according to T. H. Marshall in *Sociology at the Crossroads*) involved equal legal, political and social rights. Marshall's concept of citizenship will be used here to analyse the rights of women.

Common assumptions	Likely reality
1 Women have achieved equal legal rights with men. The Married Women's Property Act 1870 recognized women's legal rights over their own property. Women how have equal rights with men to sue for divorce.	Women's property (and women themselves) are often regarded as the property of men. Legal equality to sue for divorce does not really mean the sexes are equal. It is assumed that women will still look after the family.

Common assumptions	Likely reality
2 Women have achieved equal political rights with men. In the nineteenth century women had no political rights; this was a central grievance of the suffragette movement, which fought for women. Due to their war effort in the First World War, which challenged prejudices about women's capabilities, women over 30 got the vote in 1918, and this was extended to all women over 21 in 1928.	This common assumption is largely correct, but it should be mentioned that for most of the nineteenth century the majority of men did not have the vote either. The suffragette movement was to a large extent a middle class movement. The number of women in Parliament is still very low. Although women have full political rights, this does not mean they have equal status with men.
3 Women have more equal social rights now. In the nineteenth century their position was much more one of dependency. With industrialization women become more dependent on men – the breadwinners. This century there has been a big increase in the proportion of married women working. In 1921 only 9% of all workers were married women – but by 1971 the figure had risen to 42%.	Women's social status is not equal. Until recently factory legislation prevented them from doing night work sometimes. (This seems to assume that men, as full citizens, are capable of making contracts for the hire of their labour and can look after their own interests free of state protection in this respect.) Even now welfare and tax legislation in Britain assumes women are dependent. Much of the work available for women is menial.
4 In earlier times life for the working class housewife was all drudgery. It was not much better for the middle class housewife either. Now there are labour saving devices in the home and life is much easier.	Women still do the housework; indeed, according to Ann Oakley (in *Housewife*) housework has become an ideology. A belief that suits the economy, because the 'housewife' looks after ('services') the wage earner virtually free of charge to the employer. Expectations now for homekeeping and child care have risen.
5 With the availability of work for women, and of welfare services, and more equality, in the family woman's social status has improved.	Any increases in unemployment fall heavily on women – who are a large part of the reserve army of labour (i.e. they are the first to be made redundant and their labour is normally only sought when men are not available for the work). Finally, cutbacks in the welfare state, the stress on 'community care' and the return to 'Victorian' family values mean more (unpaid) work for women in the home.

Generally, then, whilst women *appear* to have equal rights – the rights of citizenship – they do not have equal status, as has just been shown. Thus Olive Banks (in *Faces of Feminism*) argues that the old feminist tradition was over-optimistic about the power of legislation to bring about a change in society. Reform is unlikely to change attitudes that are deeply rooted. So far, the chapter has shown that common assumptions about equality of rights and status are at least partly incorrect. However, a deeper analysis is needed to try to find out why sexual inequality persists. This analysis follows next.

What feminism does

Feminism shows that women are systematically disadvantaged in modern society and it advocates equal opportunity for both men and women. This chapter indicates the difficulties in such an endeavour.

Why do sexual inequalities persist? An investigation

It seems that the common assumption of equality or near-equality has little validity when the evidence is examined. To try to answer the question, 'why do sexual inequalities persist', one area in particular will be examined – work. Work is an important area to look at because if women had real equality at work (if all positions were open to them, if allowances were made for female careers being interrupted by a period of child-rearing) then women would have gained equality in other spheres (including sexual relations, recognition of the value of housework, full equality in education and so on). Conversely, if women had higher status in the home, or were less home-bound, they might be able to achieve higher status at work.

Firstly it is clear that in Britain women do not have equality at work, despite legislation – the Equal Pay Act 1970, the Sex Discrimination Act 1975, and the establishment of the Equal Opportunities Commission to oversee the working of the law. Why is all this insufficient to ensure equality at work? Why does inequality persist?

A few facts will help to demonstrate the continuance of this inequality at work. Table 8.1 shows women's inequality of income compared to men,

Table 8.1 Weekly earnings of
men and women, 1982 and 1988

	1982	1988
Men	£135	£207
Women	£80	£121

Source: adapted from *Employment Gazette*,
November 1988, Table 5.6

and also that this inequality persists. Not only is there inequality in income, but women are confined to certain types of work. The results of the 1981 census showed that:

33 per cent of employed women are in clerical work;

23 per cent are in service sector jobs;

14 per cent in lower professional jobs (mainly nursing, teaching and social work).

Even though it can be clearly demonstrated that inequality at work persists, most people say that the law should favour equality at work. Table 8.2 shows the response people gave when asked, 'There is a law in Britain against sex discrimination. Do you support or oppose the idea of a law for this purpose?'

Table 8.2 Level of support for law against sex discrimination

	1983	1987
Support	76%	75%
Oppose	22%	22%

Note: based on a representative sample of 3000.
Source: R. Jowell, S. Witherspoon and L. Brook (eds), *British Social Attitudes*

Finally, Table 8.3 indicates the extent to which traditionalist values about the role of women persist.

Women's jobs generally have low status (clerical, cleaning and domestic work). Even when there is equal pay, women tend to take the lower posts. Thus a report by the National Union of Teachers in 1980 showed that although women provided 44 per cent of the teachers in secondary schools they provide only 1 per cent of the head teachers.

Often the family has to take precedence and this means that paid work and a career are not central concerns for women. For this and other reasons, women tend to form what has been called 'the reserve army of labour'.

Returning now to the question at the beginning of this section – why do inequalities at work persist? Why is the legislation insufficient to counteract these inequalities? Table 8.4 is an attempt to trace sexual inequalities back to their source.

Example 1 in this table is an interesting illustration of inequality. We can investigate it further now in order to try to answer our question: why do sexual inequalities persist? This can be done by examining female careers in reverse chronological order from existing inequalities at work back to early

Table 8.3 Women's attitudes on the role of women (percentages)

	Agree (strongly or slightly)		Neither agree nor disagree		Disagree (strongly or slightly)	
	1980	1987	1980	1987	1980	1987
Traditionalist attitudes						
Wife's job to look after home	46	38	21	17	33	44
Job all right, but most women want home and children	41	24	25	19	34	57
In high unemployment, married women should stay at home	35	21	16	18	49	60
Benefits of women working						
If children are looked after, it's good for women to work	71	62	17	25	12	12
A job is the best way for women to be independent	67	65	17	21	16	14

Source: R. Jowell, S. Witherspoon and L. Brook (eds), *British Social Attitudes*

Women's position in the labour market has not improved
Source: *New Society*, 17 November 1983

Table 8.4 An analysis of the sources of continuing sexual inequality at work

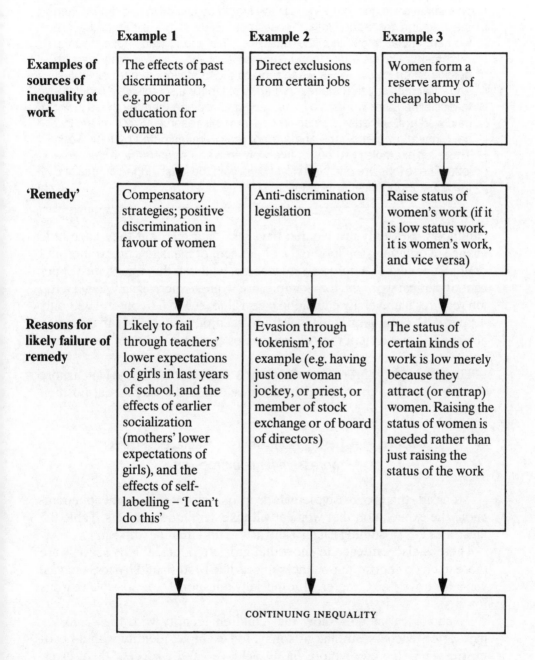

	Example 1	Example 2	Example 3
Examples of sources of inequality at work	The effects of past discrimination, e.g. poor education for women	Direct exclusions from certain jobs	Women form a reserve army of cheap labour
'Remedy'	Compensatory strategies; positive discrimination in favour of women	Anti-discrimination legislation	Raise status of women's work (if it is low status work, it is women's work, and vice versa)
Reasons for likely failure of remedy	Likely to fail through teachers' lower expectations of girls in last years of school, and the effects of earlier socialization (mothers' lower expectations of girls), and the effects of self-labelling – 'I can't do this'	Evasion through 'tokenism', for example (e.g. having just one woman jockey, or priest, or member of stock exchange or of board of directors)	The status of certain kinds of work is low merely because they attract (or entrap) women. Raising the status of women is needed rather than just raising the status of the work

CONTINUING INEQUALITY

Source: Based on a scheme used by L. and D. Nandy – 'Towards true equality for women', *New Society*, 30 January 1975

Women and the reserve army of labour

The 'reserve army of labour' refers to that part of the labour force that is only taken on in good times and is the first to be laid off in bad times when the demand for labour falls. Those most likely to be in this group are women, racial minorities, the unskilled, the young and those nearing retirement. On the other hand, members of the reserve army can be quickly taken on at low wages to replace those at work at normal wages. Thus Marxists say that the reserve army of labour also acts as a regulator to discipline other workers by threatening to replace them by these lower paid workers. Because women tend to form this reserve army they are low paid, have low status jobs and are not really emancipated by their work. Thus, for example, two out of five women wage earners have part time jobs. These jobs are often the worst paid, with the least fringe benefits and the least opportunity for promotion.

---

childhood. Not only are women paid less than men but they have little chance of obtaining top jobs; only 17 per cent of managers are women and only 18 per cent of employers are women, while on the other hand 73 per cent of clerical workers, for example, are women. Increasingly to get a top job requires a university education (see Tables 6.3 to 6.6) but in 1983 only 40 per cent of undergraduates were women despite the fact that women achieved 45 per cent of the A Level passes and 51 per cent of the O Level passes.

The stages of this process can be seen as a series of hurdles at which more women than men drop out right up to selection for managerial position itself:

O Level → A Level → University → Managerial career
Progressive female drop-out

Alongside this progressive female drop-out rate there is another phenomenon, the expectation that women will take 'feminine' subjects. Table 8.5 illustrates this (assuming English and arts to be 'feminine' subjects).

There is also evidence to show that girls attending all girls schools are more likely to choose 'masculine' subjects like Maths and Physics, and vice versa for boys (see Chapter 11, especially question 1, for possible reasons for this).

Psychological studies show that children identify with the same sex partner or teachers, so that girls may, for example, identify with a headmistress and therefore more easily achieve career success themselves. Again, studies show that where a mother works, or does not concentrate on being a wife, the daughter is more independent and more likely to enter a non-traditional career. It should also be mentioned that books and films are a source of role models; an example in Britain is the Ladybird series of

Table 8.5 Comparison of A Level choices by boys and girls (percentages)

Subject	Boys	Girls
Maths – statistics, computer science	52	26
Physics	40	11
English	17	42
Music, drama, visual arts	11	17

Source: R. Redpath and B. Harvey, *Young People's Intention to Enter Higher Education*, HMSO (Office of Population Censuses and Surveys), London, 1987, Table 5.4

books, in which Peter does the interesting things – climbing trees, discovering treasure etc. – while his sister passively looks on, or helps mother with the housework. These provide role models which can live in the memory, guiding future expectations and actions.

Secondly, there are teachers' expectations. These expectations are often unconscious, yet again guide pupils' expectations and behaviour in the long term. Girls might be asked to perform social tasks like taking messages, while boys may be asked to help in setting up technical aids. Ann Oakley in her book *Subject Women* refers to the *hidden curriculum* in schools (the unofficial consequences of teaching). Often this influences pupils through apparently little things, for example a question in a Housecraft exam paper which assumes the girl will cook and iron for a boy; an art teacher who says, 'We are now going to draw aeroplanes but the girls may like to draw birds instead'; a geography teacher who complains of a pupil's untidy map, saying 'I thought girls were supposed to be able to draw neatly'; the fact that the head teacher is usually male; if the deputy head is a woman she will usually be in charge of welfare matters. (Incidentally, Oakley concludes that women cannot escape a feminine destiny through education: 'Women's formal education mirrors rather than determines their position in society'.)

Many girls seem to be cautious at school. This caution may arise because girls think failure arises from a lack of ability rather than a lack of effort and they are afraid of appearing dumb. Sharpe suggests, in *Just Like a Girl*, that girls should be given tasks where they can monitor their own performance and gain mastery, rather than be exposed to public praise or blame. This would encourage training for independence. Sharpe also comments that a girl who competes and succeeds in a male dominated world is regarded by both sexes as not normal and unattractive. School exaggerates differences between the sexes. From the beginning, girls are seldom allowed to develop the autonomy and independence associated with analytical thinking.

Finally, and going back in time still further, there are great differences in the early upbringing of girls and boys. This was clearly demonstrated, with

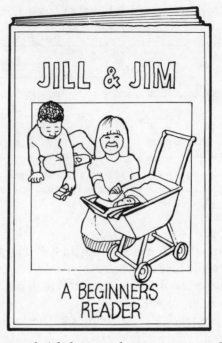

How boys and girls learn to become men and women

supporting evidence, in Chapter 3 on the upbringing of children. Sharpe says that 'by the time a girl reaches adolescence her mind has usually been subjected to an endless stream of ideas and images incorporating sexist values.' The children's books, reading primers, toys, nursery talk, play activities, television programmes, the child's contemporaries, and most importantly parents all portray these sexist values, telling her what she ought to be: feminine, submissive and unambitious. Table 3.7 on p. 48 shows the differences in parental attitudes to boys and girls of seven years of age.

The findings of the study by J. and E. Newson, *Seven Years Old in the Home Environment*, indicate that boys are considered more outgoing and aggressive and in need of less protection; mothers are harder on girls. This is in line with other studies. For example, Sharpe's studies show girls are more closely watched by mothers (and sometimes ridiculed by them). The girl taking her mother as a model and internalizing the mother's expectations will of course learn to behave like mother in general. Being less ambitious, it is not surprising that in the long run girls do less well educationally; indeed, it seems they learn to fail at school. Studies (like Sharpe's) show they even fear success.

Summarizing so far, it has been shown that the achievement of equal rights, the passing of anti-discrimination legislation and the establishment of the Equal Opportunities Commission in Britain have not ensured equality of status.

Evidence and argument have been put forward here but they still do not really answer the question: why do sexual inequalities still persist? Perhaps qualities that are thought of as being feminine, such as caring, are under-valued because they are apparently feminine qualities: but why?

Possibly one way of explaining this is through the use of the concept of *patriarchy*, meaning rule by the father, through which men have power over women as a class. This power of men over women can be economic, cultural or ideological as Table 8.6 shows.

Table 8.6 Examples of patriarchy

Patriarchy – type of power	Examples
1 Economic	a) The right to be serviced in the family – so that the cooking, cleaning and caring is done by the wife. b) The right to compulsory sex (for which the man would have to pay a prostitute). c) The woman's compulsory motherhood (although there is more choice nowadays than in the past).
2 Cultural	The devaluation of women's work and achievements.
3 Ideological	Representing women as natural biological creatures inherently different from men.

Source: based on a definition in the *Penguin Dictionary of Sociology*

Patriarchy is basically an ideology, a distortion of reality, and like other ideologies it persists because it suits the interests of the powerful in society – in this case men.

Armed with this knowledge, it may be interesting now to consider a few more common assumptions that reflect the ideology of patriarchy.

Common assumption six: *because of the biological differences between men and women, sexual equality is impossible and undesirable*

It is necessary first to distinguish between sex and gender. Sex refers to obvious physical differences between men and women. Gender refers to cultural differences which vary from society to society (Ann Oakley, *Sex, Gender and Society*). To repeat what was said in Chapter 1, the basic sociological position is that we are what we have learnt. We learn from our earliest upbringing to be men and women. What has been learnt in the home is reinforced in the school and throughout life, as this chapter has demonstrated. Because being a woman is learnt behaviour it is capable of modification, through modifying the attitudes and expectations of not only women's role models, but those of men as well.

Common assumption seven: *men have urgent sexual needs, women are sexually passive*

Again this is possibly behaviour that is learnt by both men and women. Anthropological studies show that in some societies it is the women who are sexually aggressive and the men who are sexually timid. The idea that only the man should be the active partner may be culturally based. Our Western culture assumes that the man will make the advances and that the woman is passive but in control of the situation. Thus if an indiscretion occurs it is the woman who must bear the blame. In the case of rape, the man tends to be blamed less, and the woman more, on the grounds that she did not control the situation and may indeed have provoked it (hence the court may inquire into her previous sexual life).

Common assumption eight: *women accept and prefer their existing role – to be wives and mothers*

Slaves also accept their existing role. They have learnt the required behaviour. While a woman may feel guilty if she goes out to work a man is considered anti-social if he does not work. Again the 'slavery', the drudgery, the martyrdom and the dependence are all learnt behaviour. But the ideology of housemaking and mothercraft does more harm than good, says Ann Oakley in *Housewife*. It encourages self-pity and dependence rather than partnership. The husband is relied on as a contact with the outside world and this is also a source of tension. The (learnt) concept of romantic love says women choose marriage before career. But really this is not a choice. Marriage is not a career but a partnership, and if it is a true partnership it is not for men to provide for women or women to service men. On the other hand, training and education have been shown to increase the desire for work. In other words, the more educated the woman, the less likely she is to be satisfied with the role of captive wife (Hannah Gavron, *The Captive Wife*). Hence the role of captive wife is not 'human nature'; it is a learnt role which some women resent and reject. Of course the role of housewife or mother may be an honourable one, but it is not really recognized in our society as such. It is not paid for and is usually taken for granted.

The role of mother, wife, girlfriend or daughter is not a 'natural' thing, but is culturally determined. Not only that, but a mystique is built around it – the 'feminine mystique'. Betty Friedan (in *The Feminine Mystique*) says that we have made woman a 'sex creature'. The feminine mystique is so powerful that women do not realize they have desires and capacities which the mystique forbids. On the other hand, housewifery expands to fill the time available. Women, Friedan says, martyr themselves in the role of wife and mother. At the same time, the glorification of the woman's role is in proportion to society's reluctance to treat her as a complete human being. Friedan concludes that hitherto psychiatrists have tried to cure patients by fitting them to the culture. How true this is when one considers that the overwhelming proportion of people on anti-depressant drugs are women at home. Growth requires strength to give up the past.

On the other hand it is not just a matter of women choosing to be free (as Friedan seems to imply). There are powerful constraints preventing this, as this chapter has shown in discussing the education of girls in the home and at school, and this in turn is closely linked to society generally. Thus Ann Oakley in *Subject Women* shows that the official ideology of education visible in government reports is in direct descent from the ideology that emerged in the late nineteenth century concerning the place of women. She says that capitalism by then had clearly shown itself to require the existence of two classes of labour power: productive and reproductive. Women as the bearers of children seemed naturally fitted for the latter role. But this is only what the ideology says. It does not necessarily have to be true.

Common assumption nine: *what women want is their own concern; it is up to them to fight their own battles*

The first difficulty with this assumption is that the role of women, like other roles, is provided by our culture and it is difficult to see how change can take place. This requires that the few (with sociological insight perhaps) point out to the majority how things could be different, how they could live a fuller life and so on.

The second difficulty is the assumption that women's rights concern only women. Really men too would benefit (and also lose) from female emancipation. The woman who has to work at motherhood and housework and has no career may become unreasonably depressed and so on. The man who assumes he should always be served also acts unreasonably; but in addition there is the question of ignorance of a better world – there is the man who will never know what it is like to enjoy his own emancipation.

The third difficulty is the assumption that women can become revolutionary. Because women suffer their wrongs within their own families they do not come together and share their grievances. Hence these wrongs do not become politicized; that is, they do not become matters for political action. In addition, the fear of independence is also strongly embedded in the culturally given female role.

Conclusions

Although women have equal rights with men now, this does not imply equal status. We have seen the nature of sexual inequality at work and in the home, and have investigated the reasons for it. Sexual ideologies underpin many of our common assumptions.

A criticism of this chapter

One criticism that could be made of this chapter is that it sees women as passive receivers in gender role socialization. Thus it keeps asking why women do not achieve, rather than looking primarily at male domination. Do you agree with this criticism?

One possible answer is that the criticism is valid and that we do not notice male domination because it is part of our everyday world. The reality is cloaked by the ideology of patriarchy. As with all ideologies, what patriarchy really cloaks is the power of the dominant group – in this case males (the ideology of patriarchy was explained a few pages earlier). It is necessary to be aware of your own ideological thinking (particularly if you are male, white and middle class).

Sexual equality does not of course imply that men and women are the same; of course they are not. It means treating a person as a person first rather than as a woman or man; it means respecting and valuing inherent differences. What tends to happen is that inherent feminine qualities get undervalued because they *are* feminine qualities.

In concluding her book, *The Sociology of Women*, Sara Delamont suggests that sociology has been too concerned with the masculine view of the world. Her book (and this chapter) calls for a greater understanding of the world view of women and an incorporation of that world view into sociology.

Discussion topics

1 Distinguish between sex and gender.
2 In what respects did the suffragette movement differ from the modern feminist movement?
3 Why do you think sexual inequality persists?

Case studies and past examination questions

1   'Good evening, this is the ten o'clock news and Mary Lyon reading it. First, the news headlines.

The Chancellor of the Exchequer, the Right Honourable Frances Buss, has announced today that there will be a mini-budget on 19 June before the summer recess.

The results of the Democratic presidential primary in Georgia show Bella Azburg a clear winner over Shirley Chisholm.

The Derby was won today by Blakeney's Niece at seven to four, ridden by Emma Willard, trained by Annie Kenny and owned by Lady Hester Stanhope, the millionaire industrialist.

The Secretary of State for the Environment, Prudence Crandall, announced that the Royal Commission on the Road Haulage Industry is to be chaired by Dame Lucy Larcom, President of the Royal College of Surgeons.

The President of Yorkshire County Cricket Club, Phillippa Fawcett, has made it clear that the club is to discipline Geoff Burkett over the controversial incident at Hove last Sunday.

At Question Time the Prime Minister, Dorothea Beale, faced tough questions from Opposition Leader Rhoda Nunn, over the new wages settlement for the airline pilots. Nunn claimed that the settlement was highly inflationary, but this has been denied tonight by Captain Catherine Beecher, leader of BALPA the pilots' union.

Our Middle East correspondent, Louisa Lumsden, has reported further fighting from the Iraq/Iran border tonight.

The Archbishop of Canterbury's visit to Dover today was disrupted by women demonstrating for the right to be ordained full priests of the Anglican Church.

Finally, good news for consumers. Julia Ward Howe, chief executive of the giant food manufacturers CapCorp, has promised to cut 5p in the kilo off coffee next Monday.' (From *The Sociology of Women*, by Sara Delamont.)

1   Does this news bulletin strike you as odd?

2   Would it still strike you as odd if all the people mentioned were male?

3   Are all the posts mentioned capable of being held by women? If so, why are there not more women in these positions?

4   Who holds the positions of power in your local community – on the council, in schools, in local firms? (The public library and local newspaper may be of help.)

Suggestions

The news bulletin only strikes us as odd because we are conditioned by our culture to see these high posts filled by men.

2   In the light of the sociology you have studied, what conclusions would you draw from Table 8.7?

Suggestions

The item to concentrate on is the increase in the percentage of married women at work. What does this mean for women's position in the home? For independence? For the position of the male? And why have not the results of this apparent emancipation been greater?

Table 8.7 Economic activity in Great Britain, 1921–1971; all ages over 15

	All males and females			All males		
Year	Number occupied/ economically active; in thousands	Population, in thousands	Activity rate %	Number occupied/ economically active; in thousands	Population, in thousands	Activity rate %
1921	19,357	33,339	58.1	13,656	15,672	87.1
1931	21,055	34,662	60.7	14,790	16,341	90.5
1951	22,610	37,908	59.6	15,649	17,862	87.6
1961	23,810	39,360	60.5	16,071	18,677	86.0
1966	24,857	40,041	62.1	15,994	19,030	84.0
1971	25,103	41,048	61.2	15,917	19,560	81.4

	All females			Married females		
Year	Number occupied/ economically active; in thousands	Population, in thousands	Activity rate %	Number occupied/ economically active; in thousands	Population, in thousands	Activity rate %
1921	5,701	17,667	32.3	733	8,434	8.7
1931	6,265	18,320	34.2	953	9,492	10.0
1951	6,961	20,045	34.7	2,658	12,228	21.7
1961	7,740	20,683	37.4	3,886	13,070	29.7
1966	8,863	21,011	42.2	5,063	13,296	38.1
1971	9,186	21,488	42.7	5,799	13,729	42.2

Note: Activity rate is defined as the proportion of those occupied or economically active to the total population.

Source: Central Office of Information, *Occupations and Conditions of Work*, p. 42; based on Department of Employment Gazette, Census of Population

University of Oxford Local Examinations, A Level, Summer 1984

3

1 Look at the cartoon (Item A). What does the wife do which embarrasses her husband? (1 mark)

2 A sociologist might call the husband's reaction an attempt to conform to social pressure. Briefly explain the meaning of the term 'social pressure'. (2 marks)

3 What is meant by 'role conflict'? Give an example. (3 marks)

4   Explain why the mothers of the female engineering candidates find it difficult to accept the career choice made by their daughters (Item B).   (6 marks)

5   Examine the table (Item C). Which O level subjects had a mainly male entry? Discuss the extent to which schools are responsible for continuing this pattern of entry.   (8 marks)

Southern Examining Group, GCSE Specimen Question

Suggestions

1   The wife embarrasses the husband because of her ability to mend the lawn mower.

2   Social pressure could mean the disapproval of the group, in this case the other men with whom the husband associates.

3   The role of 'helpless' wife conflicts with the role she would like to play.

4   We are socialized by society (by our parents, teachers, peers etc.) to accept or reject certain gender roles. Some mothers do not see the role of engineer as a suitable gender role for their daughters, though really there is no logical reason why women should not be engineers. (Explain the difference between gender and sex, and what is meant by socialization.)

5   The culture indicates that certain subjects accord with the female gender role. What does this mean? It means mothers tell girls this is what they could or should do – be a nurse, mother etc. This is reinforced by the girl's friends, the media and by the school which in counselling girls (for GCSE and GCE subject choices) may guide them towards 'feminine' subjects (say, English Literature). On the other hand, even if the school counsels a girl towards 'masculine' subjects, the advice may be questioned and possibly ridiculed by the girl's friends and parents.

Item A
Source: *New Society*, 15 March 1983

Item B

Source: *New Society*, 15 March 1983

Jonathan Steinberg

The candidate flushed. I had clearly embarrassed her but how? All I had asked was how she intended to spend the time between the end of her work with a well-known engineering company and starting university the following October. It's the sort of dull question that all interviewers ask when they cannot think up anything brighter. She took a while to answer and this is what she said:

"Well, my mum thinks, after all this engineering, that I ought to do some normal things . . . you know, cooking and sewing . . ."

There was an awful silence. Both of us were embarrassed now. We had touched the delicate issue of the "female engineer", the collision of two opposing role models could be seen in my poor candidate's red face. Other female engineering candidates had told me similar stories, of mothers who allow bumbling dads to make messes of their toasters but won't allow daughters to change a plug.

Item C

Source: *New Society*, 15 March 1983

O Level entries
England, 1979

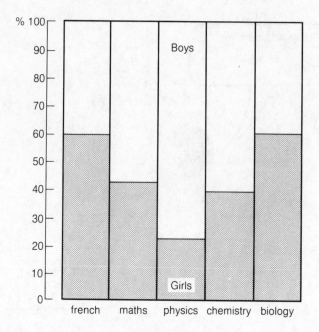

4 **The following passage comes from Colette Dowling's book *The Cinderella Complex: Women's Hidden Fear of Independence* pp. 143 and 144. After reading the passage, answer the questions that follow.**

The 'Good Woman' syndrome

The woman who devotes her entire life to keeping her husband straight and her children 'protected' is not a saint, she's a clinger. Rather than experience the terrors of being cut loose, of having to find and secure her own moorings, she will hang on in the face of unbelievable adversity. If she's really good at it, she doesn't even appear to suffer much. This is the woman who 'looks on the bright side'. Who appears tough and sinewy in situations where most would be reduced to mush. Who is, at all costs, 'terrific with the children'.

The Good Woman does her damnedest to please others. In terms of her own development tasks, she's got about as far as high school. She 'uses marriage in the service of regression', as the psychologists put it, meaning that she unconsciously hopes to return, through her relationship with her husband, to an earlier, safer time. For the Good Woman, according to ego psychologists Rubin and Gertrude Blanck, marriage becomes 'a way of being taken care of and supported . . . a way of acquiring a home instead of making one . . . an opportunity to relieve conflict instead of mastering it'.

A cover-up that's used to mask inner neurotic drives, such a relationship must be continuously and delicately manipulated. 'Some women who come into treatment with me have a very finely tuned sense of what's going to work in their marriages,' says Marcia Perlstein. 'Of course the arrangement doesn't really work or they wouldn't be starting therapy in the first place. Outwardly the mechanism may seem to be functioning, but inwardly these women aren't happy. They feel an acute lack of meaning in their lives. Their only sense of competence is tied up with being able to control – to get what they want through dependency.'

1   What is meant by the 'Good Woman' syndrome?
2   What is meant by regression?
3   What is meant by dependency?
4   What advice would feminists offer to break this syndrome.

Suggestions

1   It should be remembered that there are several versions of the Cinderella story. In one, Cinderella is offered the chance to come out of the coal corner, but she refuses. Why do you think she does this? (Perhaps she wants to remain a martyr.)
2   See A. Oakley, *Housewife*, which shows the grip of housework on the lives of many women.
3   Show how the dependency role comes from society and how girls are socialized to the role (as discussed earlier).

5 **A woman's place is in the home. How accurately does this describe women's lives since the onset of the Industrial Revolution?**

University of Cambridge Local Examinations Syndicate, A Level, Paper 2, June 1987

Suggestions

'Milestones for women', mentioned earlier, may help, and historical literature. See also S. Rowbotham, *Hidden from History: 300 Years of Women's Oppression and the Fight against It*. (See also suggestions for previous question.)

6 **Why do women take different jobs from men?**

University of Oxford Delegacy of Local Examinations, A Level, Paper 1, May 1988

Suggestions

High status jobs tend to be 'male' jobs (although women can do virtually any jobs done by men, as was demonstrated in wartime).

Discuss the reserve army of labour, dual labour markets (see box on p. 163), socialization to the task (discussed earlier).

7   In today's society, girls are still expected to be sweet, pretty and passive, destined only for domesticity and motherhood. They are reminded of it wherever they look. It is not a matter of choice. Hard luck if they are born creative and intelligent. Parents and teachers need to be more aware of the problem if this unjust division of people into active and passive roles is to stop.

1 What expectations might society have of boys?

2 Explain what is meant by 'active and passive roles'.

3 Describe *two* ways in which girls may be socialized into a mother/housewife role.

4 In what ways may schools help to reduce the influence of gender differences?

University of London, GCSE, Paper 2, May 1988

Suggestions

Becoming socialized to a role means other people have expectations of you. They expect you to behave like a girl or boy, etc.

See also Chapter 3 for different methods of child care. Sue Sharpe's book *Just Like a Girl* may be useful here.

See earlier in this chapter and Chapter 11 for the hidden curriculum. See 'socialization' and 'role' in Glossary.

Further reading

*S. Delamont, *The Sociology of Women*
 A. Holdsworth, *Out of the Doll's House*
 M. Mead, *Male and Female*
 J. Mitchell, *Woman's Estate*
*A. Oakley, *Housewife*
*A. Oakley, *Subject Women*
 A. Oakley, *Taking It Like a Woman*
 I. Reid and E. Wormald, *Sex Differences in Britain*
 L. Segal, *Is the Future Female?*
 S. Sharpe, *Just Like a Girl*
 M. Stanworth, *Gender and Schooling*
*'Sex and Gender', *New Society*, 12 May 1985 (Society Today series)
*'Women and Work', *New Society*, 7 March 1985 (Society Today series)

9 Race

This chapter describes how a sociologist might view racial discrimination. The first part of the chapter briefly sets out the facts (as distinct from the myths). The second part examines some questions that are often asked. (The arrangement of this chapter is based partly on the approach used by the Runnymede Trust in *Britain's Black Population*.)

Introduction

This chapter examines the position of black people in Britain. This means people whose origins are in what is called the New Commonwealth, which includes the West Indies, India, Bangladesh and also Pakistan, which actually left the Commonwealth. It includes immigrants from these countries, together with those born here. Usually it is referred to as NCWP – New Commonwealth and Pakistan.

Space does not permit a discussion of other minority groups, for example Poles, many of them ex-servicemen and their families who, perhaps for political reasons, did not wish to return to their native land; Italians, including ex-prisoners of war and their descendants, and others attracted to the catering trade, brickmaking and other industries offering employment when there was none at home; about half a million people of Irish descent, most of whom would regard themselves as fully British; Greek Cypriots, Chinese and Jews. Like the blacks, these groups have experienced their share of prejudice and discrimination. Imagine the difficulties of a Chinese person in being fully accepted in British society, and the pull of ties with home. Whilst some might live in Chinese communities in London or Liverpool, for example, others are more scattered; how will a family of restaurateurs, the sole Chinese family in an English country town, cope with British society?

Or to take the Jews as an example, Jewish people came to this country in three main groups. Firstly, a comparatively small number came to Britain after Cromwell allowed their return. Many of these were of Spanish or Portuguese descent. Another wave came at the turn of the century following persecution in Tsarist Russia; and finally German Jews came to Britain following Nazi persecution in the 1930s.

It might appear that anti-Semitism has become unfashionable now, that the centuries of Christian persecution have ended. After all, millions of Jews were murdered by the Nazis; surely we have learnt our lesson – we know now where the madness of racism can lead. Furthermore, Jews seem to have blended in with the community and to have succeeded in the public and business life of the nation.

Certainly the position has improved since Sir Oswald Mosley and his British Union of Fascists marched through Cable Street, in the heart of the Jewish East End of London in 1936. Yet anti-Semitism (which is, of course, just one kind of racism) still persists. Any Jew who attends a National Front meeting may be in for a nasty shock; National Front speakers deny that six million Jews were killed and seek to perpetuate the myth that Western economies are controlled by an international network of Jewish bankers etc.

Despite improvements, even today prejudice against Jews still exists – not of the blatant kind but more subtle, for example not getting the jobs they apply for or being passed over for promotion. The Jewish experience is described here as that of a non-black minority; however, the emphasis throughout this chapter will be on the black experience.

One of the aims of this chapter is to give the facts about racism, compared with the assumptions of the host community. What does it feel like to be racially prejudiced? What do prejudiced persons really think, for example members of the National Front?

One of the tasks of the sociologist is to show the situation as it really is; to try to answer the question 'what is really going on here?' in this case: why does prejudice exist? What are the effects of discrimination? Who benefits from discrimination?

Verstehen

A useful sociological tool in this kind of investigation is the concept of *Verstehen*, or understanding, used by Max Weber. Weber stressed that sociology should look at the meaning of the act to the actor – *Verstehen*. This should be the central concern of the sociologist, rather than trying to analyse human action from the outside. Once we know clearly the meaning that people (actors) give to their acts, we can perhaps say what causes street riots, poor performance at school by black pupils, etc. (See project 4 at the end of this chapter.)

One word that ought to be defined before going any further is *racism*. A possible definition is that it means treating a person on the basis of his or her race first, rather than as a person. In this respect racism is akin to sexism and ageism. Once people are distinguished on the basis of their race, sex or age they may be treated differently and we may have special expectations of them – that they will perform poorly or that they are not like us. Thus racism also implies a theory of racial superiority/inferiority; as usual, the theory contains the appropriate ideology, seemingly justifying it. (See Chapter 1, p. 3 for a comparison of racism with sexism and ageism.)

The dimensions of the alleged 'problem' in Britain

The question of what is a 'problem' in sociology is interesting. Sociologists talk of the social construction of reality (see Glossary), meaning that reality is what we believe it to be. In this case, if there were no racism there would be no 'problem' to speak of (i.e. we have constructed the race 'problem' because of our beliefs). The same could be said of sexism, ageism and deviance (we as a society define what is deviant and then punish the deviant). It will, therefore, be useful to study a few facts first.

Facts on immigration

'We cannot go on taking immigrants, we are only a small island.' 'We will be swamped.' 'We are a monoglot race.' 'We have been here for centuries – uninterrupted.'

The statements are familiar in the immigration debate; but then how English are the 'English', in that they are an amalgamation of several races – Celts, Romans, Scandinavians, French people, Jews and so forth? What in any case is nationality? Is it inherent or is it an arrangement developed by people over time? Finally, how many readers can trace their own families back for more than 100 years?

The Runnymede Trust in its book *Britain's Black Population* begins by noting that the political debate about the black population starts with the 'facts' about immigration. The Trust feels we should begin by presenting statistics on the size of the black population in Britain and not immigration statistics. By using 'facts' about immigration as their starting point, the political debates assume that all black people in Britain are immigrants and that all immigrants in Britain are black. Both assumptions are false. Table 9.1 shows the number of white and black people in the country, both immigrant and born here (43 per cent of the people of NCWP – New Commonwealth and Pakistan – descent were actually born in Great Britain as Table 9.1 shows).

Most NCWP immigrants are dependants of citizens already here. Overall total acceptances have declined from 42,500 in 1974 to 24,000 in 1986 according to *Social Trends 1985* and *1989*. New Commonwealth born citizens congregate in certain areas, e.g. Leicester, 8.2 per cent of the population and Haringey (London), 14.49 per cent of the population (Runnymede Trust, *Britain's Black Population*). Really, the proportion of the black population is quite small, but because black people are concentrated in 'black' areas they are more 'visible'.

Table 9.1   British population by ethnic origin, 1984–86

Ethnic group	Total all ages (=100%) (thousands)	Percentage UK born	Percentage resident in English metropolitan areas
White	51,107	96	31
All ethnic minority groups	2,432	43	69
All groups	54,230	93	33

Source: Labour Force Survey, combined data for 1984–86 inclusive, Office of Population Censuses and Surveys; reprinted in *Social Trends 1989*

The Runnymede Trust predicts that after the year 2000 the proportion of black people will stabilize at about 6 per cent of the population. The age structure of the black population will resemble that of the white (so too will the birth, death and fertility rates, probably). Future black immigration will continue to decline. Almost all dependants of UK passport holders will have come here by the year 2000 and signs of the run-down can be clearly seen already. The future balance of the sex ratios will reduce the need to find a fiancée from abroad. Table 9.2 confirms the decline in the fertility rates of mothers born in the New Commonwealth and Pakistan.

Table 9.2   Fertility rates by country of birth of mother (thousands)

Area/country of birth of mother	1971	1986
UK	2.3	1.7
Total New Commonwealth and Pakistan	3.8	2.9

Source: *Social Trends 1988*

Facts on employment

There is great inequality in employment between the white community and the minority racial groups. This inequality in employment is shown by the fact that:

blacks get the worst jobs;
they are paid less;
they are more likely to be unemployed;
blacks are subject to racial discrimination in the job search and at work.

Blacks have always had to take the worst jobs; black immigrants have had to take jobs at the bottom of the heap, jobs which white people did not want to do. The employment situation however is changing, though not necessarily improving. As mentioned in the previous section, about 40 per cent of blacks were born in Britain; expectations are rising. There are many more black businessmen who, in turn, employ blacks. Nevertheless, most black people still work in the same industries as their parents – transport, textiles and the NHS – in poorly paid jobs. Table 9.3 illustrates this unevenness in employment and indicates that career prospects (as measured by manual/non-manual occupations) for ethnic minority groups are worse than those of whites.

Table 9.3   Males in employment by ethnic group and occupation, Great Britain, 1984–86

Occupation	Ethnic group			
	White	West Indian or Guyanese	Indian/ Pakistani/ Bangladeshi	Other
Total non-manual	46%	21%	48%	57%
Total manual	54%	78%	51%	43%
All occupations (=100%) (thousands)	12,911	107	253	133

Source: Labour Force Survey, combined data for 1984–86 inclusive, Department of Employment – *Employment Gazette*, March 1988

Even in more prestigious careers black people do not seem to progress in many cases, apparently due to prejudice. Thus black teachers tend to stay in lower grades; black consultants tend to be in the least prestigious specialisms, such as geriatrics and mental health.

Again, blacks in the 16–24 age group are worse hit by unemployment. According to the *Employment Gazette*, 1988 (a government publication), 17 per cent of the white labour force in this age group were unemployed against 32 per cent of the ethnic minorities in the labour force. Finally, people from the ethnic minority groups tend to be less qualified for work (perhaps due partly to poor education, see last line of Table 9.4).

There are some hopeful signs, for example the ise of black owned businesses in the London Borough of Brent. Personnel managers in large organizations such as Ford and BP are taking their anti-discrimination duties seriously, according to David Thomas, but there are two main difficulties. Firstly, the rise of unemployment which makes any improvement difficult; secondly, there are what Thomas calls layers of discrimination. Take for example the way job vacancies become known. Many manual job vacancies are not formally advertised; instead they become known by word of mouth via an informal network and blacks are not

Table 9.4 Highest qualifications of males (Great
Britain, 16–64) by ethnic group

	White	Ethnic minority groups
Higher qualification	14%	16%
Other qualification	53%	44%
No qualifications	33%	40%

Note: for a definition of the terms 'higher' and 'other' qualifications, see
source.
Source: *Employment Gazette*, December 1988

members of these networks. They do not get past the first layer of discrimination.

Blacks seem to form what Marx called a reserve army of labour. In good times their services are required (usually in the jobs white people do not want), in bad times they are made redundant or not employed in the first place. Often they are not unionized and generally not powerful. They are not powerful because they are not in work or are not in higher jobs. Thus the cycle of deprivation is self-perpetuating.

Summarizing, it is clear that blacks suffer racial discrimination both in work and when applying for work. A survey by Political and Economic Planning (now renamed the Policy Studies Institute) *The Extent of Racial Discrimination*, showed that a third of black job applicants were discriminated against; while other studies show that blacks tend to get lower level jobs than their white counterparts with the same educational

---

Under class; dual labour markets

It seems that black people form part of a reserve army of labour. (See p. 144 for further explanation of 'reserve army of labour'.) They can also be seen as an *under class*. This consists of workers who do the least desirable jobs and who are denied basic legal rights or who are in poverty. Black people are quite likely to be in this under class. So too are women, the unemployed and the elderly. One thing these groups have in common is that they are not treated as full members of society.

Dual labour markets is another concept used to describe the fact that in most national labour markets there are two sub-markets for labour. Firstly, the primary market comprising the better jobs, for example those offering career prospects. Secondly, the secondary labour market comprising the unskilled, lowly paid jobs. This division can be seen as a division within the working class itself, with the poorly organized, non-unionized, unskilled workers being trapped in the secondary labour market. Again, such workers comprise mainly blacks and women.

qualifications. In David Smith's survey (*Unemployment and Racial Minorities*), 82 per cent of West Indians thought that employers discriminated racially in recruitment, compared with 59 per cent of Asians and 65 per cent of whites. In view of the inequalities in employment described here it is surprising how quietly these injuries are taken by the black communities.

Blacks seem to form a reserve army of labour

Facts on housing

Generally blacks live in inner city areas where housing standards are low, where properties are overcrowded or do not have basic amenities like sole use of baths. Black people are also less likely to own the property they live in. Table 9.5 illustrates the poorer housing endured by black people.

Note the high rate of owner-occupiers in the Indian/Pakistani community. This may be an assertion of independence. On the other hand the standard of the accommodation may be poor – see the last row in the table.

Apart from the quality of the houses themselves, these inner city neighbourhoods assume a ghetto-like character; they tend to be inhabited by one racial group. Moreover, it is difficult to get out of these ghettos and people feel trapped. The Runnymede Trust concluded that because they tend to occupy the bottom end of the labour market, blacks could only afford cheap accommodation. Further, because they congregate in these poorer areas, black people are seen as the cause of the decline of these areas rather than the victims of it.

In the 1960s most non-white people tended to live in private rented accommodation, but the situation has now changed considerably. Compared with the white population, many more Asians are buying their own homes. In contrast, an increasing proportion of West Indians rent their accommodation from local councils. Although this is an improvement, blacks have difficulty in getting a bank or building society loan and this is only partly due to their having poorer jobs. There is evidence of widespread

Portrait of a 'dump' estate
Source: Commission for Racial Equality, *Race and Council Housing in Hackney*

Table 9.5 Household tenure and housing standards: by ethnic origin of head of household

	White	West Indian or Guyanese	Indian/Pakistani Bangladeshi	Other	Not Stated	Households
Tenure (percentages):						
owned outright	26	5	24	9	27	26
owned with mortgage or loan	36	30	51	28	35	36
all owner-occupied	62	35	75	37	62	61
rented from local authority or new town	26	52	13	29	23	26
rented from housing association	2	5	2	6	2	2
rented privately unfurnished	8	4	4	10	9	8
rented privately furnished	3	4	5	18	5	3
Sample size (=100%) (numbers)	34,506	330	558	343	322	26,059
Housing standards (percentage of households): lacking sole use of:						
fixed bath	2	5	3	8	2	2
wc inside building	3	5	5	9	3	3
below bedroom standard (overcrowded etc.)	3	14	25	7	6	4

Source: *Social Trends 1987*

discrimination by other institutions – estate agents, councils, etc. Discrimination in council housing may take subtle forms. The Commission for Racial Equality interviewed a random sample of 1292 Hackney Council tenants, including 197 cases from the waiting list. Table 9.6 shows which of these obtained accommodation. The waiting list comprised 45 per cent blacks and 49 per cent whites, but overall whites got 79 per cent of the houses and 88 per cent of the new properties. (The CRE's study is described by Paul Harrison in his article entitled 'How race affects council housing'. Paul Harrison is the author of *Inside the Inner City*, which is also about Hackney.) The CRE study also showed a high proportion of black people on what it called the 'dump estates' (older estates and estates due for demolition). This study is interesting in that it is based on hard statistical evidence rather than on personal experiences and individual acts of discrimination. The study makes a number of recommendations, including: checking regularly on how housing is allocated, increasing the proportion of housing officers from ethnic minorities and informing all clients of their full range of rights. This may not be enough, since black people have more economic and social disadvantages than whites, including low income, one parent families etc. Hence these too should be taken into account for both blacks and whites, in order to ensure that inequalities in council housing do not reinforce these other inequalities and so create social as well as racial semi-ghettos on the worst estates.

Table 9.6 A comparison of black and white council housing in the London Borough of Hackney

	Houses and maisonettes	Newer properties (post-1976)	Ground or first floor properties
Whites	16	25	34
Blacks	4	3	19

Source: adapted from *Race and Council Housing in Hackney*, by the Commission for Racial Equality.

Facts on education

Schools seem to operate on the assumption that the pupils are white and speak English. This seems to be the basis of the so-called education 'problem'; but the 'problem' may lie not so much with the black children as with the rigid education system and its failure to respond to the differing needs of its charges. School books and the curriculum often seem to have a racial bias, presenting, for example, a highly favourable view of the British Empire. Overwhelmingly, the teachers are white and tend to expect less from black children. This, in turn, is a source of black underachievement. Again, as this book stresses, IQ tests, which are supposed to be fair and scientific, are really culture bound. What they really test are those items valued by the dominant white culture. And as black and white children are brought up quite differently, it is not surprising that many West Indian children fare badly in them. (Asian children seem to fare rather better.)

Some of the factors in black underachievement at school are listed here. Firstly, a language barrier: many Asian pupils come from families where English is not the usual language of everyday conversation; whilst some West Indian pupils speak a dialect not always clearly understood by teachers. (See for example W. Labov, 'The logic of non-standard English'.) Secondly, tests and exams assume the pupils come from a white middle class background. (These tests also work against white working class children – see Chapter 11.) Thirdly, there is the attitude of the teachers, who themselves were academically able at school and find it difficult to adjust their own teaching for different kinds of pupil. Finally, some West Indian children are subject to a rather stricter discipline at home and the younger children tend to be quiet and not to participate positively at school. Moreover, West Indian parents tend to blame the child, rather than the school, for low achievement.

It has been said many times in this book that being a good sociologist means asking the right questions. At this point it may be interesting to ask: are blacks really all that different from whites in this country? Or as Gaskell and Smith ask in their article of the same title, 'Are young blacks really alienated?' They say that the right sees blacks as work-shy and generally predisposed to delinquency. The left sees blacks' behaviour as a result of their treatment by society – of prejudice, harassment by the police, poor housing and high unemployment. Viewed from right to left, blacks are seen as remote from society. However, the findings in this article showed that West Indians shared many of the same aspirations as whites. They wanted the same types of jobs; a similar proportion of blacks and whites aspired to professional or managerial careers. Blacks wanted to succeed and the researchers concluded that in reacting strongly to the police in Brixton, West Indians were not expressing wholesale rejection of white society but of the perceived prejudice of the police (particularly stopping and searching).

What then needs to be done to ensure that all people of whatever race develop their potential as fully as possible? What should a multi-racial education really be aiming at? So far as multi-racial education is concerned there seem to be three basic models (C. Mullard, *Multi-Racial Education in Britain*, and J. Tierney (ed.), *Race, Migration and Schooling*):

The *assimilationist model* which was dominant in the mid-sixties sees the nation as a unitary whole. The adherents to this viewpoint suggest immigrant groups should be absorbed into the main culture.

The *integrationist model* rejects the racist assumptions underpinning the assimilationist model and stresses equal opportunity accompanied by cultural diversity and mutual tolerance. One difficulty here is that equal opportunity tends to be interpreted in the school as the provision of services and resources in order for all 'to have an equal chance to attain the middle class social and educational objectives revered by the school'.

Finally, there is the *cultural pluralist model*. This maintains that our society consists of different groups which are culturally distinct and separate. In such a society there is a commitment to preserve group culture. The only thing that is acknowledged as binding on all groups is the political authority of the state.

The Swann Report of 1985 could be taken as an example of the cultural pluralist approach, as its title '*Education for All*' implies. The report says that blacks are capable of higher achievement at school, although Asian pupils (except Bangladeshi) do as well as white pupils. The lower performance of many black pupils cannot be explained by genetically determined IQ and the Committee felt that no single factor is likely to explain such a complex issue. Probably the difference in IQ scores is best explained by social factors and the best way of improving school performance would be an improvement in the economic circumstances of the families, i.e. better housing, employment etc.

The Committee emphasized the importance of *cultural diversity* in education. This should be 'a central feature of the current debate on the balance and breadth of the school curriculum'. Thus, for example, history should not be taught solely from an English viewpoint. In accordance with the stress on cultural diversity the Committee felt that religious education should be non-denominational (rather than solely Christian); but the Secretary of State for Education did not accept this.

The Swann Report is unanimous that a good command of English is vital and this should be provided for in ordinary schools, not special units. The Report is also against separate schools – again this is seen as inconsistent with the ideals of cultural diversity.

Better ethnic statistics will be needed to monitor black performance at school and schools should employ more teachers from the minority communities.

Commenting sociologically on the Swann Report, it should be emphasized that what schools can do to reduce racial inequality is limited. The will to bring about improvement must be in society itself. In this case more money will be needed, both inside the education system and for improving the circumstances of blacks.

Facts on relations with the police

There is likely to be trouble between any immigrant group and the police, because the police reflect the values and assumptions of the host communities towards outsiders. The fact that immigrants have a different way of life makes them more visible. In addition, street crime tends to be higher in immigrant areas and this itself draws a stronger police response and does not necessarily imply police prejudice. The police may concentrate on more visible crime, such as robbery in the street, while being less strict with other 'white' crimes, thereby confirming the possible prejudice that blacks are more crime prone while confirming also the black view of police harassment. Thus, for example, drugs may be a normal part of the cultural scene in black communities while against the law of the land. Even-handed enforcement of the law is therefore often seen as harassment to blacks. (In all this the expression 'the social construction of reality' seems particularly relevant because what is reality – and what is justice – to one group may not be to another.)

There is a tendency for the press and public to focus on the immediate factors which contribute to incidents between blacks and the police, on riots, and on crime; and to advance quick remedies whilst ignoring underlying factors. Thus, for example, riots are seen as lack of parental control, lack of respect for law and order, as 'copycat' riots due to the effects of televi-

Do we really try to understand what causes antisocial behaviour?

sion coverage, as the result of outside agitators coming into the area to make trouble, or simply as 'senseless' riots. All this implies that no further explanation is required and the usual clichés then follow about trouble-makers, outsiders, ringleaders and conspiracy. Even emphasizing the importance of improving police training and of policing by consent does not tackle the roots of the real 'problem'.

What then is the real problem in the relationship between the police and blacks? How do black youths and the police view each other? It is clear that blacks are much more likely to be stopped, questioned and sometimes searched by the police than whites. George Gaskell, in his article 'The young, the black and the police', examines the research and concludes that blacks feel there are too many stops with insufficient justification, but more important than this, Gaskell believes, is the cultural difference between the blacks and the police. Basically, blacks accept British values and aspirations but reject a society which denies them opportunities. The gap between aspiration and achievement has widened recently and the author concludes: 'With unemployment levels of up to 50 per cent among black young men there is scope for conflict which goes well beyond questions of policing.'

It is wrong therefore to blame the police for the frustration and injustices that have their roots deep in our society. Nevertheless, it is necessary to study police attitudes and behaviour as part of an understanding of race relations.

The Policy Studies Institute in their report 'Police and people in London' show that policemen tend to be very conventional and denigrate those whose views or lifestyles depart from their view of the acceptable. This report concludes that whilst two out of three Londoners have no, or only minor, doubts about the police, 62 per cent of young blacks think the police often use threats, 53 per cent said they used excessive force and 41 per cent said they fabricate records.

The Policy Studies Institute suggests three improvements:

1 More community policing, in which the police would really get to know the groups they were policing with an emphasis on collaboration, understanding and crime prevention.

2 When people are stopped they should be told the reason clearly, verbally and in writing (on a form); the Police and Criminal Evidence Act provides for this.

3 People need the confidence to complain more. Gaskell quotes Home Office research. In a sample of 800 people, 111 said they had wanted to complain about the police but no-one did so. Perhaps the proposed Police Complaints Authority will be more successful in helping people to express their complaints.

One of the best known official reports on racial discrimination is the Scarman Report 1981, which followed the Brixton riots (most of the

Report concerned the police). Lord Justice Scarman said that racial discrimination was a fact of life in modern Britain and a significant factor in the clashes between blacks and the police in Brixton; whilst institutional racism, its nasty associate, has not been eliminated. The police, said Lord Scarman, do not create social deprivation or racial disadvantage, yet their role is critical. The police must be seen as adhering to the traditional principles of British policing. If they neglect consultation and cooperation with the local community, unrest and riot become probable. The attack on racial disadvantage must be more direct, for example by using positive discrimination (in which the poorest get most help). Scarman found widespread racial discrimination in Brixton, for example 20 per cent of the population there lived in sub-standard accommodation.

Whilst acknowledging that the police had a very difficult job, Scarman had to make some criticisms. He felt there was evidence of harassment by young officers, arising not so much from what they did but the way they did it, for example the way they stopped people in the street to question and perhaps search them (for drugs etc.). Sometimes the policing was un-imaginative and the complaints procedure inflexible. There was over-reaction to some disorders and lack of rigour in handling others. Lord Scarman stressed the need for consent and balance in policing, the need for better recruitment, training and monitoring in order to eliminate prejudice in the police.

Common question one: *what are the reasons for black immigration?*

Immigration should be seen in its historical context. West Indians are descended from American slaves whose own culture was destroyed. They were socialized to the slave owners' culture. Ken Pryce, in the first chapter of his book *Endless Pressure* notes that the economy of the West Indies depended on plantations which were owned by absentee landlords in Britain; they used the profits for a comfortable life at home rather than for improving their plantations. The abolition of slavery in the Empire in 1833 did not change this situation but, of course, after-effects of the Empire do affect attitudes, as the next section indicates. After the Second World War many West Indians saw Britain as a land of opportunity, compared with home. Some had served in the armed forces in Britain and they and others told their friends of the good employment prospects here. All had been socialized to a British culture during their upbringing and education and considered themselves to be British citizens.

For immigrants from the Indian subcontinent the situation is basically similar (although the people had not been uprooted like the West Indians). Indeed, most of the economies of the poorer countries of the third world are adapted to (or distorted to) the needs of the wealthier industrialized

> **Effects of the Empire**
> Colonialism not only distorted economic and political relationships
> between peoples, it also distorted people's views of each other. Like other
> cases of the rule of one group over another there were appropriate
> ideologies – ideologies which justified the exploitation of the 'native'. The
> 'natives' were treated as second class citizens in their own land. This was
> justified by the ideology that the white man brought peace and economic
> development, and this was represented (by Kipling for instance) as part of
> 'the white man's burden'. This despite the fact that *peace* came after
> colonial wars which dispossessed the people of their land, while the price
> of *economic development* was the destruction of agriculture to provide
> cash crops for the Western economies, rather than food.
>
> The distortions caused by colonialism persist today in the relations
> between black and white people, including the assumption by some white
> people that they are somehow superior.

countries. Generally, the poorer countries supply cheap raw materials such
as sugar and, in turn, import manufactured goods. The rich countries stay
rich, the poor countries remain poor, and many of their inhabitants would
like to emigrate. Thus immigrants came to this country because of extreme
poverty at home, because many felt themselves to be British and also
because other countries, especially the USA, had restricted black immigration.

As shown earlier in this chapter, many reports of immigration are
exaggerated, not only implying invasion, but emphasizing that the new-
comers are quite different from 'us' and will overwhelm us. However,
another way of looking at the 'problem' is that immigrants tend to be the
most adventurous groups in a population. In the British case many of them
were deliberately recruited in the fifties and sixties to fill posts which white
people would not accept, in the hospitals, on the buses and in unpleasant
factory work. In effect, their entry at the bottom of the occupational
hierarchy enabled whites to move up a rung on the ladder (and sometimes
to despise those at the bottom). (See the box on p. 163 for a description of
'under class' and 'dual labour markets'.)

Common question two: *what is racial prejudice?*

Prejudice is a state of mind, an individual attitude. According to psychologists an attitude may have three components – thinking (cognitive),
feeling (affective) and acting (behavioural). A prejudiced person may have
the first two components but not necessarily act on them. An important
aspect of prejudice is the use of *stereotypes* by the prejudiced person, for
example 'all blacks are like this'. Using stereotypes is a lazy way of thinking;
it saves the prejudiced person the trouble of making further investigations.

When a person who is prejudiced also acts on the prejudice, it becomes open. So *prejudice* is a state of mind, *discrimination* is an actual act, such as not taking on a black worker simply because that worker is black.

Possibly the most famous research done in this area was that by Theodor Adorno and his colleagues in *The Authoritarian Personality*. The authoritarian personality is a cluster of related traits. They constructed a composite scale, known as the 'F-scale', to measure these traits and found that a person scoring high on this scale would possess the following characteristics:

adheres strongly to conventional values;
has, for example, an exaggerated concern with sexual goings on;
is submissive to authority yet very hard on subordinates;
is preoccupied with power and status;
is generally hostile to outgroupers, especially of a different race;
is *over*-patriotic.

Adorno was interested, among other things, in the rise of anti-Semitism before the war. It seems that many of the findings are still applicable to racism today. One of the findings was that the same people who disliked Jews also disliked black people, Mexicans and 'foreigners' generally.

Although Adorno's work is very interesting, it has been criticized. For example it seems that what the F-scale really measures is education; the higher your education the lower your score on the F-scale. In addition, does the cluster of traits used by Adorno actually exist in the real world? Perhaps you might like to make tests yourself, looking for example at associates, at the popular newspapers and at National Front literature, to see where these traits exist together.

Prejudicial attitudes seem to be self-confirming. If black or coloured people are forced to take inferior jobs, then seeing them in these jobs confirms the prejudice – this is the only kind of job they can do. An interesting example of this kind of prejudice came in the Suez Crisis of 1956, when it was widely reported in the press that Egyptian pilots would be incapable of taking ships through the Suez Canal. Naturally, this was proved to be untrue. Today throughout Africa and the Indian sub-continent black civil servants, business and professional people carry out responsible jobs. In Britain the National Health Service would be in serious difficulty without its black employees.

Common question three: *what is racial discrimination?*

Discrimination means acting out the prejudice. Discrimination and prejudice are closely linked. Prejudice means pre-judging. An applicant does not get the job because of racial prejudice, but this discrimination confirms the prejudice: there are no blacks doing this kind of work, therefore it would be unwise to take on this black applicant. This is an example of the self-fulfilling prophecy. Here is one possible explanation of prejudice – that it is part of a discrimination–prejudice syndrome, the discrimination and the prejudice each confirming the other.

A distinction that has to be made is between direct and indirect discrimination. Direct discrimination might be when a black person is not offered a job because he or she is black. Indirect discrimination has occurred where, for example, an employer has devised a test which a black person is more likely to fail and the test is not justifiable as a means of getting the job (Griggs *v.* Duke Power, USA 1971).

Institutionalized discrimination occurs where the struggle between the discriminator and discriminatee becomes crystallized, for example by establishing black and white parties (like the National Front), by establishing black trade unions etc.

Three theories that could help in analysing prejudice and discrimination may be mentioned here. Firstly, there is *W. I. Thomas's theorem*. (Thomas was an American sociologist and psychologist.) The theorem says: 'if men define situations as real, they are real in their consequences.' In other words, social reality, what is actually going on, comes about as a result of our beliefs. If it is believed that black people are in some way inferior, then our beliefs will make it come true.

Secondly, and similarly, *labelling theory* may be a useful analytical tool here (although it is more commonly used in the sociology of education and the sociology of deviance). Labelling theory shows that if individuals are defined in a certain way they will live up (or down) to these definitions. Basically, the labeller awards the label and makes a prediction (that black children will do poorly at school for example) and the labelled persons (the pupils) will see that little is expected from them and will fare poorly – another case of the self-fulfilling prophecy.

The third theory that could be helpful here is Marx's view of *false consciousness*. Marx believed that true consciousness was class consciousness, whereby a class recognized its true position in society and instead of being just a class in itself became a class for itself. Thus, in particular, the working class or proletariat would become aware of, and fight against, its exploitation by the bourgeoisie. On the other hand, false consciousness meant lack of awareness of one's true class position. A common reason for false consciousness was divisions within the working class, particularly racial divisions. This was quite common in capitalist societies as employers brought in cheap foreign labour in order to cut costs. Marx cited, as an example of this, the anti-Irish riots that took place in Liverpool during his stay in Britain.

Finally, it could be argued, based on these insights, that there is a close relationship between discrimination and the class structure. Here it is worth mentioning again the concept of dual labour markets (described in the box on p. 163). Because of discrimination many black people can only compete for jobs in the secondary job market. In this way the racial divide becomes also a class divide with black people (and others) forming an under class.

Common question four: *what does it feel like to be a National Front supporter?*

Clearly black people suffer much prejudice in their everyday life (and this is made the subject of project 4 at the end of the chapter). It is also interesting sociologically, however, to view the social world through the eyes of a prejudiced person, in order to get the inside view and to try to answer the question: what is really going on here? (– to gain what Max Weber called *Verstehen*, understanding). David Jones, in his article 'Belonging to the Front', describes the viewpoint of a National Front member (he has since left). He says that when he joined he was not conscious of having racist views; he and his associates found the whole thing rather exciting. Marches especially were something to look forward to – a chance to prove their courage. It gives poor white youths (who themselves have had an unfair deal and are victims of inequality) a sense of adventure.

'I'm not National Front myself, but ...' is the title of an article by R. Cochrane and M. Billing. The authors studied 2500 15- and 16-year-olds in the West Midlands, and found that the supporters of the National Front knew little of the party's policy or even who the leaders were. Their support could be seen as 'symbolic politics', the symbol in question being the policy of expelling non-whites from Britain. The appeal is that it is a quick and 'final' solution to a complex problem. (The Nazis talked of the 'final solution of the Jewish problem', by which they meant the extermination of all Jews.) The researchers found a strong feeling of hopelessness and pessimism among the young people they interviewed.

The main political parties have failed to inspire any idealism in the young and the researchers feel that the real damage comes not from the National Front itself, but from a political party self-consciously adopting a 'genteel fascism' and deliberately seeking the support of those prepared to say 'I'm not National Front myself, but ...'

Common question five: *why has legislation against racial discrimination been a comparative failure?*

Try to answer the question in the heading yourself before you read this section.

The Race Relations Act 1976 enabled the Commission for Racial Equality to counteract instances of racial discrimination more vigorously through prosecution, persuasion and education. However, the Commission faces many difficulties. It has been suggested that the Commission should concentrate on the prosecution of cases of racial discrimination and not attempt to persuade or change deeply embedded attitudes. The relatively few prosecutions to date is a sign of failure in this respect.

Another difficulty is that much of the anti-discrimination law in Britain is unenforceable. This is because discrimination is often hidden and requires vigorous techniques to expose it – and here the will and the means to act are lacking. Further, some people feel that vigorous enforcement may be counter productive and produce a 'white backlash'.

The comparative failure of the Commission for Racial Equality could be explained by the tendency of British judges and juries to defend the right of the individual to discriminate.

Legislation can be seen as reflecting the norms and values of a society. Where this close relationship is lacking the law will not, or cannot, be enforced. (On the other hand, some people would argue that the law can change values, can be a trail blazer; that it can, in this instance, make discrimination unfashionable and not the done thing.) However, there is no doubt that where the law and the values of a society are out of step, difficulties will arise. For example, the Commission for Racial Equality relies on other institutions of law enforcement, in particular central and local government, the police, the director of public prosecutions etc. There is abundant evidence that cooperation is lacking in this respect. In addition, there should be a healthy respect for the law from discriminators – from employers, landlords, teachers and police; again, this seems to be lacking. Further, black people themselves appear to have little confidence in the Commission for Racial Equality. Their attitudes may range from resignation to defiance of the law – but do not include cooperation with the Commission. Finally, it seems the state operates a rather hypocritical set of policies on race, with racist legislation regarding immigration but 'liberal' policies when determining discrimination legislation.

The deep roots of discrimination, referred to above, can perhaps be seen more clearly when considered alongside discrimination against women. Here it may be useful to see the work of the Commission for Racial Equality alongside that of the Equal Opportunities Commission. Table 8.4 on p. 143 attempted to analyse the reasons for continuing inequality in the treatment of women at work and the reasons for the failure of the various remedies. Similarly, another reason for the failure of anti-discrimination legislation could be the earlier socialization of discriminators and discriminatees into accepting prejudice as a way of life. This may be another reason for the comparative failure of the Commission for Racial Equality.

Common question six: *what is the response of black people to the 'problem'?*

Many blacks and Asians may not be seeking acceptance and assimilation into the host community. In the USA the Black Power Movement grew as a response to discrimination and the ineffectual nature of attempts to check it. The Movement was an assertion of black consciousness. In Britain it seemed that the earlier West Indian immigrants were like black Britons. Yet their children are becoming more ethnocentric, more conscious of their roots, partly as a result of discrimination. This is shown, for example, by the growth of Rastafarianism, a religious cult that looks back to Africa for the black cultural heritage.

Other black responses have already been discussed in this chapter. They include outright defiance, such as the riots in Brixton, Toxteth, St Pauls in Bristol, Handsworth and Tottenham. At the less visible end of the scale is the success of many Asian businessmen and the high rate of owner-occupation of houses now, compared with the sixties. Money and property give some independence and help to ward off the worst effects of discrimination. However, the white community must change too and this is discussed in the next section.

What can be done?

Two reports will be considered here. Firstly, the report of the Commission for Racial Equality, which makes general recommendations. Secondly, the report of the Policy Studies Institute, which sets out the key issues.

'Loading the law'

The Commission for Racial Equality published a booklet in 1982 entitled *Loading the Law*, in which it said the problem was one of transmitted deprivation. If you are at the bottom, then your children will be too, hence the cycle of deprivation referred to earlier in this chapter.

There is a big gap between blacks and whites, as this chapter has demonstrated. The Commission for Racial Equality argues that transmitted deprivation must be eliminated in the interests of justice and social peace (bearing in mind, for instance, the street riots). The Commission advocates the following measures:

1 *Racial monitoring* in order to clarify the evidence of deprivation. The Commission would have liked a question on ethnic origin in the 1981 Census, asking not just where you were born (because many blacks were born in Britain) but, for example, where your parents were born. This would have helped in answering such questions as what sort of accommodation black people have and what kind of jobs they do.

2   *Area based positive discrimination*, in which poorer areas get greater government aid.
3   *Group based positive discrimination* for disadvantaged groups like blacks. The Commission argues that we already have this for people with special health or education needs – why not for blacks?
4   *Local authority initiatives* in housing and education, for example, would help. Again, these items have been discussed in this chapter.
5   There might have to be *stricter enforcement of legislation*, like the Race Relations Act 1976.

'Black and White Britain'

The Policy Studies Institute in its report *Black and White Britain* (by Colin Brown) does not propose detailed policies, but instead seeks to draw public attention to the following key issues:

1   Vigorous positive action is needed to prevent inequality persisting, for example in housing and employment (it is not enough just to pass laws outlawing discrimination).
2   A particular effort is needed in the private sector of industry. Barriers that prevent the recruitment of blacks to higher jobs must be removed.
3   Limited fluency in English continues to be strongly associated with economic disadvantages and vice versa. More courses in English are necessary to break this spiral of inequality.
4   The move among Asian workers to self-employment is not taking place among West Indians. Obstacles must be removed, for example there should be easier access to finance and advice.
5   There is a mismatch between the needs of black council tenants and the type of property allocated to them, as shown earlier in this chapter.
6   The council property allocated to black tenants is generally worse than that allocated to whites, and this may be the result of discrimination.
7   Local authority boundaries tend to preserve the geographical distribution and housing disadvantage of black council tenants. (A black council tenant has difficulty in getting a council house in a better area.)
8   Living in the poorer inner city areas perpetuates inequalities generally, for example living in a poor area hinders black people's chances of getting a better job.
9   There is a comparatively large proportion of West Indian families that are one parent families, and this needs special attention if we are not to witness the growth of multiple disadvantage in this group.
10   There is a lack of confidence in the protection offered by the police.
11   Overwhelmingly, blacks want integration, but there is a strong commitment to preserving their own ethnic culture.
12   While blacks are cautious of accusing whites of discrimination, most want full enforcement of the laws against discrimination.

Conclusions

Again, it might be useful and interesting to conclude this chapter by contrasting the apparent problems of race relations with reality – a reality which sociologists, among others, should help to expose.

Apparent problem	Likely reality
1 Immigration law defines the presence of black people as the problem.	The real problem is white racism. Making concessions to white racism makes the problem worse by regularizing (institutionalizing) racism in the law (Paul Gordon, *White Law*).
2 Black people are seen as a law and order problem. Consequently, the police have to behave in a special way to deal with this exceptional problem.	This could be part of a process of criminalization: of turning a section of the population into criminals, thereby providing an excuse for the abuse of that section (Gordon). Black muggings get a lot of coverage in the press and in broadcasting, but not much is said about discrimination and lack of opportunity for young blacks (T. Bilton et al., *Introductory Sociology*). The media create 'folk devils' out of a few cases and the moral panic that ensues justifies the existing social order in society with all its inequalities and discrimination (e.g. S. Cohen, *Folk Devils and Moral Panics*).
3 There must be more black criminality! Black people appear in court more often.	In reality, arrests depend on what the police are looking for and this, in turn, reflects what the public is most worried about, for instance 'muggings'. Thus, Operation 'Swamp', which preceded the Brixton riots in 1981, involved a massive police presence, 943 people were stopped and 118 arrested. Basically, the police did not respond to a problem, they created one.
4 As soon as blacks move into an area they lower the tone and property values tumble.	Often blacks move to neighbourhoods that are already in decline because property prices are

Apparent problem	Likely reality
	lower there. Being trapped in inner city areas causes both frustration and lower property prices.
5 We need the immigration laws, otherwise we should be overrun.	The idea of being swamped exists only in the mind; in any case, not many more blacks want to come here. If there were true equality we would not notice the migrants' skin colour. The legacy of British colonialism was the promise to these 'natives' that they shared our citizenship.
6 Blacks are the cause of the race relations problem.	This is like blaming the victim for the crimes committed against him. It is really racial discrimination that makes blacks feel trapped in ghettos: badly housed, unemployed, less educated and generally poor (and sometimes rebellious).
7 You cannot stop discrimination. Whites have always discriminated against blacks.	Twenty years ago the southern states of the USA used a policy of open segregation, where blacks could only sit in a blacks only part of a bus, could not use whites' toilets, etc. This has now gone; blacks are being elected to public office and schools are becoming integrated. This was fought for by civil rights campaigners (like Martin Luther King) and followed by legislation. Reality is socially constructed; what seems unchangeable can be changed if there is the will. This, in turn, depends on our beliefs and values.

Self-examination questions

1   What is meant by 'discrimination', 'prejudiced', 'the authoritarian personality', 'ethnocentric', 'institutional racism', 'Commission for Racial Equality'?
2   What are the reasons for the post-war immigration to Britain?

Discussion topics

1 What should be the policy of the Commission for Racial Equality?
2 What do you think will be the response of black people to their difficulties?

Projects

1 **Using Table 8.4 on p. 143 as a model, analyse the difficulties in achieving racial equality.**

2 **Ascertain the latest figures on immigration, black unemployment, housing and crime. Comment on the trends over the past few years.** (You will find the following useful: *Social Trends*, reports by the Commission for Racial Equality, the Runnymede Trust and so on.)

3 **Mention has been made several times in this chapter for the need to understand (what Weber called *Verstehen* – understanding the meaning of the act to the actor).**

If there are black people in your group at school, college etc. who are willing to describe their experiences, it might be interesting to ask them to give examples of prejudice they have encountered, and how they actually felt about it. (White people too can give examples of prejudice they have encountered.)

Past examination questions

1 **Distinguish between racial discrimination and racial prejudice. Which do you believe to be more significant in race relations in contemporary Britain?**

Oxford Local Examinations, A Level, Summer 1984.

Suggestions

See 'Common question two' for the distinction. 'Common question five' shows the problem of the Commission for Racial Equality – should they prosecute (against overt discrimination in, say, jobs) or should they try to educate to reduce covert prejudice?

There is no correct answer. As shown in 'Common question two', prejudice refers to beliefs and values. These are the springs of action, hence education is needed; but the roots of prejudice lie in the social structure – you could use the three theories in 'Common question three' to explain this (see also 'Common question two').

2   **Who benefits from racial discrimination in Britain?**

University of Cambridge Local Examinations Syndicate, A Level, Paper 2, Summer 1983.

Suggestions

Go through the list of people affected. Blacks, white youth, employers, police, teachers, etc. You might conclude (and if so, clearly demonstrate) that nobody benefits.

3   **'Ethnic minorities in Britain, blacks in particular, are trapped at the bottom of the social ladder with fewer opportunities, fewer possessions and fewer exercisable rights than the great majority of whites.' Discuss.**

Associated Examining Board, A Level, Autumn 1984.

Suggestions

You could use the sections of this chapter – employment, housing, education, etc. – to demonstrate that blacks are 'trapped' even though the law says they are equal citizens.

4   **What do sociologists mean by racial discrimination and how do they explain its occurrence? Illustrate your answer with examples of discrimination in any *one* country.**

University of Cambridge Local Examinations Syndicate, A Level, Paper 2, June 1988.

Suggestions

You could contrast 'discrimination' with 'prejudice' (see text) using evidence quoted in this chapter, and 'Further reading' (see also question 1).

5   **Write an essay about the UK as a multi-cultural society. You may choose to include reference to any of the following:**

1   An explanation of how the various groups came to live in the UK.
2   Immigration policies.
3   The experience of various groups in employment, education, housing.

Northern Examining Association, GCSE, Paper 2, May 1988.

Suggestions

See 'Common question one' in text, and also sections on employment, education and housing in this chapter. What are the obstacles to integration? Is it desirable?

6 **In advanced industrial countries to what extent can the position of women be compared to the position of ethnic minorities?**

University of Cambridge Local Examinations Syndicate, GCSE, Paper 1, 1987.

Suggestion

Both groups share a lower status.

Both are subject to prejudice and discrimination (define).

Discuss dual labour markets and research on the failure of legislation to improve the position of women and of blacks – especially in the labour markets.

Further reading

M. Anwar, *Between Two Cultures*
M. Banton, *Racial and Ethnic Competition*
M. Banton, *Racial Consciousness*
L. Barton and S. Walker (eds), *Race, Class and Education*
*C. Brown, *Black and White Britain*
E. Cashmore, *The Logic of Racism*
*E. Cashmore and B. Troyna, *Introduction to Race Relations*
E. Cashmore and B. Troyna (eds), *Black Youth in Crisis*
Commission for Racial Equality, *Annual Report*, 1988
*Commission for Racial Equality, *New Community: Journal of the Commission for Racial Equality*
P. Gordon, 'Hidden Injuries of Racism'
C. Husbands, *Racial Exclusionism and the City*
V. S. Khan, *Minority Families in Britain*
A. Little and D. Robbins, *Loading the Law*
J. Rex, *Race and Ethnicity*
J. Rex and S. Tomlinson, *Colonial Immigrants in a British City*
*Runnymede Trust and Radical Statistics Race Group, *Britain's Black Population*
D. J. Smith, *Unemployment and Racial Minorities*
J. Tierney et al., *Race, Migration and Schooling*
S. Tomlinson, *Ethnic Minorities in British Schools*
R. Willey, *Race, Equality and Schools*
Different Worlds
'Education and Race', *New Society*, 17 February 1985 (Society Today series)
'Race and Prejudice', *New Society*, 17 January 1986 (Society Today series)
Scarman Report: The Brixton Disorders
TUC Workbook on Racism

10   Old People

It is as though walking down Shaftesbury Avenue as a fairly young man I was suddenly kidnapped, rushed into a theatre and made to don the grey hair, the wrinkles and the other attributes of age, then wheeled on-stage. Behind the appearance of age I am the same person, with the same thoughts, as when I was younger.
J. B. Priestley (at age 79 on being asked – on the occasion of publication of his 99th work – what it is like being old)

Introduction

We often speak of 'the *problem* of old people'. But why is it a problem? For whom is it a problem – the old people themselves, the carers or the rest of society? To what extent are the genuine problems of old age worsened by our prejudice? In the same way as society seems to have racial prejudice ('racism') and prejudice against women ('sexism'), so there seems to be prejudice against the old – and this can be called the ideology of 'ageism'. This chapter shows that the ideology serves political interests and exaggerates the natural problems which old people and those who care for them undoubtedly do have.

Having examined the roots of ageism, the chapter then proceeds to examine a number of common assumptions arising from ageism:

1 work is the principal good in society (the work ethic);
2 because of welfare provision by the state, families are taking less care of their old people;
3 we help old people by treating them as a separate group and according them special privileges;
4 an older population means higher taxation for the rest of us – to pay for pensions and welfare.

The chapter concludes with a brief discussion of the sort of policy changes necessary to help us move away from our present ageist society. Finally there is a short table summarizing the contrast between common assumptions and reality on this subject.

Key issues

There are two ways of seeing the 'problem'. At one level there is in the West the 'problem' of an ageing population and all that this entails in terms of increased pensions, disability and ill health, and increased reliance on families, neighbours and on the state for health and welfare provision. At another level however, the sociologist must persist with the questions posed earlier: why is this a problem and to whom is it a problem? Obviously increased financial provision by society for old persons is involved. In addition it is also a real problem for relatives who have to care for the infirm and elderly. But this is not the crux of the problem. It will be argued that the problem is substantially one of our own making.

Clearly the population is ageing – but is this a problem? Firstly, it must be good that people are living longer and are available to their families. Further, it reflects a healthier population, not just in medical terms but also in terms of better diet and housing. Not much of a problem here! Moreover, instead of saying that we have an ageing population it would be more accurate to say that in the nineteenth century the population was abnormally youthful, due to poor health and premature death. Put this way the 'problem' of old age appears already to be less of a problem.

In approximate figures a hundred-strong cross-section of the nation taken a century ago and today would suggest the converse pattern shown in Table 10.1.

Table 10.1 Moving from an abnormally youthful population to a long-lived population

	Under 20 years	20–60 years	Over 60 years
1880s	50%	45%	5%
1980s	30%	50%	20%

Source: E. Midwinter, *Redefining Old Age*

Of course there is a genuine problem of increased dependency. In 1911 there were fewer than three million people of pensionable age in the UK. In 1951 the figure was seven million and in 1975 it was 9.5 million, according to Peter Townsend in *Poverty in the UK*. An increasing proportion of these older people will be over 75. In 1926 80 per cent of men over 65 were in full time employment; the fraction had fallen to less than a fifth by 1971 (Townsend).

A combination of factors put older people at a material disadvantage. Firstly, they usually have to retire from paid employment in order to receive the state pension. Secondly, the pension itself is low, about a third of average industrial earnings; this fraction has remained constant since 1950. All this results in a low income for the elderly.

Table 10.2 shows the increase in elderly people (65 and over) living in residential accommodation.

Table 10.2   Residential accommodation for the elderly (thousands)

	1976	1986
Number of residents in:		
homes provided by local authorities	106	121
registered voluntary and private homes	46	113

Source: adapted from *Social Trends 1988*

Reflections on Table 10.2: it seems *public* provision has increased very little, especially bearing in mind older people are living longer. Perhaps the 'excess' are 'living in the community'! Meanwhile wealthier people can apparently buy shelter and care privately.

The social construction of old age

The following is an attempt to introduce some sociological theory to help to see the 'problem' of old age more clearly.

Berger and Luckman in their book *The Social Construction of Reality* suggest that reality is socially constructed and that the sociology of knowledge must analyse the processes by which this occurs. Crucially, 'old age' is not simply a matter of accumulated years and decrease of physical capabilities. Rather it is a set of expectations and beliefs that are socially created: that the old are a 'problem' for the young; that they have declining intellectual powers; that they have little interest (other than perverse) in sexuality.

Fennell, Phillipson and Evers see old age as a social status rather than a biologically determined status (*The Sociology of Old Age*). Hence we see what we want to see or have been taught to see whether this is retirement and old age, deviance (p. 274), the manufacture of news (p. 298), or any other social phenomenon.

The following quotation comes from Fennell's book (p. 53):

Retirement, poverty, institutionalization and restriction of domestic and community roles are the experiences which help to explain the structured dependency of the elderly. [In this analysis it is] society [that] creates the framework of institutions and rules within which the general problems of the elderly emerge or, indeed, are 'manufactured'. In the everyday management of the economy and the administration and development of social institutions, the position of the elderly is subtly shaped and changed. The policies which determine the conditions and welfare of the elderly are not just the reactive policies represented by the statutory social services but the much more generalized and institutionalized policies of the state which maintain or change social structure.

The ideology of ageism

According to 'Search', an organization concerned with welfare rights for the elderly, the ideology of ageism which so distorts our thinking comprises seven *deadly myths*. These are:

the myth of chronology;
the myth of ill health;
the myth of senility;
the myth of inflexible personality;
the myth of rejection and isolation;
the myth of misery;
the myth of unproductivity.

These will now be considered in turn. (Much of this section is based on a Search report of 1983: *Welfare Rights for the Elderly*.)

The myth of chronology:
'she's not the woman she was'

There is no universal law of ageing. There are big differences in ageing and the differences may be physiological, psychological and social. Hence it is misleading to talk of 'the elderly'.

Nor do old people form a homogeneous group, for example not all 70-year-olds are alike.

The myth of ill health:
'what can you expect at your age?'

The health of people between 65 and 74 is not generally inferior to the group immediately below that age. Further, the elderly have fewer acute cases than the young.

The Search report argues that there is no automatic deterioration of health with age. Yet old people sometimes seem to be written off by their doctors. The elderly should beware of diagnoses like: hardening of the arteries; senility; organic impairment.

Many older people seem to accept poor hearing, poor sight, back pain as inevitable. To refer patients to a geriatric department in a hospital may be seen as a way of discarding them. Geriatrics as a medical specialism has low status. Often hospital posts go unfilled. On average 7.9 applicants compete for a vacancy as a senior registrar in any other specialism compared with 1.7 in geriatrics.

The myth of senility:
'he is entering his second childhood'

It is a myth that the brain inevitably 'wilts' with age. Unfortunately some older people do suffer from dementia, a clinical condition, but the numbers are not that great:

Dementia sufferers: 6% of 65-year-olds;
                      29% of 80-year-olds and over.

One third of old people said to be forgetful actually improved with age, showing that the condition is not irreversible. Or that the forgetfulness could have causes other than dementia.

Of these causes, depression is the most common – and the most treatable. Early treatment is necessary, however, so the elderly should not be fobbed off with ideologically based advice.

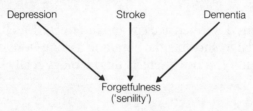

The causes of 'senility'

The myth of inflexible personality

Older student: 'Don't expect too much of me – you can't teach an old dog new tricks.'

Tutor: 'So long as you believe that, it will work on you like a spell.'

Really there is no sharp discontinuity in personality with age. The old appear to be more cautious but this may be due to greater experience – they have burnt their fingers in the past. Again, the old are not necessarily more serene – in fact they may get more frustrated, which is not surprising considering the ideology of ageism in our society.

The myth of rejection and isolation

Old people are often assumed to be isolated, and separated as a group from the rest of society; and this is assumed to be a 'mutual process'. In fact the Search report says that 80 per cent of over-65s are not living alone.

The myth of misery

Unable to love the old, we approach them via sentiment and duty with an eye to our own eventual decline (says Search). But Age Concern showed in one study that old people are happier than we think (*Inequality and Older*

People). Only 7 per cent of their sample felt they had nothing to look forward to (and one third would have gone on working had they been allowed to).

The myth of unproductivity

People are forced to retire at 65 or 60, yet many 70-year-olds have produced excellent work (Lords Shinwell and Stockton, Churchill, De Gaulle, Bertrand Russell and so on).

Why use the word retirement anyway? We don't say we retired from school. Retirement implies lack of role and lack of usefulness. Really retirement could be seen as a new creative career, yet our expectations are that older people will wind down (and be 'sensible'). Sometimes we assume they cannot be trusted with important responsibility.

Our ideologies and prejudices weigh down heavily on the old. And we are all the losers.

This section has described ageism and its effects. Much of the rest of the chapter is devoted to showing the common assumptions associated with it and trying to identify whose interests this ideology really serves.

Common assumption one: *work and the work ethic are the principal good in society*

'The ways in which older workers are treated, the frequency of retirement and the particular forms it takes, are not random occurrences – they are the result of deliberate policies formulated and carried out by people with political, economic or other persuasive power to do so' (according to Stanley Parker, a sociologist who has written extensively on the theme of creative retirement, in his book, *Work and Retirement*). Thus, for example, there was a period when retirement was discouraged, and then from the mid-1960s a period when retirement was encouraged, especially in the 1980s when there was severe unemployment. Generally it can be said that retirement policies have been based more on the alleged needs of the economy than on the needs of real people.

What do people miss most when they retire? For many it is the loss of status, the loss of a role, the loss of contact with people at work. This is illustrated in Table 10.3, which compares the views of workers on what they think they will miss when they retire with what people already retired say they do miss. It is interesting to note that the retired miss people more than the money. If we single out special groups we get different answers. For example, Jacobson found that among those workers whose jobs entailed heavy strain, 82 per cent were willing to retire at pensionable age, compared with only 39 per cent of those whose jobs entailed only light strain. (D. Jacobson, 'Fatigue producing factors in industrial work'.)

Oscar Zarate

Thousands dying of boredom

A CAMPAIGN is being launched to stop thousands of people dying of boredom.
It's the idea of David Simmonds, a research fellow at Surrey University, Guildford.
Mr. Simmonds' research shows that one in four National Health Service workers who retire at 65 die within six months because their life loses meaning without work.

One foot in the grave (or the myth of misery)
Source: *Search* Report, 1983

Naturally the prospect of a good pension leads to a more favourable attitude to impending retirement.

One major theme of Parker's book is that older people need a useful working role. Another is that we should all feel less guilty about having leisure. If leisure is defined only as the opposite of work, and if retirement is

BENNETT GROUP OF COMPANIES

Financial Controller / Director Designate

Oxfordshire Road Haulier and forwa

c. £15,000

Applications are invited from qualified accountants for the above post preferred age 25-35 full responsibility for the accounting function of the groups subidary company concerned with International Road Haulage.

Board appointment envisaged within 12-18 months, remuneration package include early entry into contributory pension company car, membershi assistance with relo

Please telephone fo
Mrs Shirley Hodges,
Common Road, Tha
2JB. Tel. Thame (08

OFFICE EQUIPMENT SALESMAN/WOMAN

Privately owned commercial stationery and office equipment retailing firm is looking for a sales person, aged between 30-45, to join a small sales team

Applicants must have a fairly extensive knowledge of the industry and experience in selling to the end user

Basic salary plus generous commission and company car, etc

Please write in the first instance to Barry Thearle, Managing Director, J. Colegrove Ltd, 2/4 Marcham R Abingdon, Oxon OX14 1AB

27 Jan 10T

SMITHS GORE
CHARTERED SURVEYORS

BAMPTON LANES TRUST RESIDENT WARDEN/MANAGER

Active person, preferably married and aged 40 to 60, sought to manage this imaginative new development of houses and flats for retired people at BAMPTON, NR WITNEY, OXFORDSHIRE

High quality accommodation provided rent and rates free and realistic salary paid for general caretaking duties and providing help for residents.

The post is open from the beginning of April

Applications please to:—
Messrs Smiths Gore, Eastgate House, Eastgate Street, Winchester, Hampshire SO23 8DZ. Tel. (0962) 51203

849Jan 10T

**SALES MANAGE
IN SCREEN ADVERTISIN**

£14K base — £21K OTE + car

Arising from considerable UK expansion, this major sc advertising company now has a unique opportunity fo talented sales manager to play a key role in its Northe operations.

Your prime responsibility will be to head up a team of seven/eight executives. In doing so, you will aim to achieve personal and group targets, train and motivate what is already a successful sales team.

Ideally, you will be between the ages of 28-40, with previous sales management experience, preferably within the media. Your efforts and experience will not go unrewarded The company offers an excellent basic salary, achieveable targets, a company car, and other benefits.

For a confidential discussion call Elizabeth Riding on 01-408 1616.

**IPP MARKETFORCE
16 DOVER STREET, LONDON W1X 3PB**

Spot the common assumptions: age matters in employment

the opposite of work, then the scene is set for the traumatic change from full time work to its opposite condition of retirement which so many 'endure' today. Retirement and leisure have low status because we are still a work orientated society. Mary Stott in *Ageing for Beginners* argues that the strongest reason for reluctance to prepare for retirement is that in our ageist society retirement is not an honourable estate, and certainly the view is borne out by much of this chapter. Jenkins and Sherman in *The Collapse of Work* comment that 'work is rather like the air we breathe and take for

Table 10.3 What the retired miss from work

	Workers %	Retired %
Would/did miss most:		
The money the job brings	48	31
The people at work	24	36
The feeling of being useful	10	10
The work itself	8	11
Things happening around	3	5
The respect of others	2	3
Other answers	5	4

Source: S. Parker, *Older Workers and Retirement*

granted, it is undramatic, certainly not funny and yet is an inbuilt part of life.' What is taken for granted (what is 'like the air we breathe') is what the sociologist investigates. Whether or not one accepts the views of Weber (see accompanying box), Thompson, Jenkins and Sherman and others on the work ethic, it seems clear that the ethic is a cultural thing rather than instinctual. If this is the case, then we can unlearn it if necessary and in so doing feel less guilty about not working. Creative leisure may become a substitute for creative work.

The work ethic

The sociologist Max Weber wanted to understand why industrial capitalism developed in the Western world. Weber thought there was a connection between religion and the attitude to work. People of different religions saw work in different ways. In Protestant countries Weber noted that hard work and the accumulation of profits and wealth seemed to be approved of, whereas spending and unwillingness to work were seen as signs of moral weakness. Weber further noted that there was a connection between the Protestant ethic and the spirit of capitalism. The central feature of the Protestant ethic is that we are predestined to Heaven or Hell. We do not know which, but hard work in this life is a sign of election to Heaven. This was the link between the Protestant ethic and the spirit of capitalism. It required self-discipline and application to work. It could be argued that what we now loosely call the work ethic is derived from the Protestant ethic.

The work ethic seems to have affected both master and workman from the early stages of the industrial revolution onwards. Thus E. P. Thompson in his article 'Time Work: discipline and industrial capitalism' says that 'without time disciplines we could not have the insistent energies of industrial man.' The problem of leisure, says Thompson, may consist in unlearning some of the urgency of factory life; an urgency imposed earlier on the agricultural labourer.

Thus in *Work and Retirement* S. R. Parker argues the case for an expansive, creative, radical approach to retirement, as opposed to a restrictive, conformist, conservative one. There are policies based on the needs of the economy, which stress decreased working ability with age, have a narrow concern with employment and separate work and leisure. On the other hand there are retirement policies based on the needs of people and on continuity of lifestyle that combat ageism and have a wider concern with the integration of work with leisure. The differences in the two approaches are summarized in Table 10.4. Compulsory retirement at a fixed age is still the norm in our society. Some of the common assumptions that this implies are described in this chapter. Parker points the way to a different approach to old age.

Table 10.4 Differing approaches to retirement

Topic	Approach	
	Restrictive/conformist/ conservative	Expansive/creative/ radical
Retirement policy based on	'needs' of the economy	needs of people
Theory of retirement	disengagement	activity
Retirement preparation	'top table', instructive	'round table', participative
Stress on	age decrements	combating ageism
Key activity concept	employment	work
Relation of work and leisure	separation	integration
Timing of retirement	fixed age	flexible
Retirement decision	compulsory	voluntary
Degree of retirement	complete	gradual
Preferred lifestyle	linear (progressive)	flexible

Source: S. Parker, *Work and Retirement*

Common assumption two: *because of welfare provision by the state, families are taking less and less care of their old people*

Are families shirking their responsibilities to the old? In fact, in all social classes families still care for the old, as Chapter 2 showed. Many old people see their adult children daily or at least once a week. The poorest old people, both financially and socially, are those without an active family – the isolates. Often these are the very elderly. Table 10.5 gives some idea of the extent of informal contact between elderly people and their relatives. It shows that old people are frequently visited by relatives and friends and that isolated people are visited more frequently.

Table 10.5 Relationship with relatives or friends

	Older persons living alone	Older persons living in married pairs
Seeing relative outside household most or all days of the week	31%	24%
Seeing relative outside household at least weekly	38%	38%
Receives help from relative, neighbour or friend	52%	16%
Helped in illness in last 12 months	43%	25%
Total number on which percentages are based	223	401

Source: P. Townsend, *Poverty in the UK*

In an earlier study, *The Aged and the Welfare State*, Townsend and Wedderburn show that only 4.5 per cent of old people lived in hospitals:

33 per cent were unmarried, compared with 10 per cent in the whole elderly population.

26 per cent had no child, compared with 16 per cent in the whole elderly population.

40 per cent had no brother or sisters, compared with 22 per cent in the whole elderly population.

39 per cent had sons only, compared with 26 per cent in the whole elderly population.

In other words, there is often a reasonable explanation for an old person ending up in a hospital for the old and apparently not being cared for by the family. (See case study at the end of this chapter for a further example of residential care.)

On the basis of these and other figures, there is little evidence to suggest that families are shirking their responsibilities to the old – so where does this idea come from? Perhaps it is a way of making people feel guilty and therefore making them tend to old (and handicapped) people at home, even though sometimes they should really be cared for in a home or hospital (for example, some badly incapacitated old people). This idea might be a way of saving the state some money, while placing a heavy burden on the 'carers' and the rest of the family.

Common assumption three: *we help old people by treating them as a separate group and according them special privileges*

Much of the alleged problem of old age is created by society itself. In particular it comes from needlessly separating old people from society by making them retire, by rehousing them away from their families and generally by treating them as a separate and helpless category. Another example of this is old people's homes. Many are of course well run; others are a legacy of the old poor law institutions, with bare day rooms and little respect for individual dignity (see P. Townsend, *Last Refuge*). *Sheltered independence* is a preferable solution, based on the determination not to separate old people from society if at all possible. To this end, money spent on domiciliary services such as home helps and meals on wheels is money well spent; yet it is these local authority services that are hit by expenditure cuts, rate capping, etc.

The basic trouble is that older people are forced by society to act the *role* of old persons, to give up work, withdraw from society, be dependent and so on. Old people themselves act in ways expected of them, and so they collude in a social construction of reality in which society sets them apart and they in turn expect and accept that they are a group apart. The following quotation from Townsend's book *Poverty in the UK* describes this loss of status through social labelling.

> That retirement brings relatively lower income has been demonstrated, in relation both to adults under the pensionable ages and the small numbers of adults over the pensionable ages who continue in paid employment. That retirement brings relatively lower social status might be demonstrated at some length, with examples of the social labelling of 'pensioners' through customs like cheap afternoon tickets for the cinema, cheap travel in off-peak hours on local bus routes, cheap seaside holidays in May or October, condescending gifts of gold watches after forty or fifty years' employed service, cheap butter and government doles (in the early 1970s) of £10 at

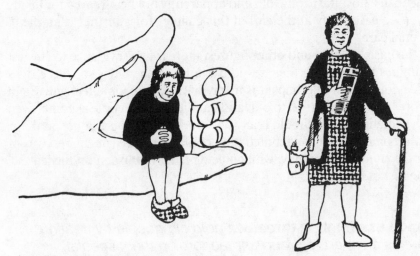

In traditional homes, old people don't need to do anything for themselves.

In progressive homes they are encouraged to organise their own lives.

Sheltered independence should be the aim
Source: *Search* Report, 1983

Christmas. That the retired recognize their depressed status might be demonstrated from evidence adduced earlier of the numbers feeling worse off than their families, neighbours and the population at large, and, in particular, worse off than at previous stages in their lives.

All this is supported by the ideology of ageism discussed earlier.

Common assumption four: *an older population means higher taxation for the rest of us – to pay for pensions and welfare*

The problem that is said to arise from an ageing population, that of increased taxation to pay for its welfare, arises partly from the flat rate nature of national insurance contributions, which are only slightly graduated. They act as a sort of poll tax hitting the lowest paid hardest. To be equitable, contributions should be on the basis of progressive taxation, with the well off paying a proportionally higher part of their income towards pensions. Private pension schemes for the well off work against this principle (and make insurance companies and pension funds the arbiters of welfare rather than the community).

To some extent therefore this is another problem created by society. As Townsend puts it:

> More of the elderly than of the young or middle aged are poor because they have been excluded from employment and therefore from the rates of income associated with employment, without adequate substitution through the state's social security system ... Some old people are poor by virtue of their low class position. Others are poor by virtue of society's imposition upon the elderly of 'under class' status. (*Poverty in the UK*)

Again, in a more equal and less ageist society many of these problems might disappear.

Trends in the sociology of old age

Fennell, Phillipson and Evers discern three trends in the sociology of old people: segregation, rising living standards and widening social cleavage – that is, a widening of the gap between the elderly poor and wealthy elderly.

1 *Segregation*: housing areas become occupied by people sharing similar patterns of construction; for example, the southern and eastern coastal strips of England have a high proportion of retired people. This segregation in housing may mean, for example, that grandparents become impoverished as family ties break.

2 *Rising living standards*: more people belong to pension schemes, though the main areas of poverty are increasing in the very old, or those previously in lower paid jobs. Many old people have experienced a

dramatic improvement in their position during their own lifetimes. Nevertheless many old people experience hardship through low income, as the evidence presented in this chapter shows.

3 *Widening social cleavage*: the poor become poorer and this applies especially to the low paid, the unemployed, one parent families, or families containing a physically or mentally handicapped member. As these disadvantaged people get older their plight becomes worse. For instance, as car ownership becomes more common and public transport declines, those without a car become relatively worse off. Overall these people participate in society less and become less 'visible' because of increasing segregation.

ANGELA RIPPON FACES RETIREMENT

Talking to John McCarthy, Chairman, McCarthy & Stone plc.

'John, it seems that retirement doesn't mean the same thing to McCarthy & Stone as it does to other companies?'

'You're right, because we believe retirement is the start of a new and active life, not the end of the world.'

'So is the secret simply looking to the future?'

'To a great extent. More and more people are reaching retirement age and they all have their own ideas of what they want to do with their lives. What we do is listen. We listen to their dreams, we listen to their hopes, we listen to peoples' daily experiences through our Consumer panels. We listen – and then we act.'

'All right, John, so what role are you going to play for the future?'

'Just as the home is the nucleus of retirement living and the centre piece of family life – so designing purpose built quality homes will remain the heart of our business.

'But, with our understanding of retirement lifestyles, don't be surprised to see us moving more and more towards many other needs.'

Source: *Radio Times*, 17–23 September 1988

QUESTION: what does the above advert tell us about retirement?

Suggestions

You could argue that there are basically two types of people who retire: those who can afford it and those who cannot. Then show the attributes of each group, using the text and 'Further reading'. It seems care for the elderly is big business, part of the service economy – what do you think? What should the state be doing (if anything)?

Conclusions

The chapter started by outlining what to the lay person, the politician and the administrator are the main problems of an ageing population, the problems of dependency and of the costs involved. It then contrasted this viewpoint with that of the sociologist, for whom the central interest lies in the ideology of ageism (while not denying the problems of increased dependency).

Clearly ageism measures up to the working definition of ideology used throughout this book:

it is a belief;
it is a distorted belief;
it flies in the face of the facts;
it is part of our taken for granted world;
it therefore forms part of the basis upon which our common assumptions
   are made hence upon which *social* policy is made.

But if ideologies serve the interests of the powerful, whose interests does ageism serve? Usually ideologies are seen as serving the interests of the few over the many, and in so doing as justifying the power of the few. At first sight ageism appears to contradict this, since it appears to serve the interests of the many (the non-retired) over the few (the retired). The key to this riddle lies in the concept of power. Decent provision for the old requires money (taxes), hence it is really a political decision – and there are not many votes to be had in higher taxes to help the old. Inadequate provision for the elderly is really just another aspect of inequality in society. (The wealthy few benefit from lower taxation for lower pensions.) It is not solely a question of money. It is also a question of attitudes too: non-ageist attitudes. The following quotation from Maggie Kuhn, founder of the Grey Panthers in the USA, illustrates this point:

> The aged are a part of society. Discrimination against the elderly reflects society's values. This is why small measures – providing for example larger pensions, more meals on wheels, vocational training etc. – however admirable in themselves are never in the long run enough. Unless society changes itself, rethinks its values, its purpose and direction the long range forecast for the elderly is very bleak indeed. *In an unequal world the powerless can always expect to be sans everything.* (Reprinted in the Search report, *Welfare Rights for the Elderly.*)

We have seen what the implications of our present ageist assumptions are. Would it help to attack ageism openly? Search recommends an Age Discrimination Act on the lines of the Sex Discrimination Act 1975 and the Race Relations Act 1976. However, it must be said that these acts have had limited success for the reasons mentioned in chapters 8 and 9. This chapter has sought to show the roots of ageism in an unequal society. Perhaps the realization that it exists is a first essential step.

The following summary of common assumptions discussed in the chapter also indicates the sort of changes, particularly policy changes, required for a more equal society for the old. (See how far you agree with the 'common assumptions' before you look at the possible realistic assessments.)

Common assumptions	Possible realistic assessment
1 We have an ageing population giving rise to increased dependency in the form of ill health, increased pensions and so on.	It is good that people are living longer. We make the old into a problem by making them dependent through inadequate pensions etc.
2 It is a fact that the old are a greater burden, e.g. in ill health etc. You cannot expect them to be as efficient as younger people.	The seven deadly myths of ageism outlined here demonstrate that often we make old people wards of the state unnecessarily through prejudice and discrimination.
3 Work and the work ethic are the principal good in society. Without work you are without a role in society and without status.	As things stand there is a lot of truth in this. But it could be different. The work ethic is not an instinct. It is learnt and varies from culture to culture. Education for leisure and self-development might lessen the importance of the work ethic.
4 Because of the welfare state families are shirking their responsibilities to their old folk.	There is little real evidence to suggest that families are shirking their responsibilities. The ideology of 'shirking' may come from the call to care for the old and handicapped 'in the community' and a 'return to Victorian values'. Often these are excuses for saving money. They usually mean the woman of the house, e.g. the adult daughter, has the sole burden of caring. It all places more strain on the family – much of this is hidden from polite society; the carers have to 'cope'.
5 We help the old ('senior citizens') by giving them special privileges (such as free bus passes).	If the old had adequate incomes they would not need these handouts. But this is only likely in a less unequal society. The handouts are a way of covering up this inequality.
6 We help the old through training for retirement, provision of centres for the retired etc.	Parker comments that the higher status the occupational group, the greater the likelihood that pre-

Common assumptions	Possible realistic assessment
	retirement plans would have been made. The lower the status of the people retiring, the more they worry about retirement but the less they do about it, partly no doubt because of limited opportunities for appropriate action. (Comment – even within the retired as a group there is still great inequality.)

Self-examination questions

1 What is meant by 'ageism', 'social labelling', 'isolation', 'prejudice', 'stereo-typing', 'progressive taxation', 'poll tax'?

2 Divide the page in half and draw up a table entitled 'The problems of old age'. In the left hand half write down the 'real' problems of old age, e.g. ill health. In the right hand half write down what you think are the socially created problems (which may be just as real in their way).

Discussion topics

1 'The major cause of poverty in contemporary Britain is old age'. Discuss.

Oxford Local Examinations, A Level, Summer 1982.

2 This chapter suggested that the alleged problems of an ageing population are to some extent artificially created by society itself, and it asked: why do we do this? Why are old people separated from society, allowed to become needlessly wards of state, treated as different and separate, paid low pensions? How would you answer these questions?

Project

Taking Table 10.4 ('Differing approaches to retirement'), expand the table by showing, with examples, what each item means. You will find this chapter and Parker's book *Work and Retirement* useful for this.

Case study and past examination questions

1 **Read the passage and answer the questions that follow.**

Care of the elderly

The low status attributed to carers, whether paid or unpaid, inevitably affects the way in which they perceive themselves, their work and the status of those they care for. This has been vividly illustrated by many studies in institutional settings. For example:

We witnessed many scenes in which old people were subjected to the indignity of being treated like inanimate objects. They were so frequently, and so much ignored by other members of staff that we can only conclude that the staff involved were not exceptional in their thoughtlessness. Once more we seem to be describing a way of life.

It is 1.35 p.m. in a geriatric rehabilitation ward. An auxiliary brings a patient who has just been bathed back to the ward and puts her to bed. As she is doing this an enrolled nurse comes to tell her not to put the patient to bed – 'Because she'll soak the bed and who's going to change her?' The fact that it is only 1.35 p.m. seems to be of no relevance.

An auxiliary in a geriatric ward pushes a patient off in a wheelchair – without a word. The patient says, 'I don't go to bed at this time.' 'OK,' says the auxiliary, and continues to wheel her off to bed.

It is not only empathy with the suffering that old people may have to endure that we avoid. We expect all their human responses to be muted. An elderly man who shows any signs of sexual interest is called 'dirty', and older women who make themselves sexually attractive are 'mutton dressed as lamb'.

Our denial of the physical and emotional reality of older people's lives continues into a denial of their expectation and experience of death. Most people's reaction when an elderly person makes some remark which shows that they are thinking about impending death, such as 'I'd like you to have this when I'm gone', or 'I don't suppose I shall be here this time next year', is to shut them up. 'You've got years yet', 'you mustn't talk like that'. If this is the reaction when there is no immediate terminal illness, it is even stronger if the person is indeed dying. In spite of the growth in hospice care, most people who do not die at home, die in hospital, and about 70,000 a year die in geriatric wards. Many studies have shown that medical and nursing staff distance themselves from patients they know to be dying. (A. Norman, *Aspects of Ageism*, pp. 13 and 15.)

1 Why is the status of carers low?

2 Why do you think these old people were subject to indignities?

3 How might a sociologist be able to suggest ways for treating the dying?

Suggestions

Carers, whether at home or in institutions, are usually women, and the work they do is often not highly valued.

There is a tendency for some organizations to be run for the benefit of the staff. In this example, patients are put to bed early because this seems to suit the staff better (not the residents). (On the other hand staff are poorly paid and not respected.)

We should not distance ourselves from the dying. They should be treated as full members of society as far as possible and their problems should be discussed not dismissed (instead we impose the role of dying patient on them and expect them to play that role – to be sensible etc.).

Role theory may be useful. What role are we expected to play as patient, nurse, carer, etc? See Glossary for 'role'.

2   **'Behind all the talk about the problems of an ageing society there is the forgotten question of the class structure. The old are not a classless tribe.' Discuss.**

> *University of Cambridge Local Examinations Syndicate, A Level, Summer 1984.*

Suggestions

Show how we make ageing a social problem, for example by separating old people off from the rest of society. Then show how within this group the middle class are better equipped for retirement.

3   **From a sociological viewpoint what are the problems of old age?**

> *District Nurses Examination, Oxford Polytechnic, March 1985.*

Suggestions

Dealt with in the chapter.

4   **In 1951 there were 11 per cent of the population beyond retiring age. In 1981 there were 17 per cent. Examine the causes and effects of this ageing population.**

> *London and East Anglian Group, GCSE, Paper 2, May 1988.*

Suggestions

Emphasize the sociological viewpoint. It is not just a question of numbers, resources used, etc. Rather it is a question of our attitudes. For example, do we regard them as a 'problem'? Examine the 'problem' of ageing (a) in terms of the social construction of reality and (b) in relation to the ideologies surrounding old age, notably 'ageism'. (See text for the causes and effects of an 'ageing' population.)

Further reading

M. Abrams, *The Elderly*
Simone de Beauvoir, *Old Age*
P. Berger and P. Luckman, *The Social Construction of Reality*

*N. Dickson (ed.), *Living in the 80's: What Prospects for the Elderly?*
G. Fennell, C. Phillipson and H. Evers, *The Sociology of Old Age*
D. Hobman (ed.), *The Social Challenge of Ageing*
A. Norman, *Aspects of Ageism*
S. R. Parker, *Older Workers and Retirement*
S. R. Parker, *Work and Retirement*
Search, *Welfare Rights for the Elderly*
*P. Townsend, *Poverty in the United Kingdom* (chapter on old age)
British Journal of Social Work
New Age (a quarterly magazine)

Part V

Social Life and Social Control

11 Education

A sociology of education would comprise, among other things, the following:

1 a sociology of inequality of opportunity;
2 a sociology of curriculum development (which can also be seen as a branch of the sociology of knowledge);
3 the analysis of classroom behaviour;
4 the school as an organization;
5 the teaching professions;
6 the sociology of special, further and higher education.

As can be seen, this is a vast subject in its own right, and only part of it can be considered here. This chapter concentrates on the first three items in the list, making only passing reference to some of the others.

A sociology of inequality of opportunity

Equality of opportunity has been a key theme in education policy. For example, the Education Act of 1902 was intended to extend the possibility of secondary education to all – to offer a ladder to the bright child, irrespective of social class, to climb from secondary school to university. In the continuing debate on education policy two distinct views may be discerned: firstly, what may be called the 'elitist' view, which stresses excellence and implies that more means worse; and secondly, the equality or 'pool of talent' view, which stresses the need for education for everyone in order to develop each person's full potential. These two opposing views on education may be summarized as in Table 11.1.

Education policy in Britain could be analysed in terms of these two viewpoints. The Education Act 1944 appeared to open up secondary education for all in Britain. The state system was based on three types of school (which allegedly had parity of esteem). At the top was the grammar school for the academically able, next technical schools and last the largest section, secondary modern schools for the less able. Allocation to each kind of school was decided by examination at the age of 11.

A large scale study by Halsey, Heath and Ridge (*Origins and Destinations*) concluded that since the beginning of the century, inequalities of

Table 11.1   The excellence and equality views on education

Elitist view (stresses excellence)	Pool of talent view (stresses equality)
Only the very able should be given the opportunity of higher education.	We must prevent leakages from the pool by promoting equality of opportunity.
Stress on academic excellence.	Stress on education as a means of self-development of the individual.
Example: The Black Papers on Education whose theme is: 1 Without selection the clever working class child in a deprived area stands little chance of real academic education. 2 You can have equality, or equality of opportunity, but you cannot have both. (Equality would mean holding back the bright child.) 3 If the non-competitive/equality ethos dominates our schools we shall fall behind in international competition.	*Example*: The Education Act 1944 which, in adopting a pool of talent approach, laid down that any who could benefit from a grammar school education should be given the opportunity. (Note the date – the Act was part of the wartime social reforms which, together with the Beveridge report etc., can be seen as forming the basis of the post-war welfare state.)
Assumes: 1 that talent can be measured, e.g. through IQ tests and A levels; 2 that public school and Oxford and Cambridge Universities represent the best in education.	*Assumes*: 1 that the 1902, 1944 and other Acts really helped to bring about equality of opportunity in education; 2 that education can change society.

opportunity in schools have remained remarkably stable. This is shown by Table 11.2. Despite its best intentions the Education Act of 1944 did not reduce this inequality (although it did relieve more affluent parents from the need to pay for secondary education). The question that recurs throughout Halsey's book is: can education change society? To the authors this seems also to imply: can education make society fairer, more equal, more open, develop each individual's full potential, provide access to the best jobs for all those capable of doing these jobs?

Because of this continuing inequality, Labour governments in the past have introduced comprehensive schools open to all children in the neighbourhood (thus doing away with the eleven plus exams for grammar schools in many areas). But can these comprehensive schools bring about more equality in education – doing away with these perpetual class divisions referred to above?

If the comprehensive movement is to achieve its goal of an educated

Do we have equality in education?

society with a common culture, then there must be a common curriculum, as well as common schools. But it must also be a curriculum that appeals to all social classes. It should include the vocational ethos of the technical schools, and the literary and scientific ethos of the grammar school.

However, bringing the subject up to date, there are many difficulties preventing presentday comprehensive schools achieving the sort of ideals

Table 11.2 Attendance of selective schools by birth cohort
(percentages)

Father's class	Birth cohort				
	1913–22	1923–32	1933–42	1943–52	All
	%	%	%	%	%
Professional and managerial (upper middle class)	69.7	76.7	79.3	66.4	71.9
Intermediate	34.9	44.0	43.3	37.1	39.9
Working class	20.2	26.1	27.1	21.6	23.7
All (numbers in samples)	1,873	1,897	1,890	2,351	8,011

Note: Attendance by the sons of the upper middle class has remained near the 70 per cent mark – while the working class figure has remained near the 20 per cent mark.
Source: Halsey, Heath and Ridge, *Origins and Destinations*.

described by Halsey (an educated open society with a common culture). Among the difficulties facing comprehensive schools are the following:

1   Comprehensive schools in the more desirable neighbourhoods attract the best teachers and pupils, and this leads to the other comprehensive schools becoming second class comprehensives.
2   The existence of independent schools often 'creams off' the most able pupils and their absence weakens the comprehensive schools.
3   Most comprehensive schools have streaming in one form or another rather than mixed ability teaching. This will now be considered further.

In their book *Fifteen Thousand Hours*, Rutter et al. survey the studies of streaming in secondary schools, and note that 'the net effect of streaming on attainment amounts to the equivalent of no more than five IQ points – a small difference but not a trivial one.' Probably the most famous study of the effects of streaming was done some years ago by J. W. B. Douglas in *The Home and the School*. Douglas showed that the ability of pupils in an upper stream increased while those in the lower stream decreased relatively, as Table 11.3 shows.

Sociologists have taken this as an example of the effects of labelling. Teachers try to predict how well a pupil will make out. If a pupil is labelled a bottom streamer he or she will tend to act accordingly. ('I must be thick, that is my label.') The teacher's professional reputation is on the line too: teachers try to show that their original labelling was largely correct. Thus labelling becomes a self-fulfilling prophecy.

Streaming seems to affect pupils' attitudes and behaviour as well as ability. Pupils in lower streams are labelled as failures and perceive themselves as failures. Many form an anti-school subculture, a few become delinquent. However, Lacey noted that when a school which had been

Table 11.3 The effects of streaming

Measured ability at eight years	Upper stream change in score, 8–11 years	Lower (B) stream change in score, 8–11 years
41–45	+5.67	−0.95
46–48	+3.70	−0.62
49–51	+4.44	−1.60
52–54	+0.71	−1.46
55–57	+2.23	−1.94
58–60	+0.86	−6.34

Source: J. W. B. Douglas, *The Home and the School*.

streamed changed to mixed ability groupings, the less able boys improved their exam performance whereas the change made no difference to the pass rate of the most able group (in 'Destreaming in a pressured academic environment'). The difficulty in making comprehensives genuinely comprehensive and in attaining equality of opportunity in education generally is basically due to the continuing effect of class. If 'the hereditary curse upon English education is its organization upon class lines'; this would seem to be as true now as when Tawney wrote these words in *Equality* in 1931.

Halsey, Heath and Ridge (in *Origins and Destinations*) conclude that education can bring expansion – higher standards more fairly shared:

> Education has changed society in this way, and can do more. It does so slowly against the stubborn resistance of class and class related culture. But it remains a friend of those who seek a more efficient, more open and more just society.

QUESTION: what would you do to achieve (a) equality and (b) excellence in the education system?

A sociology of the curriculum

For much of the post-war period the sociology of education dealt mainly with inequality of opportunity and tended to neglect what was actually being taught. In some of the literature which showed that working class children fared poorly at school it was implied that their home background did not prepare them for school and that this was due to inappropriate socialization at home (see Chapter 3 on the effects of early upbringing). Thus the further implication was that the home should adjust to the school rather than vice versa. Now the focus is more on the organization of knowledge at school, the key question being: how does the school through its control of the curriculum also control opportunity? (The sociological breakthrough in this new emphasis in the sociology of education was achieved with the book edited by Michael Young, *Knowledge and Control*, and this section draws on the book.)

At the outset it should be said that knowledge is not neutral or 'free floating' – it is defined, categorized, owned, controlled and patrolled. This is made clear in the next chapter, when the nature of medical professional knowledge is analysed, but at this stage the following propositions, based on Young's book, are advanced:

1 Some kinds of knowledge have higher status than other kinds. Knowledge is thus stratified by status – there is a hierarchy of knowledge (corresponding roughly to the social stratification of society generally).

2 Generally the higher status knowledge has an emphasis on:

    literacy;
    individualism (i.e. individual achievement);
    abstractness (theoretical);
    and it is not part of daily life.

    To illustrate this, consider which kind of knowledge or learning has the higher status in the following pairs:

    English literature or woodwork;
    an essay or a group project;
    pure maths or applied maths;
    a book on the theories of childhood socialization or a book on the practice of bringing up children.

3 Knowledge is controlled by its 'owners'. Each profession, for example, has its own area of expertise, each discipline its own knowledge.

4 The owners and controllers of the knowledge also control access to it. Thus a profession decides who shall be allowed to become student professionals. A school decides who shall be allowed to enter the top stream. It *appears* that these decisions are 'rational', 'scientific', and based on merit – but often they are not, as will be shown later.

5 Access to knowledge is controlled by status and not just by merit. A profession admits applicants on the basis of their GCE A Level results which *appear* to be a matter of merit. However, it is really a matter of the applicant having attended the right schools. This is because independent schools and high status comprehensive schools attain the best A level results. Similarly access to the top streams in a comprehensive school may be on the basis of IQ and aptitude tests and tests of maths and English, and again this *appears* to be a matter of merit. However, what these tests measure are mainly numeracy and literacy rather than manual dexterity, for instance (which is a lower status knowledge). These qualities are in turn the qualities developed in a middle class family, so that what these tests measure is in fact 'middle

classness' rather than the inherent intelligence of the child. Thus admission to the knowledge of the higher streams in a school (which in turn ensures admission to universities etc.) is again on the basis of status rather than of a true measure of merit. In short, 'definitions of intelligence arise from the power of certain sections of the middle class to define as worthy of high esteem (i.e. to define as intelligent) those skills that they themselves hold in comparison with skills held by others.' Thus:

IQ is not neutral;
it is based on values;
it is based on ideologies;
it is a management decision (it controls access to resources);
it is political (because it involves the use of power);
it is merely dressed up as a neutral, scientific/technical measure.

6 So far, then, the chapter has suggested that there is a hierarchy of knowledge, that is, that some kinds of knowledge have higher status than other kinds (for example, theoretical knowledge has higher status than practical knowledge). It has also suggested that, generally, higher status people are admitted to higher status knowledge (even though the admission tests –like IQ and A levels – purport to be fair, rational and 'scientific').

It follows that the hierarchy of knowledge in schools and throughout society corresponds to social hierarchy. A profession insists on high grade A level entrants not because this is essential for the professional skill but because it needs to attract high status entrants – generally those who have attended high status schools (which in turn get better A level results). It does not want to be known as a GCSE profession. This is not, of course, to suggest that you could become a doctor without understanding basic scientific concepts, for example. Nevertheless, it is the high status of the medical profession that attracts high status recruits. The high status of the medical profession comes from the high status of its members and the high status of the knowledge they possess.

The figure depicts a very simple classification of knowledge with its corresponding practitioners.

Having developed the concept of the sociology of knowledge as applied to the school curriculum, what is the usefulness of it? What does it tell us about what goes on in school and in society generally?

Firstly, it gives an indication of what the school classifies as higher status knowledge, for example, theoretical knowledge having a higher status than practical knowledge. Generally it will be found that higher status students are in the upper streams doing higher status subjects. In this way the focus may be changed from the alleged inadequate socialization in the working class home to the way knowledge is organized in the school. It helps to answer the question asked at the beginning of this section: how does the

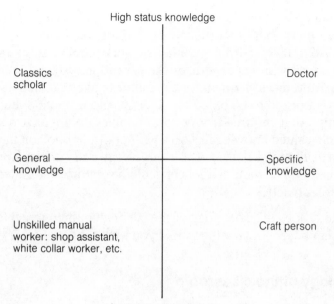

school, through its organization of knowledge and access to it, control opportunities? In all, it will be seen that schools are both people-processing organizations, and also knowledge-processing organizations.

Secondly, a sociology of knowledge shows that what is knowledge is what is defined as knowledge by powerful people or institutions – headteachers, universities and professional organizations for example. Here again one could contrast the 'elitist' and the 'pool of talent' viewpoints. The elitist viewpoint would stress the need to preserve excellence. It accepts the hierarchy of subjects and stresses that access to the highest status subjects, for example the classics, should be limited to the 'excellent'. There is thus an emphasis on exclusion (of the non-excellent). The pool of talent or equality viewpoint would show that we tend to mystify students with this hier-archical fragmentation of knowledge and thereby exclude able students of lower status. Supporters of this view would emphasize the inclusion of students.

Thirdly, in taking what is knowledge as problematic (questionable and to be investigated), new insights can be developed. For example, maths is what the teacher defines as maths and what the pupil accepts as maths. It depends on the power of the teacher to define a subject as maths. In general, the status of maths as knowledge is maintained by making it abstract. Twenty years ago maths problems were specific – what volume of water does a swimming pool hold? Nowadays the new maths emphasizes such abstract subjects as sets, base numbers, probability theory and so on. (This was the general comment by a group of inspectors from the Department of Education and Science in 1985.)

Young has shown how knowledge is defined, evaluated and controlled.

Later writers have built on this. Thus Bowles and Gintis in *Schooling in Capitalist America* show that school reproduces the social relationships of everyday life. It socializes people to work contentedly, rather than providing them with real expertise. The education system therefore reproduces and legitimizes inequality and attributes poverty to individual failing. All this is supposed to be based on objective merit – school performance. The reality is that children from poorer families do not have access to the more highly valued knowledge. (Another important book on the sociology of the curriculum is Michael Apple's *Ideology and Curriculum*, in which the author shows how the school curriculum supports and reflects existing ideologies in society.)

QUESTION: does this sociology of the curriculum help to explain what is going on in your school (or the school you went to)?

A sociology of the classroom

The sociology of the classroom looks at the different meanings given to the classroom situation by the pupils, teachers, headteachers and parents. It should be stressed that there is not one reality in a situation but several; what to the teacher is a matter of discipline is to the pupils a laugh, a break in the tedium.

Some writers have shown that pupils try to find out what teachers want in order to gratify their wishes and bask in their acceptance. Sometimes pupils concentrate on pleasing the teacher at the expense of the work, for example by giving wild answers. Cheating might be an example. For the pupil who has not done the homework, cheating can mean possible rewards and the avoidance of certain punishment. The teacher, of course, clamps down on cheating but does not notice feigned enthusiasm (it would be a threat to the teacher's professional competence). Feigning enthusiasm could be an example of the hidden curriculum – it is partly the result of pupils being taught to hide their feelings. Learning to give right answers is a further example of the hidden curriculum; as a result teaching becomes answer centred and therefore rigid.

The hidden curriculum
The formal curriculum comprises the official syllabus, for example the GCSE or A Level syllabus. This is what the student is officially expected to learn. But students also acquire the values and attitudes of the hidden syllabus. These are the values and attitudes that please the teacher, such as hard work and enthusiasm. Although these appear to be good values to acquire, this hidden curriculum could be seen as a means of social control: students are trained to conform, to be 'good', to accept authority unquestioningly. (See pp. 144–6 for more on the hidden curriculum.)

This desire to please may be especially true of middle class children. The middle class child may go on wanting to please even if the work is meaningless, but this is less true of the working class child who may prefer to 'play' in some way. 'Mucking about' may not be pointless to the child. It may be a means of overcoming the unpleasantness or boredom of school life. (The sociologist should not label any behaviour as 'pointless', 'mindless', 'senseless' or 'aimless' – the behaviour is something that needs to be understood.) Children may take part in the 'pointless' activity as a group, because it emphasizes togetherness and fortifies the group. So it is not really pointless at all.

The researcher may be interested in discovering what is good teaching or why some pupils have learning difficulties, but the first task of the sociologist is to discover what is really going on. Here is a sample of the methods of investigation that may be used:

1   Linguistic approach, studying the language used by participants to analyse hidden meanings.
2   Interactionist approach, studying how pupils and teachers define and give meaning to the situations in which they find themselves.
3   Sociometry. This is used to identify and measure relationships, showing for example who associates with whom. It could be used for identifying 'outsiders' and their characteristics.
4   Participant observation, living among the people you are observing. In this way the researcher can perhaps feel what it is like to be a pupil. (This could be a problem for ageing sociologists!) Participant observation ensures that the researcher's methods are '*grounded*' in reality (see pp. 318–19 for a more detailed description of participant observation).

Hammersley has argued that the classroom is the key site in which to explore the nature of schooling. It is surprising that until recently sociologists have shown little interest in classroom interaction, perhaps because it is so familiar. When we do look closely, it is clear that the parties have sharply differing perspectives: that features of classroom behaviour which seem unremarkable are by no means 'natural': they tell us a lot about the nature of the education system and the nature of society.

Trends in education policy

At the beginning of this chapter it was suggested that education policy could be analysed in terms of two viewpoints: the elitist view, which stresses excellence, and the pool of talent view, which stresses equality – that the full potential of students should be developed. Since the Education Reform Act 1988 there are many reasons for saying that government policy favours the elitist view, for example:

1   Allowing schools to 'opt out' of local education authority control and be financed from central government may result in two kinds of state

school: those under local authority for the mass of pupils, and the opted-out for the more able, or more socially 'privileged'.
2　The emphasis on examinations at 7, 11, 14 and 16 means extra hurdles, and in the past this has meant that pupils from poor backgrounds have a higher drop-out rate. Again the emphasis on exams is consistent with an elitist view of education.
3　The proposed City Technology Colleges, supported by local business people, are likely to become colleges for the more able, draining resources from remaining schools.
4　The national curriculum (of important subjects) is for the mass of schools, but independent schools are not affected; they can teach as they choose and they may emphasize more prestigious, non-vocational subjects such as the classics (see section headed 'A sociology of the curriculum').
5　There may in the long run be fewer university places in relation to college places overall. If this is the case it will again emphasize the elitist view of education. Polytechnics and other higher education colleges may be expanded on the cheap. However, this is conjectural at this stage.
6　There seems to be an increasing emphasis on education for work. Schools and colleges should prepare their students for work (rather than educate their students generally). This has been called the 'new vocationalism' and is for the mass of students. These students therefore will go on to such things as the Youth Training Scheme and the Technical and Vocational Education Initiative. The elite will continue to go to Oxford and Cambridge to do 'Greats' (Classics), PPE at Oxford (Politics, Philosophy and Economics), history and so on.

Sociologists have commented on the new vocationalism, for instance:

it is intended for the 14–18 age group;
it is aimed at the lower two-thirds of the ability range;
the new vocationalism does what the educational system has always done – it legitimizes inequality in society whether the inequality is based on ability, class, race or sex;
it is opposed by many educationalists, teachers and young people themselves.

(See, for example, A. Pollard, J. Purvis and G. Walford (eds), *Education, Training and the New Vocationalism*.)

Conclusions – what do schools really do?

This chapter has indicated that some of the common assumptions concerning education may not be completely true. Summarizing and evaluating these common assumptions may be a good way of concluding this chapter.

Common assumptions	Possible realistic assessment
1 There is a greater equality of opportunity now, especially since the 1944 Education Act and the introduction of comprehensive schools.	Virtually all the evidence shows that inequality of opportunity is as great now as it was at the beginning of the century.
2 Access to knowledge is open to those who seek it. Knowledge is or can be 'neutral' and/or 'rational', 'scientific' etc.	Some kinds of knowledge have higher status than other kinds. Access to knowledge is not open. Generally the higher your status, the higher the status of knowledge to which you have access.
3 The school is a rational organization whose main function is to educate the children.	The school as an organization is pervaded by managerial and professional ideologies which distort reality. Hence control (by the school) rather than, say, self-improvement may be emphasized; and similarly teaching rather than learning is stressed.
4 One of the main problems in the classroom is discipline. Truancy, vandalism and 'mucking about' in class seems to be pointless behaviour.	The main problem in the classroom in many schools is how to get through the day when it is the curriculum that seems pointless. Disruptive behaviour is not pointless to the sociologist who must try to investigate its true meaning.
5 The main tasks of the school are: a) to transmit useful knowledge and skills; b) to educate the pupils by introducing them to all kinds of knowledge and new experiences; c) to include the right values; to provide moral education.	The school does many other things as well, for example: a) pupils meet, form groups and widen their circle of friends; b) the school sometimes acts as a sort of marriage agency; c) schools act as a free baby sitting service – this is important for freeing mothers to go to work; d) in times of high unemployment, schools and colleges perform an important function in reducing the labour supply, thereby hiding the true extent of unemployment. QUESTION: would it be fair to say that this is one of the functions of the Youth Training Scheme?
6 Schools help to preserve the best in our social heritage, passing on what	Schools also preserve intellectual systems and the existing hierarchy of

Common assumptions	Possible realistic assessment
is best in our culture.	knowlege. They pass on accepted knowledge and tradition.
7 School prepares children for the world of work by providing a good education, vocational skills and self-discipline.	Children are socialized to the occupational role they are to fill. Thus schools in a working class neighbourhood help to socialize their pupils to a lifetime of manual work (see P. Willis, *Learning to Labour*). It follows that prestigious schools mould elites, socializing these children for leadership roles.

Overall the education system can be seen as a sorting and selecting agency for both people and knowledge, preserving and handing on traditionally accepted knowledge and selecting people for their place in the occupational hierarchy, thereby maintaining and reproducing the existing arrangements in society.

QUESTION: how much of all this is true of the school or college you attend (or used to attend)? For example, does your school emphasize 'control' rather than 'self-improvement' and 'teaching' rather than 'learning'?

For a discussion of gender and education, see Chapter 8. For a discussion of race and education, see Chapter 9.

Self-examination questions

1   What is meant by: 'equality', 'equality of opportunity', 'the curriculum', 'the sociology of the curriculum', 'streaming', 'labelling', 'self-fulfilling prophecy', 'hierarchy of knowledge', 'IQ tests', 'a sociology of the classroom'?
2   Argue the case for and against (a) the elitist view of education and (b) the equality or pool of talent view of education.
3   In what respects would you say this chapter relates to Chapter 3 on the socialization of young children?

Discussion topic

What measures would you advocate in your own school (or the school you went to) in order to encourage greater equality? You should examine especially any inequalities due to ability, class, race and gender.

Table 11.4 School leavers in England with A Level passes in selected subjects

Subject	Percentage of the 17-year-old age group						Percentage change 1976-77 to 1986-87		
	1976-77			1986-87					
	Boys	Girls	Total	Boys	Girls	Total	Boys	Girls	Total
Any subject	17.0	14.6	15.8	16.9	16.3	16.6	−1	+12	+5
English	3.3	6.5	4.9	2.6	6.4	4.5	−21	−2	−8
Maths	6.0	2.2	4.1	7.1	3.6	5.4	+18	+64	+32
Physics	5.5	1.2	3.4	5.6	1.6	3.6	+2	+33	+6
Chemistry	4.4	1.9	3.2	4.5	2.5	3.5	+2	+32	+9
Biological sciences	2.6	2.9	2.8	2.5	3.5	3.0	−4	+21	+7
Craft, design, technology and other sciences	1.2	0.2	0.7	1.4	0.4	0.9	+17	+100	+29
French	1.3	2.9	2.1	1.0	2.7	1.8	−23	−7	−14
History	3.4	3.5	3.5	3.0	3.2	3.1	−12	−9	−11
Geography	3.6	2.5	3.0	3.4	2.5	2.9	−6	–	−3
Creative arts	1.5	2.4	1.9	1.4	2.6	2.0	−7	+8	+5
Commercial and domestic studies	0.1	0.8	0.5	0.5	1.1	0.8	+400	+38	+60
General studies	3.8	2.4	3.1	4.4	3.3	3.8	+16	+38	+23

Source: *Department of Education and Science Statistics Bulletin*, December 1988

Projects

1 A number of concepts have been introduced in this chapter such as 'streaming', 'labelling', 'creaming off', 'vocationalism', 'hierarchy of knowledge', 'equality'. If you are a pupil or student, demonstrate whether these concepts apply to your own school or college and show their effect generally.

2 **Study Table 11.4 and answer the following questions.**

1 Are there some subjects that could be called 'girls' subjects and some that could be called 'boys' subjects? If so, identify them.
2 Is the gap between boys and girls getting bigger?
3 Can you relate this table to the concept of the hidden curriculum discussed earlier in this chapter, and also in Chapter 8?

Suggestions

The concept of the hidden curriculum may be important here – 'girls do this and not that'. Look at expectations of pupils, parents and teachers. Give examples – from your own experiences and from the reading.

For discussion of the hidden curriculum see pp. 144–6 and 214, and Glossary.

Past examination questions

1 **'The power of education systems to transform societies has been much exaggerated.' Discuss.**

Associated Examining Board, A Level, Autumn 1984.

Suggestions

Education alone cannot transform society because class is deeply entrenched – see Halsey et al. *Origins and Destinations*, as well as the earlier part of this chapter and Chapter 5 on stratification.

2 **There is a poor match between education and the world of work. We are less 'efficient' than our competitors overseas. Only 5.5% of the labour force in the UK are graduates compared with 7.1% in West Germany. Only 30% of British people have intermediate vocational qualifications (including apprenticeships), compared with about 60% in West Germany. (Adapted from *Society Today*, February 1982.)**

1 According to the above information, what percentage of the work force in Britain are graduates?   (1 mark)
2 According to the above information, what percentage of West Germans have intermediate vocational qualifications?   (1 mark)

3 Identify and explain two ways in which a British government might attempt to improve the 'efficiency' of education as a preparation for work? (4 marks)

4 Identify and explain the *other* functions of education apart from the preparation of young people for the world of work. (6 marks)

5 Many studies have shown that children from working class homes are less successful at school than those from middle class homes. Suggest reasons why this may be so. (8 marks)

Southern Examining Group, GCSE Specimen Question.

Suggestions

1 and 2 seem clear.

3 Many people would stress the need for education to be more attuned to the needs of industry and commerce. However, it might be argued that the real need would be to open up education more for the working class and to *try* to achieve more equality in education. This would avoid the present high waste of talent due to the fact that the education system does not enable students to develop their full potential. Also to try to improve the quality of education by making it less conventional and boring, and instead encourage critical thinking (as in sociology) and encourage students to work energetically at projects that interest them.

4 See list of common assumptions at end of chapter.

5 See text – also Chapter 3 on infant care.

3 **'Education merely reproduces the status quo.' What evidence from studies can be used to support or refute this statement?**

University of Cambridge Local Examinations Syndicate, A Level, Paper 2, June 1988.

Suggestions

See suggestions for question 1 and 'Trends in education policy' in this chapter.

4   *Item A*

The middle class parents take more interest in their children's progress at school than the manual working class parents do, and they become relatively more interested as their children grow older. They visit the school more frequently to find out how their children are getting on with their work, and when they do are more likely to ask to see the Head as well as the class teacher, whereas the manual working class parents are usually content to see the class teacher only. In this study, the level of the parents' interest in their children's work was partly based on comments made by the class teachers and partly on the records of the number of times each parent visited the schools to discuss their child's progress with the Head or class teacher. At both 8 and 11 years, but particularly at 11, the highest average scores in the tests are made by the children whose parents are the most interested in their education and the lowest by those whose parents are the least interested. (J. W. B. Douglas, *The Home and the School*.)

Item B

The following extract is from tape recordings made by a young teacher in her first term of teaching in an inner city New York elementary school with a high Negro/Puerto Rican enrolment.

'Mrs Jones, the 6th-grade teacher, and I were discussing reading problems. I said, "I wonder about my children. They don't seem too slow; they seem average. Some of them even seem to be above average. I can't understand how they can grow up to be 5th and 6th graders and still be reading on the 2nd-grade level. It seems absolutely amazing." Mrs Jones (an experienced teacher) explained about environmental problems that these children have. "Some of them never see a newspaper. Some of them have never been on a subway. The parents are so busy having parties and things that they have no time for their children. They can't even take them to a museum or anything" ... you have to remember that in a school such as ours the children are not as ready and willing to learn as in schools in middle class neighbourhoods.' (E. Fuchs, 'How Teachers Learn to Help Children Fail', in *Tinker, Tailor*, ed. N. Keddie.)

Item C

'Stanworth's (1983) analysis of A Level classes reports that, from the pupils' point of view, it is boys who stand out vividly in classroom interaction. Boys are, according to the pupils' reports, four times more likely than girls to join in discussion, or to offer comments in class. They are twice as likely to demand help or attention from the teacher, and twice as likely to be seen as 'model pupils'.

These sorts of differences were of equal relevance in the classes taught by women teachers. Boys were still the focus of attention. In addition, teachers reported that they identified more readily with boys and were more attached to them. They were more likely to reject girls and often assumed routinely that they would not pursue their studies because of marriage. (Adapted from Stephen Ball, *Education*.)

1 What criticisms could be made of the method, described in Item A, which is used to measure parents' interest in their children's work?   (4 marks)

2 Illustrating your answer with material from Items A and B, explain what is meant by 'cultural deprivation'.   (6 marks)

3 How useful is the concept of cultural deprivation to an understanding of differences in educational achievement?   (7 marks)

4 Using material from Item C and elsewhere, examine the influence of the 'hidden curriculum' on gender differences in education.   (8 marks)

Associated Examining Board, Specimen A Level Question for 1991 Syllabus

Suggestions

1 The middle class parents feel at home in the school and therefore visit often. The opposite is true of working class parents. The teachers appear to award labels according to their (middle class) values.

2   See Labov, 'The Logic of Non-Standard English', p. 38 (there is more than one culture).

3   Working class children and those from ethnic minorities fare poorly because they are judged by middle class (alien) standards – see also Swann Report, pp. 149–50.

4   See hidden curriculum – mentioned several times in text.

Further reading

S. Ball, *Education*

L. Barton and S. Walker (eds), *Gender, Class and Education*

L. Barton and S. Walker (eds), *Schools, Teachers and Teaching*

L. Barton, R. Meighan and S. Walker (eds), *Schooling, Ideology and the Curriculum*

R. G. Burgess, *Sociology, Education and Schools*

K. Chapman, *The Sociology of Schools*

M. Hammersley and A. Hargreaves, *Curriculum Practice*

D. Lawton, *Education, Culture and the National Curriculum*

*R. Meighan, *A Sociology of Educating*

A. Pollard, J. Purvis and G. Walford (eds), *Education, Training and the New Vocationalism*

*I. Reid, *Sociology of School and Education*

*P. Robinson, *Perspectives on the Sociology of Education*

*M. Stanworth, *Gender and Schooling*

B. Troyna, *Racial Inequality in Education*

G. Walford (ed.), *Doing Sociology of Education*

P. Woods, *Sociology and the School*

12   Medicine

Introduction

Sociology is now included in the curricula for medical students and other health professions. The General Medical Council (one of the governing bodies for doctors) has recommended that medical students should study social problems and the social context of the practice of medicine. One of the points emphasized in this chapter is that trends in disease and mortality may often have social origins; for example that people of a certain social class are more likely than people of another class to be affected by some diseases. The social context of medical practice is clear from a glance at the following topics to be dealt with in this chapter.

1   The relationship of social class to disease. Here investigations focus on groups at risk of certain diseases; for example bronchitis is prevalent among working class people.
2   The professions in medicine – in particular the dominant position of the doctors.
3   The hospital as an organization. The dehumanizing effects of the hospital, and the dominance of the medical ideology in hospitals.
4   The doctor–patient relationship. Does the doctor always understand the patient's problems?

There are of course other important areas that could be investigated under the heading of the sociology of medicine, for example the drug industry, medical research and so on; but to keep the subject matter within reasonable limits, it is the four areas listed above that will be examined here.

The relationship of social class to disease

Taking the first item, the social causes of disease, it can be shown that in the West there is a strong connection between social class and rates of illness and death. To examine this connection one could start at the beginning, the health of newly born babies and young children.

Table 12.1 shows that despite improvements in infant mortality rates over the years, the gap between the highest and lowest social classes

Table 12.1 Infant mortality by occupational class, 1975 and 1984

Deaths	Social class I and II		Social class IV and V		Rate for IV and V as percentage of rate for I and II	
	1975	1984	1975	1984	1975	1984
per thousand total births						
Stillbirths	7.9	4.2	12.6	7.2	159	168
Perinatal deaths	15.0	7.7	22.7	12.3	151	159
per thousand live births						
Neonatal deaths	8.3	4.3	12.3	6.5	148	148
Postneonatal deaths	3.1	2.5	6.4	4.5	202	178
Infant deaths	11.5	6.9	18.7	11.0	162	159

Source: calculated from Office of Population Censuses and Surveys data, by M. Whitehead in 'The Health Divide', Health Education Council, 1987, now published by Penguin.

remains very wide. Although these infant mortality rates have been related to social class, they also relate to poverty, stress in pregnancy, poor diet, housing, sanitation and poor educational attainment. In general, studies both in the USA and Britain demonstrate that working class women:

marry younger;

have more children;

have more illegitimate children;

suffer more overcrowding;

suffer more stress during pregnancy (an index for this is taken to be a higher accident rate among working class women).

More infants and young children are lost to working class mothers through:

respiratory diseases;

gastroenteritis;

accidents;

and all other major causes of infant death.

Furthermore, as the Newson studies (for example *Patterns of Infant Care*) and others show, working class mothers make substantially less use of:

antenatal clinics;

hospitals;

health visitors and other facilities;

immunization;

welfare foods (when these are available).

It is interesting to note that babies born into working class families are likely to have as many colds as those born to middle class parents, but are much more likely than babies from middle class families to suffer from pneumonia and all infectious diseases. It seems that infant sickness is likely to take a more serious turn, the lower one goes in class terms.

Turning from infant mortality and disease to the health of the population generally in Western society, it is clear that the better start in life given to middle class infants will result in their better health throughout their lives. In addition the same social factors that operate in their favour during their mother's pregnancy and in their infancy continue to operate into adulthood. Thus the effect of better diet, housing, education, and so on will continue to ensure better health to middle class people and a wide difference between the death and sickness rates for middle class people compared with the working class.

Thus Graph A confirms that standard mortality ratios are highest for social class V (unskilled manual workers). Standard mortality ratios compare the death rate within one group – say unskilled workers – with the population as a whole. Hence, for example, if the death rate within the group is the same as the population as a whole, the standard mortality ratio will be 100 (SMR = 100).

Graph B shows manual working class people consult the doctor more and report more chronic illness than non-manual workers.

Looking at the social causes of these class differences, two factors could be examined: *diet* and *stress*. Studies show that the poor eat:

less fruit than the rich;
fewer green vegetables;
less carcass meat;
more potatoes;
more cereals and white bread;
more sugar.

Such a diet may be deficient in some essential elements, especially vitamins and fibre, while containing too much 'stodgy' food (for example white bread and sugar). Table 12.2 shows that the lowest income group – D – consumes more of the less nutritious foods.

There is also evidence of higher consumption of sweets by children in lower social groups.

The links between nutrition and health are many and varied, ranging from effects on growth to links with specific diseases like coronary heart disease and obesity, to general resistance to infections, most of which are also class related.

It might be objected that diet is not a *social* cause of disease. Diet is surely just the items of food that people eat? Just persuade poorer people to change their diet, through advertising campaigns and health education, and thereby ensure better health.

Graph A Mortality of men of working ages (16–64) by social class in England and Wales, 1981–83.

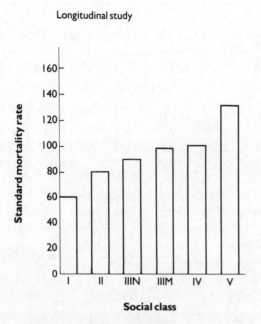

Source: drawn from Office of Population Censuses and Surveys data, see references 17 and 19.

Graph B Percentage of male population reporting chronic sickness by socioeconomic group, 1984.

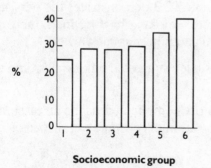

Source: General Household Survey; reprinted in M. Whitehead, *The Health Divide.*

Table 12.2 Food consumption in Great Britain by income group, 1976 and 1984 (ounces per person per week)

Food	Income group							
	A		B		C		D	
	1976	1984	1976	1984	1976	1984	1976	1984
White bread	19.8	12.3	26.2	18.3	30.4	23.0	29.9	26.0
Brown bread (including wholemeal)	4.1	8.0	3.0	6.0	3.0	5.9	2.7	5.2
Sugar	12.3	8.0	13.4	9.4	14.5	10.9	15.7	11.5
Total fats	9.8	9.1	10.5	9.5	11.0	10.4	11.0	10.0
Fruit (fresh)	22.5	25.3	18.3	19.0	15.2	16.0	15.2	13.0
Vegetables (fresh)	27.3	30.7	24.0	24.4	24.8	25.5	24.9	21.5
Potatoes	29.8	33.4	35.0	36.5	38.2	42.4	42.3	48.3

Note: A is the highest income group.

Source: MAFF, *Household Food Consumption and Expenditure* for 1976 and 1984, references 172 and 173.

In practice it is not as simple as that. Diet is not just a collection of foods. It is a social phenomenon. It reflects a way of life. Three extreme examples illustrate this, heavy drinking, heavy smoking (which is part of diet) and overeating. Diet generally can be looked upon as a habit. This habit is passed on in the family, especially from mother to daughter. To some extent we are what we eat, but we also eat certain foods because we are that kind of person and this in turn reflects our social class, race and religion. (Think of kosher food, Moslem non-drinking, the importance of fish and chips in a working class diet and so on.) Table 12.3 demonstrates the persistence of habit. It shows that whilst cigarette smoking has declined, there are still great differences between manual and non-manual workers.

So far a simple proposition has been suggested linking class and disease:

Class → Disease

But really the true position is more complicated, as the discussion of diet indicates, and the following proposition may be more realistic:

Social class → { Diet, Stress, Working conditions, Housing, Education } → Disease

Table 12.3 Adult[1] cigarette smoking in Great Britain: by sex and socioeconomic group

Socioeconomic group	Percentage smoking cigarettes			
	Males		Females	
	1972	1986	1972	1986
Professional	33	18	33	19
Employers and managers	44	28	38	27
Intermediate and junior non-manual	45	28	38	27
Skilled manual and own account non-professional	57	40	47	36
Semi-skilled manual and personal services	57	43	42	35
Unskilled manual	64	43	42	33
All persons[2]	52	35	42	31
Average weekly cigarette consumption per smoker (numbers)	120	115	87	97

[1] Persons aged 15 or over in 1972, but 16 or over in later years.
[2] Includes members of the armed forces, people in inadequately described occupations and all people who have never worked.
Note: based on sample size of 10,304.
Source: *Social Trends 1989*.

Caution – stress can damage your health

When examining the causes of illness it would probably be true to say that the professions in medicine and indeed the public itself would concentrate on the physical aspect of disease, including diet and genetic inheritance. We use what has been called 'the medical model'. This focuses on the organic disorder and specific symptoms, and often omits the patients' thoughts, social background, social status and social class. It emphasizes pathology (the cause of the disease), even though for most of the 'killer' diseases we do not know the cause.

What can sociology offer here? Basically it can show the effects of stress in the patients' lifestyles leading to disease. Thus stress is greatest among the poor because it is associated with bad housing, and poor conditions at work. It is reflected in higher accident rates both at home and work. This is the theme of Jeannette Mitchell's book *What is to be Done about Illness and Health?*, in which she tries to show how stress damages our health. She carried out a survey asking people about their work in order to try to find out the relationship between stress and illness.

In thinking about what damages our health and what keeps us well, eight key dimensions emerge:

1 *How much we are exposed to a hazardous environment*, both inside and outside work. Andrew's story (one of the interviewees in Mitchell's study) graphically illustrates how hazardous work can be. He points out how many untested chemicals are currently in use in factories and how many products now in use may also turn out to be dangerous to the consumer.

2 *How exhausted our work inside and outside the home makes us*, and how much time and space we have for recuperation. Ethel (another interviewee in this case study) remarks that since bonus schemes were introduced her sons seem to come home more tired than her husband used to. Shan describes the exhaustion of sweatshop work, especially where there is no union protection. She also points out that where women are working a double shift – going out to work then doing the housework, as Ethel was, particularly in the period when she was going twice a day to do office cleaning – the exhaustion is intensified. Looking after children can be exhausting in itself, especially if it means losing sleep.

3 *How much money we take home*. Overtime, bonus schemes and the rest may be exhausting, but they are often the only way to make enough money to live on. Money buys housing, which also means space so we don't get on top of one another. It buys gardens, which means having somewhere safe for children to play. It buys weekends in the country and holidays for relaxation. *It brings freedom from financial worries* and opens up the number of choices you can make about your life and thus the degree to which you can feel in control of it. All of these are very important to health.

4 *How many worries we have* and how deep and sustained they are. Worries about work, about losing your job, about your children's future, about the dangers of walking in the streets, about how to pay the bills, about getting the gas cut off, about breaking the law to make ends meet, and about illness can all affect our health. It is worse when they all come together and if there seems no way out.

5 *How hopeful or hopeless we feel*. How hopeful we feel for the future affects how much we are prepared to invest in our own health now. Feeling positive about things is a precondition of taking exercise, changing what you eat, or giving up addictions, including tranquillizers, food and tobacco. If you don't see things getting better, if you can't look forward to holidays, or getting a job, or being able to enjoy having children or retirement, if you feel stuck, taking an interest in your own wellbeing is the last thing you want to do.

6 *How powerless or powerful we feel*. Both Ruth and Vera identify their own powerlessness as a factor in their ill health in Mitchell's book. Vera

talks of women not feeling they have a right to influence events beyond their own front door. What we want is to be powerful not in the sense of controlling other people, but in the sense of feeling in control of our own lives.

7 *How bored or alienated we feel.* George and Baden describe how destructive monotonous work can be, and how not feeling in control of what you are making, whether it is a tractor or a machine tool, leaves a hollow feeling. They both say that making something you can take no pride in is soul-destroying.

8 *How lonely or loved we feel.* The loss of someone close to you, as Ruth lost her friend, has long been recognized as having consequences for our health. Spouses often die within a short period of one another. Loss is also a major factor in depression and in increasing vulnerability to illness. Equally, having someone to talk to and share our feelings with can make us less likely to become ill. But it is not just very intimate and family relationships which affect us; so does having workmates and neighbours to be friends with. Vera contrasts the isolation of the tower blocks with the friendliness of the old neighbourhoods. Ethel also regrets her present isolation, looking back on the time when she was able to sit out with her neighbours.

We tend to concentrate on the negative poles of the eight dimensions. But their positive poles – a clean and safe environment, time for rest and recreation, reasonable living standards, freedom from chronic worry, hope for the future, self-confidence and autonomy, fulfilling work and opportunities for friendship, support and intimacy – also provide a framework for thinking about the minimum conditions for health a reasonable society should work for.

Sociologists and psychologists are also interested in the link between individual life events and disease and this will be considered next.

Life events and disease

Life events such as divorce, a death in the family, loss of a job, moving house and so on have been associated with the onset of disease. The theories seem to be of two main kinds (as is pointed out in D. Tuckett (ed.), *An Introduction to Medical Sociology*):

1 The *triggering* effect of life events on disease. This states that the disease would have occurred sooner or later and that the life event merely triggered off the disease. This can be seen as a *genetic* theory of disease. The disease was, so to speak, part of the person, presumably passed on from parents, and it was the life event (such as a bereavement) that 'set it off'.

2   The *formative* role of the life event: life events play a formative role over
    a long period, gradually predisposing the person towards the disease.
    Clearly this is an *environmental* type of theory of disease.

Possibly both types of theory have some validity; but the differences in
mortality and disease between the social classes seem to indicate the
importance of formative factors over a lifetime. In other words, people in all
social classes are likely to experience similar life events (loss of a parent
etc.); therefore the fact that people in lower social classes have higher death
and disease rates seems to point to environmental factors as being most
likely to account for these differences.

The following example illustrates the type of study made of social causes
of disease (quoted in *An Introduction to Medical Sociology*). Japan has one
of the lowest rates of coronary heart disease in the world and the USA has
one of the highest. However, Japanese people living in the USA have the
same rates of heart disease as the general population of the USA (in Hawaii
the heart disease rate for Japanese people is half way between the
American and Japanese rates). Here we have people of the same race with
different rates of heart disease. What explanation would you give?

Summarizing so far, it has been emphasized that:

1   Disease is closely related to social class.
2   Infant mortality is lowest for the professional and managerial classes
    (and correspondingly highest for the unskilled manual class).
3   The mortality rates for *all* major diseases are lowest for the professional
    and managerial classes.
4   Sickness rates are lowest for the professional and managerial classes.
5   These differences are related to the different life styles that the different
    social classes experience (and endure). Thus the greater mortality in
    working class people has been related to their poorer diet and greater
    stress.
6   Sociologists tend to emphasize that disease may be brought on by a
    poor environment (bad housing, poor diet etc.) rather than genetic
    factors alone.

The professions in medicine

What is the importance of the professions? Why are they studied here in a
chapter dealing with the sociology of medicine?

Professions are important in the study of the sociology of medicine
because of the overwhelming influence of the medical profession: its
influence over other professions like nursing; and its influence over all of
us, especially during our encounters with doctors.

Two basic questions will be considered in this section. Firstly, why is the medical profession so influential? Secondly, what is the ideology of the medical profession? The next two sections then continue this theme by looking at the influence of the medical profession in hospital, and finally by examining the doctor–patient relationship.

Why is the medical profession so powerful?

Professions are strong partly because their members are socialized to their professional role during their training. Thus during the course of training they have acquired not only technical expertise but also the 'correct' professional personality. The training, the examinations, the transition from lay person to professional, are like a shared ordeal which binds aspiring professionals to their chosen profession and to each other. In this way medical students become committed to the medical profession. If this is true of most professions, how much more true is it of the medical profession with its long training period, heavy work overload at medical school, and the stress of life or death decisions?

Two well known studies of medical schools in the USA illustrate these points. Firstly Howard Becker and his associates in their book *Boys in White* show the importance of the student group. In the face of stressful problems, particularly work overload, medical students turn to each other for support and this helps to bind the members of the group to one another. Mutual support helps to give a sense of identity and common purpose and all this helps to make the medical profession strong.

In another study Robert Merton and his associates showed the importance of professional socialization (the process by which the student acquires the values of the profession). It helps the medical student to deal with anxiety and uncertainty. It also instils correct medical values and helps the individual to be self-reliant. (See *The Student Physician*.)

The medical profession is further strengthened by the actual circumstances of practice. It is natural that a professional person is in a powerful position *vis-à-vis* the lay person. Not only does the professional possess knowledge not available to the client, but the client when consulting a professional is usually in an emotional state of mind. Something needs putting right, and the professional has to be trusted. This is true when seeing the dentist, optician, lawyer or accountant. Again, how much more true this is when seeing the doctor; the knowledge gap is greater and the matter is usually of more vital personal concern. (In addition a doctor has a legal monopoly. Only a doctor can practise medicine; medical records are usually secret from the patient; etc.)

If the medical profession itself is strong, the other professions in medicine are weak. They are what Etzioni called semi-professions, especially nursing (see A. Etzioni (ed.), *The Semi-Professions*).

The characteristics of a semi-profession are that the period of training is short, the majority of members are women, and the employers are large bureaucracies (e.g. hospitals). Nursing, like social work and teaching, has all these characteristics (though in the USA it is becoming more professional-ized through graduate entry). In Britain some nurses are members of the Royal College of Nursing, which is a professional body and does not support strikes; others are members of health service trade unions. A profession that has a secure status does not need to rely on a trade union type organization to support its power. The nursing profession does not quite fit into this category.

Finally the medical profession is influential because, having a high status itself, it tends to attract high status recruits.

Because the medical profession is so powerful it tends to influence the way the rest of us think. The consequences of this are considered in the next section.

What is the ideology (if any) of the medical profession?

Really all professions have ideologies or beliefs about themselves and their work; they tend to see the world through their 'occupational spectacles'. These ideologies, while not untruths, tend to be distortions or exaggera-tions of the truth. Because the medical profession is so powerful its profes-sional ideologies tend to be accepted by the rest of us.

What is the ideology of the medical profession? Probably its basic ideology is the 'cure' ideology – that is, the overemphasis on cures, rather than emphasizing preventive medicine and the improvement of social conditions.

One way of showing what the ideology of the medical profession is and how it affects patients and the rest of us is to examine some of the common assumptions many professionals seem to make. These common assump-tions will now be considered (they are based on Ian Kennedy's book *The Unmasking of Medicine*). (Again, readers should ask themselves whether these really are common assumptions.)

Common assumption one: *'normal' is an objective observable fact*

At the beginning of the century the 'normal' life expectancy for men was about 48 years. This is the 'normal' life expectancy in many parts of the world today. It is 'normal' to expect people under stress like the harassed or isolated mother or the factory worker with heavy boring work to 'cope' instead of rebelling. ('Coping', like 'normal' is another 'good' word.) It is clear though that what is normal is not an objective fact. It is defined by society and by institutions in society, like the medical profession, and the definition of normal changes over time and between societies.

Normality versus mental illness

'Very often, people who deviate from society's norms are classified as mentally ill. In this sense it is a means of social control. Thus, Victorian women who deviated from that society's chaste norms were "nymphomaniacs"; Soviet citizens who are not unreservedly devoted to the ideals of the Marxist–Leninist system are described as "schizophrenics".

What is happening here, sociologists say, is that people are becoming labelled – a social process that can have a devastating effect on an individual. Once a Soviet dissident, say, has been labelled as mentally ill, then everything he subsequently does can be seen in that light. Despite his denials, he begins to feel uncertain, not least because his perception of himself is affected by the way other people see him. It may not be long before he really does start to suffer from mental illness, which is exactly what the authorities want.' (*New Society*, 8 November 1984.)

Common assumption two: *illness is a technical term, a matter of objective fact*

To say a person is ill implies there is a normal state of health, but just as normality is not an objective fact, neither is normal health, and neither is the definition of illness. It has been shown that the poor suffer worse health than the better off, but we accept this higher rate of illness as normal. Quite often, therefore, people are 'ill' because they are poor, badly housed, badly fed or work at depressing jobs. The doctor cannot cure this but we abdicate to the doctor the power to define health, with the result that it is predominantly defined in terms of illness – definitions which the medical professions themselves create – rather than bad social conditions.

Common assumption three: *doctors should 'cure' patients who are ill*

Of course they should! But this overstresses the power of science, seeing the sick person like a car that needs repairs. Really, the ills that kill us before our time are not readily amenable to cure. Medicine tends to ignore how this state of affairs has come about. The emphasis on cures is part of a medical ideology. This can be seen in the quantity of resources that goes into hospitals, and their expensive equipment, compared with the resources of preventative medicine. Hospitals are the epitome of the cure ideology, yet if school health care, antenatal care, health education, community health care and so on were given greater prominence, less would need to be spent on hospitals. Even more fundamental than this, if there were less inequality in society there might be less disease, as the first part of this chapter indicates. Thus if people in social class V had the same life and health chances as people in social class I this would considerably raise life expectancy overall. This does not require new scientific research, better cures, or even better preventative medicine. Perhaps what is really required is a determination to work for a more equal and just society.

Common assumption four: *good health is largely a matter of good luck – especially in having healthy parents*

There was a considerable improvement in health in Western countries in the nineteenth century through better housing, diet and sanitation. This was not good luck (nor especially due to the advance of medicine). Today some of the main causes of ill health are diet, smoking, alcohol, accidents, bad working conditions, monotonous jobs and unemployment. The doctor cannot improve these, but society can if it has the will. But there are powerful lobbies against improvement – food manufacturers, tobacco manufacturers, brewers etc., and commercial pressures which limit funds.

Every reduction in the school meals subsidy and in state benefits for food, fuel and clothing, or every time school crossing wardens are dispensed with, increases ill health and death in children. This is especially true in social class V, where five times as many children as in class I die between the ages of one and ten.

Common assumption five: *the doctor knows best – he (or she) is the expert*

Of course the doctor is the expert, but on the other hand the patient is the consumer and should be able to complain and take court action where there is negligence. At present this is difficult and the medical profession says, quite rightly, that it safeguards professional standards itself. However, professional self-policing may not be an adequate safeguard. The consumer should have more power (we should not be put off consumerism by some of the sensational court cases in the USA where high damages are awarded against doctors for negligence).

Instead of consumerism we seem to have the opposite in Britain, the idea that the professional knows best. The lay person (patient, client, pupil, etc.) is more or less helpless. This is a theme of Ivan Illich's writings, particularly *Disabling Professions* and *Medical Nemesis*. He describes, for example, the patient who is helpless in the face of the expert knowledge of the doctor. A similar theme is pursued by Ann Oakley in *Women Confined*, which speaks of the medicalization of childbirth: the emphasis on its technical aspects rather than the mother's feelings. She calls for an end to unnecessary

Patients should complain more
Source: *New Society*, 3 May 1984

medical intervention in childbirth, a redomestication of birth and a return to female-controlled childbirth.

These five assumptions – and the list could be lengthened – can be seen as part of the ideology of the medical profession. They are what most doctors (and most lay people) believe to be true. But these beliefs and common assumptions are ideological, not because they are inherently untrue (there is a strong element of truth in all of them) but because of the objections set out in Chapter 1, in particular that they are exaggerations of the truth and are used to justify power, in this case the power of the medical profession.

Physicians, heal yourselves

'Since September 1981, patients have had a new right to complain about their treatment in hospital. For the first time they could question a doctor's clinical judgement without having to sue him through the courts.

It was an important development for the consumer. The health service ombudsman regularly had to reject most complaints made to him because they were clinical matters which were outside his jurisdiction. Pressure to have them brought within his jurisdiction, from the Parliamentary Select Committee on the Ombudsman among others, was strongly resisted by the doctors.

Most complainants want nothing more than to be dealt with on equal terms: to be told exactly what happened and why, to be offered an apology where appropriate, and an assurance that the same thing won't happen to anyone else. But the ethos of medical paternalism dies hard.' (Jeremy Laurance, *New Society*, 3 May 1984)

None of this is to deny the professional altruism of the vast majority of doctors. However, medical ideology (summed up in its overemphasis on 'cure') could be a barrier to better health. The task of the sociologist is to show the real situation, that while the medical view is not untrue there are other 'truths', other realities, and that a realization of these other 'truths' will lead to improvements in health.

The effects of medical ideologies will now be examined in two settings, the hospital and the doctor/patient relationship.

Hospitals – a sociological view

Sociologists would probably stress two particular aspects of the modern hospital. Firstly, it is a large organization with many interdependent parts. Secondly, the medical profession (with its ideology) is dominant.

On the first point, the growing complexity of the modern hospital could itself be seen as an aspect of medical ideology, the emphasis on cures. This in turn leads to more 'scientific' hospitals, new technology, new specialisms, greater division of labour and the remoteness of the patient.

The growing complexity of the hospital as an organization can lead to the sort of malfunctions that affect all organizations. For example, there is what has been called 'goal displacement'. This simply means that the means have become more important than the ends. Thus there may be an overemphasis on procedure. Bed making, cleaning, meal time routines, all important things in themselves, become overemphasized so that the hospital loses sight of its goal, the well being and cure of the patients and their restoration to good health. Take one example, the waking of patients at 6 or 7 a.m. Despite protests from nurses that 'it has changed now' this is still common practice. (This denial is itself an interesting phenomenon to investigate, if the staff concerned have closed their eyes to the facts.) But why in any case wake patients who have been sedated (perhaps because of pain) and new and expectant mothers who need the sleep? The answer is basically that this suits the needs of the organization (not the patients' needs). In this example, it may be that the consultant is likely to visit the ward at about 11 a.m. Everything then works back from this time, allowing, say, half an hour each for washing patients, changing bed linen, breakfast, medicaments, cleaning the ward and so on, which brings reveille back to about 8 a.m., but say 7 a.m. to be on the safe side.

The hospital as an organization suffers other defects arising from the effects of oligarchy. Oligarchy is rule by the few at the top – with the many following set instructions. Oligarchy also implies hierarchical rules, chains of command with orders filtering down and information going up. This again is likely to result in depersonalization of the patient – in treating the patient as a case. Studies show this is most marked where the patient is helpless or where choice is the exclusive prerogative of management. Here the patient's rights are determined by management's interpretation of the rules. Thus, Tuckett reports a study that suggests that if patients were defined by the hospital as terminal cases, then this gave the clue as to how they should be treated, with a custodial type of treatment; plans to discharge them were seen as disruptive activities (in R. Coser, *Alienation and the Social Structure: A Case Analysis of a Hospital*). Clearly bureaucracy, labelling of patients, strict medical discipline, hierarchy, and the helplessness of the patient, are part of the everyday life of the hospital.

Is 'democracy' or 'consumer sovereignty' possible in a hospital? Possibly not, because hospitals are mostly large organizations and because of the necessity of medical discipline. In addition the patients, because they are relatively helpless, may not notice that their helplessness is increased by the 'logic' of the organizational requirements of the hospital.

As in the previous section on the medical profession, it is not intended that these comments should be seen as censuring the conscientious staff of hospitals. However, it is the task of the sociologist to describe what is really going on, especially from the patient's viewpoint. This is what is being attempted here.

" Could you tell me how Mr Smith in ward 10 is doing ? "

Patients should be kept informed
Source: *Sunday Express*, 20 October 1985

Another aspect of the hospital as an organization is the dominance of the medical profession. Much of the decision making is either by the doctors or takes account of doctors' wishes (although the medical profession accounts for only about 4 per cent of the staff of hospitals in Britain).

This may seem natural enough at first sight. The doctors are in the front line. But again this implies a 'cure' ideology – doctors can cure disease if given the right tools and enough resources. However, because much ill health is due to environment and to our habits, diet, smoking, alcohol,

monotonous work etc., a cure ideology and the complex medical technology that go with it may be inappropriate to deal with this kind of health
problem. Yet hospitals with their expensive equipment, specialist staff and
cure ideology take up 70 per cent of national health service resources in
Britain. Incidentally there are few applicants for posts dealing with the care
of non-curable patients – the mentally handicapped and the elderly.

QUESTION: what is the reason for the lack of interest in posts dealing with
non-curable patients? (A possible answer is that these posts lack status
because there are no medical 'cures' in this type of work.)

One other aspect of hospitals should be mentioned. Doctors have their
careers to think of. Many, quite understandably, are ambitious and may
wish to become consultants. Table 12.4 shows that teaching hospitals seem
to have higher prestige and get more interesting patients than other
hospitals. Will doctors be hurt if we ask: is medicine blind to class and
prestige?

QUESTION: it seems teaching hospitals get the 'fitter', high status patients
and more medically 'interesting' patients. Do you agree?

Finally, consider the quotation given in the box, which seems to be
saying: spend less on the latest medical technology but spend more and
more on improving the quality of life of the chronically sick.

Table 12.4 Admissions to hospitals

Kind of hospital	Planned admission	Emergency
Teaching	72%	23%
Other	18%	77%

Kind of hospital	Social class I or II	Social class IV, V
Teaching	70%	40%
Others	30%	60%

Kind of hospital	% Up to age 64	% 75 or over
Teaching	59%	28%
Others	41%	72%

Kind of hospital	% Congestive heart failure	Other
Teaching	12%	66%
Others	88%	34%

Source: R. Meighan et al., *Perspectives on Society*

Why does the cost of the NHS keep rising?
'It is this combination of an increasingly elderly population, and the growing scope for alleviating even those conditions which cannot be cured, that may help to explain some of the current frustrations within the NHS. Technology is just about the ability of doctors to save lives expensively: heart transplants and such-like. But it is also about improving the quality of life: plastic joint replacement surgery is perhaps the best example (and a warning that yesterday's "high" technology can become today's routine procedure). So the sense of crisis within the NHS may reflect not so much a fall in standards or a cut in service, but a growing gap between what can be done and what could be done.' (R. Klein, 'Is the NHS really in crisis?', *New Society*, 3 November 1983)

An important question in the sociological view of hospitals is who controls the expensive technology in a modern hospital – who decides to buy it in the first place?

Navarro has argued that technology, including medical technology, depersonalizes relationships between the expert and the client. Thus Oakley (see above) has written of the medicalization of childbirth, a natural occurrence that has become medicalized, making the mother helpless. Some sociologists believe that technology, rather like science and medicine itself, is not neutral or natural but can be used to further the power of highly influential managers and professionals (doctors in this case). Waitzkin suggests that medical workers simplify the working of the body, use jargon in their explanations and reproduce relations of super-subordination with patients. Thomas McKean in *The Role of Medicine* shows that contrary to popular belief medical technology has done little to reduce deaths from infectious diseases in the last 150 years. It was public health measures like sewers and clean water that did this. Today we can keep people alive longer with improved technology, but really we should also try to improve the quality of their lives – help the infirm, ensure adequate income, provide home helps, etc. – a shift from curing to caring.

The doctor/patient relationship

Two assumptions in particular about this relationship will be considered, and they will be considered together.

Common assumptions six and seven:
sick people will see the doctor and have their sickness diagnosed; medicine is blind to class

Before receiving medical treatment there are a number of stages to pass through:

Does the person have a disease?
Is he or she aware of it?
Report it to the doctor.
Is it acted upon?

This appears to be obvious and should not cause any difficulty. However one American study showed that for every person receiving medical treatment for a given illness, there was at least one other person who was not getting treatment for the disease. Generally studies show there is much under-reporting of disease to the doctor. Often people without disease symptoms consult the doctor, while many with disease symptoms do not consult. The recognition of symptoms, the tolerance of pain, and the tolerance of disruption in daily life are cultural matters. One study indicated that when in pain Italian patients called for pain relief and were mainly concerned with the analgesic effects of the drug. Jewish patients were reluctant to accept the drug due to a concern about the effects of the drug on general health. Other studies confirm these cultural differences in the experience of pain and the reporting of symptoms. The experience of childbirth, for example, seems to differ from culture to culture. In some societies women till the fields soon after bearing a child.

The interview with the doctor is a social accomplishment which some people achieve more easily than others. Some people are not good at getting to the point quickly, others do not report fully and so on. Studies show that doctors cut short interviews, often unintentionally.

The sick role
Being sick seems to be a natural event, yet Talcott Parsons thought this process should also be studied sociologically. He saw the sick role as a sort of deviance (from the 'normal'). The doctor legitimates the sick role and the patient is exempted from normal social responsibilities (can take time off from work etc.). Three criticisms could be made of the concept of the sick role. Firstly, as shown in the main text, not all people who are ill claim the sick role. Secondly, it assumes doctor and patient agree to the sick role whereas it is really the doctor who decides; and thirdly, sometimes the sick role is conferred when it should not be, for example, the worker or housewife under stress. They may be given medicine, whereas really a change in the social conditions that oppress them is what is really required (yet it would be cruel of the doctor not to offer medicine for their condition).

What would you say is wrong in the following tape recorded conversation?

Doctor: Apart from these palpitations you're really very healthy, aren't you?

Patient: Yes, yes. Well, I mean, I have varicose veins, you know?

Doctor: Oh yes.

Patient: And I've got a small ulcer, but it's dry now.

Doctor: Mm.

Patient: On my right leg I have a small ulcer.

Doctor: Yes, that's very good.

Patient: But it's drying up gradually. One day I think it's gone completely but it hasn't. It comes back. But . . .

Doctor: Now here's the letter to see about your eyes . . . Righto, well that's it. Very good.

Patient: One or two other aches and pains, but I suppose that's old age, I suppose? A bit of rheumatism in my shoulder.

Doctor: OK.

Patient: As I say, the thing is that, well, this here, though I've had these pains I've felt so good in myself, you know . . .

Doctor: That's right.

Patient: I've had – well . . .

Doctor: That's right, if you develop further trouble come back. Otherwise you don't need to, just keep going.

(A. Cartwright, 'Social Class Variation in Health Care', reproduced in D. Tuckett (ed.), *An Introduction to Medical Sociology*, p. 204.)

Generally, working class people are less likely to consult the doctor and various reasons have been suggested for this:

they are more stoic;
they may be less health conscious;
they cannot take time off from work;
they experience the medical profession as alien;
there is a greater emphasis on 'coping' in the working class;

Table 12.5   General practice consultations with middle and working class patients aged 65 and over

	Middle class	Working class
Average length of consultation (minutes)	6.2	4.7
Average number of questions asked by patient	3.7	3.0
Average number of problems discussed with doctor	4.1	2.8
Average number of symptoms mentioned to interviewer prior to consultation	2.2	3.0

Source: Patrick and Scrambler in *Sociology as Applied to Medicine*

Table 12.6 People with no natural teeth: by social class and age, 1968 and 1978, England and Wales (percentages)

Age groups	Social class						All persons	
	Professional, intermediate, and skilled (non-manual)		Skilled manual		Partly skilled and unskilled			
	1968	1978	1968	1978	1968	1978	1968	1978
16–24	1	–	2	–	–	1	1	–
25–34	2	1	7	5	13	6	7	3
35–44	12	7	24	14	34	14	22	12
45–54	31	18	43	34	49	38	41	29
55–64	51	39	64	51	72	61	64	48
65–74	65	65	87	76	80	85	79	74
75 and over	81	81	92	84	91	95	88	87
All ages	27	21	34	28	46	37	37	29

Source: Office of Population Censuses and Surveys, *Adult Dental Health*, Volume 1

many services are not easily available, e.g. on a housing estate without
  public transport;
lack of information.

Table 12.5 suggests that doctors may spend less time with working class
people.

Finally, there is also severe under-utilization of preventative services by
working class people, for example, various screening services, chiropody,
immunization, dentistry and the optician. Table 12.6 helps to illustrate this
point. (What does this table indicate?)

Once again, the aim here has been simply to try to describe what is really
going on. This is difficult in medicine because of the mystique surrounding
it and because it is so personal. Generally it has been shown that health is
not solely a medical matter. The sociologist has much to contribute.

Conclusions

1   The Health Education Council in 1981 set out the inequalities of health
    in the report of that title. The 'Health Divide' 1987, another report of
    the Health Education Council, demonstrates that these inequalities
    persist.
2   Little action has been taken to reduce these inequalities in health.
3   The medical profession is very powerful and its 'cure' ideology
    permeates the health service.
4   Following from point 3 above, we tend to accept the 'medical model'
    with its 'scientific' approach to disease and its emphasis on 'cures' rather
    than the importance of preventative medicine, good housing and
    improvements in the standard of living.
5   Perhaps we should concentrate more on how individuals feel, how they
    define illness; how they decide whether or not to see the doctor in the
    first place.
6   Overall, we need to attack poverty and gross inequality in society. This,
    more than 'miracle cures', will substantially improve the health of the
    nation.

Self-examination questions

(See text for answers)
1   What sort of topics would the sociology of medicine examine?
2   What is meant by: 'illness', 'normal', 'standard mortality ratio', 'diet', 'stress',
    'triggering effect', 'formative effect', 'professional socialization', 'the semi-
    professions', 'preventive medicine', 'consumerism', 'medical ideologies',
    'sick role', and 'epidemiology'?

3   What are the reasons for the predominance of the medical profession and what are the effects?

Projects

1 **Read the following passage and answer these questions:**

1   Do inequalities in health persist? Are they greater or less than in the past? Produce evidence to support your view.

2   What were the main recommendations of the Working Group (see passage and *Inequalities in Health* by Townsend and Davidson)? Why could not the Secretary of State support these recommendations?

3   What are the present government policies for the NHS? What are the likely results of these policies?

Foreword by Patrick Jenkin
The Working Group on Inequalities in Health was set up in 1977, on the initiative of my predecessor as Secretary of State, under the Chairmanship of Sir Douglas Black, to review information about differences in health status between the social classes; to consider possible causes and the implications for policy; and to suggest further research.

The Group was given a formidable task, and Sir Douglas and his colleagues deserve thanks for seeing the work through, and for the thoroughness with which they have surveyed the considerable literature on the subject. As they make clear, the influences at work in explaining the relative health experience of different parts of our society are many and inter-related; and, while it is disappointing that the Group were unable to make greater progress in disentangling the various causes of inequalities in health, the difficulties they experienced are perhaps no surprise given current measurement techniques.

It will come as a disappointment to many that over the long period since the inception of the NHS there is generally little sign of health inequalities in Britain actually diminishing and, in some cases, they may be increasing. It will be seen that the Group has reached the view that the causes of health inequalities are so deep-rooted that only a major and wide-ranging programme of public expenditure on the scale which could result from the report's recommendations – the amount involved could be upwards of £2 billion a year – is quite unrealistic in present or any foreseeable economic circumstances, quite apart from any judgement that may be formed of the effectiveness of such expenditure in dealing with the problems identified. I cannot, therefore, endorse the Group's recommendations. I am making the report available for discussion, but without any commitment by the government to its proposals.

Patrick Jenkin, Secretary of State for Social Services, August 1980

Suggestions

You will find the following useful:

Social Trends;
The Health Divide;
Annual Abstract of Statistics;
General Household Surveys;
Inequalities of Health, by Townsend and Davidson;
Party Manifestos and statements by politicians, doctors, etc.

2 The NHS is constantly in the news. Who runs the NHS? – is it the government, doctors, health service administrators or patients? Examine the effects of large hospitals and their expensive equipment; the control of the medical profession over the other professions; the managerial power of the administrators; and the lack of power of patients. What is the effect of allowing hospitals to 'opt out'? Should group practices work to a budget? Use examples of disputes, currently or recently in the news, to work through this project. It might be more interesting to work in small groups of three or four. (See p. 2 for suggestions.) You may find the following useful:

E. Freidson, *Professional Powers*;
E. Freidson, *Profession of Medicine*;
A. Etzioni (ed.), *The Semi-professions*;
I. Illich, *Disabling Professions*;
I. Illich, *Medical Nemesis*;
Keesing's Record of World Events;
British Medical Journal;
I. Kennedy, *The Unmasking of Medicine*.

Past examination questions

1   When we think about sickness and health we tend to assume that they are not difficult to define – that we are either healthy or we have unpleasant symptoms and are therefore sick. If we are sick, we tend to assume that it is a chance occurrence rather than something produced by the society in which we live.

(Doyal: *Demystifying Social Statistics*)

Examine the ways in which sociologists have challenged both these assumptions.

Associated Examining Board, A Level, Autumn 1984.

Suggestions

Emphasize that health and illness are not just natural occurrences, they are sociological too. Thus sickness is defined by society (see Talcott Parsons' views on 'the sick role', described on p. 92). Also this chapter has emphasized that sickness is not a matter of chance: it is a reflection of the sort of society we are (why do some countries have higher sickness rates than others – even among advanced Western societies?). This chapter has emphasized that social inequalities seem to be the root cause of a lot of disease and premature death.

2   What explanations have sociologists offered for the social distribution of health chances and health care in Britain?

Associated Examining Board, A Level, Summer 1984.

Suggestions

See last question and text.

3   Account for the differences in mortality rates between social classes since 1900.

Oxford Local Examinations, A Level, Summer 1983.

Suggestions

Stress that although the mortality rates for the whole population have fallen, the gap between the classes is wide. The text suggests reasons for this. See also suggested sources of information for the project.

4   In what ways could the sociology of medicine improve the practice of medicine generally?

Health Visitors' Examination, Oxford Polytechnic, 1985.

Suggestions

Improving hospitals, seeking miracle cures for cancer and heart disease etc. probably would not do much to improve or reduce sickness and mortality rates. The biggest improvement is likely to come from raising the life expectancy of the poorest members of society and this means reducing social inequalities. This is where sociology could help by highlighting these inequalities.

5   What is the relationship between social class and disease?

District Nurses' Examination, Oxford Polytechnic, 1985.

Suggestions

See text.

6   Study the information given in the Evidence and then answer the questions which follow:

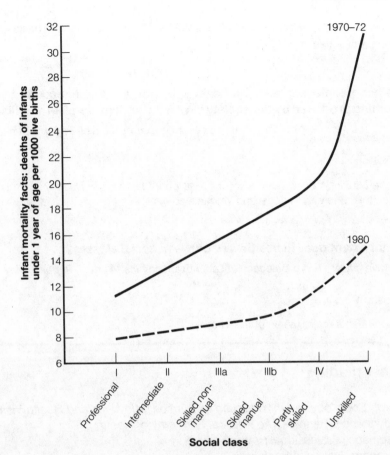

Evidence: Infant mortality rates in England and Wales, 1970–72 compared with 1980, by social class of father

1 To which social class (I–V) do the following occupations belong?
   a) doctor; (1 mark)
   b) road sweeper; (1 mark)
   c) carpenter. (1 mark)

2 Which social class experienced the greatest reduction in its Infant Mortality Rate between 1970–72 and 1980? (2 marks)

3 How would you explain that in both 1970–72 and 1980 Social Class V had a much higher Infant Mortality Rate than Social Class I? (5 marks)

   Total 15 marks

   Part of a specimen question, Southern Examinations Group GCSE (Social Science paper)

Suggestions

1 a) Social Class I   Professional
   b) Social Class V   Unskilled manual
   c) Social Class III   Skilled manual

2 Social Class V, Unskilled manual (but it still has the highest infant mortality ratio).
3 Dealt with in text.

7 **'Whether people are sick or healthy is not a chance occurrence but something produced by the society in which they live.' Explain and discuss.**

Associated Examining Board, A Level, Paper 2, June 1988.

Suggestion

Jeanette Mitchell's book *What is to be Done about Illness and Health?* is particularly good on this. See also suggestions for question 4.

8 **To what extent does ill health vary between social classes?**

University of Oxford Delegacy of Local Examinations, A Level, Paper 2, May 1988.

Suggestion

This has been a major theme of this chapter.

Further reading

*C. Cox, *Sociology: An Introduction for Nurses, Midwives and Health Visitors*
L. Doyal and I. Pennell, *The Political Economy of Health*
E. Freidson, *Professional Powers*
H. Graham, *Issues in Sociology*
N. Hart, *The Sociology of Health and Medicine*
I. Illich, *Medical Nemesis*
B. Ineichen, *Mental Illness*
*I. Kennedy, *The Unmasking of Medicine*
D. Mechanic (ed.), *Readings in Medical Sociology*
J. Mitchell, *What is to be Done about Illness and Health?*
M. Morgan et al., *Sociological Approaches to Health and Medicine*
V. Navarro, *Crisis Health and Medicine*
D. L. Patrick and G. Scrambler (eds), *Sociology as Applied to Medicine*
M. Stacey, *The Sociology of Health, Illness and Disease*
*P. Townsend and N. Davidson (eds), *Inequalities in Health*
*D. Tuckett (ed.), *An Introduction to Medical Sociology*
D. Tuckett and J. M. Kaufert (eds), *Basic Readings in Medical Sociology*
M. Whitehead, *The Health Divide*

13   Urbanism

This chapter takes a sociological approach to the problems of our cities. Some of the key concerns of urban sociology are:

the meaning of community;
urbanism as a way of life;
the problems of the inner city;
the sociology of housing;
the sociology of architecture and town planning.

These topics will be discussed in turn. But an important concern of this chapter, as of others, is to expose and examine hidden assumptions, and to show how these assumptions affect decision making – for example, town planning decisions, design decisions and the allocation of money for urban problems. In so doing the chapter also exposes the ideologies underpinning these assumptions – that they may be distortions of reality, serving the interests of the powerful.

The meaning of community and urbanism

Traditionally, a central concern of urban sociology has been that of community. 'Community' means more than the local area or neighbourhood; it is not solely or mainly a concept of space. Rather, community implies a group sharing a culture and having the same beliefs and values. Thus people of the same religion or profession can be said to be of the same community. Community therefore implies emotional attraction and continuity. One reason why the feeling of community is so strong among miners, for example, is that they share a culture, a common memory of hardships, and they share a neighbourhood, often one that is isolated such as a mining village.

In the past sociologists have often distinguished between the strong sense of community in rural areas, and its weakness in urban areas. One of the most famous books on this subject is *Gemeinschaft und Gesellschaft – Community and Society* – written by Ferdinand Tonnies around the turn of the century. In this he contrasted rural life (with its strong sense of community) with urban life, as shown in Table 13.1.

Table 13.1 A comparison of community and society

	'Gemeinschaft', community	'Gesellschaft' society
Dominant social relationship	Based on natural impulse – because of the importance of kinship, locality, common friends	Based on rational calculation – because the individual is isolated
Main social institutions	Family life Village life	City and cosmopolitan life
Forms of social control	Family law and extended kinship group (see Chapter 2 on the family)	Public legislation Public opinion
Status	Status is given – ascribed (see Chapter 5) (if you are born a peasant you stay a peasant)	Status has to be striven for or achieved (by hard work you could become a manager or professional person)

Many other sociologists have written on this difference between town and country (the urban–rural continuum), notably Robert Redfield and Louis Wirth. Wirth saw urbanism as a way of life. People were not merely attracted to the city, but came under its spell and adopted a distinctive way of life. The chief characteristics of the city and its urban way of life were as follows, according to Wirth:

Size: The larger the city, the more you are among strangers (in contrast to the village, where everyone knows everyone else).

Density: The larger the city, the more you need formal controls such as the police (in contrast to the village, where being known to all ensures 'correct' behaviour).

Heterogeneity: The larger the city, the more it will attract different kinds of people (in contrast to the village, where people are alike and know their place).

Although this distinction between town and country sounds reasonable and although Wirth's view of urbanization sounds plausible, how relevant is it in Western society now? Often the country inhabitant is socially indistinguishable from the town dweller. (Possibly Wirth's theory of urbanization may be applicable in the underdeveloped countries of the third world.) The country dweller may well commute to the large town and work at some specialized job in industry or in commerce, alongside a town dwelling colleague.

Again, the people who care for the environment may live equally in the countryside or towns. Thus the environmental lobby, sometimes known as 'the greens', has increased apace since the sixties and in Britain includes Friends of the Earth, Greenpeace and the Civic Trust. There are protests about housing development in the green belts (rural land surrounding the cities on which housing is prohibited), protests against polluted air and water, and damage to plants and trees; to repeat, the protesters may come equally from town or country.

From a sociological viewpoint one could be critical of the environmental (green) movement. Thus some might argue that the real problem is the nature of capitalism which unquestionably exploits the earth's resources. To understand the nature of the environmental problem we should start with people and their desires rather than the physical problems. Over-emphasis on the harm to the planet could be termed 'planetism' to denote that it is or may be an ideology. The term 'environmental determinism' may also be appropriate here, implying that all you have to do is tidy up the environment, rather than concentrating on the greedy society we appear to be and trying to change society's values. If this change in values were achieved there would be no need to impose and police 'green' solutions (of course, many members of the green movement are aware of these dangers).

To summarize, probably the most important factor influencing the way people live today is not the locality they live in but their social class and all that this entails. The wealthier middle class people can buy their environ-ment, whether it be a flat in a good central area or a house in a fashionable village. Poorer people, however, who tend to be of the working class, must live in cheaper housing near their work. Usually this means in an inner city area. Often they are dependent on council housing.

Perhaps the more important concept is not *urbanization* but rather *industrialization*. Industrialization means more than transforming an agricultural economy to an industrial one. In Britain the Industrial Revolu-tion was accompanied by a widespread division of labour in which workers did specialized jobs and acquired special skills. Fundamentally, industrial-ization is modernization. What Wirth is really describing when he talks of urbanization as a way of life is really modern society, rather than a specifically urban society. One example may explain this. The economy of New Zealand is based largely on agriculture, yet it is a modern, industrial-ized society because it uses scientific means of production and has wide-spread division of labour involving many different kinds of people doing different kinds of jobs.

Thus rather than studying urbanization as such, sociologists are more interested in the impact of industrialization and the way in which different types of industrialization affect the character of the city. Hence in the West we have the advanced capitalist type of city which grew mainly for commercial reasons. On the other hand, in the poorer countries of the third world the city is a sort of enclave. Here most of the country is poor, but with this type of city there is limited prosperity. Many of the people in this type of city work for foreign multinational enterprises, who pay them a wage which is above prevailing local wages yet well below Western wages. For the companies the advantage is a cheap, satisfied labour force which enables the company to undercut competition. For the workers, newly attracted to the city, the advantage is steady work at a higher wage. It is not surprising that there is an explosive population growth in most third world cities. Unfortunately, these enclaves undermine traditional industry crafts and agriculture in the rest of the economy of these poor countries. Finally, another type of city that must be mentioned is the socialist planned city of Eastern Europe, where the government decides which cities shall grow and how many resources shall be allocated to them. These countries are now adopting market economies with less central planning.

The inner city

In the past the differences between town and country (the urban–rural continuum) have been a major concern of sociology. Today the main interest is in the inner city and its social problems. An interesting early analysis of how the city works comes from a book called *The City*, a collection of essays edited by Parks and Burgess and based on actual experiences in the Chicago of the twenties. In one essay Burgess conceived of the city as having concentric zones, each having a characteristic social structure and pattern of growth. He also investigated what he called 'natural areas' – little worlds which touch in a mosaic but do not interpenetrate, each having its own subcultural values. Examples of this can be seen in ghetto inner city areas which each contain different immigrant groups. Individuals and groups are sorted out in a city by competition, that is, by the struggle for land which allocates people to their position in society and their position in space. Thus when, for example, an immigrant group becomes more prosperous it may move from the ghetto area of the inner city to the smarter suburbs, while the next wave of immigrants comes in to take its place in the poorer old ghetto area. This is why these inner areas are called the 'zone in transition' in the diagram. The immigrant inhabitants thus saw their stay as only transitory. ('Immigrant' does not of course refer just to black immigrants or even those from other countries. There is a considerable amount of internal immigration in many countries; in Britain, for example, many young single people come from the North to get work or get away from home. Again, many people move from the big cities to country areas or the new towns to attain a pleasanter environment.)

This has been a brief introduction to the inner city. There are many social problems in the inner city and the outlying housing estates, for example:

impersonal housing estates on the edge of town used to rehouse people dumped from the inner areas;

run-down transport systems which make it difficult for poorer people on

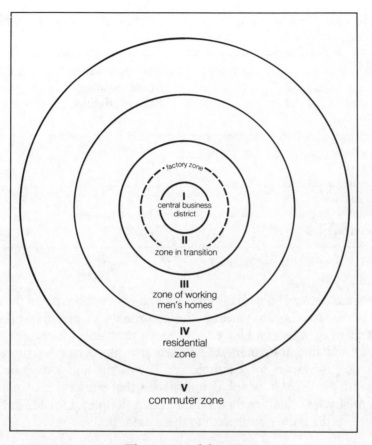

The zones of the city
Source: Park and Burgess, *The City*

outlying estates to get inner city jobs or see their relatives;
new roads cutting off districts and bringing traffic problems, noise and
   pollution into the city;
encroachment on the countryside.

Looking now at the problems of the inner city itself, Table 13.2 compares
the death rates in two towns: Salford, one of the poorer cities, and Oxford, a
prosperous city. Table 13.3 shows the social composition of four poor

Table 13.2 Comparison of death rates in two
towns (per thousand of population)

	Salford	Oxford
Infants under 1 year	28	17
Men 45–64	20	12
Women 45–64	10	6

Source: P. Townsend, *Poverty in the UK*

Table 13.3 Social composition of four poor city areas as shown by their occupational structure

	Four poor urban areas (Neath, Salford, Belfast, Glasgow) %	UK as a whole %
Professional	0	6
Managerial	0	5
Supervisory and routine non-manual	13	32
Skilled-manual	41	31
Partly skilled manual	21	16
Unskilled manual	24	10

Source: P. Townsend, *Poverty in the UK*

urban areas compared with the country as a whole. Looking at the areas, it could be said that because most of the inhabitants are manual workers they are likely to earn less and have more social problems (due for example to low pay and unemployment). They are also likely to have more health problems (as shown for example by Townsend and Davidson's book *Inequalities in Health*, which demonstrates that working class people are substantially less healthy than middle class people). Indeed, Table 13.4 seems to confirm the poor health in these areas.

Table 13.4 Percentage of households with sick or disabled people

	Four poor urban areas (Neath, Salford, Belfast, Glasgow)	UK as a whole
Disabled child	3	1
Disabled adult under 65	15	10
Person sick or injured for more than 8 weeks	18	9

Source: P. Townsend, *Poverty in the UK*

Paul Harrison in his book *Inside the Inner City* lists some of the features of inner city areas. His list can be used here to summarize this section on the inner city. He shows that:

1   Inner cities are areas of older dying industries; often formerly prosperous, these areas are beset by the problems of low pay and unemployment.

2 They are areas of particularly bad housing comprising worn out Victorian houses and badly designed council blocks of flats. An environment full of dereliction and dehumanized concrete.
3 They are areas of low skilled, lowly paid workers, and high unemployment.
4 They are areas in which the local council lacks money, where schools are poor and health services below average (whereas all these local services should be better than average because of the greater need).
5 They are areas in which all other social problems are greatest, including crime, vandalism, ill health, many elderly, infirm people, racial tensions, one parent families, and so on.

So far the discussion of the problems of the inner city has been mainly descriptive and factual. The problem now needs to be analysed more deeply by looking at the common assumptions that seem to be made by housing managers, architects and town planners. Some of the main assumptions appear to be that:

1 you can get rid of slums by demolishing them;
2 good architecture and design will produce a good environment;
3 town planners will act as fair umpires in the proper allocation and use of land and help to prevent bad development caused by private greed, etc.

Examining these common assumptions will also serve as an introduction to the sociology of housing and town planning. But first of all, how far do you yourself agree with the three common assumptions mentioned above – and if you do not, why not?

Common assumption one: *you can get rid of the slums by demolishing them*

This also assumes that building good housing with modern amenities like central heating will reduce poverty. In this better housing the ex-slum dwellers will live fuller lives. This seems sensible, and the drive for better housing has always been part of the Labour Party's policy in Britain. With better housing, the old slum areas can be demolished and forgotten.

Unfortunately, the actual results of such housing policies have often been socially disastrous. The slum clearance and rehousing policies have been applied by municipal authorities, charities and other public benefactors who had little understanding of the social consequences of their actions (and apparently no knowledge of sociology). The new public housing has often taken the form of high rise flats, inconvenient to families and a source of vandalism in the public spaces, lifts and staircases. The new housing becomes a new ghetto, publicly marking the inhabitants as unworthy or inadequate. The old slums have been replaced by high cost, dehumanizing housing. Old communities have been broken up, old people separated from their families and old institutions extinguished.

The American urban sociologist Herbert Gans argues that:

1 Good modern housing does not eliminate poverty; but removing people's poverty will enable them to buy housing which is truly better.
2 Constructing new public housing for the poor stigmatizes them and reduces their dignity and their ability to live where they choose.
3 A public anti-poverty policy will do more in the long run to improve the physical environment than urban renewal. This would involve supplementing the income of the poor.
4 Public housing policies do not cater for the poorest people, delinquents, discharged prisoners, deserted wives, immigrants and others who form no powerful interest group. These people are often housed, if at all, in the old inner city areas in poor, private, rented accommodation.

Public housing policies have been implemented by professionals – planners, architects, housing managers, surveyors, and the councillors they advise. It is not safe to assume that these professional 'housers' and others have learnt from past mistakes. As is the case with other professionals, the audience for whom they perform is not the ultimate client (the municipal housing tenant), but other professionals – fellow architects for example.

Slums, then, are not the result of ageing housing, but they exist when the poor cannot compete for housing, cannot articulate their wants in the market place, and are forced into overcrowded buildings. Moreover it is sociologically naive to assume that crime, for example, is produced mainly by the physical environment – rather, it is an expression of lack of opportunity and lack of hope. The real way to clear slums and enable the poorest to live in good housing is to eliminate unemployment, raise incomes, reduce racial discrimination and improve education and social services.

> Council housing grew up in a period when building was cheap, simple and durable, not plagued with condensation and maintenance problems, when it was occupied by respectful, regularly paid small earners (never the poorest of the poor) and administered and cared for by rent collectors who would give advice on hygiene and floor scrubbing and caretakers with a background of the armed forces who kept everything shipshape. (Colin Ward, *When We Build Again*, p. 86.)

Common assumption two: *good architecture and design will produce a good environment and social harmony*

This assumption is based on the fallacy known as architectural determinism or physical determinism (or sometimes as the ecological fallacy), which holds that a good physical environment will in itself produce good social results. In other words, given good physical surroundings people will be happier. Thus architectural determinism assumes that people are determined by their environment. Two architects in particular could be mentioned here, Gropius and Le Corbusier.

Gropius had the concept of the 'total architecture': the creation of an environment for all human activities. In this view, sociology would be seen mainly as a method of social investigation to help the architect to control the environment, rather than as a critique of what they do.

Le Corbusier is famous for bequeathing to our urban environment the tower block. Indeed he had the concept of the tower city, living in the sky. Many tower blocks look like architects' dreams and some of these have in fact received awards from the Royal Institute of British Architects. They are not dreams of inhabitants though – rather, nightmares. The mother who cannot watch her children play from the twentieth floor, the old person trapped in the flat when the lift is vandalized, the sterile public land between the blocks. How could so little thought be given to the people who live there? Again the answer seems to be related to the idea of professionalism and professional ideology. Receiving an architectural award is a symbol of approval from your peers, allegedly the only people truly competent to judge your professional work (rather than the actual consumers, the tenants of these flats). Architects, like other professionals, tend to see the world through their own professional spectacles in the same way as the lawyer may view, say, divorce in terms of the law only, the policeman may see society in terms of law and order, the planner in terms of future plans (and therefore the architect may look at a neighbourhood in terms of the pleasingness or even beauty of the buildings). Thus the architect may notice the slag heap rather than the lack of footpaths; or derelict eyesore rather than the lack of shops. It may well be that architects can provide pleasing surroundings, but they cannot transform society by this or even predict the ways inhabitants will use their buildings or what new demands people will make of their buildings. As M. Broady puts it, in *Planning for People*, phoney social theory is likely to produce phoney expectations and spurious designs.

Common assumption three: *town planners will act as fair umpires in the proper allocation and use of land and help to prevent bad development caused by private greed, etc.*

Planners are influential because before development can take place the builder or developer must obtain planning permission from the council's town planning department.

Town planning in Britain is often associated with the concept of the garden city, created at the turn of the century – Welwyn Garden City,

Letchworth Garden City, Hampstead Garden Suburb. After World War II new towns were created where the mistakes due to lack of planning and haphazard private development would not be repeated. Town planners have tended to be social idealists, heirs to a tradition of utopian thinking. They have tried to create ideal balanced communities through the estab-

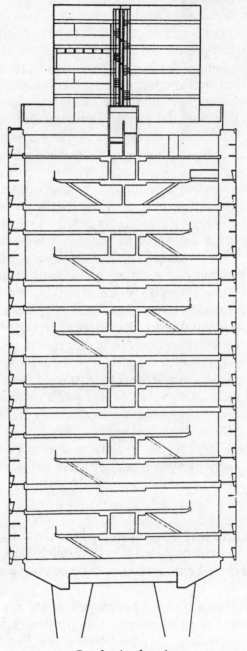

Castles in the air
Source: V. Scully Jr., *Modern Architecture*

Le Corbusier's 'Unité d'Habitation'
Source: Scully, *Modern Architecture*

lishing of classless neighbourhoods, and by bringing the countryside to the town. The tools at their disposal have been architectural design and popula- tion density control.

However, planners as allocators of space have been more concerned with demographic and ecological facts than with sociological insight, and have tended to look on people as recipients of services – how many shops, hospitals, etc. are required for a given population. There are also certain ideologies, beliefs, which town planners seem to have and which affect their decisions. One of these is a kind of anti-urbanism which comes, perhaps, from the idealistic garden city roots to the profession. This seems to assume that bringing the countryside to the town is good planning. Coupled with this is an implicit belief in social happiness and social integration through the bringing together of different people in balanced communities (see M. Broady, *Planning for People*).

There appear to be three basic ideologies in the planning profession. These are:

1   that planners see themselves as impartial umpires reconciling com- peting uses of land;
2   that the physical environment can be improved through better architec- ture and lower population densities;
3   that better physical conditions can create a better basis for community life.

These beliefs are ideological.

Firstly, they may be either untrue or exaggerations of the truth and secondly, they serve the interests of the powerful – in this case the interests of wealthy property owners and occupiers. This will now be explained further.

The idea of the planner as impartial umpire assumes that there is a scientific/rational body of knowledge or expertise called 'planning', of which the town planner is the trustworthy custodian. This further implies that planning decisions are impartial and scientific. The fact is that planning decisions are basically political decisions about the use of land. Planning decisions may be about the line of a new road, where to build a new sewage works, whether or not some new housing development shall take place. However, those most able to affect planning decisions are generally those with most land, who will themselves be most affected, and often these are wealthy property owners. They will object most strongly to, say, a new airport near their property and will be able to pay for an advertising campaign, employ the best lawyers and so on. Again, property owners seeking commercial development, spurred on by profit, may be able to influence planners to advise their council to grant planning permission for offices rather than homes. Thus, for example, such property owners may be able to offer the council land for new roads.

The assumption that improving physical conditions will also improve social conditions can also be seen as ideological. This was discussed in connection with architects' ideologies. It is no accident that many of the plans used look like photographs taken from a helicopter. They imply control and allocation, whereas planning should be for people not build-

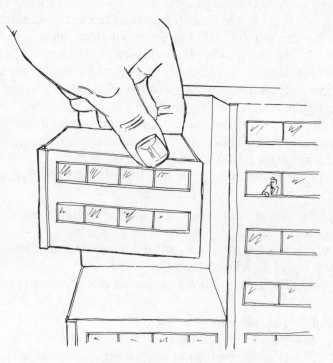

Planning from above
Source: Based on an original drawing in M. Broady, *Planning for People*

ings; planning should begin with people's goals (not geography or population densities).

The new towns in Britain are an example of the consequences of planning ideologies. Most were started just after the war to relieve overcrowding in the old inner city areas and many of the inhabitants were happy with their new homes. One of the aims of the new towns was to mix the classes; to have socially balanced neighbourhoods comprising both middle class and working class inhabitants. This did not work, as a study of Crawley New Town by B. J. Heraud showed.

The planners at Crawley tried to spread the social classes evenly throughout the new town so as to obtain a balanced community. However, it was found that in time some suburbs became more working class and working class people from all parts of the town would move to these suburbs. Similarly, middle class people would move to more middle class suburbs. It was a case of birds of a feather . . . By looking at what people really want, it seems clear that most families are seeking an ordinary suburban house and garden. They move to the suburbs not to become part of a community or live in a beautiful tower block but to buy a house suitable for the family, as was shown by Gans in his book *Levittowners*.

The people of Levittown have deliberately chosen to buy their house there, and Gans argues that we should listen to what people really want rather than what planners think is best:

> The essence of sociology . . . is that it observes what people really do and say. It looks at the world from their perspective . . . Sociology is a democratic method of enquiry; it assumes that people have the right to be what they are.

Criticism

Some readers may feel that this chapter is unfair to architects and town planners, who after all generally have the best of intentions. Le Corbusier's blocks of flats, for example, contained all manner of facilities as well as the living units, and were well maintained; later tower blocks had to be built much more cheaply.

What do you think? If you work through the project at the end of this chapter, you may be able to make a clearer judgement on the role of architects and town planners, and others concerned with development.

Castells and the new urban society

Manuel Castells, a Spanish sociologist and a Marxist, says in a well known book on urbanization that any analysis of the urban scene should start with the analysis of urban social movements. These movements arise when access to local public services such as education, transport, health and especially housing becomes restricted. Castells quotes some examples. Thus the rent strike in Glasgow in 1915 was a popular demonstration backed by the withholding of rent following a large increase. The government had to freeze rents at their earlier levels. These social movements become politicized, that is, people come to realize that they have grievances in common, and this affects all classes. Castells challenges Wirth's view of society. What Wirth, Tonnies, Park and Burgess and others are describing is not urbanism but the culture of capitalist urbanization. Castells concludes we need a new theory of social movements – one that looks at the provision of local services from a consumer's viewpoint. We need to know what the conditions for their development are. How are they inter-related? Finally, the state itself is not neutral but is an expression of the wider society with all its inequalities in wealth and power.

Conclusions

The following table sets out the conclusions of this chapter.

Everyday interpretations	A sociological viewpoint
1 Community is based on neighbourhood.	Community means more than this: it means people sharing similar values and life styles.
2 There is a big difference between town and country.	It is more likely that the differences between town people and country people are related to social class rather than locality.
3 The problems of the inner cities are the slums, bad schools and medical services, and unemployment etc.	The problem of the inner cities is poverty. The slums etc. are symptoms of this. These problems are inter-related. You do not get rid of slums by just demolishing them and building council housing. Similarly you cannot really improve education by building more schools. Rather you must tackle the root cause of all these problems – poverty. But this means redistributing income to the poor through higher taxes on the rich, hence it will be strongly opposed.
4 Good design will help create a happy neighbourhood.	People like what they are used to, especially 'normal' houses – and not tower blocks.
5 Town planners try to allocate land to its proper use.	The wealthier, more powerful people can influence planning decisions in their favour.

Everyday interpretations	A sociological viewpoint
6 Serious poverty has been eliminated in Britain.	All the statistics show the poor are getting relatively poorer. We are constantly rediscovering poverty, especially in the inner city.
7 The poor are cushioned against extreme poverty by the welfare state.	The welfare state deals with acute cases now (a genuine welfare state would ensure that none of its citizens lived in want).
8 There is less class distinction now.	'The divide between manual and non-manual workers is deeper here than in almost any other Western country . . . with most neighbourhoods segregated by income, leading to considerable segregation in schools' (P. Harrison, *Inside the Inner City*).

Self-examination questions

1 What is meant by 'urbanism' (or 'urbanization'), 'density', 'heterogeneity', 'industrialization', 'community', 'zone in transition', 'ecological fallacy', 'ghetto', 'architectural determinism'?

2 Why is the demolition of slums not necessarily the best way to get rid of them in the long run?

3 In what sense are large council housing estates on the edge of town really a problem of the inner city?

Project

What do you think is the ideology (if any) of architects, town planners, property developers, local councillors (and other groups concerned with housing and property development) in your area? Illustrate your views by reference to actual examples of redevelopment (public or private) that has taken place in your area. You will probably find the following useful:

a camera;

the local newspaper, past and present editions (from the public library);

council minutes, housing committee minutes, town planning committee minutes, etc. (from the public library);

the views of council tenants and owner occupiers about their housing;

the views of town planners etc.

Case studies and past examination questions

1 **After reading the passage, answer the questions that follow.**

Dismantling the fiefdoms

Council housing is under frequent attack. It is caught up in the conflict between a government hostile to the traditional power of local authorities and Labour councils bitterly resistant to a reduced housing role.

Britain is unique in running the vast majority of its rented housing stock under direct political control, with large bureaucratic town halls exercising a virtual monopoly over subsidized housing for rent. But massive organizational changes are taking place in our society (and not just ours), leading to new styles of organization – less hierarchical, less authoritarian, more diverse, more flexible, more collaborative, more autonomous. For a century, council housing has been run more as a 'municipal fiefdom' than as a service to tenants. If for no other reason, its organization was bound to change towards more choice and diversity.

But not all council tenants are enthusiastic about the government's proposals to break up local authority landlords. According to a recent survey carried out by the National Consumer Council, most council tenants simply do not want to change their landlord. This suggests that the government's plans to transfer a million council properties out of council ownership might be far less popular than its earlier right to buy legislation, which led to one million council tenants becoming owner-occupiers. Nonetheless, a further one million council properties might be transferred out of council ownership – a massive shift in the structure and organization of council housing.

The government will use five main mechanisms to transform council housing.

a) The declaration of Housing Action Trusts – government sponsored bodies – with power to take over compulsorily the ownership and management of most run-down inner city council estates.

b) The transfer to independent landlords of council housing on condition that the majority of existing tenants do not object.

c) Strong support and an expanding role for housing associations and tenant cooperatives.

d) Targeting additional resources through the Department of the Environment's Estate Action Programme to the most needy council estates, where the local authority is prepared to innovate and establish estate-based management to ensure an effective local service.

e) The continued expansion of owner-occupation.

There are several uncertainties and doubts about the government's strategy, particularly over the role of housing associations and tenant cooperatives, which will play a small but symbolically significant role. With only half a million dwellings, housing associations and cooperatives have shown immense variety and flexibility, if on a minuscule scale: they have been popular, local and responsive. But the terms on which they will be expected to expand rapidly, doubling or tripling their stock, will be far less favourable than in the past. Their rate of expansion is fraught with uncertainty.

There are other difficulties. Private landlords operate for profit, but without subsidy it is very difficult to make it profitable to rent to low-income households. American and German governments, with a far larger and more successful private rental market than we have, know this. Besides, to transfer council properties to alternative landlords, there need to be alternative landlords ready to take over. There are few signs of such a proliferation. Quality Street, the independent landlord sponsored by Nationwide Anglia Building Society, is uniquely interesting precisely because it is unique.

Intense social problems in large areas of council housing may deter would-be landlords. The government has no clear strategy for youth unemployment, homelessness, one parent families, racial tensions, crime and policing. Problems like these need sensitive and localized responses which involve residents and outside support. The government's timescale does not fit the slow uncomfortable processes of deep social change.

There is a further danger that the government's housing initiatives will be seen to concentrate on the conversion from low-income renting to high-income owner-occupation or up-market renting, displacing low-income households and reducing the size of the rental market. (A. Power, *New Statesman and Society*, 17 June 1988.)

1 Summarize the government's five main mechanisms for transforming council housing.
2 What are the main obstacles to the government's policy from a sociological viewpoint?

Suggestions

The claim that the control of council housing will become less authoritarian in the future needs questioning or at least confronting. Really, 'solving' the housing problem is not just a matter of reorganizing housing authorities; poor housing should be seen as an aspect of poverty. Thus, for example, a housing policy stressing owner-occupation may not help poorer 'natural renters' in housing need, for whom the choice is between public authority housing or homelessness.

2 **Read the passage and attempt the questions that follow.**

Living loose

An estimated 80,000 young people are homeless in Britain today, reeling from sordid squat to night shelter, sleeping rough for a spell before resorting to cramped bed-and-breakfast lodgings. They are largely invisible as they attempt to extricate themselves from the downward spiral of no home, no job, no security, no self-respect.

The figure of 80,000 is only an estimate – nobody really knows how many young homeless there are, or their exact age; some suggest that this is because if the figures were available, something would have to be done. What is known is that there are runaways as young as 7 and, more commonly 14 and 15: legally, such youngsters have to be returned home or into care. But there are also thousands of homeless 16 and 17 year olds, many intent on concealing how young they are.

At a time of stretched resources, the thinking seems to be that all young people should remain in their parents' home until they can set up on their own, and that those who leave are up to no good or are scrounging.

Everyone working in the field is keen to explode this myth. In her book *Homeless Young People in Britain* Barbara Saunders writes: 'British society is inconsistent in its attitudes towards young people. On the one hand they are encouraged to show initiative, to seek opportunities away from home and set off in search of work. On the other, they are criticized if they move and find themselves homeless, being considered feckless, workshy and abusers of the social security system.'

Homelessness is not necessarily a matter of sleeping rough. If all those in squats, shelters, hostels and bed-and-breakfast accommodation are to be counted, a broad definition of homelessness must be found to measure the problem. As a starting point, a definition that you are homeless is if there is nowhere that you have a RIGHT to stay.

The lack of rights begins with local housing authorities. Most will keep single people way down their lists until they are 30, a few until 40. Even those who put 16 or 17 year olds on the waiting list suffer from lack of resources. Basically we do not spend enough on public housing.

The question of housing priority is a vexed one. The Homeless Persons Act lays down guidelines that any homeless young person who is vulnerable to sexual or financial exploitation should be housed. It is easy to argue that ALL homeless teenagers are open to exploitation, but very few authorities recognize this. A survey by the National Children's Home has found that only 15 per cent of the 83 per cent of councils who responded will house 16, 17 and 18 year olds as a priority. Among these are Glasgow, Newcastle and Liverpool. Young people in other areas remain homeless and can find themselves living in a nightmare, drifting towards the big cities to find help and a job. (Jane Hodgkin, *New Society*, 18 September 1987.)

1 Why is the figure of 80,000 homeless only an estimate?
2 In what ways is British society inconsistent in its attitudes towards young people?
3 What are the main problems facing the young homeless?
4 What do you think are likely to be the main problems facing the middle-aged and elderly homeless?

Suggestions

Many in this group have 'lost their way' – lost their job, lost contact with their family, etc. We may not have the right to change their way of life, but at least we could provide decent shelter. See also suggestions for previous question. People have housing *needs* even if they cannot pay to have them met. We should not tackle homelessness on its own but rather see it as an aspect of poverty, together perhaps with crime, drug addiction, etc. It might be useful to ask the question – what sort of societies have the highest rates of homelessness?

Table 13.5 Housebuilding performance, seasonally adjusted, in Great Britain (thousands of dwellings)

Year	Starts			Under construction at end of period			Completions		
	Public sector	Private sector	All	Public sector	Private sector	All	Public sector	Private sector	All
1985	34.2	162.8	197.0	49.2	222.4	271.6	40.0	152.1	192.1
1986	33.0	176.1	209.0	47.3	235.3	282.7	34.8	163.2	198.0
1987	31.8	181.3	223.1	47.0	256.0	303.0	32.1	170.7	202.8
1986 2	7.9	43.7	51.6	47.1	228.7	275.8	8.1	40.1	49.2
3	8.8	46.7	55.5	47.8	234.1	281.9	9.1	41.3	49.4
4	8.2	44.5	52.7	47.3	235.3	282.7	8.6	43.2	51.8
1987 1	8.1	47.6	55.7	47.9	240.5	288.4	7.6	42.5	50.1
2	8.4	45.5	53.9	47.8	243.2	291.0	8.5	42.8	51.3
3	7.6	48.1	55.7	47.2	248.1	295.3	8.2	43.2	51.4
4	7.7	50.1	57.8	47.0	256.0	303.0	7.9	42.2	50.1
1988 1	7.7	56.8	64.5	47.1	263.6	310.7	7.6	49.1	56.7
2	6.8	55.0	61.8	45.8	273.9	319.7	8.1	44.7	52.8

Source: Department of the Environment, Housing and Construction Statistics, 1988 June Quarter, Part 1

3 **Table 13.5 was issued by the Department of the Environment in 1988.**

1   From this table, what would you deduce to be the government's housing policy?
2   How far is the policy likely to be successful?
3   What comment might sociologists offer?

Suggestions

The cutting down of housing in the public sector may increase homelessness. It should be recognized that some people are 'natural renters'. For them the choice might be public housing or homelessness (as mentioned in the suggestions for question 1).

4 **'There is not one crisis in the inner city but many.' Discuss.**

University of Cambridge Local Examinations, A Level, Summer 1984.

Suggestions

Demonstrate that the problem is not just bad housing and the physical deterioration of the inner city.

Show there are other problems as indicated here, such as low income, unemployment, ill health, racial tension.

Finally, you could show that really there is one underlying problem – poverty.

5 **Either (a) 'A spirit of community depends upon shared values and interests. As cities become more socially mixed, maintenance of community spirit becomes impossible.' Discuss.**

Or (b) 'Britain has succeeded in providing adequate housing in terms of physical comfort but only at the expense of causing social and environmental problems.' Discuss.

University of Oxford Local Examinations, A Level, Summer 1984.

Suggestions

a) Show you know what is meant by 'community'.
   Could say that the idea of community spirit may be a planning ideology.
   Stress the birds of a feather argument as outlined here in connection with Crawley New Town. Perhaps people do not want a community spirit – just a home.

b) Could show that these environmental problems arise partly from the ideologies of architects and planners (bad planning decisions etc.). Discuss green belts, the green movement, etc.

6 Either (a) 'The problems of the inner cities are essentially those of poverty and unemployment; the problems would disappear if poverty and unemployment were eliminated.' Discuss.

Or (b) What factors determine the pattern of residential segregation in cities?

Oxford Local Examinations, A Level, Summer 1983.

Suggestions

a) Really this has been the main theme of this chapter.

b) Again – see text – use Park and Burgess, and also birds of a feather argument, etc.

7 'The concept of "community" tells us more about how we might like the world to be than how it actually is.' Discuss.

Associated Examining Board, A Level, Autumn 1984.

Suggestions

It seems safe to agree with this statement, but put arguments for and against this view first.

Define community and show that in the past it has been associated with a supposed rural way of life. Show that many of us, especially town planners, might overestimate the virtues of the country and of community.

Could show why the key term is not 'urbanization' but 'industrialization'.

8 a) Explain why people are drawn to the South East of England. (8 marks)

b) Why are people moving away from the cities and what are the consequences? (12 marks)

Southern Examining Group, GCSE Specimen Questions.

Suggestions

a) People move to the South East because there is less unemployment there, better housing and a higher standard of living.

b) People move away from the big cities when employment moves away. To a large extent the inner city is where the poor live. The consequences of this shift of population are the break-up of communities, disruption of families – leading to further urban decay and more migration from the cities. Describe the social conditions in the inner city (as in the text), and show that these unsatisfactory conditions are both the causes and consequences of migration from poor inner city areas, often aggravated by the well-meaning but misguided efforts of planners etc. – who seem to know little of sociology.

Further reading

M. Castells, *City, Class and Power*
R. Frankenburg, *Communities in Britain*
M. Harloe, *New Perspectives in Urban Change and Conflict*
*P. Harrison, *Inside the Inner City*
P. Lowe, and J. Goyder, *Environmental Groups in Politics*
S. Lowe, *Urban Social Movements*
J. R. Mellor, *Urban Sociology in an Urbanized Society*
R. E. Pahl (ed.), *Whose City?*
R. E. Park and E. W. Burgess, *The City*
B. Saunders, *Homeless Young People in Britain*
P. Saunders, *Urban Politics*
J. Seabrook, *Landscapes of Poverty*
C. Ward, *When We Build Again*
*'Community', *New Society*, 22 November 1984 (Society Today series)
*'Inner Cities', *New Society*, 1 March 1984 (Society Today series)

14 Deviance

Introduction

The sociology of deviance studies any departure from the norms and values which usually regulate behaviour in any society. In this sense both the criminal and the saint could be regarded as deviants since they are both exceptions to normal behaviour in society. However, the sociology of deviance usually concentrates on behaviour that most people consider wrong or disturbing and therefore worthy of punishment or treatment or notice. To the lay person there is not much of a problem here. We know (from the Sunday newspapers for example) what behaviour is wrong and what punishment should be accorded. What is the problem?

As in other aspects of social life, what every lay person knows is not the end of the matter; for the sociologist it is the start. Thus there is firstly the problem of defining deviance, then of describing it and finally the problem of explaining and understanding deviance.

It has been suggested that deviance is a departure from the norms and values of society. Because we are members of a society we take its norms and values for granted. 'Normal' behaviour is common sense behaviour. Abnormal or deviant behaviour is in some way 'senseless'. Therefore, the deviant needs to be taught 'sense', usually by punishment, to bring the message home. However, there are at least two reasons for not accepting this as the end of the matter.

Firstly, what is normal in society varies over time and between societies. Up to the last century in England it was quite normal for ordinary soldiers and seamen to be awarded a hundred lashes for minor breaches of discipline. The type of 'crime' perceived by a society is related to its dominant values at a particular time. Erikson in *Wayward Puritans* demonstrates that in seventeenth century New England religious crime was the most easily perceived of any sort of crime and economic crime the least harshly treated – thieves were treated leniently if they repented. In the West today it is economic crime that is harshly dealt with, stealing usually carrying heavier penalties than blasphemy.

Deviance and crime change in accordance with the changing values of society. In Britain the possession of soft drugs, if not tolerated, is not so severely punished; while in recent years homosexuality and attempted

> **'Deviance': a label**
> According to labelling theory (described more fully later in this chapter) deviant behaviour is not just the violation of a norm. Rather it is behaviour that gets labelled as deviant. Thus, in different societies different acts get labelled as deviant – hence the expression that the crime statistics are 'socially constructed'.

suicide have ceased to be criminal offences (with the exception of male homosexuality with a person under 21).

A second problem in defining crime comes from the crime statistics. The fact that crimes of violence have increased by, for example, 20 per cent in the last year seems to present no problem in understanding at first. However, to the sociologist crime and crime statistics are socially constructed. (See Glossary for the 'social construction of reality'.) But if a person is assaulted, where is the social construction in that? Surely it is a fact and should appear in the crime statistics as one assault? However, increases in crimes of violence may be partly explained by our greater sensitivity now to violence. For example, domestic violence is more likely to be reported now. Crime figures refer to crimes known to the police, but many crimes are not reported. Much shoplifting and pilfering by staff is undetected or, if detected, not reported. Crimes of great social stigma such as sexual offences by middle class men may be under-reported. Even major crimes like murder may be under-reported; for every murder there may be a dozen names on the missing persons records which could be the subject matter of murder enquiries. Again, some types of crime are more visible than others. Burglary is visible but fraud and embezzlement (mostly middle class crimes) are not very visible. Thus Sutherland in *White Collar Crime* has shown that what business people may call sharp practice could be seen as criminal practice if viewed from a different perspective.

Some crime is more dramatic and therefore more reported. By this criterion there is an over-reporting of crimes of violence, which in fact account for only 2 per cent of offences in Britain. These crimes of violence are often misrepresented, in that many of them are minor and about two thirds of them are domestic violence. In other words, the assailant in a murder or rape case is more likely to be known to the victim than be the feared image of the evil stranger. It has been said that in locking the outer doors at night you are locking the assailant in rather than keeping the criminal out.

There is then in criminal statistics the problem of the 'dark figure', crime that is unreported or undetected or not counted as criminal even though technically an offence has been committed. Those who are caught and prosecuted tend to be:

poor;
ill educated;

unemployed or in marginal jobs;
socially inadequate;
visible – especially blacks;
male.

Once a criminal is caught it is more likely that he or she will continue to be caught in the future, having passed from the invisible to the visible. S/he is known to the police and therefore a regular suspect, while those who have never been caught may continue to commit crimes which are part of the 'dark figure'.

We are now in a better position to see why sociologists talk of the social construction of crime and the social construction of crime statistics. What the crime figures show is not social reality but an interpretation of that reality. If the public is more interested in certain types of crime, the police will become more sensitive to those crimes and this will usually be reflected in the law too. There is an interconnection between society's values, the law, police action and criminal statistics. This in turn determines and defines:

what is crime;
what is hidden;
what is known;
what is visible;
what is tolerated;
how much crime there is.

It now remains to try to explain and understand crime. To try to see what exactly is happening rather than what the lay person thinks is going on. The first difficulty is to define crime.

The problem of defining deviance

Under-reporting – 'the dark figure'

What is the problem in trying to define crime? Table 14.4 seems clear enough. It appears to show in a simple, straightforward way the amount of crime committed in England and Wales.

Why not accept these figures at their face value? The trouble is that these figures show only the crime reported to the police, not the 'dark figure' – hidden crime. Thus taking all types of crimes of violence, Young and Lea estimate that there are five times as many crimes as are officially recorded.

How can the 'dark figure' be explained? Before an event becomes officially recognized as a crime (and therefore eligible to enter the crime statistics), it has to go through a number of stages, for example:

stage 1   Is the event worth reporting to the police?
stage 2   Do the police think it is a crime?
stage 3   Do the police think it is worth prosecuting?
stage 4   Do the courts consider it a crime?

At each stage an interpretation of the event has to be made, and this interpretation is made in accordance with the prevailing culture of society. The following example may illustrate this process.

A wife is assaulted by her husband in their own home. She may feel too embarrassed to tell the police so it does not reach stage 1. Or she may tell the police, who may tell her to sort out her own problem (up to stage 2), or the police may just warn the husband, and so on.

Supposing now the prevailing patriarchal culture of our society has changed (due partly perhaps to pressure from the women's movement), and this kind of violence becomes unacceptable. The assault is now much more likely to pass through the final stage and get recorded as a crime. Then the official statistics on assault will increase due to greater reporting and more vigilance and action by the police, even though the actual number of assaults has not increased.

Media exaggeration and our own fears

Another source of distortion in our perception of crime arises from media exaggeration and the way we often tend to frighten ourselves about the extent of crime in society.

Stan Cohen in his book *Folk Devils and Moral Panics* shows how the media and the public exaggerate the violence and the damage to property that occurs occasionally at seaside resorts in the summer. But the British Crime Survey shows that the average person can expect:

a robbery once every five centuries;
an assault resulting in injury (even if slight) once every century;
a family car stolen once every 60 years;
and a burglary (in the home) once every 40 years.

(On the other hand, the Islington Crime Survey, quoted towards the end of this chapter, does indicate that people's fears of crime are justified to some extent.)

While not wanting to minimize the prevalence of crime, Tables 14.1 and 14.2 indicate that what we fear most is least likely to happen. There is an

Table 14.1 Fear of street crime

Women	Percentage likely to be victims of 'street' crime	Percentage feeling very unsafe
Age 16–30	2.8	16
31–60	1.4	35
61+	1.2	37

Source: British Crime Survey and adapted from J. Young and J. Lea, *What is to be Done about Law and Order?*

Table 14.2 Fear of crime compared with actual rate of crime

Type of crime in 'fear' order	Percentage of people fearing the crime	Actual rate of crime per 100,000 of the population
Burglary	44	410
Robbery (including 'mugging')	42	34
Sexual assaults	23	16
Assault	16	396
Vandalism	1	1490

Source: adapted from J. Young and J. Lea, *What is to be Done about Law and Order?*

inter-relationship here (as shown in Chapter 15 on the mass media). The types of crime we fear get reported more and this alerts the police more to these crimes, hence more arrests and an increase in the statistics for these crimes. Exaggeration and dramatization sell newspapers; they can also distort reality.

In summary then, official crime statistics cannot be taken at their face value for three main reasons. Firstly, there is the under-reporting of crime, known as the 'dark figure'. Secondly, the definition of deviance changes over time and from society to society. Thirdly, there is the distortion of the media and of our own fears, which hides any clear view of what is really going on.

The *conservative approach* to crime (the term used by Young and Lea) is largely the reverse of radical criminology, described later. In essence it is illustrated every day in the mass media by the way crime news is reported; by emphasizing the details of the crime itself rather than putting it in a social context.

Thus for the conservative, crime is not seen primarily as a problem of poverty, since the vast majority of the poor are honest. Crime is seen as the action of a person unwilling to restrain himself or herself, hence the need for punishment.

The ideological component in this is, firstly, that it is an exaggeration (in that you cannot explain crime solely in terms of individuals' actions) and, secondly, it virtually ignores the social causes of crime, the multiple deprivations. By so doing it implies that the wealthy in society need not pay more taxes for social reforms since the cause of crime is individuals' wickedness. (Thus, the answer to crime is more police and harsher punishments rather than costly social reforms like better housing.)

Supposing you adopt this view of crime; that crime is committed by individuals and that individuals must be held responsible for their be-haviour. How then would you explain Table 14.3?

Clearly the difference cannot be explained solely by reference to

Table 14.3 Homicide rate per 100,000 of population

Developed countries		Less developed countries	
Australia	1.8	Brazil	10.8
Canada	2.5	Colombia	25.5
England and Wales	1.1	Guatemala	14.0
Scotland	1.5	Mexico	22.0
Switzerland	0.7		
United States	10.3		

Source: adapted from Young and Lea *What is to be Done about Law and Order?*

individuals, for example that some individuals are wicked by nature. There is a job for the sociologist here. What is there about the cultures in developing countries that causes these differences? Again, within the league of developed countries, why is the murder rate so much higher in the USA? In 1975 in New York there were 1645 murders, compared with 629 murders in the whole of England and Wales in 1979. What is the explanation of this?

A possible sociological explanation might begin by demonstrating that in the USA success is very highly prized (the American dream) yet success is of course a limited commodity. Those who do not succeed in the usual way, through hard work perhaps, may choose illegitimate ways or short cuts to achieve success, such as crime (the murder rate being one indicator of the general crime rate). This is not the full explanation, but it may be a start.

A sociological approach to deviance then may enable us to see more clearly the true social nature of crime. A 'commonsense' approach to crime suggests more should be spent on police and prisons, together with longer sentences. But, as Tables 14.4 to 14.7 show, the crime rate is rising despite the increasing amount spent on law and order, more police, more prison officers, more prisons and longer sentences.

QUESTION: why is the crime rate rising despite the increasing amount spent on law and order?

First of all, it *is* true that crime rates are rising. Consider Table 14.4.

Secondly, it *is* true that more is being spent on the police and on prison officers, as Tables 14.5 and 14.6 show.

Thirdly, the prison population *is* increasing and convicts are serving longer sentences, as Table 14.7 shows.

Finally, despite the increase in police strength, the clear-up rates for notifiable offences have not improved substantially since 1971.

What lessons can we learn from these statistics? See if you agree with these comments.

1 Increasing the strength of the police force does not seem to reduce crime.

Table 14.4   Notifiable offences recorded by the police in England and Wales: by type of offence (thousands)

Notifiable offences recorded	1971	1986	1987
Violence against the person	47.0	125.5	141.0
Sexual offences	23.6	22.7	25.2
of which, rape and attempted rape	–	2.3	2.5
Burglary	451.5	931.6	900.1
Robbery	7.5	30.0	32.6
Drugs offences	–	7.3	7.1
Theft and handling stolen goods	1003.7	2003.0	2052.0
of which, theft of vehicles	167.6	411.1	389.6
Fraud and forgery	99.8	133.4	133.0
Criminal damage	27.0	583.6	589.0
Other notifiable offences	5.6	9.4	12.2
Total notifiable offences	1665.7	3846.5	3892.2

Source: Criminal Statistics, Home Office; adapted from *Social Trends 1989*

Table 14.5   Strength of police forces in the UK (thousands)

	1961	1971	1981	1987
UK total	87.9	112.2	140.0	145.7

Source: Home Office; adapted from *Social Trends 1989*

Table 14.6   Prison service staff in Great Britain

	1971	1981	1988
Prison officer class	13,087	19,441	22,512
Governor class	532	614	649
Other non-industrial staff	3,027	4,358	4,689
Industrial staff	1,825	2,426	2,350
Total staff in service	18,471	26,839	30,200

Source: Home Office, Scottish Home and Health Department; adapted from *Social Trends 1989*

Table 14.7   Male prisoners in England and Wales: by length
of sentence

	1971	1981	1987
Prisoners aged 21 or over serving:			
up to 6 months	2,970	3,970	2,920
over 6 months and up to 18 months	8,230	7,480	6,110
over 18 months and up to 4 years	9,580	8,010	9,890
over 4 years (excluding life)	3,320	3,700	6,590
Life sentences	770	1,530	2,170
All sentenced prisoners	24,870	24,690	27,680

Source: Home Office; adapted from *Social Trends 1989*

Table 14.8   Clear-up rates for notifiable offences in England and
Wales: by type of offence (percentages)

Notifiable offences recorded	1971	1986	1987
Violence against the person	82	71	75
Sexual offences	76	71	75
of which, rape and attempted rape	–	62	71
Burglary	37	26	27
Robbery	42	20	21
Theft and handling stolen goods	43	31	32
of which, theft of vehicles	–	22	25
Fraud and forgery	83	67	67
Criminal damage	34	21	23
Other notifiable offences	92	93	96
Total notifiable offences	45	32	33

Source: Criminal Statistics, Home Office and *Social Trends 1989*

2   Increasing the strength of the police force does not seem to increase the
clear-up rate.
3   Increasing the length of prison sentences (i.e. punishing the offender
more) does not seem to have reduced the crime rate – although the
government thinks it will, hence (partly) it is embarking on a big
programme of prison building.

What contribution can the sociologist make to these problems? The
approach here is to outline some sociological theories that have been put
forward to try to explain deviancy from a sociological view. Then some
common questions (hiding some common assumptions) are 'answered'.

Finally, a case study based on the well known Islington Crime Survey is
quoted, showing the effects of crime from the victim's viewpoint.

Types of deviance theories

One difficulty in estimating and accounting for deviance in society is that there are many different theories of deviance. The main types of theories are:

deviant subculture;
anomie;
differential association;
labelling theory;
radical criminology.

Each type of theory will now be explained briefly in turn.

Deviant subculture theory

A society may be viewed as an entire group which has its own culture – its norms and values. Within a society there may be many smaller groups which, though subscribing in the main to the culture of the society of which they are a part, have their own subculture, their own particular values. Three examples of this would be minority religious sects, immigrant groups and the professions.

Another example of subcultures would be various deviant groups. Albert Cohen in *Delinquent Boys: The Culture of the Gang* shows how non-academic working class boys deal with their lack of success at school (at least according to the middle class 'measuring rod' applied at school – see Chapter 11). Denied success at school, they seek it in the gang. This could, for example, help to explain acts of vandalism. The boy may commit such acts for the 'applause' of the other gang members, thereby obtaining success, but here success is defined according to the culture of the deviant subgroup. Each member feels that the values of this subgroup are his values and therefore vandalism, seen as 'senseless' vandalism by the wider society, makes sense to him and the deviant subgroup which accepts him as a member.

Merton's anomie theory of deviance

Robert Merton (in *Social Theory and Social Structure*) argued that individuals have goals, and try to attain these goals in approved ways. Thus, for example, different societies would have different goals and means of attaining these goals, as shown in Table 14.9.

Merton thought that in a well regulated society the goals and the means of achieving them were in harmony; for example if most people believed in financial success, the opportunity to work hard to achieve this was available. Where, however, the goals and the means of achieving them were not in harmony (not integrated), then the individuals in such a society would suffer *anomie*. Hence, where the cultural goal was financial success but

Table 14.9 Examples of different cultural goals and means

	Cultural goals	Cultural means
Society A	Military success	Courage
Society B	Saintliness	Prayer
Society C	Financial success	Hard work

many people would have to cheat or steal to achieve it, then there would be widespread anomie in Merton's sense of the word. (Merton argues that cheats, thieves etc. appear because some people find that the institutional means for success, such as a good job, are not available to them.)

Merton's theory of anomie is based on the effects of a disjunction between the cultural goals of a society and the means of achieving them. Table 14.10 explains this.

Table 14.10 Merton's theory of anomie

		Cultural goals	Cultural means
I	Conformity	+	+
II	Innovation	+	−
III	Ritualism	−	+
IV	Retreatism	−	−
V	Rebellion	±	±

+ means people believe in society's cultural goals or use cultural means of achieving their goals;
− means they do not.

Conformity implies that the individual approves of society's goals and of the means of achieving them. American society lays much emphasis on success. Hence the cultural goal could be seen as success and the means of achieving it might be hard work.

The *innovator* may approve of society's goal, success, but not adopt the usual societal means for achieving it, hard work. Instead such a person may steal, for example, or commit acts of vandalism to gain success, as the Albert Cohen study describes. Such persons may feel no guilt, as they are socialized to the values of the deviant subculture which says such means are permissible.

An example of a *ritualist* may be an apparently religious person who goes through the motions, going to church on Sunday, but is not truly religious in everyday dealings. Merton gives other examples, the overzealous bureau-crat and the frightened employee.

The *retreatist* is the person who has withdrawn from society, accepting neither its goals nor the means of achieving them. This category may include tramps, alcoholics, drug addicts. It is seen as an individual adapta-tion, in contrast to the innovator's deviant subculture solution to society's pressures. On the other hand it would be possible to see commune dwellers in this category, with their group emphasis on, say, a 'hippie' life style with its togetherness, romanticism, identity with the poor. Quite often these life styles seem to be a response to the authoritarianism of 'established' middle class parents.

Finally *rebellion* could, for example, refer to the political rebel: the revolu-tionary who seeks to change both society's goals and its means of achieving them, as the table indicates. Quite often these people come from families which are politically radical.

Merton's theory has been criticized by Taylor, Walton and Young in *The New Criminology* for concentrating too much on individual adjustment and not enough on, for example, deviant subcultures and the power of the state to define crime (see section on 'radical criminology' on pp. 284–5).

Thus, according to Taylor, Merton does not say what caused this disjunc-tion between goals and means in the first place. Merton's theory implies that the poor are likely to commit crime because they do not possess the means to achieve success, hence they are more likely to 'innovate'. But this does not convincingly explain the over-representation of the lower class amongst apprehended offenders. This could also be explained by the way the police are organized, the bias of the courts and so on. Again, if most of the poor are under pressure to 'innovate' (commit crime in order to gain success) – how is it that such a small proportion do actually commit crime?

Differential association

Sutherland (in *The Principles of Criminology*) has argued that delinquency depends on who you associate with. In a 'criminal area' you tend to associate with others from a criminal background. Cloward and Ohlin, however (in *Delinquency and Opportunity*), show that not all people living in 'bad' areas become criminals and ask: why do delinquent norms develop? Combining the theories of Sutherland and Merton, they argue there are three basic kinds of subculture. Firstly, there is the criminal subculture. This is available to youths living in poor areas where there are the means available to commit crime, such as a fence to handle stolen property and criminal adult role models to copy.

Secondly, there is a conflict subculture. This may arise where there is no adult role to copy. Youths then innovate. In this subculture gang fights are commonplace.

Thirdly, there is a retreatist subculture where roles are not available, for example the youth of poor physique or the person who may turn to drug addiction.

In contrast to Cohen's deviant subculture theory, this theory indicates that there is not one single deviant subculture, but several.

Merton has criticized this theory on the grounds that it stresses the importance of place (or milieu). It also omits the notion of human purpose and meaning. People are not shaped solely by where they live or with whom they interact. Individuals also have purposes, plans and intentions.

Labelling theory

Labelling theorists see deviance as more than the violation of a rule (or norm): it is any behaviour that gets successfully defined by others as deviant. In other words the deviance lies not in the act itself but rather the response of others to the act. The deviant then responds to other people's reaction. Thus there are two stages according to Lemert:

1 primary deviance: the original act that gets defined as deviant;
2 secondary deviance: the deviant's response to society's definition of the original act.

Take, for example, the homosexual who is deprived of a respectable career by the discovery of his primary deviance. He may then drift into unconventional marginal (or unusual) occupations where his deviance does not make much difference. These marginal occupations could be called secondary deviance.

(Howard Becker sees such a deviant as embarking on a deviant career. In our normal use of the word 'career' the individual is seen as entering an occupation or profession, undergoing training, passing exams perhaps, starting actual work, becoming successful and so on. Becker uses this as an analogy to show what happens when an individual becomes a deviant.)

Labelling theory can be useful in understanding the relationship between deviance and the reaction to deviance, and between reaction and the results of that reaction. Labelling theory is not very good for explaining primary deviance, i.e. the original deviant act. But it is helpful in explaining secondary deviance, as perhaps shown by the example quoted here.

Radical criminology

This rejects all the theories so far described here on the grounds that they do not really show the relationship between the criminal and the state. According to this approach the criminal is seen as a product of the kind of society we live in. To understand crime in society it is no good just describing crime, criminals, the law, criminal statistics, the police or the victims. What is really necessary is to look at the *relationship* between the 'criminal' and the (repressive) state.

Thus Young and Lea argue that

working class crime is generated within the system. It is part of an individual-istic response to the brutalization created by multiple deprivation. And then it further contributes to this brutalization. To grow up 'hard', to be willing to stand up against difficult circumstances, only too often creates and contrib-utes towards adverse circumstances.

This process is illustrated by the accompanying diagram.

Perhaps this helps to explain why the overwhelming majority of men in prison come from social class V – unskilled manual workers; or why a labourer is 14 times more likely to be arrested than a professional person (Young and Lea).

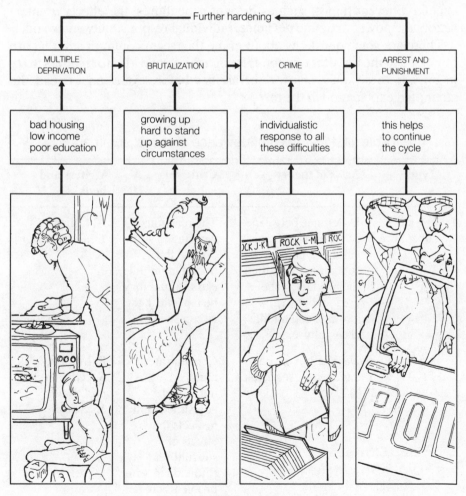

The making of a criminal: the spiral of deviance (or deviance amplification)

If the real causes of crime lie in the social structure, then punishment will only harden the criminal. As Young and Lea say, children may drift in and out of delinquency but those who then pass through the penal system are systematically broken: they are rendered inadequate by the system rather than rehabilitated by it (hence the futility of the idea of the 'short sharp shock').

Radical criminology therefore sees crime as only one of a number of related social problems, all of which arise from inequality in society. Thus the problem of crime cannot be solved by tackling it on its own. Clearly, punishment of the criminal will not solve the crime problem.

Theories of deviance: summary

Table 14.11 summarizes the theories of deviance described in this section. In criticizing these theories it is worth mentioning that they are seeking to explain different things, such as deviant subcultures, the effects of inter-action, the power to define deviance, individual responsibility and so on.

There are some questions about crime that seem common and that are discussed in the rest of the chapter. It might be a good idea for readers to try to answer these questions for themselves before going on to read the attempted explanation in the text.

Table 14.11 Types of deviance theories: summary

	Type	Basis of theory	Criticisms	Writers and books
1	Deviant subculture	Difference between subculture and main culture. Delinquent subcultures are often the product of the conflict between working and middle class culture.	The reaction of working class boys to the dominant middle class culture may be realistic in the circumstances.	A. Cohen, *Delinquent Boys*.
2	Anomie	Disjunction of goals and means (see Table 14.9).	Concentrates too much on individual adjustment and neglects the effects of subcultures. (Individuals with problems create solutions together.)	R. Merton, *Social Theory and Social Structure*.

	Type	Basis of theory	Criticisms	Writers and books
3	Differential association	Opportunity to associate with groups which reinforce individual's deviant tendencies – similar to 1 above but emphasis on conditioning.	Attempts to account for a wider range of deviant subcultures than 1 or 2 above but fails to encompass the full diversity of deviance.	E. H. Sutherland, *The Principles of Criminology*; Cloward and Ohlin, *Delinquency and Opportunity*.
4	Labelling theory	Labels are awarded during interaction between people. The individual may then take on the label – and may in future embark on a deviant career.	Cannot account for secret acts of deviance (where there is no-one to award the labels). It says little about serious crime.	H. Becker, *Outsiders* and *The Other Side*; and (possibly) D. Matza, *Becoming Deviant* and *Delinquency and Drift*.[1]
5	Radical criminology	The criminal is the product and victim of social relations. Labelling and punishing him serves the interests of the establishment.	Says little about individual morals and responsibilities.	I. Taylor et al. (eds), *Critical Criminology* (especially article by P. Q. Hirst).

[1] Not everyone would classify Matza as a labelling theorist.

Common question one: *crime is rare, so why all the interest in it?*

Is it true, crime is comparatively rare. As mentioned earlier, the average person can expect a robbery once every five centuries. Why then is it of such interest to sociologists, the police, the political parties and governments? For the sociologist, crime is the tip of the iceberg. It is a real problem in itself but it is also an indicator and symbol of greater problems. The following quote from Young and Lea gives some idea of this.

> Crime is the end-point of a continuum of disorder. It is not separate from other forms of aggravation and breakdown. It is the run-down council estate where music blares out of windows early in the morning; it is the graffiti on

the walls; it is aggression in the shops; it is bins that are never emptied; oil stains across the streets; it is kids that show no respect; it is large trucks racing through your roads; it is streets you do not dare walk down at night; it is always being careful; it is a symbol of a world falling apart. It is lack of respect for humanity and for fundamental human decency.

Common question two: *are blacks more deviant than whites? The crime statistics seem to show this*

The mention of 'crime statistics' should put the reader on guard now. Firstly, crime statistics reflect what the police and public are sensitive to. It may be robbery, a 'black' crime, rather than fraud, a 'white' crime. Like the rest of society the police have their prejudices, and in any case blacks are more visible. Again, 'swamping' an area, as the police tend to in black parts of the inner city, will obviously produce many arrests (and provoke further 'arrestable' acts). If white areas were similarly swamped 'high white crime rates' might also be discovered.

There is, however, another question that should be asked. Faced with discrimination and prejudice, poor housing, poor education, unemployment, provocation by the police and white youths – how is it that the crime rate for blacks is so low? It seems that black people are in fact well socialized, and that this enables them to overcome the very real frustrations referred to above.

Common question three: *why are crimes of violence increasing?*

It may be true that violent crime is increasing, but to some extent this may also be due to greater sensitivity. Thus we do not now tolerate wife beating, a violent crime that may previously have gone unreported. Another reason for the increase is the need to succeed, the greater stress on affluence and competition. Those at the bottom of society, who cannot succeed in the conventional way in an unequal society, may increasingly resort to violence as a way of life – to get rich quickly by robbery or to show prowess by being fearless, or as an aspect of male 'machismo' – the masculine mystique. Thus, as shown earlier, American rates of crimes of violence are much higher than European and this may be due to the greater emphasis on success in American society (as argued earlier in the chapter).

Finally it was also shown earlier in the chapter that the fear of crime, especially assault, is far greater than the actual rate of crime – see Tables 14.1 and 14.2.

Common question four: *why do women commit fewer crimes than men?*

Women do commit far fewer crimes than men. Such crimes as they commit are often connected with women's roles, such as housewife and mother.

Women seldom commit violent crime and if they do they are more severely punished for it.

Women are of course socialized to their role and this means socialized to their role *in the family* as wife, mother, carer and provider. All this means that women have less to do with the wider world and less opportunity and less desire to participate in criminal activity. On the other hand many crimes of violence do occur in the home as Chapter 2 on the family showed. Women are nearly always on the receiving end of assault, rape and incest. In such a case, the woman still has to prove in court that she did not provoke the man, such is the prejudice of our society.

Wife beating and rape are connected with male control in the family (patriarchy). It is worth repeating that in most cases of rape the rapist is known to the woman or girl, the offence usually occurs at the family home, or the home of the rapist or the woman. A woman may turn to a man for protection, yet it is within marriage that the woman is most likely to experience violence (wife battering is estimated to occur in 30 per cent of marriages). (Eva Gamarnikov in *The Macmillan Student Encyclopedia of Sociology*.)

Thus it is true that women commit fewer crimes, but instead of asking why, it might be more interesting sociologically to ask firstly, what is there in the *culture* of our society that could account for this difference, and secondly, why are crimes against women under-recorded and concealed? (Good sociology asks the right questions.)

Common question five: *what is the cause of football hooliganism?   why cannot sociology give an explanation?*

In Stan Cohen's words, we make folk devils of football hooligans and work ourselves into moral panics. But what is really happening at matches?

In *Rules of Disorder* Marsh, Rosser and Harré show how apparently 'senseless' behaviour makes sense to those involved. The book seeks to interpret the behaviour of youths in the classroom and on the football terraces. These actions are rule governed; there are unspoken rules concerning the use of violence, for instance, which put bounds on the interaction. The authors demonstrate that the incidence of violence is grossly exaggerated anyway – about nine arrests per game at Leeds.

The authors show that the ritual on the terrace is related to the age old problem of proving that one is better at being a man than one's rivals. There are usually two stages to this ritual. The first consists of insults which portray the rivals as feminine. Once this has been achieved the rivals can be challenged, chased or even in some cases beaten up, but usually this stops short of serious injury. It is therefore a way for youths to assert themselves, and especially their masculinity, in a (for them) dehumanizing society. 'The fact that the process of dehumanization is largely absent in the conflicts between rival football fans provides a basis for cautious optimism.'

The authors do not seek to excuse the football fan or the classroom trouble maker, but try to show that the events that outrage us have a different reality for the actors. Perhaps magistrates and police in fact threaten social order when they refer to fans as animals? The book shows that there are at least rules of disorder. The disorder comes from society itself, its inequalities, meaningless schools, boring jobs and of course unemployment. (The fact that a few fans flaunt their money should not hide the reality that most come from the working class.)

(Note: the worst example of football violence in recent times was the Liverpool–Juventus match in Brussels in May 1985 in which 32 people died. However, most of these deaths were accidental due to the collapse of a brick wall which was under pressure from panic stricken fans.)

Common question six: *why do working class people commit more crime than middle class people?*

Again, it is largely true that the crime rate is highest in social class V (unskilled manual worker). A labourer is 14 times more likely to be arrested than a professional person.

One explanation tentatively put forward here (when discussing radical criminology) was the 'brutalization' and 'hardening' process associated with the types of life styles of poorer people.

Another explanation is that the differences are not as great as they might appear because a lot of crime committed by middle class people does not get reported. Edwin Sutherland in his book *White Collar Crime* shows that white collar crime is widespread, highly organized, and very costly. It includes breaches of anti-trust legislation (against monopolies), breaches of safety regulations, pollution and so on. Sutherland showed that the largest corporations in America were law breakers.

There have been several further studies of white collar crime in the USA confirming Sutherland's findings. The President's Commission on Law Enforcement showed that while traditional property crimes (theft etc.) got most notice in the mass media, they took up only 8.6 per cent of the cost of crime. On the other hand, white collar crimes like fraud, committed by people of high repute, got little media attention and yet accounted for 14.5 per cent of the cost of crime, with very few arrests.

Finally, Sutherland suggested that crime should be defined on the basis of social injury; that is, hurt to society.

A case study

The Islington Crime Survey: Crime Victimization and Policy in Inner-city London by T. Jones, B. MacLean and J. Young

This survey differs from most others in criminology in that it focuses on the *victim*. It was commissioned by the Islington Council and is based on 2000 door to door interviews; it was undertaken by the Middlesex Polytechnic Centre for Criminology.

The study showed there was a great fear of crime, particularly among vulnerable groups such as blacks, women, the elderly and the poor in this run-down inner city area. (See also Tables 14.1 and 14.2.)

The researchers found that over 70 per cent of Islington residents see crime as a 'problem'. This is not just panic – their perception of risk is related to their vulnerability. Only 8 per cent saw race as a problem; about half the women worried about rape or being sexually molested; 68 per cent thought burglary has become more common in the last five years; 53 per cent thought vandalism had become more common. Many residents would like to join a crime prevention scheme but could not afford it.

The following summary, quoted from the Report of the Islington Crime Survey, confirms that the people of Islington see crime as a big problem – a problem for the poor.

Summary and policy recommendations of the Islington Crime Survey
1   Taking the public seriously
We have shown that crime is perceived by the people of Islington to be a problem of major dimensions. Indeed, crime and vandalism are seen as the second greatest problems in the Borough after unemployment, on a par with poor youth and children's facilities and housing – and way ahead of schools and public transport.

The impact of crime is considerable and it is far from a rare event. 31 per cent of households in Islington had a serious crime committed against them in the last year – and it shapes their lives. For example, over a quarter of all people in Islington always avoid going out after dark because of fear of crime and this rises to over one third in the case of women. We have a virtual curfew of the female population.

2   The crisis of crime control and policing
There can be little doubt that we face a crisis of extraordinary proportions in the policing of the inner city. At present the clear-up rate per officer per year in the Metropolitan Police Area is four crimes at the staggering cost of £6076 each crime. In areas such as Islington the clear-up rate for burglary has fallen to 9 per cent and this refers, of course, only to the crimes known to the police. As our survey shows, many people simply do not bother to report crime because little good is likely to come from it. Meanwhile, substantial sections of the population are alienated from the police. We have traced the evidence

of this in detail. It is certainly a time for change. (But this is not solely a police problem.)

3 Public estimation of police effectiveness

We have seen that there is widespread public scepticism about the ability of the police to combat the crimes which are of greatest public concern. This is reflected in the extremely high proportion of people who simply do not report offences to the police because they feel that it would do no good. As we have indicated throughout, the key to police efficiency is public cooperation.

The point to stress here is that detective work is rarely of a Sherlock Holmes variety and is much more often dependent on good public relations. Criticism of police efficiency is *ipso facto* criticism of police–public relations. It is for this reason that arguments about the necessity of the police to act scrupulously within the letter of the law and in a courteous fashion in their relations with the public, are not only important on a level of democratic sensibility. They are also so in terms of police effectiveness. This is clearly recognized in the excellent 'Principles of Policing and Guidance for Professional Behaviour' published by the Metropolitan Police.

'Any unreasonable, abrupt and over-zealous action by us will not achieve an orderly society, except perhaps in the very short term, but will rapidly lose for the Force its public support. And, since a police service without public support will not be able to police by consent, and in the long term will not be able to police at all, one of the very cornerstones of democratic government will have been put at risk.'

4 Curbing stop and search

A specific police activity which involves largely an 'order maintenance' function is stop and search. Our survey indicates that in Islington a third of young white males have been stopped in the last 12 months and over a half of young black males. The yield of such procedures is extremely low in terms of the main public priorities with regard to crime. We argue that with the important exception of breathalyser checks on suspected drunken drivers (a high public priority) stops should be severely curbed.

5 Conclusions

The approach we have outlined to combating crime must be multi agency, it involves reforms both in public policy and in policing, it must involve both local and Borough level initiatives and it should strive towards the greatest level of popular participation and democratic accountability.

Some sociologists might see the problem of crime in the inner city as forming part of the wider problem of poverty. They may therefore advocate higher incomes, better housing and so on.

Another approach might be that of community policing as advocated by John Anderson, formerly Chief Constable of Devon and Cornwall, with closer contact between the police and the community. This was also advocated in the Islington Crime Survey.

A third approach was advanced by Kinsey, Lea and Young in their book

Losing the Fight against Crime. They suggest what they call minimal policing (pp. 207 and 208), based on the following propositions.

1   The vast majority of crimes cleared up by the police are, in fact, those in which individual members of the public have provided the critical information and have initiated police action. Thus, by emphasizing public initiation we maximize that aspect of police work which is most effective.

2   Minimal policing encourages contact between the police and the public in those circumstances where cooperation is most forthcoming, that is, where police presence has been deemed necessary and desirable and has been requested. Conversely, it minimizes those instances which most clearly undermine public confidence in the police – that is, where police are seen to be 'interfering', or acting officiously.

3   Minimal policing emphasizes that policing is and should be about crime and law enforcement, and restricts police activity to this clearly defined area. In other words, it cuts out that whole ill-defined grey area of 'pre-emptive policing' with its emphasis upon covert 'intelligence collection', surveillance and random stop and search.

4   Finally, within the concept of the public initiation of police action, minimal policing emphasizes the principle of democratic accountability and the protection of individual rights and civil liberties as an integral element of overall policing strategy.

QUESTIONS: do you think minimal policing will work? Will it reduce crime? Improve the clear-up rate? Gain the cooperation of the public?

Suggestions

The citizens of inner cities suffer many disadvantages; crime is just one of them (see 'Common question one', p. 287). Just to concentrate on policing alone may be inadequate.

   The police have their own methods, their own professional code and perhaps their own ideologies. They may not take to ideas like minimal policing.

   Try to be as sociological as possible, when answering these questions. For example, will minimal policing change the circumstances in which labelling occurs? (See definition of labelling theory in this chapter.)

Conclusions

The main function of the sociologist is to try and show what is really taking place in society and thereby offer a critique of society. Supposing the crime rate increased sharply. Would better policing, bigger prisons and stiffer sentences really be the answer? The appeal of simple solutions to complex problems is very strong, hence, for example, the continuing debate on whether to restore the death penalty. The majority of people favour restoration; it is seen as a simple solution to the problem of violence in society.

Yet the problem of violence is too complex for these simple solutions to work. One of the tasks of sociologists is to show these complexities, for example that high rates of violence are often associated with inequality in society. To draw attention to this makes sociologists unpopular with those people who think they know the solution (and also those people who do not really want less inequality in society).

Self-examination questions

1 What is meant by: 'deviance', 'crime', 'norms', 'values', 'normal', 'religious crime', 'economic crime', 'anomie' (as used by Merton)?
2 Briefly outline the main types of sociological theories of deviance.
3 What are the main difficulties in determining the amount of crime in a society?
4 To what extent is society responsible for crime?
5 What are the areas of the sociology of deviance discussed in this chapter? What further topics might a sociology of deviance embrace?

Project

Compare the statistics for crime now with those for, say, ten or twenty years ago. Show trends in crime and try to account for them. Try to assess society's attitudes, looking, for example, at statements by judges and magistrates, police and probation officers, politicians, newspaper editorials, victims and so on. You will find *Social Trends* useful as well as back numbers of newspapers and magazines (like *New Society*). Finally attempt a sociological analysis of the data you have collected. Try to answer the question: what is really going on?

Past examination questions

1 **Examine the view that crime is predominantly a working class phenomenon.**

Associated Examining Board, GCSE, Paper 2, July 1988

Suggestions

A lot of middle class crime is hidden – fraud, etc. (see E. Sutherland), 'the dark figure'. Deviance in the working class is more likely to be treated as crime. Working class men are more likely to be caught. See 'Common question six'.

2   Either (a) Compare two theoretical approaches to deviance.

or (b) Explain the major differences between men and women in the level and pattern of recorded crime.

University of Oxford Delegacy of Local Examinations, A Level, Paper 2, Summer 1988

Suggestions

a) See text, pp. 281–7, especially Table 14.11, for summary, and also 'Further reading'.
b) See p. 289 and 'Further reading', especially Carlen and Elliott.

3   What is labelling theory? Critically assess its contribution to the sociological understanding of crime and deviance.

University of Cambridge Local Examinations Syndicate, A Level, Paper 2, June 1987

Suggestions

Again, see Table 14.11 and writers in this area.

4   Study the information given below and then answer the questions printed after it.

Every eight seconds, there is another innocent victim

CRIME FILE

**LAWLESS
BRITAIN!**

THE CRIMINALS HAVE
NEVER HAD IT SO GOOD

RAPE	UP 24%
ROBBERY	UP 9%
BURGLARY	UP 7%
THEFT	UP 6%
VIOLENCE	UP 3%
VANDALISM	UP 8%

TABLE OF SHAME

The shocking truth about lawless Britain was exposed by official Government figures yesterday.

They show that the country is in the grip of its worst-ever crime

REGION by region these were last year's biggest crime increases: 1. City of London – up 16%; 2. Avon and Somerset – 15%; 3. Cleveland – 14%; 4. South Wales

wave. There was a 7% overall increase in crime in England and Wales last year.

Crimes of violence, including rape, are soaring. Robberies, burglaries and theft are all up.

What lies behind the tide of lawlessness sweeping Britain and the rest of Europe?

The police say it's being fuelled by the consumer boom, television, drug-taking and unemployment.

– 12%; 5. Bedfordshire, Greater Manchester, Suffolk – 11%. 6. Cumbria, Essex, Humberside, West Midlands –10%; 7. Lancashire, Surrey, Thames Valley – 9%; 8. Merseyside, South Yorkshire, Staffordshire – 8%.

Three police forces reported a fall; Gwent – down 5%; Derbyshire – 3%; Cambridgeshire – 1%.

MIRROR COMMENT
A Double Disgrace

Two issues cry out for sympathetic and urgent action in today's Budget.

They are the record rise in crime - and the continuing brutality of unemployment, which is the root of much of that crime.

Source: quotations from the *Daily Mirror*.

1 a) Which area shown in the table had the greatest fall in the crime rate in 1986? (1 mark)
  b) What was the overall percentage increase in crime in England and Wales in 1986? (1 mark)
2 Why is some deviant behaviour seen as criminal? (2 marks)
3 Why may statistics for crime be unreliable? (4 marks)
4 To what extent do you agree with the statement in the information above that unemployment is the main cause of the increase in crime? (6 marks)
5 Men are six times more likely than women to be convicted of a criminal offence. Explain why this is so. (6 marks)

Midland Examining Group, GCSE, Paper 2, May 1988.

Suggestions

Whether some deviant behaviour is seen as criminal depends on the culture of the society concerned (see text).

Criminal statistics may be unreliable because of the changing definition of crime, the number who get away, or where crime is unrecorded, etc. (Mention the 'dark figure'.)

On question 4 it could be argued that both crime and unemployment are aspects of the same thing – poverty – but this would need testing.

On question 5 see text.

Further reading

*H. Becker, *Outsiders*
S. Box, *Deviance, Reality and Society*
M. Brake, *Comparative Youth Culture*
P. Carlen (ed.), *Criminal Women*
A. Cohen, *Delinquent Boys*
S. Cohen (ed.), *Images of Deviance*
J. Douglas (ed.), *The Sociology of Deviance*
*D. Downes and P. Rock, *Understanding Deviance*
D. Elliott, *Gender, Delinquency and Society*
S. Hall and T. Jefferson (eds), *Resistance through Rituals*
R. Kinsey, J. Lea and J. Young, *Losing the Fight against Crime*
D. Matza, *Becoming Deviant*
P. Rock and M. McIntosh (eds), *Deviance and Social Control*
E. Sutherland, *White Collar Crime*
I. Taylor, P. Walton and J. Young, *The New Criminology*
I. Taylor, P. Walton and J. Young (eds), *Critical Criminology*
*J. Young and J. Lea, *What is to be Done about Law and Order?*
*'Deviance', *New Society*, 16 February 1984 (Society Today series)
*'Social Control', *New Society*, 28 April 1983 (Society Today series)

15　Mass Media

The mass media include newspapers, radio and television (together with video, cable television and new channels). Basically, this chapter will argue that the mass media are a conservative influence, reinforcing the status quo; that the mass media do not cause people to change their beliefs and opinions; and finally that the mass media perhaps 'manufacture' and systematically distort the news. But readers are invited to form their own judgement on these issues. These themes will be examined in terms of the following common assumptions made about the mass media:

1　The mass media have an important influence on people's lives, and in particular influence and sometimes change their beliefs and opinions.
2　The mass media reflect a variety of viewpoints.
3　The mass media try to give an unbiased account of the news, faithfully separating news from comment.
4　Television has a bad influence on children; violence on television is a possible cause of delinquency.

These common assumptions will now be examined in turn.

Common assumption one: *the mass media have an important influence on people's lives and in particular influence and sometimes change their beliefs and opinions*

The influence of the mass media is often overemphasized. Frequently the media, especially television, are seen as:

1　encouraging crime;
2　leading to political demagogy;
3　having a 'copycat' effect (seeing crime or riots will encourage others to do likewise);
4　influencing people to change their views.

These criticisms are often based on an oversimplified view of the mass media, as in Diagram 1. Really the model should take into account the effects of the structure of society, its prevailing values and attitudes, and the influence of the groups to which the individual belongs, as in Diagram 2.

Thus, Klapper (in *The Effects of Mass Communication*) and Lazarsfeld

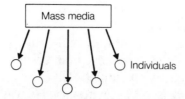

Diagram 1   *The simplified view of the mass media*

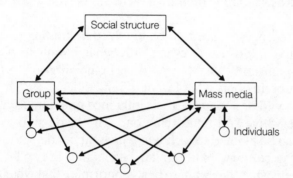

Diagram 2   *A more realistic view of the mass media*
Source of Diagrams 1 and 2: Secord and Blackman, *Social Psychology*

(in *The People's Choice*) suggest that there is a two step flow of information. The 'message' is mediated (or judged) by opinion leaders who in effect act as gate keepers (or censors) of information. Examples would include political and religious leaders, trade union leaders, company directors, leading professionals such as doctors, colleagues at work, your family and friends and so on.

The pronouncements of such people may be awaited before any change of view. In addition, of course, viewing television is usually a family affair so that the family group also mediates the message. In any event, Diagram 1, the simplified view of the influence of the mass media, should be rejected.

QUESTIONS: Who mediates the news for you? Who mediates the news for me?

Generally people are reluctant to change their views if such a conversion means leaving the group and giving up the satisfaction obtained from being a member of that group. An interesting example for this is the study by Shils and Janowitz of German army units in the closing stages of World War II. ('Cohesion and disintegration of the Wehrmacht in World War II'.) These soldiers discounted allied propaganda because the unit met their needs, giving both physical and moral support. Another example of this reluctance to change is the fact that most people vote the same way as their parents. To change may seem to imply some sort of break and a loss, to some extent, of family group support.

Lazarsfeld and his colleagues showed in a well known study of an American presidential campaign (*The People's Choice*) that viewers and listeners do not change and that they 'tune out' what they do not want to know (i.e. information likely to change their opinion). Some years ago there was a series on BBC television entitled 'Till Death Us Do Part'. The central character was sexist, racist and reactionary. He was depicted as a fool and his views were held up to ridicule, yet a considerable part of the audience saw the series as validating their own racist views – they saw only what they wanted to see.

Three main processes seem to be involved in limiting the effects of the media: selective exposure (viewing only what I want to view), selective perception (seeing only what I want to see in the programme) and selective recall (remembering only what I want to remember).

Turning now to newspapers, their influence on people's opinions tends to be a conservative and reinforcing one. The readership for a particular newspaper can be likened to a club in which the readers, though scattered throughout the country, have similar beliefs and life styles. Their newspaper tells them what they want to hear, confirming that what they define as news is news; what they define as shocking is shocking and so on. Newspaper loyalty is therefore another aspect of selective exposure, selective perception and selective recall. Table 15.1 indicates the strong class basis of choice of newspapers in Britain. (The ownership of newspapers etc. is discussed in the working of project 1.)

On the first common assumption then, that the mass media influences and can sometimes change people's opinions, the sociologist must be very cautious. Klapper (in *The Effects of Mass Communication*) suggests that the main influence of the media is to confirm views already held.

Newspapers help to confirm the views their readers already hold
Source: *New Society*, 1 December 1983

Table 15.1 Reading of national newspapers in Great Britain: by sex and social class, 1987

Daily newspaper	Percentage of adults reading each paper in 1987		Percentage of adults in each social class reading each paper in 1987						Readership (millions)		Readers per copy (numbers)
	Males	Females	A	B	C1	C2	D	E	1971	1987	1987
The Sun	28	23	5	10	20	32	37	27	8.5	11.3	2.8
Daily Mirror	23	18	4	8	16	27	29	19	13.8	9.1	2.9
Daily Mail	11	10	14	14	14	9	6	5	4.8	4.5	2.5
Daily Express	10	9	9	12	13	10	6	6	9.7	4.3	2.5
The Star	11	7	2	2	6	12	15	9	–	3.9	3.2
The Daily Telegraph	7	5	28	16	8	3	1	2	3.6	2.8	2.4
The Guardian	4	3	9	10	4	1	1	1	1.1	1.5	3.1
The Times	4	2	16	8	3	1	1	1	1.1	1.2	2.7
Today	3	2	1	2	3	3	3	1	–	1.1	3.3
The Independent	3	1	6	6	3	1	1	–	–	0.9	2.8
Financial Times	3	1	8	5	2	1	–	–	0.7	0.8	3.5
Any daily newspaper	73	63	74	67	67	70	72	59	–	68.0	–

Note: class A corresponds to class I in Chapter 5.
Source: National Readership Surveys, 1971 and 1987, Joint Industry Committee for National Readership Surveys; Circulation Review, Audit Bureau of Circulation; reprinted in *Social Trends 1989*

Common assumption two: *the mass media reflect a variety of viewpoints*

'Common sense' suggests there is great variety in the mass media: many newspapers and, in the USA, literally dozens of broadcasting stations, many different kinds of programmes and articles etc. In addition, new technology would appear to increase media variety: video, cable TV and automated printing. But might this variety in the media be more apparent than real? Do the media really reflect a variety of viewpoints or merely a variety of different ways of saying the same thing?

The first point is that for the mass media in a free enterprise society the message is mainly *entertainment*, according to Klapper. This is what the audience wants, and therefore this is what is supplied – supplied by programme contractors, sponsors, financiers, and those concerned with programme ratings. Entertainment means in the main comedy, sex and violence, but in any case it usually avoids genuinely controversial issues. Thus again the media can be seen as having the effect of reinforcing the status quo, since these entertainments reflect the beliefs and values approved of by the mass media. The audience gets what it wants and this in Britain is assured by the competition among the contracting companies and the BBC – all competing for high audience ratings.

News itself can become entertainment and any serious political import in the news can become reduced to this level. Television news bulletins are usually introduced by dramatic music and presented by attractive newscasters. Consider the following passage from John Hartley's book *Understanding News*. It concerns the storming of the Iranian Embassy by the SAS, shown live on television.

> Ideology and entertainment are not incompatible. If you're not looking for it [entertainment], that doesn't make it go away. In fact it can be argued strongly that the more entertainingly an ideological message is encoded, the more we are likely to be 'subjected' to its ideology. The SAS example is relevant here. For once defined as entertainment, politics and cause have disappeared. Few people can have known very much about the situation in Arabstand, and after the siege we knew very little more. The event became an isolated 'dramatic' act, into which all sorts of patriotic pro-SAS 'meanings' were then inserted. It may well have been a dramatic triumph for the British military, but that is by no means all that it meant.

In following an item of news on television, or in a newspaper, readers might like to make these tests for themselves:

1 How far is this news item concerned with what is dramatic and immediate rather than what is important? For example, a difference of views in a political party may be presented as a dramatic happening (which it might well be), yet the reasons why the protagonists hold the views they do might be neglected.

2   How far is important news trivialized by presenting it in terms of personalities rather than issues? For example, an election campaign may be presented in terms of Maggie versus Neil rather than comparing the policies of the political parties.

3   How far is the item concerned with attention to the details of the event (say a hijacking), rather than with underlying motives for the event?

Coming back to the common assumption that is the heading of this section, a general question could be asked: how far does this news item really challenge people to think deeply about the event (and perhaps change their views), and how far does it reinforce existing beliefs?

QUESTION: what do you think will be the result of the government's intention to open up the airwaves and increase competition among television companies?

Common assumption three: *the media try to give an unbiased account of the news, faithfully separating news from comment*

The challenge to this common assumption is that the news is consistently biased, and that this bias reflects what would loosely be called the 'official' viewpoint.

In their book *Really Bad News*, the Glasgow University Media Group demonstrate a bias in what is reported; for example, there is consistent over-reporting of strikes. They claim that the news is presented from the viewpoint of the Treasury, and of managers. Thus the Group found that all the television channels offer a remarkably similar product. The types of stories and their presentation varied only slightly and the news was very selective, for example only 2 per cent of Britain's work force makes vehicles, yet it had one quarter of the general industrial coverage on television news. Again, there is constant reference to disputes – the dustcart drivers' dispute, the civil servants' dispute, the laggers' dispute – without reference to the other side, the employers. The implication seems to be that trouble comes from low status groups, from the bottom of society rather than the top.

QUESTION: how true is this implication of strikes, street riots, and crime? Give actual examples from the media.

The media – newspapers and television – seem to be committed to a consensus view of society, the nation and the community; yet they have to report news that challenges this consensus view – strikes, inflation and unemployment. Often this involves closing off radical (and sociological) views of what is really happening in society.

Do the media use stereotypes in presenting the news?

Suggestion

Check for yourself whether this is true – especially in industrial disputes, street riots and crime.

Finally, the Glasgow University Media Group comment that most of the mass media, books, records and films are owned by only 12 companies in Britain, including household names like EMI and Rank. 95 per cent of the total circulation of national daily newspapers is controlled by just five companies. Naturally this financial control affects what the newspapers produce. Newspaper proprietors like Beaverbrook and Rothermere in the past and Murdoch today have great influence and power (though this chapter suggests that the effect of the media generally is to confirm people's existing beliefs rather than to change their views).

The Glasgow University Media Group conclude that 'ideologies are the connecting link between the so-called facts of the news and the background assumptions which enable us, the audience, to understand those "facts".' Broadcasters, on the other hand, say that the events in the news are real and that they are newsworthy. Summarizing, the argument could be presented as follows:

A possible broadcaster/journalist's viewpoint

1 We try to report the news and to separate facts from comment.

2 We report as news what everyone says is the news. Make the test for yourself – ask the man or woman on the Clapham omnibus whether they agree that what we have selected as news accords with their definition of what the news is.

3 We report the news, we react to the news, we do not make the news.

4 The media does not impose consensus – it reflects it.

5 We try to give 'balance' in our news presentation, to reflect all sides of an issue. The fact that we have strong critics from Left and Right confirms our view that we do strike a proper balance.

A possible sociological viewpoint

It is impossible to separate fact from comment. For example, wife beating is reported as a newsworthy fact now whereas before the war it would not have been.

This is probably true, but to use the same metaphor, the person on the Clapham omnibus does not want to go very far. What is lacking is real analysis. Again, selection of the item as newsworthy reflects the values of the selectors (broadcasters) and their audience.

The media does indeed manufacture news. How does crime get selected from the pool of events? *Answer* – the selective portrayal of crime by the media shapes the public definition of the crime problem. Thus the journalist reports those items the public is sensitive to, and this confirms the selection of the item as newsworthy.

This is probably true. By reporting mainly what the person on the Clapham omnibus wants to know, you support the status quo. Even the manufacture of news (in 3 above) probably supports the status quo.

Balance is really an ideological word (along with 'moderate' and 'common sense'). Balance supports the status quo. It levels everything down, diluting and making safe what appears to be threatening, e.g. a point of view which strongly challenges conventional wisdom. The concept of balance assumes an omniscient broadcaster and a single definable truth. It might be better for professional broadcasters to stand aside, allowing contending groups to present their own news programmes – but this might be seen by broadcasters as an attack on their professional integrity.

Can we, however, be more specific about what gets selected as news? Steve Chibnall in *Law and Order News* lists eight items which guide the selection of items as news. They are:

1 Immediacy: news is about what has just happened.
2 Dramatization: news must be dramatic (millions of people slowly starving is not dramatic).
3 Personalization: for example, important political issues get trivalized, e.g. 'Maggie versus Neil' in a general election.
4 Simplification: an editor of the *Daily Express* defined a bad news story as one that cannot be absorbed at first reading.
5 Titillation: for example, 'Shock Horror Probe'. It fascinates and titillates and then reassures us by finally condemning the act. (See Stan Cohen's book *Folk Devils and Moral Panics*.)
6 Conventionalism: the journalist does not just report the news, but 'translates' it so that it can be understood by 'normal' people.
7 Structured access: those in authority get more access to the media – hence news tends to be what those in authority define as news.
8 Novelty: there must be an 'angle' which another paper or programme has not got.

Representations in the mass media

As people we are constantly using signs and symbols to make sense of our social world. The meaning of these symbols is widely shared; for example, people in Britain readily associate Jaguar cars with high status, skinhead haircuts with rough youths, pin-stripe suits with upper middle class males.

The following discussion of the representation of gender and race in the media shows how the media use popular symbols and portray groups of people to the viewing and reading public.

The representation of gender in the media

Sociologists may look at the ways in which *women* are represented in the media. These might include housewife, mother, woman as a sex symbol for men (e.g. page 3 girl in *The Sun*), professional women, the carefree girl, the beautiful woman, and so on (see T. Millum, *Images of Woman*). Margaret Fergusson has studied the representation of gender in the media. In *Forever Feminine* she shows that the media, in representing women, often mentions irrationality and feminine unpredictability. She surveyed best-selling women's magazines *Woman*, *Woman's Own*, and *Women's Weekly* and found that the ones that survived seemed to be those that stressed traditional feminine values and promoted the ideal of the exemplary woman. This ideal has its own beliefs, including beautification, child rearing, housework and cooking. There appeared to be two main themes: firstly, getting your man, and secondly, self-perfection.

Fergusson's view is that women's image of themselves is reinforced by these representations and this is ideological since it supports the interests of the powerful in society – namely, men – and so helps to maintain the subordination of women.

The representation of race in the media

The representation of *race* in the media usually stresses trouble. Little attention is given to the real problems black people suffer, such as poor housing, education, poor employment prospects, poor health facilities, a fear to go out at night. (D. Glover, *The Sociology of the Mass Media*, pp. 31–3.) Often the press give exaggerated reports, for example, 'School Mobs in London Race Riot' (held by the Press Council as being inaccurate and unjustified).

In his study of press reporting on race (*Public Awareness and the Media*) Troyna showed that black people were represented as 'outsiders'. Despite a big decline in black immigration, this was seen by the press as the crucial issue. Black people were represented as a problem and as being essentially different from the mainstream in society.

Other representation by the media

The previous chapter has shown how deviance is represented in the media, and perhaps here it is worth mentioning a study that brings together the representation of race and deviance. It is by Stuart Hall et al. and called *Policing the Crisis: Mugging, the State and Law and Order*. Hall accuses the media of inventing a crime previously unknown in Britain. The crime is called mugging – where black men attack white victims.

The social construction of the news

The concept of the social construction of reality may prove useful in understanding the self-confirming nature of the news. Berger and Luckman, in their book *The Social Construction of Reality*, argue that what is real is what society takes to be real and what is knowledge is what society says is knowledge. Thus what is real to, say, a monk, differs from what is real to an American businessman. We all become 'institutionalized' or habituated to our place (role) in society, and in this way order in society is maintained. We adopt (internalize) the beliefs of our society, including our societal role, our society's principal beliefs, our society's definition of what constitutes knowledge and finally our society's definition of what constitutes 'news'. It may be helpful here to refer back to pp. 303–4, where the social construction of news is discussed. The Glasgow Media Group demonstrate the similarity of output, the similarity of news stories and their presentation.

Note: the social construction of reality is a useful social tool used several times in this book; see Chapters 10 and 14 and Glossary.

Common assumption four: *television has a bad influence on children. Violence on television is a possible cause of delinquency*

As shown earlier in this chapter, we cannot really say that television alters people's attitudes. Himmelweit, Oppenheimer and Vince showed (in *Television and the Child*) that television tended to make no impact on the child where it could look to other sources of information such as parents, books or friends. They also showed that those children who were influenced would have been easily influenced by other media anyway.

Halloran, Brown and Chaney in *Television and Delinquency*, compared a group of male delinquents with non-delinquents and showed there was only a slight difference in their preferred programmes. However, they did find that as a group the delinquents tended to come from 'socially disorganized families' (one parent families, or father unemployed etc.). They usually did not have girl friends. These researchers concluded that television was not a cause of delinquent behaviour, but played a minor contributory part.

Winick and Winick in *The Television Experience* show that the child's viewing is an active, not a passive, experience. The child relates the programme to its own world, dismissing for example some programmes as 'kids' stuff'. The child views what it is ready for and wants and these researchers conclude: 'By 15, most surely 17, the youngster would probably have formed a personal code that involved management of aggressive and violent feeling.'

Finally, W. A. Belson in *Television Violence and the Adolescent Boy* concluded that though high exposure to television violence did lead to real violence, this was probably a releasing effect: it did not actually *cause* the violence.

The principal findings of the Belson study were that:

1 High exposure to TV violence may increase the degree to which boys engage in serious violence. However, there was no evidence that high exposure to television violence leads to a *general* preoccupation with violence or leads boys to feel more willing to commit acts of violence.

2 There is no evidence to show that exposure to television hardens boys – makes them more callous about violence in the real world.

Table 15.2 Comparison of 'qualifiers'
(heavier exposure to violence) with
'controls' (lighter exposure to violence)

'Score' for involvement in serious crimes	Exposure to TV violence	
	Qualifiers	Controls
0	411	429
1	95	91
2–3	77	95
4–9	92	87
10–39	66	56
40–69	29	17
70–99	4	3

Source: W. A. Belson, *Television Violence and the Adolescent Boy*

3 There was no evidence to show that watching TV violence:
   a) causes boys to consider violence part of 'human nature';
   b) causes boys to see violence as a way to solve their problems;
   c) leads to sleep disturbance;
   d) reduces boys' consideration for other boys;
   e) reduces boys' respect for authority.

4 Table 15.2 seems to show that heavy exposure to TV violence does not necessarily lead to a higher 'score' for involvement in serious violence.

As can be seen, the evidence is not all that clear. All that can really be said is that it is unlikely that television violence directly causes real violence. Perhaps one good way of examining the common assumption above is to subdivide it into four parts and deal with each part.

Common assumption four	Criticism
1 Television will make people passive: they will just want to be entertained.	Himmelweit shows that the first people to buy television sets in the past were previously avid cinema goers and radio listeners. Viewing only became a habit when the person had few other interests to fall back on. Television did not cause children to stay at home; they went to friends' houses to view.
2 People and especially children will become non-selective and just view anything.	In homes where parents were selective in their viewing, so too were the children (Himmelweit). 'The content of the screen only

Common assumption four	Criticism
	assumes meaning through the child's readiness and ability to receive and interpret it' (Winick and Winick). Television does not *cause* the child to be satisfied with rubbish.
3 The coming of video and cable and satellite television will cause even more passive viewing of television.	Again, Himmelweit shows that in the past when new television channels were opened, the amount of actual viewing increased little.
4 Television violence causes real violence.	Halloran shows it might have a contributory effect, and Belson that it might have a releasing effect. But it does not seem to have a direct causal effect.

Conclusions

1 We tend to exaggerate the influence of the mass media. Primarily they seem to confirm the status quo and they concentrate on entertainment.
2 The mass media try to maintain 'balance' when presenting the news, yet, as sociological studies (such as the research of the Glasgow University Media Group) show, their presentation of news is highly selective.
3 The effect of television on children is often exaggerated. (The really important influence is the home.)
4 The media tend to use stereotypes; for example, women are often represented as irrational, race is associated with trouble.
5 The ownership and management of newspapers and television companies is concentrated in a few hands (see project 1 at the end of this chapter).

Self-examination questions

1 What is meant by: 'status quo', 'political demagogy', 'copycat effect', 'the two step flow of information', 'selective exposure', 'balance'?
2 In this chapter a newspaper's readership is referred to as a sort of 'club'. What does this mean?
3 What do you understand by 'the manufacture of news'?

Discussion topics

1 What effect does television have on its viewers? What effect do the viewers have on television? (Refer to 'Further reading' for further evidence.)

2 Argue the case for and against the view that newspapers influence people's opinions.

3 Do the mass media of communication change or merely reinforce attitudes and behaviour?

Oxford Local Examinations, A Level, Summer 1982

Projects

1 Using college and public libraries etc., ascertain the circulation of the main newspapers, their political viewpoints, and their owners. Similarly ascertain details of the governors of the BBC, members of the Independent Broadcasting Authority and the chair of the main programme contractors. Give details of personal backgrounds such as school and university attendance.

Suggestions

1 You will find the *Directory of Directors* useful. This gives the names of company chairpersons and directors. Having ascertained the name of the chairperson of a board of directors of a newspaper, say, look up their details in *Who's Who*, then tabulate the results as was done in Chapter 6.

2 Read the preface or appendix in whatever directory you use to find how the directory was compiled.

3 When selecting a company to be investigated, you will need its precise name – for example, Granada Television Ltd or Guardian Newspapers Ltd.

4 As mentioned, the *Directory of Directors* and *Who's Who* are useful. So too is *Benn's Media Directory*; *Writers' and Artists' Yearbook*; *Kompass*; *Who Owns Whom*, etc. Consult the library's catalogue for further reference works in this area.
   Here is a list giving further details:
   Benn's Media Directory, Tonbridge (annual)
   Who's Who, Black, London (annual) (when people die their details are transferred to *Who Was Who*)
   Who Owns Whom, Dun and Broadstreet, London (annual)
   Key British Enterprises: The Top 20,000, Dun and Broadstreet, London (annual)
   Current Biography Yearbook, H. W. Wilson, New York (annual)
   Directory of Directors, Thomas Skinner Directories, East Grinstead (annual)
   Writers' and Artists' Yearbook, Black, London (annual)

5 *Example*: the following details of *The Independent* come from *Benn's Media Directory*

   The Independent
   Est. 1986
   Head Office: 40 City Rd, London EC1Y 2DB
   01 253 1222. Telex: 9419611 INDPNT.
   Fax: 01 608 1552 Ade Doc: DX 38460

   SOUTH CROYDON
   Fax: 01 608 1149 (Editorial); 1205 (Business and City); 1552 (Advertising)
   Publishers: Newspaper Publishing plc
   Editor: Andreas Whittam Smith

The directory goes on to give even more detailed information.

Now ascertain the board chairperson and chief editors in other cases and then find out from *Who's Who* the school and university attended. This should give some idea of the social background of the people in charge of the media and what their values are likely to be.

2 Take an item now in the news. What criticisms might a sociologist make of the selection and presentation of the item? What replies might a journalist make?

Suggestions

Use the table on p. 305 to help you. You could, for example, see how minority groups are represented. Check on how news items are taken up by the media and then dropped.

Past examination questions

1 **Assess sociological explanations of the cause of 'bias' in the mass media.**

Associated Examining Board, A Level, Paper 2, November 1988

Suggestions

This has been a major theme of this chapter.
  Discuss the possible causes of bias in the mass media: for example, the social construction of the news, the concentration of the newspaper industry in a few hands, the similarity in social status of many newspaper directors and so on.

2 **Assess the extent to which the mass media can influence the content of the mass media.**

Associated Examining Board, A Level, Paper 1, June 1988

Suggestions

See projects 1 and 2 and the table on p. 305. Glover's book is useful.

3 **Read the following passage carefully and then answer the questions printed after it.**

By the term 'mass media' we mean ways of communicating with large numbers of people without face-to-face personal contact. They include television, radio, newspapers, magazines, comics, books, films and advertising billboards. The mass media are an important way of getting information and ideas from other people. These can shape people's attitudes and perhaps influence their behaviour. Many sociologists have seen the mass media in modern industrial society as an agent of social control. In particular the media are seen to support the main norms and values of society and the established order.

1 From the passage, give two examples of the mass media.   (1 mark)
2 From the passage, what are two of the functions of the mass media?   (1 mark)
3 Explain, using examples, the following terms:
   a) norm;   (3 marks)
   b) socialization.   (3 marks)
4 Explain how the mass media may influence either the attitudes towards women in society; or voting behaviour; or attitudes towards ethnic minorities.   (6 marks)
5 Explain the ways in which social control takes place in society.   (6 marks)

Midland Examining Group, GCSE, Paper 2, May 1988

Suggestions

For 'norm', 'value', 'social construction of reality', 'socialization', see Glossary. For question 4 see the representation of race and gender, earlier in this chapter. On 5, social control implies compliance with society's norms and playing your role correctly (see Glossary for 'role'). Social control is achieved through 'correct' socialization in the family. Family and school are the main agents of social control. The main latent function of the mass media is to confirm beliefs (or ideologies), thereby helping to maintain social control. Do you agree?

Further reading

H. Christian (ed.), *The Sociology of Journalism and the Press*
J. Curran and J. Seaton, *Power Without Responsibility*
*Glasgow University Media Group, *Really Bad News*
Glasgow University Media Group, *War and Peace News*
D. Glover, *The Sociology of the Mass Media* (also in H. M. Haralambos (ed.), *Sociology: New Directions*)
M. Gurevitch et al. (eds), *Culture, Society and the Media*
M. Harrison, *Television News: Whose Bias?* (for a criticism of the Glasgow Media Group)
*John Hartley, *Understanding News*
M. Hollingsworth, *The Press and Political Dissent*
D. Moreley, *Family Television*
J. Root, *Open the Box*
B. Troyna, *Public Awareness and the Media*
M. P. Winick and O. Winick, *The Television Experience*
*'Television', *New Society*, 1 December 1983 (Society Today series)
*'The Press', *New Society*, 17 November 1983 (Society Today series)

Part VI

Research

● Chapter 16　Research

16   Research

Introduction

The opening chapter of this book outlined three basic themes:

1 the question: what is really going on here?
2 the unmasking of ideologies because they distort our view of what is really going on;
3 'doing sociology' because it invites the reader's active participation; using sociology in everyday life rather than just learning it from books.

It is the third theme that is emphasized in this chapter.

There are two important questions that we can ask about *doing* sociology: how do you apply your sociological knowledge to your everyday social world? And how do you relate what happens in everyday life to your knowledge of sociology? This two way flow of ideas should be the aim of every sociologist, according to C. Wright Mills in *The Sociological Imagination*.

Erving Goffman in *The Presentation of Self in Everyday Life* provides further insight into sociology and everyday life by showing how we try to present desirable images of ourselves. Using the theatre as an analogy, there is a 'back region' where the show is prepared and we rehearse our parts; and a 'front region' where the performance is presented for an audience. Do you think this is true in your own experience? Take for example the professional person. The 'back region' may be in the family, mixing with other professionals at meetings and less formal occasions, recollecting past professional experience and so on. The 'front region' is where the professional faces the client, presenting an appropriate front and performing the role correctly. The same could apply to a long list of situations, for example the funeral, the employment interview (the job seeker dressing 'correctly' for the interview), the lecture, the political speech, the car showroom and so on. Understanding Goffman's drama model enables us to follow the show and so gain a clearer insight into what is really going on.

Readers can be their own researchers living their sociology in their daily lives. For example, we all like to present ourselves as reasonable, fair-minded people. However, some very 'nice' people can be quite

Some hints on starting a research project or course work assignment

Before embarking on a study, a researcher will often use a pilot survey. A questionnaire may be tried out first on just a few people, to see if the questions are clear, simple to answer, and unambiguous. A pilot survey is a test of the methods the researcher will be using. The researcher must also be satisfied that the project can be carried through to completion and must be satisfied on the following points.

1 The researcher must have a clear idea of what the research is trying to achieve. What is its aim?

2 The project should have some sociological significance, to avoid what C. Wright Mills called 'abstracted empiricism' (that is to say, just collecting facts and figures). So, for example, rather than just asking people if they are satisfied in their work, it would be better to build the project around a sociological concept such as 'alienation': do workers feel alienated in their work? (See p. 124 for a definition of alienation.) Furthermore, the researcher should ask what *original* contribution the work makes to knowledge in that area.

3 The researcher should try to imagine what the end results will look like. One way of doing this could be to draw up tables of imaginary results. However, the tables should not just be descriptive statistics (just measuring absences from work, for example, or the number of exam passes). Ideally, they should help to prove something, or test a hypotheses, as in Table 16.1. (A hypothesis is a proposition that is going to be tested.) Table 16.1 is an example, showing that the hypothesis that the children of higher status parents fare better in professional examinations would have to be rejected. Do you agree with this interpretation?

Table 16.1   Relationship of exam results to father's status in a class of surveying students

	Students in the top half of the class in surveying examinations	Students in the bottom half of the class in surveying examinations
Student's father in a high status occupation	43%	67%
Student's father in a lower status occupation	57%	33%
	100%	100%
	n = 75[1]	n = 75

[1] n = 75 means there were 75 people in the sample.
Source: this and other data given in the chapter from the author's unpublished D. Phil. thesis 'Professional socialization'. These students were studying estate management surveying (which includes the valuation of property etc.).

authoritarian – it does not always show; and we all have our own hidden, unexamined assumptions. Constant analysis of our everyday world lies at the heart of doing sociology and living the part of a sociologist. You do not have to be a religious person to appreciate that the only Christianity that is worthwhile is an everyday Christianity (rather than a Sunday morning Christianity). In the same way, the sociology that is really worthwhile is an everyday sociology.

Methods of research

Five methods of research are outlined here, and there are many more. You should aim to include at least three of them in any piece of research. The methods of research (or social investigation) described here are:

1 participant observation;
2 experimental method;
3 informal interviews;
4 diaries;
5 formal questionnaires containing *open* questions and usually administered by an interviewer;
6 formal questionnaires containing *closed* questions to which there is a definite answer, such as 'yes' or 'no'.

Participant observation

In this case the researcher lives among the people being studied. The researcher should ideally accompany them wherever they go and should generally merge into the background listening to and taking part in conversations and other activities, and if possible eavesdropping. Being present during stressful situations – such as the approach of exams, or promotions boards in an organization – may be useful. It is best to enter the field without predetermined hypotheses (or propositions to be tested). Rather, these hypotheses should emerge from your observations and then continually be retested by looking for negative cases (cases that may refute your original propositions). This is done by reinterviewing people or by eavesdropping again. The researcher needs to have empathy with the people being studied, but should be careful not to be too sympathetic. The aim is to be objective, while always recognizing that absolute objectivity is not possible. (Reliability tests and validity tests are discussed towards the end of this chapter.)

One example of participant observation is Howard Becker's study of medical students (*Boys in White*). He and his co-researchers went to lectures with the students, listened to their conversations, followed them to their common rooms, accompanied them on their rounds of the wards, dined with them and so on. Another example is Colin Lacey's study

Hightown Grammar. As a teacher there himself, Lacey was able to study what was really going on in the classroom, which pupils adhered to school values and which were isolated. Thus Lacey was both a participant in and an observer of classroom activity.

The term *ethnography* is sometimes used to describe this type of research. Ethnography means the direct observation of the activity of members of a particular social group, for example a class at school, or a group of people at work, or members of the same race or tribe.

QUESTION: what makes a teacher or lecturer effective and interesting? How would you as a student (and hence a participant observer) carry out research on this question?

Experimental method

In the physical sciences change may be made deliberately and observed – for example by heating a substance. Another example would be when one group of patients suffering from a certain disease were given a drug and another group suffering from the same disease were not. The experimenter would then observe any changes in the two groups. The second group here, which would not receive the drug, is known as the control group. It is seldom possible to conduct experiments in sociology because we cannot use control and experimental groups. We cannot recreate in a laboratory the childhood conditions that lead people to hold the views they do. Also it is impossible deliberately to establish social institutions, such as religion, which influence the ideas and behaviour of individuals.

Informal or unstructured interviews

In informal interviews the researcher may ask a number of open questions. The researcher should have a rough idea of what he or she wants to ask, but should also encourage the interviewee to do most of the talking. It is very useful (with the interviewee's permission of course) to tape record these informal interviews. When I replayed interviews in my own research, I was surprised how much I butted in and put words into the interviewee's mouth, and how much I missed by just writing notes of the interviews. This highlights the problems of selective perception and selective recall. The interviewer may be 'hearing only what he or she wants to hear'. Listening to the tape carefully at least twice helps to reduce these problems. So does making verbatim transcripts (not necessarily to be reproduced in full when the research is written up). It may be interesting to ask interviewees such questions as what the main faults of their course or their job etc. are – that is to say, questions on which they have direct knowledge and a strong desire to express a viewpoint.

Your overall objectives might be: firstly to gain insights and to form hypotheses to be tested. Secondly, to try to see the world from the interviewees' viewpoint. Thirdly, to look for recurrent words such as 'practical', 'sensible', 'professional', 'independence' and so on, and try to see which are the 'good' words and which are the 'bad' words in many groups. Sociologists are very interested in the language people use. Thus if a student kept on saying a course was too 'academic', it might be that he or she was overestimating the importance of practicality, and this would need investigating. Fourthly, these informal interviews might be useful in formulating questions for the formal questionnaires – by using the wording that the interviewees themselves use.

Diaries

In my own research, concerned with estate management surveying students, I asked 15 volunteers to keep diaries for two weeks. The diaries were divided up according to the teaching timetables, and the students were asked to record in each division what they thought the object of each lecture or seminar etc. was, and their own evaluations.

Respondents should be asked to keep their diaries private. It is then interesting to look for recurrent features, such as complaints. The findings can then be tested later through a formal questionnaire.

Formal questionnaires containing open questions

Here the interviewee is asked in private a range of questions without a specific response in mind; the questions must be put to the interviewee without prompting and the reply recorded in full. At the end of the interview the interviewee can be asked to read over what has been noted to see if the replies have been correctly recorded. If a reply is too brief, the interviewer can ask 'is there anything else?' or 'why do you say that?' but the prompting should not go further than that. You should try to code (or categorize) the replies, as Table 16.2 shows, grouping together replies

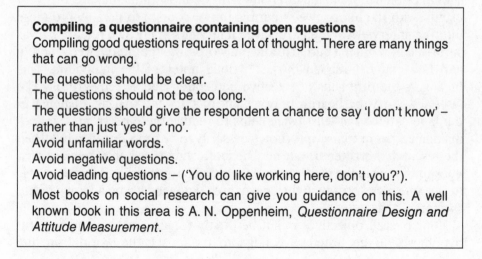

Compiling a questionnaire containing open questions
Compiling good questions requires a lot of thought. There are many things that can go wrong.

The questions should be clear.
The questions should not be too long.
The questions should give the respondent a chance to say 'I don't know' – rather than just 'yes' or 'no'.
Avoid unfamiliar words.
Avoid negative questions.
Avoid leading questions – ('You do like working here, don't you?').

Most books on social research can give you guidance on this. A well known book in this area is A. N. Oppenheim, *Questionnaire Design and Attitude Measurement*.

Table 16.2   Coded replies to the open question: what would you say constitutes a good course at the Polytechnic?

Coded replies to the question	Percentage of mentions	
	Surveying students	Social studies students
1 It should have variety.	13	7
2 The subjects in the course should be related.	5	14
3 It should be interesting.	10	31
4 The course should be educational/'fulfilling'.	2	22
5 The course should be practical (and prepare you for the 'real world').	32	7
6 The course should lead to a qualification.	23	2
7 Other items.	15	17
	100%	100%
Number of mentions	105	86

which are basically similar. The table shows the coded replies given by surveying and social studies students to the open question: What would you say constitutes a good course at the Polytechnic?

QUESTIONS: 1   How would you code the reply: 'A good course should help you to do your job better when you leave the Polytechnic'? (In the author's research it was coded as 5.)

2   What do you think these findings indicate?

Formal questionnaires containing closed or fixed questions

Table 16.3 is an example of a closed questionnaire, where the respondent is asked to tick the appropriate box. The replies are shown in Table 16.4. It is important to comment on the results and say what you think they demonstrate. In this study of surveying and social studies students one of the issues I was trying to explore was whether or not 'freedom' had the same meaning to these two groups of students. It appears from the results of the questionnaire that the two groups have two different concepts of freedom. For the surveying students it is freedom of the market place, freedom to buy what you want, freedom of choice. For the social studies students it seems that freedom means freedom for self-expression, for example freedom to squat. Do you agree with this interpretation of the results set out in Table 16.4? In particular, do you agree that these two groups of students have differing views as to what constitutes 'freedom'?

By using closed questionnaires, researchers can collect data from many people. Suppose, for example, you wanted to know the voting intention of

Table 16.3 Questions on the housing problem and economic freedom (the freedom to choose in the market place): 'closed' or fixed questions

Now a question about your general approach to the housing problem. Please tick the appropriate box for each item.[1]

	Strongly agree	Agree	Neither agree nor disagree	Disagree	Strongly disagree	Any comments
More encouragement should be given to owner occupation in order to ease the housing problem.						
Building more council houses will not really solve the housing problem.						
More encouragement should be given to the private landlord (for example, by easing rent restriction legislation).						
Squatters should be more firmly dealt with.						
The government itself should build more houses to rent.						

	Strongly agree	Agree	Neither agree nor disagree	Disagree	Strongly disagree	Any comments
The government should nationalize the building societies.						
More encouragement should be given to housing associations to build more houses.						

[1] Students were asked a number of specific *indirect* questions about economic freedom rather than the direct question: 'Is economic freedom a good thing?' This seems to be a more reliable way of getting accurate results, by asking a number of questions, you can come to an overall conclusion.

The formal questionnaire: a useful research tool

Table 16.4 The housing problem and economic freedom

		Surveying students column%	Soc. Studs students column%	Statistical test significance levels[1]
1 More encouragement should be given to owner occupation in order to ease the housing problem.	Agree/ strongly agree Otherwise	83 17	59 41	 .01
2 Building more council houses will not really solve the housing problem.	Agree/ strongly agree Otherwise	50 50	29 71	 .01
3 More encouragment should be given to the private landlord (for example, easing rent restriction legislation).	Agree/ strongly agree Otherwise	76 24	30 70	 .01
4 Squatters should be more firmly dealt with.	Agree/ strongly agree Otherwise	62 38	18 82	 .01
5 The government itself should build more houses to rent.	Agree/ strongly agree Otherwise	26 74	27 73	
6 The government should nationalize the building societies.	Agree/ strongly agree Otherwise	15 85	39 61	 .01
7 More encouragement should be given to housing associations to build more houses.	Agree/ strongly agree Otherwise	97 3 n = 164	96 4 n = 125	

[1] In the statistical test, .01 means that there is only one chance in a hundred of the result occurring by chance, so the result can be accepted.

the whole population of Britain. One way to do this would be to ask people which party they would vote for. However, it would not be necessary to ask the whole population. You could take a random sample of, say, 3000 people and infer from the results the voting intention of the whole population; that is provided:

1 you have a good response rate – over about 70 per cent;
2 the question is clear;
3 the proportion of 'don't knows' is relatively small.

Your sample should be a *random* sample in order to be representative of the population as a whole. The accompanying box describes how a large scale random sample survey is carried out.

The methods of social research described so far may be summarized as in Table 16.5. It is clear that the more mathematically (statistically) accurate

---

How are large scale random sample surveys designed?

Selection may, for instance, be made from the Register of Electors in an area. This is an example of what is called a *sampling frame*, that is, a list of people from which a sample is selected. In a *simple random sample*, every person in the sampling frame has an equal chance of being selected, say, one chance in a hundred.

You can have more complicated designs, for instance, a *multi-stage sample*. For example, the first stage might be to select a number of regions; the second towns chosen at random within the selected regions; the third stage might be households selected at random; and the final stage individuals within the households, again chosen at random.

A *stratified sample* may sometimes be used in order to select a group (of, say, women) according to a number of characteristics thought to be significant – e.g. age, religion, employment status. The purpose of this is to ensure that a sampled group represents the characteristics of the group at large, in order that it may be adequately investigated.

Multi-stage samples and stratified samples are used to reduce costs and identify the target population more accurately than a full nationwide sample survey.

How do you think you could design a survey for:
1 investigating poverty and/or street riots in an inner city area;
2 investigating the relationship between mothers and young children.

Suggestions

1 As a first stage, you could select, say, four regions (this will save costs). Then within the regions select only the poorer towns and cities, and then only inner city areas. Then use the register of electors in those areas as the final sampling frame from which to select interviewees (at random).
2 You could look up the appendix in the book by J. and E. Newson, *Patterns of Infant Care*. This describes how the researchers selected the mothers to be interviewed.

Table 16.5 Types of research methods

Type of methodology	Brief description	Advantages	Disadvantages
1 Participant observation	Becoming part of the group you are studying.	The researcher can get to know what group members are really thinking, saying and doing in a way which is not possible using formal questionnaires.	a) There is a danger of becoming too sympathetic to the group you are studying. b) The results cannot be checked.
2 Experimental method	Comparing an experimental group with a control group.	The researcher can obtain scientifically testable results.	Cannot really be used in sociological research (though it is frequently used by psychologists in controlled experiments).
3 Informal or unstructured interview	The researcher has a rough idea of what he or she wants to ask and encourages interviewees to talk.	Useful for ideas. Interviewees may say many things that the researcher has not thought of.	The results cannot be tested.
4 Diaries	Respondents are asked to keep a diary.	Encourages respondents to record in a methodical way what happens to them.	It depends on the respondent's diligence.
5 Formal questionnaires with *open* questions	The interviewer asks set questions. Interviewees reply in their own words.	Covers the research in a methodical way. The interviewees' replies can be coded and quantified.	It is difficult to really test the respondents' deeper feelings. How strongly do respondents really feel on these questions?
6 Formal questionnaires with *closed* questions	The interviewee may, for example, be asked to tick appropriate boxes or just give 'yes' or 'no' answers.	The answers are definite and can be measured mathematically. This type of questionnaire can be used in surveys.	As above. The questions must be clear and precise.

Reliability and validity tests

After the data (results of surveys etc.) has been collected, the researcher should apply reliability and validity tests.

Reliability of a test means the extent to which repeated measurements produce the same results (it may be helpful to remember reliability as repeatability).

Validity means the extent to which particular questions or a particular method of data collection measure what they are supposed to measure – are they valid? For example, in Table 16.3, do the questions really measure the students' attraction to economic freedom? One way of establishing validity would be to use different methods, for example, formal questionnaires together with informal interviews. However, there are difficulties in this. As the next section shows, when you decide on one method of research you usually have to buy the 'package' of everything that goes with it.

---

the methodology used, the less likely it is to measure the respondents' deeper feelings about the research topic – and vice versa.

What method should a researcher use?

This depends on the theories being used by the social researcher and the type of data being investigated.

Supposing a researcher wants to be as scientific as possible, to *explain* and be able to *prove* what is happening, then he or she may decide on a large scale survey using a formal questionnaire with closed questions. Such research will not only record the findings, but also try to see if certain *laws* of behaviour can be discerned. This is sometimes called 'scientific' or 'positivistic' sociology.

On the other hand, the researcher's aim may be to *understand* what is going on. What are the beliefs of the people he or she is studying? This is sometimes called 'interpretative' sociology.

Table 16.6 compares these two approaches.

Can sociology be a science?

It is difficult for sociology to be an exact science; for example, as explained earlier in the chapter, it is not possible to use the experimental method to establish the sociological facts of life. But another and deeper problem is the problem of what Max Weber called 'value freedom'. Value freedom implies that sociology can exclude ideology; that the sociologist's beliefs will not intrude into the research. This is very difficult; for example, a

Table 16.6 A comparison of research methods

	Positivist or 'scientific' sociology	Interpretative sociology
1 Aim of research	To explain what is going on in a law-like, proveable way.	To understand what is going on. To accurately assess and record the respondents' feelings.
2 Methods used	The large scale social survey. Uses *quantitative* data (such as statistics etc.).	Informal conversation and participant observation. Uses *qualitative* data (such as understanding how people feel about a problem).
3 Examples of studies	a) Blauner's study *Alienation and Freedom*, in which he tried to relate the degree of alienation at work to the type of technology being used. b) Goldthorpe's social mobility study, in which the researchers tried to measure rates of social mobility (see Chapter 5).	a) Whyte's study *Street Corner Society*: in which the researcher lived among poor Italian immigrants in order to understand their life styles. b) Colin Lacey's study *Hightown Grammar*, in which he tried to show the values of his pupils. He compared those pupils who were attached to the school's values with those who were not.
4 Advantages	a) The large scale study covers many people; especially if a representative sample is used, you can make generalizations about a wide population. b) By using statistical tests you can assess the probability of your results being accurate.	You can assess how deeply people feel about something that affects them personally, such as their college course, marriage or bereavement.
5 Disadvantages	There is a danger of what C. Wright Mills called 'abstracted empiricism', in which we become too concerned with methods and trivia.	Usually the results cannot be tested. We have to have confidence in the researchers and trust their word.

	Positivist or 'scientific' sociology	Interpretative sociology
6 Examples of the forms that studies may take:		
a) infant care	Comparing birth weights with class (what could be the purpose of this?).	Seeing how carefree or otherwise the mother's interaction is with the child. (See the Newson studies – Chapter 3).
b) divorce	Trying to account for the increase in the number of divorces.	Finding out what divorce means to the couple (e.g. do they see divorce as a sign of failure?).
c) poor productivity at work	Does this relate to the type of work, type of plant, type of employee, type of union, etc.? (An example of this is the Blauner study, *Alienation and Freedom*, referred to above.)	How do individuals react to their work – for example, strict management control at work? (See H. Beynon, *Working for Ford* – Beynon got a job at Ford in order to be a participant observer.)
d) race relations	Study job discrimination by comparing rates of unemployment of blacks and whites (as the Commission for Racial Equality has done).	Study prejudices by ascertaining what prejudiced people really think (as Adorno and his colleagues did in *The Authoritarian Personality*).

sociologist researching into, say, unemployment may unconsciously be 'siding' with the unemployed.

As far as possible, sociologists should make their own values clear and should not advocate particular values. A scientific sociology really means a value free sociology. Even though a researching sociologist can never achieve complete value freedom, it should still be the goal.

A check list for research

Patrick McNeill in his book *Research Methods* provides a useful check list for evaluating a piece of sociological research (p. 125). Most of these points are discussed in this chapter.

A research report should show how it was done so that the reader can assess it. The reader should ask the following questions (not every question is applicable to every piece of research).

Primary and secondary sources
A primary source of evidence is, for example, what people actually do or say – what an eye witness to an accident says, for example. A secondary source would be an interviewee telling you what someone else said happened at the accident. Here are some more examples.

Primary source	Secondary source
1 A boy telling you about a fight he had with another boy.	A teacher telling you what happened.
2 A husband or wife giving an account of a quarrel they had had.	A neighbour's account of the quarrel.
3 The Treaty of Amiens 1802 – the actual document.	A historian's description of the document.
4 What an interviewee actually says.	The researcher's account of what the interviewee said.
5 A completed census form (stating who lives in the house etc.).	The census tables showing the distribution of the population.

Normally primary sources are the best evidence.

---

1 Why did the researcher choose to study this topic? Was it for money? To attain a PhD?
2 How was the research paid for?
3 What were the research methods used?
4 How was access gained to the subjects of the research? Did anybody's permission have to be asked?
5 Does the study use all primary data, or secondary data, or both? If secondary data is involved, how is it used?
6 Is there any clear preference for survey methods, or for ethnographic methods, or for experiments? If there is such a preference, is it explained or justified? How?
7 Does the researcher operationalize any concepts?
8 Does the researcher discuss problems of objectivity, bias (such as racial minority or gender, and value-freedom)?
9 Are the questions of validity and reliability discussed?
10 Does the researcher discuss any ethical problems raised by the research? Are there problems of secrecy, or of anonymity?
11 How is evidence presented? Is it mainly in quantitative form, in tables and graphs? Or in qualitative form, with many quotations direct from those studied? Or is there a mixture of these, and are they used to complement each other?

Some further advice on sociological research

This chapter began with some general advice on doing sociology, suggesting for example that the only sociology that is really worthwhile is an everyday sociology. It seems fitting to conclude this chapter, and this book, with the following advice from C. Wright Mills (from *The Sociological Imagination*).

1   True thinkers do not split their work from the rest of their lives.
2   Scholarship is a choice of how to live, as well as a choice of career.
3   There is a continual need to examine and interpret experience.
4   Keep a file (or journal) – especially to capture your fringe thoughts.
5   Whenever you write for a wider audience, assume that it is a very mixed audience – make sure the readers can understand at once what you have written. Avoid verbiage and 'soc. speak' (i.e. jargon).
6   Try to view what is going on from a variety of perspectives. Avoid rigid procedures.
7   Try to understand people – not as isolated beings, but as social actors (thus people from a similar social background will act in a similar way).
8   Do not allow public issues, as they are officially formulated, to determine the subject of your study. Do not accept someone else's definition of the problem (for example, do not necessarily accept that there is a crime wave just because the official statistics indicate there is – there may be other explanations).

Conclusions

1   Sociological research should try to answer the question – what is really going on here?
2   Six research methods were described here: participant observation; experimental method; informal interviews; diaries; formal questionnaires with open questions; formal questionnaires with closed questions. Table 16.5 compares these methods of research.
3   Positivistic (or 'scientific') sociology was contrasted with 'interpretative' sociology. Table 16.6 summarizes this comparison.
4   Mills has suggested that sociology should be an enjoyable lifelong activity open to all who want to take part.
   Good luck with your sociological ventures.

Self-examination questions

Briefly outline the advantages and disadvantages of:
participant observation;
informal interviews;

eavesdropping;
open question;
closed question;
diaries.

'Library-based' projects

The reader might like to choose a project dealing with some conceptual/
theoretical problem in the sociology of work. Consider, for example, the
following.

1 **What is meant by 'alienation'? How useful is this concept in describing what happens at work?**

Suggestions

You could contrast Marx's view of alienation with that of Blauner. Take a number of studies, for example: H. Beynon, *Working for Ford*; C. Wright Mills, *White Collar*; Goldthorpe et al., *The Affluent Worker: Industrial Attitudes* etc.; and show whether the concept of alienation is useful in accounting for what is going on.

2 **'Ideology' as a key concept in the sociology of the professions.**

Suggestions

Ideology is discussed in most of the chapters in this book. Explain (a) how it distorts reality and (b) how it advances the interests of the powerful. (See especially Chapter 12 on medicine.)

3 **What are the key issues now in:**

the sociology of education;
the sociology of medicine;
the sociology of the family?

What were the key issues, say, 10 or 15 years ago?

Account for any changes.

4 **Compare and contrast the methods of research used in a number of sociological studies.**

(NB: quite often the research methods, including questionnaires used, are found in the appendixes of the books describing the research.)

Further suggestions

The first two examples of projects are attempts to find a key concept that will be useful in analysing research in these areas. The third example is a search for recurrent themes in the literature. The fourth example helps to establish what faith we can put in a piece of research.

Readers choosing a 'library-based' project will appreciate that a great deal of reading may be involved and the following advice is offered.

1 It is seldom necessary to read a book from cover to cover – just take what you need from the book.

2 Do not quote at length from books – it is what *you* make of your reading that is of interest.

3 Use all available libraries. Older readers may, for example, be able to use university libraries in the holidays.

4 In addition to books, make sure you are acquainted with other publications – pamphlets, journals, Open University courses, the International Encyclopaedia of the Social Sciences, dictionaries of sociology and so on.

Whilst it is necessary to read widely, it is really your own thinking and your own analysis that is of key interest. Your work should show some evidence of original thought.

Suggested practical work

1 Listen – eavesdrop on conversations. Record or recall carefully what the parties are actually saying. Then note what you think they really mean and try to account for the difference. It might be helpful to fold a sheet of paper in half. In the left hand half you can record what the parties say; in the right hand half you can write your commentary – what common and often hidden assumptions they may be making, how they could have taken the topic further and so on.

2 Take a problem at work, for instance excessive record keeping, an authoritarian person in a high position, the threat of redundancy, frustration over the lack of promotion, too much time spent in committees and so on. Attempt a sociological analysis of the problem using concepts like power, authority, role, socialization, culture, etc. Students may similarly analyse college problems, work overload, uncertainty, loneliness. Show how a sociological approach helps you to gain deeper insights.

3 Take an item in the news and see how it may become distorted. Try to find out what is really happening, for example, is it the case that:
   a) the journalist wants to dramatize (rather than, say, elucidate or analyse);
   b) the expert wants to obscure (to show the value of his or her knowledge);
   c) the politician or pressure group leader presents only one side;
   d) you yourself are conditioned by your previous socialization and see and hear only what you want to?
   Now rewrite (remake) the news item.

4 Ask yourself: how can I practise sociology in my everyday life? Consult leading practitioners if you wish, for example:

   C. Wright Mills, *The Sociological Imagination*, especially the section entitled 'Intellectual Craftsmanship';
   P. Berger, *Invitation to Sociology*;

E. Goffman, *The Presentation of Self in Everyday Life*;
H. Becker, *Sociological Work*.
Now write a piece of advice to yourself (or others).

5 Using a *sociological* analysis:
   a) account for your own political views;
   b) account for your views of men and women;
   c) account for your views of people of other races and religions.

Projects, case studies and past examination questions

1   Tony Wilkinson, a BBC TV reporter, set out to investigate living conditions among the men and women who exist in the twilight world of our large cities: the social derelicts, the 'down-and-outs'. For a period of a month, therefore, he left his comfortable and secure existence to become Tony Crabbe, an unemployed Yorkshire labourer who had travelled south to find work in London.

Great care was taken to make him and his story believable. His clothes were carefully selected and deliberately soiled. The team of three technicians who filmed him had to do so in absolute secrecy. The cameraman himself posed as a 'dosser', concealing his valuable camera in a shoulder bag. Wilkinson's own battered portable radio hid a microphone. He was given a comprehensive medical examination before the investigation started, together with a course of injections against the sort of infectious diseases with which he might come into contact. Nonetheless, soon after the start he felt feverish and found great difficulty in obtaining proper medical care.

Wilkinson's life as a derelict ranged from sleeping rough with alcoholics underneath railway arches and being threatened or physically assaulted, to the humiliation he suffered at the Government Reception Centre. He found social workers little help, charity organizations callous or overworked. Eventually he was able to obtain menial casual work in the kitchens of some of London's most famous restaurants and hotels.

The film and sound recordings together with the smuggled pieces of paper upon which Wilkinson recorded his daily experience show a way-of-life with which the Welfare State appears totally incapable of coming to terms.

The material produced was shown by the BBC on the Nationwide programme and used as the basis for a book by Tony Wilkinson called *Down-and-Out*.

1 **To the television audience, is the programme on 'down-and-outs' a primary or a secondary source?**

2 **Explain two major advantages of participant observation.**

3 **Explain two major disadvantages of participant observation.**

4 **What was one of the main conclusions of the research?**

5 **How might this conclusion be criticized on the grounds of**
   a) reliability;
   b) validity?
   Your answer should explain the meaning of each term.

6 Name one other research method which might be used to help to check the results of Wilkinson's investigations. Explain your choice.

7 How might this research project be criticized on ethical or moral grounds?

From Joint Matriculation Board, Social Science O Level, Summer 1983.

Suggestions

1 To the television audience the programme on down-and-outs is a secondary source, since it is mediated by the film itself.

2 and 3: Advantages of participant observation are that the researcher is among the people s/he is researching and is accepted by them, so that in due time they will confide in her/him, thus passing on important information and insight.

   The disadvantages are that the researcher may over-empathize (or sympathize) with the people s/he is observing, and may uncritically accept what they say as being true (hence bringing in bias).

4 He found social workers of little help and charity organizations callous and over-worked.

5 a) Reliability – would another researcher report the same findings?
   b) Validity – is the researcher really describing what the down-and-outs feel? Discuss.

6 He could have used structured interviews. The replies could then have been coded as shown earlier in the chapter.

7 There is a deception here. Wilkinson is presenting himself as a 'down-and-out', which he is not. Discuss.

2 Much social research requires the researcher to participate actively in the social world to generate his data. The experimenter recruits his subjects and tries to set up a particular kind of social situation in the laboratory to test his hypotheses. The survey researcher, or more usually one of his interviewers, solicits respondents, enters their homes and engages them in 'structured conversation'...

   Ethnography is not, then, unique among research traditions in involving the researcher as an active participant in the social world. It is unique, however, in the role it requires him to play.

   The critical difference is the degree to which the research situation is structured by the researcher. (*Block 4: Data Collection Procedures*; Open University Course DE304.)

1 Explain briefly the terms: 'experimental research'; 'survey research'; 'ethnography'. (3 × 2 marks)

2 Outline what supporters claim are the advantages of a high degree of structure in data collection. (9 marks)

3 Outline what critics claim are the disadvantages of a high degree of structure in data collection. (10 marks)

Associated Examining Board, A Level, Autumn 1984.

Suggestions

1 See text for definitions.

2 A high degree of structure using formal questionnaires with closed questions means the findings can be quantified and statistically tested.

3 The disadvantage is that the researcher may not be able to find out what the respondents really think. To achieve this understanding may require longer, unstructured conversation, participant observation and so on.

3 **Read the passage and then say what is meant by 'private troubles' and 'public issues'. How would you apply this distinction to: mass unemployment; poverty; war; crime; racial discrimination; sexual discrimination; health; marriage and divorce?**

> A trouble is a private matter; values cherished by an individual are felt by him to be threatened . . . An issue is a public matter; some value cherished by the public is felt to be threatened . . .
>
> When in a city of 100,000 only one man is unemployed, that is his personal trouble, and for its relief we properly look to the character of the man, his skills and his immediate opportunities. But when in a nation of 50 million employees, 15 million men are unemployed, that is an issue and we may not hope to find its solution within the range of opportunities open to any one individual. The very structure of opportunities has collapsed. (C. Wright Mills, *The Sociological Imagination*.)

Suggestions

Take *war* for example. Mills says that the *personal problem* of war may be how to survive it, or how to die with honour, or how to make money out of it. In short, according to one's values, to find a set of people or milieu (group etc.), and within it to survive the war or make one's death in it meaningful. But the *public issues* of war have to do with its causes: economic, political, family and religious institutions; with the unorganized irresponsibilities of a world of nation states.

Now try your hand at the other examples.

4 **To what extent do official statistics published by the government actually distort reality?**

Suggestions

Some sociologists might argue that official statistics (such as those found in *Social Trends*) really serve the interests of the state. That embarrassing statistics do not get published (or the figures get 'massaged'). The following are a few possible examples:

1 The basis of the figures for unemployment is constantly changing to make unemployment less than it really is.

2 While governments constantly call attention to 'scoungers', it is difficult to get the figures for tax evaders.

3 Official figures seldom give any idea of the unequal distribution of income and wealth. It would be revealing if, in official statistics, class was recorded by income rather than occupation.

4 Many facts and figures about education are hidden. For example, Chapter 6 on politics shows overwhelmingly that our 'rulers' were educated at public school (mostly Eton, Harrow and Winchester) and went on to Oxford and Cambridge. (Why is this not known more widely?)

5 Crime figures get distorted (see Chapter 14). There is especially the problem of the 'dark figure' – unreported and undetected crime.

6 Often women do not get recorded officially in the statistics – for example it was suggested in Chapter 8 that women form part of a reserve army of labour. They are the first to drop out of the work force when unemployment rises, but their own employment is often under-recorded.

7 Housing statistics under-record the full extent of homelessness and the ensuing miseries and 'social problems'.

8 The extent of inequalities in health is not widely known.

Further questions

1 Can you think of any other examples of distortion in state statistics?

2 Why do these distortions occur? Whose interests do these distortions and omissions serve?

3 On the whole, did the statistics in the various tables in this book come as a surprise to you? If so why?

5   Have a go at the following:

1 **'Studying a useless subject like sociology does not prepare you for anything.' Discuss.**

2 **'Sociology cannot be scientific, therefore it is not much use studying it.' Discuss.**

3 **'Sociology is just common sense.' Discuss.**

4 **Which of these statements (if any) might a sociologist find most wounding?**

Suggestions

a) Take the questions seriously.

b) For question 1, stress that sociology is not just a practical skill, rather it is a critique. You could mention and enlarge on the three basic themes of this book, which are:
'what is really going on?'
'what ideology is here?' (How does it distort reality and serve the interests of the powerful?)
doing sociology – making it part of your everyday life.

c) For question 2, it is difficult for sociology to be scientific because our values keep intruding. Thus instead of describing what is going on, in a factory say, we stress what ought to be happening. Nevertheless, sociology should strive to be scientific (which means 'value free'), to demonstrate what is really going on and to be a critique.

d) For question 3, sociology is often a questioning of common sense; for example, common assumptions – and this unsettles people and attracts criticisms.

e) For 4, you could say that it is not a sociologist's job to be popular and hence criticism should not be hurtful. On the contrary, if all the powerful, wealthy and influential people in society were saying what a 'useful' subject sociology is, this would be a fair indication that sociology was not doing its job properly – which is to be a critique (as the rest of the answers to these questions indicate).

6   **What are the main benefits and limitations of a positivist approach to sociology?**

University of Oxford, A Level, Paper 2, May 1988

Suggestions

This is discussed earlier in this chapter. Say what positivist means and give further examples.

7   **Give a critical account of the methodology employed in any *one* sociological study with which you are familiar.**

University of Oxford, A Level, Paper 2, May 1988

Suggestions

As mentioned on p. 332, the research methods used in a case study are often mentioned at the end of the study report or book.
  Set out and criticize the methodology used in your chosen study.
  Here are a few examples to start on first:

  J. Goldthorpe et al., *The Affluent Worker in the Class Structure*;
  J. Newson and E. Newson, *Patterns of Infant Care in an Urban Community*;
  J. Newson and E. Newson, *Perspectives on School at Seven Years Old*;
  P. Willis, *Learning to Labour*.

8   **The following is an account, published in *New Society* (15 January 1988), of an interview by Pat McNeill, a sociologist, and Steve Taylor, who is researching into child abuse, particularly how it comes to be recognized. After reading the passage, work in groups on the discussion topics that follow.**

Researching child abuse

Taylor believes we should not rely just on interviews but should use other methods, particularly participant observation. Thus Taylor played the role of a trainee social worker in order to get behind the scenes and make sure people were not being extra efficient for his benefit.

PM: Is it difficult to keep your own personal values distinct from the research you are doing?

ST: If we let our personal values predominate, then we cease to be sociologists. Just recently, every politician and pundit has suddenly become an expert on child abuse. If you are on the political right, it's because of the decline in family values. If you are left of centre, it's because of bad housing, stress, and the deprivations of capitalism. If you are into feminism, it's just another example of male power.

All these views are immediate political responses, and there is an important distinction between politics and sociology. Politicians only look for evidence to confirm a preconceived view. Sociology, on the other hand, is about discovery. The sociologist may have preconceived views, but research must be structured so that there is always the chance of discovering the unexpected.

You must also keep your emotions as well as your values out of research. As a citizen, child abuse alarms me. As a social scientist, it is behaviour to be observed and analysed.

PM: What other concepts have you developed during the research?

ST: The purpose of a concept is to help clarify and analyse the mass of data that you are working with. Our key concept was the 'danger cue'. This means any piece of evidence which alerts a professional worker to a possible case of child abuse. An obvious example would be a child with severe physical injuries. But there are many other things that worry the professionals, but have nothing to do with the physical condition of the child; the background, the state of the home, the nature of the family.

From this observation we made a distinction between primary and secondary danger cues. Primary cues were those which related to the condition of the child; physical injury, anal bleeding, something like that. Secondary cues were those which related to something other than the child's condition; social class, racial origin, whether the parents had been abused as children, the nature of the family, the way the parents talked and so on.

As you move through the list you find that it is increasingly subjective, and we found that many decisions were made which had less to do with the condition of the child than with the nature of the family. So from this distinction we were able to conclude that many decisions about children at risk are taken on the basis of how families are living their lives, explaining their actions and so on.

Professionals have assumptions about the kind of people who do and don't harm their children, and it takes very strong evidence to contradict those assumptions.

In short, professionals theorize about child abuse, and these theories structure their perception of the problem. I think distinguishing between the two types of cue illustrated this in a way that would not otherwise have been so clear.

Discussion topics

Like all social research, this must be critically evaluated.

1   How valid do you think Taylor's data is likely to be?

2   How reliable is it? See text for definition of validity and reliability.

3   How likely is it that the people he talked to and observed are representative of all workers in this field?

4   How does the variety of methods used contribute to the value of the research?

9   The problem of interviewer bias in *un*structured interviews is much greater. There is no formally fixed list of questions to work through; instead the interviewer may work through an informal checklist which will remind him of the topics he wishes to cover. What topic he raises first, and how he leads on to the next, is left entirely to him, as long as he eventually covers all the issues in the guide! Clearly the training of the interviewer is very important. (Adapted from *Introducing Sociology* by P. Worsley et al.)

1   According to the above passage, what does the interviewer use instead of a fixed list of questions?   (1 mark)

2   According to the above passage, why is interviewer bias much greater in unstructured interviews?   (1 mark)

3   Identify and explain two reasons why the interviewer would need to be trained and have knowledge of sociology.   (4 marks)

4   Explain, giving examples, why a sociologist might use a postal question-naire rather than a personal interview.   (6 marks)

5   When a sociologist decided to investigate the way that husbands and wives divided domestic tasks between themselves she chose the *un*structured interview. Why do you think she chose this method and what are likely to be its limitations?   (8 marks)

Southern Examining Group, GCSE Specimen Question.

Suggestions

1   The interviewer needs a guide or list of topics to be covered. *Note* 'unstructured interview' means there is not a list of questions to be asked. A structured interview is where there is a list of questions. As mentioned in the text, these questions may be either open questions, where interviewees say freely what they feel, or closed (fixed) questions where interviewees must give a definite answer (yes/no etc.).

2   Because interviewers are left to their own devices.

3   a) A trained sociologist would know about the importance of value freedom: that by keeping the interview value free, and not making value judgements (e.g. that indiscipline in the classroom is bad) the sociologist can arrive at a true under-standing of what is really going on. (Seeking value freedom is one way of avoiding bias.)

   b) The trained sociologist can see the significance of the casual remark, for example could be looking for 'good' words and 'bad' words which will indicate how the respondent really feels.

   c) In an unstructured interview the trained sociologist can get the respondent talking freely and yet can keep to the main line of the enquiry and elicit useful information for the research.

4   Advantages of the postal questionnaires:
   a) can cover a wide geographical area where it would be expensive to send out paid interviewers to interview people personally;
   b) useful when the enquiry concerns only a simple issue;
   c) useful when the issue is personal;
   d) results can be statistically tested.

   NB a serious disadvantage is the low response rate to postal questionnaires even when a stamped addressed envelope is sent to respondents. There is also a problem of bias; only a certain type of person may reply, for example, the more conscientious type of person.

Another disadvantage of the postal questionnaire is that you can only use closed (fixed) questions.

5   Advantages of the unstructured interview:
   a) It is helpful in this sensitive type of enquiry where closed questions of the sort shown in this chapter would not enable respondents to say what they really think.
   b) It helps the interviewer to establish empathy or rapport with the interviewee so that eventually more personal questions can be asked.
   c) The interviewee may volunteer information that the interviewer had not thought of asking for or would not have sought in a formal questionnaire of closed questions.
   Disadvantages of the unstructured interview:
   a) This is an expensive method of research.
   b) It can only cover a small sample.
   c) There is a danger of bias through the researcher being too involved with the interviewee.

GCSE course work

The Southern Examining Group requires students to undertake a project which is marked at the school or college (and moderated externally).

The following is part of a list of projects suggested by the Southern Examining Group, together with part of a marking scheme proposed by the Group which shows what the examiners think is important in project work. Whether or not your particular exam requires you to do a project, you may be interested to try one, perhaps as a small group. In any case, the list of projects presented here is interesting because it seems to cover much of a typical GCSE or GCE syllabus in sociology.

GCSE projects: topics suggested by the Southern Examining Board

1   a) Any chosen topic. Construct and use a questionnaire. Assess its usefulness.
   b) Any sociological study. Look at method(s) of research used and assess alternatives.
2   a) Study of family relationships using interviews with three generations.
   b) Study of the structure of the family in modern Britain or in another culture (e.g. kibbutzim), using secondary sources.
3   a) Study of subject options within student's school including work on how choices are made. Specific reference to gender or race.
   b) Study of educational achievement, e.g. exam performance, in relation to social class, using secondary sources.
4   a) Study of attitudes to social class using questionnaire/interviews with peer group.
   b) Comparison of the social class system in modern Britain with an alternative form of stratification.

5　a) Study of media presentation of **either**
　　　(a) specific issues **or**
　　　(b) news during one week.
　b) Study of **ONE** pressure group – mostly secondary sources.

6　a) Study of the role of a trade union in a specific place of work of which the student has experience.
　b) Study of the effects of technology on specific occupations, using secondary sources.

7　a) A study of population movement in student's own area – local secondary sources.
　b) Study of specific trend e.g. deurbanization and its consequences, using secondary sources.

8　a) Study of specific 'problem' e.g. drug abuse in student's area. Secondary sources plus interviews.
　b) Study of the changing role of the police. Secondary sources plus interviews.

9　a) Study of the use made of a health clinic by different social groups using questionnaire and/or interview.
　b) A study of poverty in Britain or in a Third World country, using secondary sources.

Table 16.7 Project marking scheme (Southern Examining Board)

	Mark allocation	Mark attained
1　*Aim/hypothesis.* In planning the project, the candidate:		
a) made no attempt to pose clear questions or hypotheses;	0	
b) posed inadequate questions or hypotheses;	1	
c) made some attempt to pose appropriate questions or hypotheses;	2	
d) posed appropriate questions *or* hypotheses;	3	
e) posed appropriate and detailed questions or hypotheses.	4	
	_____	
	_____	
2　*Methodology.* The candidate:		
a) failed to choose methods appropriate to the questions or hypotheses and remained unaware that they were inappropriate;	0	
b) failed to choose methods appropriate to the questions or hypotheses but became aware that the methods were inappropriate;	1	
c) made some attempt to choose and apply methods appropriate to the questions or hypotheses;	2	

	Mark allocation	Mark attained
d) successfully chose and applied methods appropriate to the questions or hypotheses;	3	
e) successfully chose and applied methods appropriate to the questions or hypotheses and showed some understanding of why they were appropriate;	4	
f) successfully chose and applied methods appropriate to the questions or hypotheses and showed a clear understanding of why they were appropriate.	5	_____
		_____
3 *Sources*. The candidate:		
a) made no reference to sources;	0	
b) used some sources but did not relate them to the questions or hypotheses posed, or failed to relate them well;	1	
c) used a wide range of sources and related them to the questions or hypotheses posed;	2	
d) used a wide range of sources and related them to the questions or hypotheses posed;	3	
e) used a wide range of sources and related them well to the questions or hypotheses posed.	4	_____
		_____
4 *Content*. The main body of the candidate's enquiry was:		
a) irrelevant and superficial;	0	
b) superficial but of some relevance;	1	
c) relevant but did not pursue questions or hypotheses posed in depth;	2	
d) relevant and made some attempt to pursue questions or hypotheses posed;	3	
e) relevant and thorough in that it was consistently related to the questions or hypotheses posed and pursued them in depth.	4	_____
		_____
5 *Presentation*. The candidate's work:		
a) did not include any of the features listed in (e) below;	0	
b) was presented in a poor manner;	1	
c) was satisfactory and included three of the features listed in (e) below;	2	

Table 16.7 *(Cont.)*

	Mark allocation	Mark attained
d) was satisfactory and included at least four of the features listed in (e) below;	3	
e) was of a high standard and included at least five of the following features: table of contents, clear separation of chapters, good layout, clear use of language, use of diagrams and illustrations if appropriate, a detailed bibliography.	4	_____
		_____
6 *Evaluation*. The candidate drew:		
a) no conclusions;	0	
b) conclusions which lacked perception and were only marginally relevant;	1	
c) relevant but largely superficial conclusions;	2	
d) relevant conclusions;	3	
e) relevant and perceptive conclusions;	4	
f) relevant and perceptive conclusions explored in depth.	5	_____
		_____
7 *Personal contribution*. In executing the project, the candidate:		
a) relied entirely on external help and made no attempt to personalize the content;	0	
b) displayed little initiative in seeking out and using sources, and showed little personal involvement in the content;	1	
c) showed some initiative in seeking out and using sources, and some personal involvement in the content;	2	
d) showed initiative in seeking out and using sources, and some personal involvement in the content	3	
e) showed a high degree of initiative in using sources, and considerable personal involvement in the content.	4	_____
		_____
		_____
	TOTAL MARK = (Max. 30)	_____

Revised syllabus

As mentioned on p. 2, this book is intended for most students beginning sociology, including GCSE and A level students. Many of the questions and exercises come from past examination questions at both levels. Syllabuses are changed from time to time. For example, the Associated Examining Board is revising its 1991 A Level syllabus. Paper 1 will make use of structured questions of the kind shown at the end of most of the chapters in this book. For A Level the examples of structured specimen questions are: question 3, Chapter 2; question 5, Chapter 5; and question 5, Chapter 11. The AS Level Sociology syllabus is closely related to the revised A Level syllabus of the Associated Examining Board. An A level exam containing some course work will be introduced. Here is an extract from the course work syllabus.

Candidates are required to submit a sociological study undertaken in the 12 months preceding the written examination. The study will be an opportunity for candidates to carry out an analysis using primary and/or secondary data to investigate a subject of sociological interest.

Candidates may make use of primary or secondary data or both. Whatever material they use, the study must address theoretical issues. The study may be based on one or more areas of the syllabus.

It is recommended that the length of a study does not exceed 5000 words, but it is possible to meet the requirements with a smaller number of words.

Candidates should be advised that their study ought to contain the following sections clearly labelled and indexed.

Rationale	a reason for choosing the subject of the study
Context	an outline of the theoretical context of the study
Methodology	a statement of the methodology used including reasons for choosing it and recognition of associated problems
Content	presentation of the evidence and/or argument including results
Evaluation	an evaluation of the material and conclusions
Sources	a list of the sources used

Studies will be marked internally by teachers and moderated by the Board. It is the responsibility of teachers to ensure that candidates choose an appropriate subject for their study in terms of the syllabus subject content and the marking scheme.

Further details about course work can be found in the Course Work Memorandum available from the Board (Department A9).

It must be emphasized that these notes are for guidance only. You should contact your examining Board and your tutor for the full position.

Further reading

*H. S. Becker, *Sociological Work* (relevant article)
R. Berry, *How to Write a Research Paper*
M. Bulmer, *Sociological Research Methods: An Introduction*

N. K. Denzin, *The Research Act*

P. E. Hammond (ed.), *Sociologists at Work* (especially articles by Geer and Dalton)

G. Hoinville et al., *Survey Research Practice*

D. Lawton, *Investigating Society*

*P. McNeill, *Research Methods*

*P. Mann, *Methods of Sociological Enquiry*

C. A. Moser and G. Kalton, *Survey Methods in Social Investigation*

C. J. Parsons, *Theses and Project Works*

L. Schatzmand and A. Strauss, *Field Research*

*'Is Sociology a Science?', *New Society*, 29 April 1982 (Society Today series)

and any other book in these areas you find useful.

Bibliography

Adorno, Theodor, et al., *The authoritarian personality*, Harper & Bros., New York, 1950.

Age Concern, *Inequality and older people: report of the Age Concern Scotland Conference, October 1982*, Age Concern Scotland, Edinburgh.

Aggleton, Peter, *Rebels without a cause: middle class youth and the transition from school to work*, Falmer Press, Falmer, 1987.

Albrow, M., *Bureaucracy*, Macmillan, London, 1970.

Allen, Graham, *Family life: domestic roles and social organization*, Blackwell, Oxford, 1985.

Ambrose, et al., 'Men after divorce', *New Society*, 23 June 1983.

Anderson, Michael, 'How much has the family changed?', *New Society*, 27 October 1983.

Anderson, Michael (ed.), *Sociology of the family*, Penguin, Harmondsworth, 1971.

Annual abstract of statistics.

Anwar, Muhammed, *Between two cultures: a study in the relationships between generations in the Asian community in Britain*, Commission for Racial Equality, London, 1978.

Apple, Michael W., *Ideology and curriculum*, Routledge & Kegan Paul, London, 1979.

Ariès, Philippe, *Centuries of childhood*, Penguin, Harmondsworth, 1973.

Badinter, Elisabeth, *The myth of motherhood*, Condor, London, 1981.

Ball, Alan R., *Modern politics and government*, Macmillan, London, 1983.

Ball, Stephen, *Education: sociology in focus*, Methuen, London, 1986.

Banks, J. A., *Prosperity and parenthood*, Routledge & Kegan Paul, London, 1954.

Banks, Olive, *Faces of feminism*, Martin Robertson, Oxford, 1981.

Banton, Michael, *Racial and ethnic competition*, Cambridge University Press, Cambridge, 1983.

Baran, Paul Alexander, and Sweezy, Paul Marlor, *Monopoly capital: an essay on the American economic and social order*, Penguin, Harmondsworth, 1968.

Barrett, Michele, and McIntosh, Mary, *The anti-social family*, Verso Editions, London, 1982.

Barthes, R., *Mythologies*, Paladin, London, 1976.

Barton, Len, and Walker, Stephen (eds), *Gender, class and education*, Falmer, Barcombe, 1983.

Barton, Len, and Walker, Stephen (eds), *Race, class and education*, Croom Helm, London, 1983.

Barton, Len, and Walker, Stephen (eds), *Schools, teachers and teaching*, Falmer, Barcombe, 1981.

Barton, Len, Meighan, Roland, and Walker, Stephen (eds), *Schooling, ideology and the curriculum*, Falmer, Barcombe, 1981.

Beauvoir, Simone de, *Old age*, Penguin, Harmondsworth, 1977.

Beauvoir, Simone de, *The second sex*, Jonathan Cape, London, 1968.

Becker, Howard S., *Boys in white*, Transaction books, New Brunswick, New Jersey, 1980.

Becker, Howard S., *Outsiders*, Free Press, New York, 1966.

Becker, Howard Saul, *Sociological work: method and substance*, Aldine, Chicago, 1970.

Becker, Howard S. (ed.), *The other side: perspectives on deviance*, Free Press, New York, 1967.

Bell, Colin R., *Middle class families: social and geographical mobility*, Routledge & Kegan Paul, London, 1968.

Bell, Daniel, *The coming of post-industrial society*, Heinemann, London, 1974.

Belson, William Albert, *Television violence and the adolescent boy*, Saxon House, Aldershot, 1978.

Benenson, Harold, 'Women's occupational and family achievement in the US class system: a critique of the dual-career family analysis', *British Journal of Sociology* 35 (1984), pp. 19–41.

Benyon, J., *Scarman and after: essays reflecting on Lord Scarman's report, the riots and their aftermath*, Pergamon, Oxford, 1984.

Berger, Peter Ludwig, *Invitation to sociology*, Penguin, Harmondsworth, 1966.

Berger, P., and Luckman, P., *The social construction of reality*, Penguin, Harmondsworth, 1971.

Bernard, Jessie, *The future of marriage*, Yale University Press, New Haven & London, 1982.

Bernstein, Basil, and Atkinson, Paul, *Language structure and reproduction*, Methuen, London, 1985.

Berry, Ralph, *How to write a research paper*, Pergamon, Oxford, 1966.

Bettelheim, Bruno, *The children of the dream: child-rearing and its implications for society*, Paladin, London, 1971.

Beynon, Huw, *Working for Ford*, Penguin, Harmondsworth, 1973.

Bilton, Tony, et al., *Introductory sociology*, Macmillan, London, 1981.

Blackstone, T., and Weinreich-Haste, H., 'Why are there so few women scientists and engineers?', *New Society*, 21 February 1980.

Blauner, Robert, *Alienation and freedom*, University of Chicago Press, Chicago, 1967.

Bott, Elizabeth, *Family and social network: roles, norms, and external relationships in ordinary urban families*, Tavistock, London, 1971.

Bottomore, Thomas Burton, *Political sociology*, Hutchinson, London, 1979.

Bowlby, John, and Fry, Margery, *Child care and the growth of love*, Penguin, Harmondsworth, 1970.

Bowles, Samuel, and Gintis, Herbert, *Schooling in capitalist America*, Routledge & Kegan Paul, London, 1976.

Box, Stephen, *Deviance, reality and society*, Holt, Rinhart & Winston, London, 1981.

Brake, Mike, *Comparative youth culture*, Routledge & Kegan Paul, London, 1985.

Brannen, Julia, and Collard, Jean, *Marriages in trouble*, Batsford, London, 1983.

Braverman, Harry, *Labour and monopoly capital: the degradation of work in the twentieth century*, Monthly Review, New York, 1975.

British Journal of Social Work.

Broady, Maurice, *Planning for people: essays on the social context of planning*, Bedford Square, London, 1969.

Brown, Colin, *Black and white Britain*, Heinemann, London, 1985.

Bulmer, Martin, *Sociological research methods: an introduction*, Macmillan, London, 1977.

Burgess, Robert G., *Sociology, education and schools*, Batsford, London, 1986.

Burgoyne, Jacqueline, 'Married happiness', *New Society*, 10 April 1987.

Burgoyne, J., and Clark, D., 'Why get married again?' *New Society*, 3 April 1980.

Burgoyne, Jacqueline, Ormrod, Roger, and Richards, Martin, *Divorce matters*, Penguin, Harmondsworth, 1987.

Butler, David Edgeworth, and Kavanagh, David, *The British general election of 1979*, Macmillan, London, 1980.

Carlen, Pat (ed.), *Criminal women*, Polity Press, Cambridge, 1985.

Cashmore, Ernest, and Troyna, Barry, *Introduction to race relations*, Routledge & Kegan Paul, London, 1983.

Cashmore, Ernest, and Troyna, Barry (eds), *Black youth in crisis*, Allen & Unwin, London, 1982.

Castells, Manuel, *City, class and power*, Macmillan, London, 1978.

Central Office of Information, *Occupations and conditions of work*, Reference Pamphlet 139, HMSO, London, 1976.

Chapman, K., *The sociology of schools*, Tavistock, London, 1986.

Chibnall, Steve, *Law and order news: an analysis of crime reporting in the British press*, Tavistock, London, 1977.

Christian, Harry (ed.), *The sociology of journalism and the press*, The Sociological Review, Keele, 1980.

Clark, David, 'Wedlocked Britain', *New Society*, 13 March 1987.

Cloward, Richard Andrew, and Ohlin, Lloyd Edgar, *Delinquency and opportunity*, Routledge & Kegan Paul, London, 1961.

Cochrane, R., and Billing, M., 'I'm not National Front myself, but . . .', *New Society*, 17 May 1984.

Cohen, Albert K., *Delinquent boys: the culture of the gang*, Free Press, New York, 1971.

Cohen, Stanley, *Folk devils and moral panics: the creation of the Mods and Rockers*, MacGibbon & Kee, London, 1972.

Cohen, Stanley (ed.), *Images of deviance*, Penguin, Harmondsworth, 1982.

Commission for Racial Equality, *Annual Report*, London, 1988.

Commission for Racial Equality, *New community: journal of the commission for racial equality*.

Commission for Racial Equality, *Race and council housing in Hackney*, Commission for Racial Equality, London, 1984.

Cooper, David, *Death of the family*, Penguin, Harmondsworth, 1972.

Coser, Lewis, A., *The functions of social conflict*, Routledge & Kegan Paul, London, 1956.

Coser, R., *Alienation and the social structure: a case analysis of a hospital*.

Cox, Caroline, *Sociology: an introduction for nurses, midwives and health visitors*, Butterworth, Sevenoaks, 1983.

Cox, Charles Brian, and Dyson, Anthony Edward (eds), *The black papers on education*, Davis-Poynter, London, 1971.

Crewe, Ivor, 'The disturbing truth behind Labour's rout', *The Guardian*, 13 June 1983.

Crewe, I., 'Why Mrs Thatcher was returned with a landslide', *Social Studies Review*, September 1987.

Curran, James, and Seaton, Jean, *Power without responsibility: the press and broadcasting in Britain*, Fontana, London, 1981.

Dahl, Robert, A., *Who governs?*, Yale University Press, New Haven, 1961.

Dahrendorf, Ralf, *Class and class conflict in an industrial society*, Routledge & Kegan Paul, London, 1959.

Dally, Ann Gwendolen, *Inventing motherhood*, Burnett, London, 1982.

Davies, C. E., et al., *The young child at home*, National Foundation for Education Research, Windsor, 1984.

Delamont, Sara, *The sociology of women*, Allen & Unwin, London, 1980.

Dennis, Norman, Henriques, Fernando, and Slaughter, Clifford, *Coal is our life: analysis of a Yorkshire mining community*, Tavistock, London, 1969.

Denzin, Norman K., *The research act: a theoretical introduction to sociological methods*, McGraw-Hill, London, 1978.

Department of the Environment, *National dwelling and housing survey*, HMSO, London, 1978.

Dickson, Niall (ed.), *Living in the 80's: what prospects for the elderly?*, Age Concern, Mitcham, 1980.

Different worlds, Runnymede Trust, London, 1983.

Directory of Directors (annual), Thomas Skinner Directories, East Grinstead.

Douglas, Jack (ed.), *The sociology of deviance*, Allyn & Bacon, London, 1984.

Douglas, James William Bruce, *The home and the school*, MacGibbon & Kee, London, 1964.

Dowling, Colette, *The Cinderella complex: women's hidden fear of independence*, Fontana, London, 1982.

Downes, David Malcolm, and Rock, Paul, *Understanding deviance: a guide to the sociology of crime and rule-breaking*, 2nd edn, Clarendon Press, Oxford, 1988.

Doyal, Lesley, and Pennell, Imogen, *The political economy of health*, Pluto, London, 1979.

Drucker, Henry M., et al., *Developments in British politics*, Macmillan, London, 1983.

Dubois, Pierre, *Sabotage in industry*, Penguin, Harmondsworth, 1979.

Edwardes, Sir Michael, *Back from the brink*, Collins, London, 1983.

Elliott, Doreen, *Gender, delinquency and society*, Gower, Aldershot, 1988.

Engels, Friedrich, *The origin of the family, private property and the state*, Lawrence & Wishart, London, 1972.

Erikson, Kai T., *Wayward puritans: a study in the sociology of deviance*, Wiley, Chichester, 1969.

Etzioni, Amitai (ed.), *The semi-professions and their organization*, Collier-Macmillan, London, 1969.

Evans, M. (ed.), *The woman question*, Fontana, London, 1982.

Families in the future: a policy agenda for the '80s, Study Commission on the Family, London, 1983.

Farmer, Mary, *The family: social structure of modern Britain*, Longman, Harlow, 1979.

Farnham, David, and Pimlott, John, *Understanding industrial relations*, Holt, Rinehart & Winston, London, 1986.

Fennell, G., Phillipson, C., and Evers, H., *The sociology of old age*, Open University Press, Milton Keynes, 1988.

Finch, Janet, 'Family ties', *New Society*, 20 March 1987.

Firth, Sir Raymond William, et al., *Families and their relatives*, Routledge & Kegan Paul, London, 1969.

Fletcher, Ronald, *The shaking of the foundations*, Routledge & Kegan Paul, London, 1988.

Fox, Alan, *A sociology of work in industry*, Collier-Macmillan, London, 1971.

Fox, Alan, *Beyond contract: work, power and trust relations*, Faber, London, 1974.

Fox, Alan, *Man mismanagement*, Hutchinson, London, 1985.

Frankenburg, Ronald, *Communities in Britain*, Penguin, Harmondsworth, 1966.

Freidson, Eliot, *Profession of medicine*, Dodd Mead & Co., New York, 1971.

Freidson, Eliot, *Professional powers*, University of Chicago Press, Chicago, 1986.

Friedan, Betty, *The feminine mystique*, Victor Gollancz, London, 1963.

Gans, Herbert J., *Levittowners: ways of life and politics in a new suburban community*, Columbia University Press, New York, 1982.

Gaskell, George, 'The young, the black and the police', *New Society*, 24 November 1983.

Gaskell, G., and Smith, 'Are young blacks really alienated?', *New Society*, 14 May 1981.

Gavron, Hannah, *The captive wife: conflicts of housebound mothers*, Routledge & Kegan Paul, London, 1983.

Giddens, Anthony, *Sociology*, Polity Press, Cambridge 1989.

Gill, Collin, *Work, unemployment and the new technology*, Polity Press, Cambridge, 1985.

Gittins, Diana, *The family in question*, Macmillan, London, 1985.

Glasgow University Media Group, *Really bad news*, Routledge & Kegan Paul, London, 1982.

Glasgow University Media Group, *War and peace news*, Open University Press, Milton Keynes, 1985.

Glass, D. V. (ed.), *Social mobility in Britain*, Routledge & Kegan Paul, London, 1954.

Glover, David, *The sociology of the mass media*, Causeway, Ormskirk, 1984.

Goffman, Erving, *Gender advertisements*, Macmillan, London, 1976.

Goffman, Erving, *The presentation of self in everyday life*, Penguin, Harmondsworth, 1971.

Goldthorpe , John Harry, et al., *Social mobility and class structure in modern Britain*, Clarendon Press, Oxford, 1980.

Goldthorpe, John Harry, et al.:
1 *The affluent worker – industrial attitudes and behaviour*;
2 *The affluent worker – political attitudes and behaviour*;
3 *The affluent worker in the class structure*.
Cambridge University Press, Cambridge, 1968.

Goode, William J., *World revolution and family patterns*, Free Press, New York, 1970.

Gordon, P., 'Hidden injuries of racism', *New Statesman and Society*, 12 May 1989.

Gordon, Paul, *White law*, Pluto, London, 1983.

Graham, Hilary, *Issues in sociology: health and welfare*, Macmillan, Basingstoke, 1985.

Greer, G., *Sex and destiny*, Secker & Warburg, London, 1984.

Gurevitch, Michael, et al. (eds), *Culture, society and the media*, Methuen, London, 1982.

Hall, Stuart, and Jefferson, Tony (eds), *Resistance through rituals: youth subcultures in post-war Britain*, Hutchinson, London, 1976.

Hall, Stuart, et al., *Policing the crisis: mugging, the state and law and order*, Macmillan, London, 1978.

Halloran, James D., Brown and Chaney, *Television and delinquency*, Leicester University Press, Leicester, 1970.

Halsey, A. H., et al., *Origins and destinations: family, class and education in modern Britain*, Oxford University Press, Oxford, 1980.

Hammersley, Martyn, and Hargreaves, Andy, *Curriculum practice: some sociological case studies*, Falmer, Barcombe, 1983.

Hammond, Phillip Everett (ed.), *Sociologists at work*, Basic Books, New York, 1964.

Happy families? Discussion paper on families in Britain, Study Commission on the Family, London, 1980.

Harloe, Michael, *New perspectives in urban change and conflict*, Heinemann, London, 1981.

Harris, Christopher Charles, *The family and industrial society*, Allen & Unwin, London, 1983.

Harrison, Martin, *Television news: whose bias? A casebook analysis of strikes, television and media studies*, Policy Journals, Hermitage, 1985.

Harrison, Paul, 'How race affects council housing', *New Society*, 12 January 1984.

Harrison, Paul, *Inside the inner city: life under the cutting edge*, Penguin, Harmondsworth, 1983.

Hart, Nicky, *The sociology of health and medicine*, Causeway, Ormskirk, 1985.

Hart, Nicky, *When marriage ends: a study in status passage*, Tavistock, London, 1976.

Hartley, John, *Understanding news*, Methuen, London, 1982.

Heath, Anthony, *Social mobility*, Fontana, London, 1981.

Heraud, B. J., 'Social class and the new towns', *Urban Studies* 5, pp. 33–53.

Himmelweit, Hildegard Therese, et al., *Television and the child*, Oxford University Press, London, 1958.

HMSO, *Social trends*, London, 1985.

Hobman, David (ed.), *The social challenge of ageing*, Croom Helm, London, 1978.

Hoinville, Gerald, et al., *Survey research practice*, Heinemann, London, 1978.

Holdsworth, A., *Out of the doll's house*, BBC Books, London, 1988.

Hollingsworth, Mark, *The press and political dissent*, Pluto, London, 1986.

Holme, A., 'Family and homes in East London', *New Society*, 12 July 1985.

Household food consumption and expenditure, HMSO, London, 1978.

Hoyles, Martin (ed.), *Changing childhood*, Writers and Readers Publishing Cooperative, London, 1979.

Husband, Charles (ed.), *'Race' in Britain: continuity and change*, Hutchinson, London, 1982.

Husbands, Christopher, *Racial exclusionism and the city*, Allen & Unwin, London, 1983.

Hyman, Richard, and Price, Robert (eds), *The new working class? White collar workers and their organizations*, Macmillan, London, 1983.

Illich, Ivan D., *Medical nemesis: the expropriation of health*, Calder & Boyars, London, 1975.

Illich, Ivan D., et al., *Disabling professions*, Boyars, London, 1977.

Ineichen, B., *Mental illness: the social structure of modern Britain*, Longman, London, 1979.

International encyclopedia of the social sciences.

International Labour Office, *Year book of labour statistics 1984*.

Irvine, Elizabeth Ernestine, *The family in the kibbutz*, Study Commission on the Family, London, 1980.

Irvine, J., Miles, I., and Evans, J. (eds), *Demystifying social statistics*, Pluto, London, 1979.

Jacobson, D., 'Fatigue producing factors in industrial work: on pre-retirement attitudes', *Occupational Psychology* 46 (1972).

Jenkins, Clive, and Sherman, Barrie, *The collapse of work*, Methuen, London, 1979.

Jenkins, Clive, and Sherman, Barrie, *White-collar unionism: the rebellious salariat*, Routledge & Kegan Paul, London, 1979.

Jenks, Chris (ed.), *The sociology of childhood: essential readings*, Batsford, London, 1982.

Jones, David, 'Belonging to the Front', *New Society*, 4 October 1984.

Jones, Trevor, MacLean, Brian, and Young, Jock, *The Islington crime survey*, Gower, Aldershot, 1986.

Joseph, Martin, *Professional socialization*, D.Phil. thesis, University of Oxford, 1980.

Joseph, Martin, *Sociology for business*, Polity Press, Cambridge, 1989.

Jowell, R., Witherspoon, S., and Brook, L., *British social attitudes*, Gower, Aldershot, 1988.

Keddie, Nell (ed.), *Tinker, tailor . . . the myth of cultural deprivation*, Penguin, Harmondsworth, 1975.

Kennedy, Ian, *The unmasking of medicine*, Allen & Unwin, London, 1981.

Kennedy, Thomas, *European labour relations*, Lexington Books, Lexington, Kentucky, 1980.

Khan, Verity Saifullah, *Minority families in Britain*, Macmillan, London, 1979.

Kinsey, Richard, Lea, John, and Young, Jock, *Losing the fight against crime*, Blackwell, Oxford, 1986.

Klapper, Joseph T., *The effects of mass communication*, Free Press, New York, 1960.

Klein, Josephine, *Samples from English cultures*, Routledge & Kegan Paul, London, 1965.

Klein, R., 'Is the NHS really in crisis?', *New Society*, 3 November 1983.

Kompass.

Labov, William, 'The logic of non-standard English', in *Tinker, tailor . . . the myth of cultural deprivation*, ed. Nell Keddie, Penguin, Harmondsworth, 1975, pp. 21–66.

Lacey, C., 'Destreaming in a pressured academic environment', in *Contemporary research in the sociology of education*, ed. S. J. Eggleston, Methuen, London, 1974.

Lacey, Colin, *Hightown Grammar: the school as a social system*, Manchester University Press, Manchester, 1970.

Laing, R. D., *The politics of the family, and other essays*, Penguin, Harmondsworth, 1976.

Lane, Anthony David, *The union makes us strong: the British working class, its trade unionism and politics*, Arrow, London, 1974.

Larkin, Philip, *High windows*, Faber, London, 1974.

Laslett, Peter, *The world we have lost: England before the industrial age*, Methuen, London, 1971.

Lawton, Denis, *Education, culture and the national curriculum*, Hodder & Stoughton, London, 1989.

Lawton, Denis, *Investigating society: an introduction to sociology*, Hodder & Stoughton, London, 1980.

Lazarsfeld, Paul F., *The people's choice*, Columbia University Press, New York, 1944.

Little, Alan, and Robbins, Diana, *Loading the law*, Commission for Racial Equality, London, 1982.

Lockwood, David, *The blackcoated worker: a study in class consciousness*, Allen & Unwin, London, 1958.

Lonsdale, Susan, *Work and inequality*, Longman, London, 1985.

Lowe, Philip, and Goyder, Jane, *Environmental groups in politics*, Allen & Unwin, London, 1983.

Lowe, Stuart, *Urban social movements: the city after Castells*, Macmillan, Basingstoke, 1988.

Lukes, Stephen, 'The future of British socialism', in *Fabian thought*, ed. B. Pimlott, 1987.

McGregor, Oliver Ross, *Divorce in England: a centenary study*, Heinemann, London, 1957.

McIntosh, Neil, and Smith, David J., *The extent of racial discrimination*, Political and Economic Planning, London, 1974.

McKean, Thomas, *The role of medicine*, Oxford University Press, Oxford, 1979.

Mack, Joanna and Lansley, Stewart, *Poor Britain*, George Allen and Unwin, London, 1985.

Macmillan student encyclopedia of sociology, ed. Michael Mann, Macmillan, London, 1983.

McNeill, Patrick, *Research methods*, Tavistock, London, 1985.

McRobbie, A., 'Keep the girls from the boys', *New Statesman and Society*, 12 August 1988.

Mann, Peter Henry, *Methods of sociological enquiry*, Blackwell, Oxford, 1968.

Marsh, Peter, Rosser, Elisabeth, and Harré, Rom, *The rules of disorder*, Routledge & Kegan Paul, London, 1978.

Marshall, G. M., 'What is happening to the working class?', *Social Studies Review*, January 1987.

Marshall, Gordon, et al., *Social class in modern Britain*, Hutchinson, London, 1988.

Marshall, Thomas Humphrey, *Sociology at the crossroads, and other essays*, Heinemann, London, 1963.

Martin, John Powell (ed.), *Violence and the family*, Wiley, Chichester, 1978.

Matza, David, *Becoming deviant*, Prentice-Hall, Englewood Cliffs, New Jersey, 1969.

Matza, David, *Delinquency and drift*, Wiley, New York, 1970.

Mead, Margaret, *A coming of age in Samoa*, Penguin, Harmondsworth, 1971.

Mead, Margaret, *Growing up in New Guinea*, Penguin, Harmondsworth, 1970.

Mead, Margaret, *Male and female: a study of the sexes in a changing world*, Penguin, Harmondsworth, 1970.

Mechanic, D. (ed.), *Readings in medical sociology*, Collier-Macmillan, London, 1980.

Meighan, Roland, *A sociology of educating*, Holt, Rinehart & Winston, London, 1981.

Meighan, Roland, Shelton, Ian, and Marks, Tony (eds), *Perspectives on society: an introductory reader in sociology*, Nelson, London, 1979.

Mellor, J. R., *Urban sociology in an urbanized society*, Routledge & Kegan Paul, London, 1977.

Merton, Robert King, *Social theory and social structure*, Free Press, New York, 1968.

Merton, Robert King, et al. (eds), *The student-physician*, Harvard University Press, Cambridge, Massachusetts, 1957.

Michels, Robert Willy Eduard, *Political parties: a sociological study of the oligarchical tendencies of modern democracy*, Jarrold & Sons, London, 1915.

Midwinter, Eric, *Redefining old age*, Centre for Policy on Ageing, London, 1987.

Miliband, Ralph, *The state in capitalist society*, Weidenfeld & Nicolson, London, 1969.

Mill, J. S., *On the subject of women*, Dent, London, 1970 (first published 1869).

Mills, Charles Wright, *The power elite*, Oxford University Press, New York, 1956.

Mills, Charles Wright, *The sociological imagination*, Oxford University Press, New York, 1959.

Mills, Charles Wright, *White collar: the American middle classes*, Oxford University Press, New York, 1956.

Millum, Trevor, *Images of woman: advertising in women's magazines*, Chatto & Windus, London, 1975.

Mishnan, E. J., 'A sceptical view of Scarman', *New Society*, 10 December 1981.

Mitchell, Jeannette, *What is to be done about illness and health?*, Penguin, Harmondsworth, 1984.

Mitchell, Juliet, *Woman's estate*, Penguin, Harmondsworth, 1971.

Moreley, David, *Family television*, Comedia, London, 1986.

Morgan, D. H. J., *The family, politics and social theory*, Routledge & Kegan Paul, London, 1985.

Morgan, Myfanwy, et al., *Sociological approaches to health and medicine*, Croom Helm, London, 1985.

Morris, Lydia, 'The no longer working class', *New Society*, 3 April 1987.

Morrish, Ivor, *The sociology of education: an introduction*, Allen & Unwin, London, 1978.

Moser, C. A., and Kalton, Graham, *Survey methods in social investigation*, Heinemann, London, 1971.

Mount, Ferdinand, *The subversive family: an alternative history of love and marriage*, Jonathan Cape, London, 1982.

Mullard, C., 'Multi-racial education in Britain', in *Race, migration and schooling*, John Tierney et al., Holt, Rinehart & Winston, London, 1982.

Nandy, L., and Nandy, D., 'Towards true equality for women', *New Society*, 30 January 1975.

Navarro, Vicente, *Crisis health and medicine: a social critique*, Tavistock, London, 1986.

New, C., and David, M., *For the children's sake*, Penguin, Harmondsworth, 1985.

New Age.

Newson, John, and Newson, Elizabeth, *Four years old in an urban community*, Penguin, Harmondsworth, 1970.

Newson, John, and Newson, Elizabeth, *Patterns of infant care in an urban community*, Penguin, Harmondsworth, 1965.

Newson, John, and Newson, Elizabeth, *Seven years old in the home environment*, Penguin, Harmondsworth, 1978.

Newson, J., and Newson, E., *The extent of parental physical punishment in the UK*, Association for the Protection of All Children, London, 1978.

Newson, John, Newson, Elizabeth, and Barnes, Peter, *Perspectives on school at seven years old*, Allen & Unwin, London, 1977.

Norman, Alison, *Aspects of ageism*, Centre for Policy on Ageing, London, 1987.

Oakley, Ann, *From here to maternity*, Penguin, Harmondsworth, 1981.

Oakley, Ann, *Housewife*, Penguin, Harmondsworth, 1976.

Oakley, Ann, *Sex, gender and society*, M. T. Smith, London, 1972.

Oakley, Ann, *Subject women*, Fontana, London, 1982.

Oakley, A., *Taking it like a woman*, Jonathan Cape, London, 1984.

Oakley, Ann, 'The woman's place', *New Society*, 6 March 1987.

Oakley, Ann, *Women confined: towards a sociology of childbirth*, Martin Robertson, Oxford, 1980.

Occupational mortality: the Registrar General's supplement for England and Wales, HMSO, London, 1970–72, 1978.

O'Donnell, Mike, *A new introduction to sociology*, Harrap, London, 1981.

Office of Population Censuses and Surveys, *Adult dental health*, vol. 1.

Opie, P., and Opie, I., *The lore and language of schoolchildren*, Oxford University Press, Oxford, 1987.

Oppenheim, Abraham Naftali, *Questionnaire design and attitude measurement*, Heinemann, London, 1968.

Orwell, George, *Road to Wigan pier*, Secker & Warburg, London, 1959.

Pahl, Raymond Edward, 'Family, community and unemployment', *New Society*, 21 January 1982.

Pahl, Raymond Edward (ed.), *Whose city?*, Longman, London, 1970.

Pareto, Vilfredo Federigo Damaso, *The mind and society* (4 vols), Jonathan Cape, London, 1935.

Park, Robert E., and Burgess, Ernest Watson (eds), *The city*, University of Chicago Press, Chicago, 1968.

Parker, Stanley Robert, *Older workers and retirement*, HMSO, London, 1980.

Parker, Stanley Robert, *The sociology of leisure*, Allen & Unwin, London, 1976.

Parker, Stanley Robert, *Work and retirement*, Allen & Unwin, London, 1982.

Parker, Stanley Robert, et al., *The sociology of industry*, Allen & Unwin, London, 1977.

Parsons, Christopher James, *Theses and project works*, Allen & Unwin, London, 1973.

Parsons, Talcott, and Bales, Robert Freed, *Family socialization and interaction process*, Routledge & Kegan Paul, London, 1956.

Parsons, Talcott, and Shils, Edward A. (eds), *Towards a general theory of action*, Harvard University Press, Cambridge, Massachusetts, 1967.

Patrick, D. L., and Scambler, G. (eds), *Sociology as applied to medicine*, Bailliere Tindall, Eastbourne, 1982.

Penguin dictionary of sociology, Penguin, Harmondsworth, 1984.

Pizzey, Erin, *Scream quietly or the neighbours will hear*, If Books, London, 1974.

Police and people in London:
  1 *A survey of Londoners*, by David J. Smith;
  2 *A group of young black people*, by S. Small;
  3 *A survey of police officers*, by David J. Smith;
  4 *The police in action*, by David J. Smith and J. Gray.
Policy Studies Institute, London, 1983.

Pollard, Andrew, *The social world of the primary school*, Holt, Rinehart & Winston, London, 1985.

Pollard, Andrew, Purvis, June, and Walford, Geoffrey (eds), *Education, training and the new vocationalism*, Open University Press, Milton Keynes, 1988.

Poulantzas, Michael, *State power socialism*, New Left Books, London, 1978.

Pryce, Ken, *Endless pressure: a study of West Indian life-styles in Bristol*, Penguin, Harmondsworth, 1979.

Puner, Morton, *To the good long life*, Macmillan, London, 1978.

'Race and Prejudice', *New Society*, 17 January 1986 (Society Today series).

Rapoport, Rhona, and Rapoport, Robert Norman, *Dual-career families*, Penguin, Harmondsworth, 1971.

Rapoport, Robert Norman, et al., *Families in Britain*, Routledge & Kegan Paul, London, 1982.

Redfield, Robert, *The little community*, University of Chicago Press, London & Chicago, 1960.

Reid, Ivan, *Social class differences in Britain: a sourcebook*, Grant McIntyre, London, 1981.

Reid, Ivan, *Sociological perspectives on school and education*, Grant McIntyre, London, 1982.

Reid, I., *Sociology of school and education*, Fontana, London, 1986.

Reid, Ivan, and Wormald, Eileen, *Sex differences in Britain*, Grant McIntyre, London, 1982.

Rex, John, and Tomlinson, Sally, *Colonial immigrants in a British city: a class analysis*, Routledge & Kegan Paul, London, 1979.

Rex, John, et al., *Race, community and conflict: a study of Sparkbrook*, Oxford University Press, Oxford, 1969.

Richards, Martin, 'Parents and kids: the new thinking', *New Society*, 27 March 1987.

Rimmer, Lesley, *Families in focus: marriage, divorce, and family patterns*, Study Commission on the Family, London, 1981.

Robinson, Philip, *Perspectives on the sociology of education: an introduction*, Routledge & Kegan Paul, London, 1981.

Rock, Paul (ed.), *A history of British criminology*, Oxford University Press, Oxford, 1988.

Rock, Paul, and McIntosh, Mary (eds), *Deviance and social control*, Tavistock, London, 1974.

Root, Jane, *Open the box*, Comedia, London, 1986.

Rosser, Colin, and Harris, Christopher Charles, *Family and social change: a study of family kinship in a south Wales town*, Routledge & Kegan Paul, London, 1983.

Rowbotham, Sheila, *Hidden from history: 300 years of women's oppression and the fight against it*, Pluto, London, 1977.

Runnymede Trust and Radical Statistics Race Group, *Britain's black population*, Heinemann, London, 1980.

Rutter, Michael, *Maternal deprivation reassessed*, Penguin, Harmondsworth, 1972.

Rutter, Michael, et al., *Fifteen thousand hours: secondary schools and their effects on children*, Open Books, Shepton Mallet, 1979.

Sampson, Anthony, *The changing anatomy of Britain*, Hodder & Stoughton, London, 1982.

Saunders, Barbara, *Homeless young people in Britain*, Bedford Square, London, 1988.

Saunders, Peter, *Urban politics: a sociological interpretation*, Hutchinson, London, 1983.

Scarman report: the Brixton disorders, 10–12 April 1981, Penguin, Harmondsworth, 1982.

Scarr, S. and Dunn, J., *Mother care other care*, Penguin, Harmondsworth, 1987.

Schatzman, Leonard, and Strauss, Anselm L., *Field research: strategies for a natural sociology*, Prentice-Hall, Englewood Cliffs, New Jersey, 1973.

Scott, J., 'Does Britain still have a ruling class?', *Social Studies Review*, September 1986.

Scully, V., Jr, *Modern architecture*, George Braziller, New York, 1974.

Seabrook, Jeremy, *Landscapes of poverty*, Blackwell, Oxford, 1985.

Search, *Welfare rights for the elderly*, Search Report, 1983.

Secord, Paul Frank, and Backman, Carl W., *Social psychology*, McGraw-Hill, New York, 1964.

Segal, L., *Is the future female?*, Virago, London, 1987.

Segal, Lynne (ed.), *What is to be done about the family?*, Penguin, Harmondsworth, 1983.

Sharpe, Sue, *Just like a girl: how girls learn to be women*, Penguin, Harmondsworth, 1981.

Shils, E. A., and Janowitz, M., 'Cohesion and disintegration in the Wehrmacht in World War II', *Public Opinion Quarterly* 12 (1948), pp. 280–315.

Shorter, E., et al., 'The unholy family', *New Society*, 20/27 December 1985.

Smith, David J., *Unemployment and racial minorities*, Policy Studies Institute, London, 1981.

Stacey, Margaret, *The sociology of health, illness and disease*, Unwin Hyman, London, 1988.

Stanworth, Michelle, *Gender and schooling: a study of sexual divisions in the classroom*, Hutchinson, London, 1983.

Stott, Mary, *Ageing for beginners*, Blackwell, Oxford, 1981.

Sutherland, Edwin Hardin, *The principles of criminology*, 6th edn, University of Chicago Press, Chicago, 1960.

Sutherland, Edwin Hardin, *White collar crime*, Dryden Press, New York, 1949.

Swann Committee, *Education for all*, 1985.

Tawney, Richard Henry, *Equality*, Allen & Unwin, London, 1931.

Taylor, Frederick Winslow, *The principles of scientific management*, Harper & Bros., New York & London, 1911.

Taylor, Ian, Walton, Paul, and Young, Jock, *The new criminology*, Routledge & Kegan Paul, London, 1973.

Taylor, Ian, Walton, Paul, and Young, Jock (eds), *Critical Criminology*, Routledge & Kegan Paul, London, 1975.

Thomas, David, 'New ways of working', *New Society*, 30 August 1985.

Thomas, David, 'The job bias against blacks', *New Society*, 1 November 1984.

Thompson, E. P., 'Time work – discipline and industrial capitalism', *Past and Present* (1967).

Thornes, Barbara, and Collard, Jean, *Who divorces?*, Routledge & Kegan Paul, London, 1979.

Tierney, John, et al., *Race, migration and schooling*, Holt, Rinehart & Winston, London, 1982.

Tomlinson, Sally, *Ethnic minorities in British schools: a review of the literature 1960–82*, Heinemann, London, 1983.

Tonnies, Ferdinand, *Community and society*, Routledge & Kegan Paul, London, 1955.

Townsend, Peter, *Poverty in the United Kingdom: a survey of household resources and standards of living*, Penguin, Harmondsworth, 1979.

Townsend, Peter, *The last refuge*, Routledge & Kegan Paul, London, 1962.

Townsend, Peter, and Davidson, Nick (eds), *Inequalities in health*, Penguin, Harmondsworth, 1982.

Townsend, Peter and Wedderburn, Dorothy, *The aged and the welfare state*, G. Bell & Sons, London, 1965.

Tressell, Robert, *The ragged trousered philanthropist*, Lawrence & Wishart, London, 1979.

Troyna, B., *Public awareness and the media: a study of reporting race*, Commission for Racial Equality, London, 1981.

Troyna, B., *Racial inequality in education*, Tavistock, London, 1987.

TUC Workbook on Education, TUC, London.

Tucker, N., 'Unhappy childhood', *New Statesman and Society*, 8 July 1988.

Tuckett, David (ed.), *An introduction to medical sociology*, Tavistock, London, 1976.

Tuckett, David, and Kaufert, Joseph M. (eds), *Basic readings in medical sociology*, Tavistock, London, 1978.

Tunstall, J., 'The British press in the age of television', in *The sociology of journalism and the press*, ed. Harry Christian, The Sociological Review, Keele, 1980.

Values and the changing family: a final report from the working party on values, Study Commission on the Family, London, 1982.

Veblen, Thorstein, *On the nature and uses of sabotage*, Oriole Editions, New York, 1977.

Wagg, S., 'Perishing kids? The sociology of childhood', *Social Studies Review*, March 1988.

Waitzkin, H., 'Medical super structure and micro politics', *Social Science and Medicine*, vol. 13A, no. 6, 1979.

Walford, Geoffrey (ed.), *Doing sociology of education*, Falmer Press, Falmer, 1987.

Walvin, James, *A child's world: a social history of English childhood, 1800–1914*, Penguin, Harmondsworth, 1982.

Ward, Colin, *When we build again*, Pluto, London, 1985.

Watson, Tony J., *Sociology, work and industry*, Routledge & Kegan Paul, London, 1980.

Westergaard, John and Resler, Henrietta, *Class in a capitalist society: a study of contemporary Britain*, Penguin, Harmondsworth, 1976.

White, Graham, *Socialization*, Longman, London, 1977.

Whitehead, Margaret, *The health divide*, Health Education Council, London, 1987.

Whitley, R., 'Commonalities and connections among directors of large financial institutions', *Sociological Review* 21 (1973), pp. 613–32.

Whitty, Geoff, *Sociology and school knowledge: curriculum, theory, research and policy*, Methuen, London, 1985.

Whyte, William Foote, *Street corner society*, University of Chicago Press, Chicago, 1981.

Wilkinson, Tony, *Down and out*, Quartet Books, London, 1981.

Willey, Richard, *Race, equality and schools*, Methuen, London, 1984.

Williams, Raymond, *Television, technology and cultural form*, Fontana, London, 1974.

Willis, Paul E., *Learning to labour: how working class kids get working class jobs*, Saxon House, Aldershot, 1978.

Willmott, Peter, 'Urban kinship past and present', *Social Studies Review*, November 1988.

Willmott, Peter, and Young, Michael, *Family and class in a London suburb*, Routledge & Kegan Paul, London, 1960.

Wilson, P., and Pahl, R., 'The changing sociological construct of the family', *Sociological Review*, May 1988.

Winick, M. P., and Winick, Charles, *The television experience: what children see*, Sage, London, 1979.

Wirth, Louis, *On cities and social life: selected papers*, University of Chicago Press, London & Chicago, 1964.

Wollen, P., 'Do children really need toys?', *Social Studies Review*, March 1988.

Woods, P., *Inside schools: ethnography and educational research*, Routledge & Kegan Paul, London, 1986.

Woods, Peter (ed.), *Pupil strategies*, Croom Helm, London, 1980.

Woods, Peter, *Sociology and the school: an interactionist viewpoint*, Routledge & Kegan Paul, London, 1983.

Woods, Peter, *The divided school*, Routledge & Kegan Paul, London, 1979.

Worsley, Peter (ed.), *Introducing sociology*, Penguin, Harmondsworth, 1970.

Young, Jock, and Lea, John, *What is to be done about law and order?*, Penguin, Harmondsworth, 1984.

Young, Michael Dunlop, and Willmott, Peter, *Family and kinship in East London*, Routledge & Kegan Paul, London, 1957.

Young, Michael Dunlop, and Willmott, Peter, *The symmetrical family*, Penguin, Harmondsworth, 1980.

Young, Michael F. D. (ed.), *Knowledge and control*, Collier-Macmillan, London, 1971.

Glossary of Terms
(after consulting the Glossary, see Index for further details)

Achieved status: the individual can achieve a higher position in society, for example, through hard work.

Ageism: discrimination against people on the basis of their age; categorizing older people (all old people do this, etc.).

Alienation: Marx argued that we are creative and fulfil ourselves in our work. When we cannot do this and when our labour is merely bought and sold by the hour like any other commodity we are said to be alienated or separated from our true creative selves. Alienation is part of the process of exploitation of the proletariat by the bourgeoisie. (See also Blauner, *Alienation and Freedom*, Chapter 7.)

Ascribed status: the individual's position in society is fixed. They cannot better themselves. The qualities an individual has (occupation, income, status, etc.) depend on the position into which he or she is born rather than achievement.

Authority: the legitimate use of power. According to Weber there were three types of authority:

1 charismatic authority; the personal authority of a strong leader;

2 traditional authority: established authority (of, say, a pope or monarch);

3 rational–legal authority: for example, large organizations in advanced societies, such as large corporations, and the state itself.

(See Chapter 6.)

Class: in Western societies class is usually based on occupation. Thus the highest classes are in the highest occupations – such as professional and managerial occupations – while the lower class would be in the lowest occupations – unskilled manual (see introduction to Chapter 5).

For Marx there were two main classes in advanced societies – the bourgeoisie who owned the means of production, and the proletariat who did not. Weber's theory of class is based on the possession of skills. (See Chapter 5 for further details.)

Community: a group of people sharing similar values. It could be a religious community, a profession and so on. Sometimes people of the same community live together in the same neighbourhood, for example a mining village, but this is not necessary. (See R. Frankenburg, *Communities in Britain*.)

Culture: culture could be seen as comprising the norms and values of society; that is to say, ways of behaving and the ultimate goals of a society.

A wider view would be to see culture as everything pertaining to a society, including prevailing ideas, the treatment of women, old people and minorities, the technology of a society, its artefacts and so on.

Dual labour markets: in most societies there may be at least two sub-markets for labour. The primary market comprises the best jobs and the secondary market contains the low-paid, low-skilled, non-unionized jobs. Such workers are trapped in the secondary labour market.

Elaborated code: see 'restricted code of speech'.

Embourgeoisement: the process by which occupations and members gain higher social status. The opposite of proletarianization.

False consciousness: being unaware of one's exploited position – especially in capitalist society.

Fascism: an ideology which glorifies power. Fascist beliefs usually incorporate the following:

nationalism: the superiority of your country;
racism: the superiority of your race;
totalitarianism; the central power of the state over all other institutions including trade
 unions, the church, schools and virtually all other public and private organizations.

Pre-war Italy and Spain are the examples usually quoted, and also Nazi Germany.

Feminism: a social movement seeking equal rights for women through equal opportunity at work and the abolition of patriarchy and sexism. Early feminists sought equal rights within the existing 'system', particularly the right to vote. Later, in the sixties, feminism became a mass movement strongly advocating equality. One difficulty for feminists is that because women are more tied to their own families they do not come together as a strong movement, i.e. they do not become politicized and so they 'grieve' in private (see H. Gavron, *The Captive Wife*), rather than assert their right to a full life based on equality. (See also C. Wright Mills, *The Sociological Imagination*, for the link between private troubles and public issues. What appears to be a purely personal problem is in fact a public issue, for example discrimination against women in the job market.)

Functionalism: this is a major theory in sociology, though questioned by many now. It sees society as composed of parts or institutions. These parts include the family, the church, the military, the education system and so on. In a 'healthy' society all these parts work together to ensure that society remains healthy. The analogy used to explain this is that of the body, where separate organs (heart, lungs, etc.), though different, are interdependent and work together for the health of the body. (See, for example, Chapter 2, p. 18, and Chapter 6, p. 92 – the opposite of a functional world would be dysfunctional.)

Gender: sex refers to the obvious biological differences between men and women, whereas gender refers to the social and cultural differences. Thus the role of a woman varies from society to society, and the example often given is the comparison of women in Islamic societies with those from Western societies.

There is an enormous amount of feminist literature illustrating gender, sexism and patriarchy, etc. (See also 'role'.)

Hegemony: this term was used by the Italian sociologist Antonio Gramsci to show that the ruling class does not rule solely by control of the means of production but also by the control of ideas. Capitalist society is more likely to be overthrown when workers establish their own ideological supremacy, Gramsci argued.

Hidden curriculum: assumptions that are implicitly made in schools, for example that girls are neat and will choose feminine subjects like English Literature and Language, whereas boys are more boisterous and will choose masculine subjects like Maths and Physics. In these ways girls and boys learn their place – their role – in society as future women and men. In studying schools the sociologist should always search for, and expose, the hidden curriculum. (See also box in Chapter 11, and M. Young (ed.), *Knowledge and Control*.)

Ideology: a set of beliefs about the social world. These beliefs may be distorted and not based on actual facts. Often these beliefs are used to justify the position of powerful people in society, for example the power of men over women (sexism), white over black (racism), and so on (see Chapter 1). This working definition of ideology has been used in this book to analyse the social world, for example, 'scientific management' (see below), 'patriarchy' (see below and Index) and 'fascism' (see above), etc.

Further characteristics of an ideology are:

1   The beliefs and values comprising these ideologies form a set, that is to say, they are inter-connected, as was shown in Chapter 9 when racial prejudice and racial discrimination were considered.

2   Ideologies are determined by the economic arrangements of society, hence many believed the owners of the means of production (the bourgeoisie) influenced or controlled the ideas of society (see Chapter 5).

3   Ideologies are linked to the sociology of knowledge. What passes for knowledge is socially determined. (See Chapter 11 for a sociology of knowledge and a sociology of the curriculum.)

4   Karl Mannheim believed ideologies could either maintain the status quo or promote social change – hence the title of his book *Ideology and Utopia*. Anthony Giddens (in *Sociology*) shows how ideologies can be used to justify force. For example, intruders can justify their activities by seeing themselves as 'civilizing' the 'heathen' peoples with whom they come into contact.

5   See 'hegemony' above.

Industrialization: this is sometimes associated with urbanization or modernization, but really industrialization means something more specific. It includes the division of labour – a wide range of people doing different jobs – specialization at work, urbanization in most cases, and the rational use of technology. In contrast, pre-industrial societies are usually rural, traditional, and have less division of labour (see also Chapter 13).

Norms and values: norms can be seen as acceptable ways of behaving and values can be seen as the ultimate ends of society. Thus norms and values can be seen as means and ends in society. For example, financial success may be an ultimate value or end in society and hard work may be seen as a norm or means of achieving this.

Patriarchy: the dominance of the male in the home, including the control of finance and compulsory sexual demands by the male head of the household.

Pluralism: assumes society is composed of a wide variety of competing groups – economic, professional, religious, etc. The government does not interfere except to ensure that everyone keeps to the rules and that rights of individuals are upheld. But Chapter 6 shows that modern societies are less open than we think.

Polarization: a coming-together of those with similar class interests (see Chapter 5).

Politicization: a growing awareness of your class position through association with others (see also 'feminism' above).

Power: the probability that a person can carry out his or her will – Weber (see Chapter 6).

Prejudice: literally pre-judgement using *stereotypes*. In racial prejudice, for example, there is an assumption that all black people will behave in a certain way. *Discrimination* means actually acting according to your prejudice. (See Chapter 9.)

Professional ideologies: most professions – medicine, law, accountancy – have beliefs about their work. Some sociologists believe that the medical profession has a 'cure' ideology. It overemphasizes 'cures' rather than preventative medicine or making improvements in social conditions, for example reducing poverty in society, etc. (See I. Kennedy, *The Unmasking of Medicine*.)

Proletarianization: the process by which workers in higher status occupations lose this status and become absorbed in the working class (see, for example, *The Affluent Worker* studies by J. Goldthorpe et al.).

Racism: discrimination on the basis of a person's race. Beliefs about people's race determine attitudes towards them. (See also 'prejudice', 'dual labour markets', 'reserve army of labour'.)

Reserve army of labour: this is the part of the labour force that is taken on in good times only and is the first to be laid off in hard times. In most societies the reserve army includes unskilled workers, women, racial minorities and the elderly.

Restricted code of speech: this can be contrasted with its opposite – the elaborated code of speech. Bernstein argues that working class people use a restricted code of speech (some of the time), for instance short commands, while the middle class mother uses the elaborated code (again some of the time), which may use whole sentences. For example, a middle class mother may say, 'Do not go near the stairs because they are dangerous'; whereas a working class mother may say, 'Don't go there.' The restricted code of speech is said to be context dependent. Thus in the above example, the working class child knows what 'there' means without further elaboration. Many sociologists, such as W. Labov, would disagree with these concepts. (Further reading: B. Bernstein and P. Atkinson, *Language Structure and Reproduction*.)

Role: role is the behaviour expected of us. Obvious examples are the role of man, woman, mother, father, teacher, nurse, accountant. Sociologists see role mainly as learned behaviour rather than biologically determined behaviour. Some people learn their roles better than others; a few are clumsy. Societies differ in the ways these roles are performed. Goffman uses the analogy with the theatre to explain the concept of role. Thus society writes the script but the individual plays the part written. The individual is given the part and may perform it well – or not so well. (See E. Goffman, *The Presentation of Self in Everyday Life*.)

Role conflict: performing two or more inconsistent roles. Here are a few examples: a teacher is marking the exam paper of his or her child who is also his or her pupil (the role of parent conflicts with the role of an impartial teacher); a mother goes out to work (is there role conflict here? If so, can it be avoided? Yes, perhaps by providing crèches). Another example of role conflict is a factory supervisor who is also the safety officer. He or she may wish to raise production but in so doing may overlook hazards at work – the roles of production officer and safety officer conflict.

Scientific management: this holds that management has the full right to manage and that management can say not only what is to be done but how it is to be done. Management's control of the task was systematically analysed by Frederick Taylor in his book *The Principles of Scientific Management*, first published in 1911. Scientific management is seen by many sociologists (Fox, Braverman, etc.) as an ideology justifying over-zealous control by management. This is a frequent cause of bad industrial relations.

Sexism: discrimination against men and women on account of their gender; for example, the belief that women can only do certain kinds of work, a belief in male dominance (see also 'gender', 'patriarchy').

Social construction of reality: the process by which people create a personal view of social reality as they are socialized into society. This subjective view of reality becomes objectified as social institutions, that is to say regular shared patterns of behaviour. (See 'role', 'socialization', P. Berger and D. Luckman, *The Social Construction of Reality*.)

Socialization: the process by which individuals learn about their society and their place or role in it. This is achieved by these individuals learning or *internalizing* the *norms* and *values* of their society. Socialization is usually applied to young children, and indeed this is the theme of Chapter 3, 'Infant Care'. Socialization does happen in adult life too, for example immigrants learning their role in their new society. This is known as secondary socialization as distinct from the primary socialization of early childhood. (See also 'role'.)

Social mobility: moving up or down in social class is often defined in terms of one's occupation; an example of upward social mobility would be a labourer becoming a clerk. Sociologists are interested in social mobility rates as they indicate how open a society is. Thus a high rate of social mobility would indicate an open society in which people from humble positions can rise to higher positions. Intergenerational mobility compares the present position of individuals with those of their parents. Intragenerational mobility compares the positions achieved by an individual during the course of his or her life. (See Chapter 5.)

Social reality: this is what is going on in society as opposed to what some people think is going on. The sociologist is therefore always seeking answers to the question – what is really going on here? (See p. 2.) For example, many people, including some cabinet ministers, think that the importance of social class has declined, whereas sociological studies repeatedly show that class is still important (p. 84). Again, some occupational groups and professions tend to define social reality for their members (see Table 7.2). (See also 'ideology' and 'social construction of reality'.)

Taylorism: see 'scientific management'.

Urbanism: the urban way of life led to loss of primary relationships (seeing near kin, for example), weaker social controls (because you are less likely to know your neighbours and therefore are not worried by their opinion of you), greater division of labour (people specializing in one job, etc.). All this in turn is associated with greater population density and greater heterogeneity (people coming from different backgrounds). (See also 'industrialization' above and L. Wirth, 'Urbanism as a Way of Life', *American Journal of Sociology*, 1938, often repeated in textbooks on urban sociology.)

Index